Lacan and Philosophy

Anamnesis

Anamnesis means remembrance or reminiscence, the collection and re-collection of what has been lost, forgotten, or effaced. It is therefore a matter of the very old, of what has made us who we are. But *anamnesis* is also a work that transforms its subject, always producing something new. To recollect the old, to produce the new: that is the task of *Anamnesis*.

a re.press series

Lacan and Philosophy: The New Generation

Lorenzo Chiesa, editor

re.press Melbourne 2014

re.press

PO Box 40, Prahran, 3181, Melbourne, Australia
http://www.re-press.org

National Library of Australia Cataloguing-in-Publication Data

Lacan and philosophy : the new generation / edited by Lorenzo Chiesa.

9780992373412 (paperback)

Series: Anamnesis.

Subjects: Lacan, Jacques, 1901-1981. Philosophy.

Chiesa, Lorenzo, editor.

190

Designed and Typeset by A&R

This book is produced sustainably using plantation timber, and printed in the destination market reducing wastage and excess transport.

Contents

Editorial Introduction:
Towards a New Philosophical-Psychoanalytic Materialism and Realism

Lorenzo Chiesa

> I am attacking philosophy? That's greatly exaggerated!
> (Lacan, Seminar XVII)

I

Much has been written about Lacan's dialogue with philosophy as well as the reasons for his dismissal of it. Commentators often rightly argue that nowhere is psychoanalysis more vehemently opposed to the love of wisdom than in the theory of discourses formulated starting from Seminar XVII (1969-1970). Here Lacan strictly associates philosophy with the discourse of the master: a philosopher is not a master but the one who inspired in the master the 'desire to know' and, in doing so, paved the way for the discourse of the University, the contemporary figure of mastery that has appropriated the practical, almost animal, knowledge of the slave by means of a—epistemological and political—theft. Insofar as the master can be regarded as the 'other side' [*l'envers*] of psychoanalysis, which is, in spite of an as yet embryonic development, the only discourse that can function as his 'counterpoint', philosophy (by now fully phagocyticised by the University) cannot, and should not, be resuscitated. But Lacan importantly adds that, in bringing the discourse of the master to a close, psychoanalysis also remains symmetrical to it. For this, moving from the theorisations originating in its clinical practice (as a new servile form of know-how), psychoanalysis ultimately 'extend[s] the philosophical discourse very much beyond the point at which it was most properly effaced'. Such a paradoxical prolongation does not merely 'transform' philosophy, in the sense of keeping its tradition alive, but promotes a 'different discourse' that is, nonetheless, *philosophically* problematic.[1]

II

Against an increasing interest in Lacan's 'anti-philosophical' vocation witnessed by both psychoanalytic secondary literature and the independent work

---

1. Lacan 2006, pp. 20-24, p. 99, p. 146.

of well-known thinkers (*in primis* Alain Badiou's)—which is as such not mistaken yet should be adequately dialecticised—the present collection of essays primarily focuses on the fact that the condemnation of philosophy expressed in the theory of discourses goes together with the elaboration of a new ontology, or better, a para-ontology. This rather unpredictable connection is already envisaged in Seminar XVII but becomes fully evident only in Seminar XX (1972-1973). If, on the one hand, philosophy epitomises the discourse of the *m'être*, of the delusional belief of being the master [*maître*] of myself, or, more precisely, of being-me-to-myself [*m'être à moi même*],[2] on the other, psychoanalysis should replace this old ontology of mastery—which amounts to an 'I-cracy' [*je-cratie*], 'the myth of the ideal I, of the I that masters, of the I whereby at least something is identical to itself, namely, the speaker'[3]—with a discourse of the *par-être*, a discourse on being as *para*-being, as 'being beside' [*être à côté*].[4] What is para-ontology? First and foremost, it is a *lateral* ontology concerned with the contingency and materiality of the signifier (*qua* letter) and, consequently, of the linguistic laws that rest on it. Two passages from Seminar XX perfectly capture this crucial point:

> No signifier is produced [*se produit*] as eternal. That is no doubt what, rather than qualifying it as arbitrary, Saussure *could* have formulated. It would have been better to qualify the signifier with the category of *contingency*. The signifier repudiates the category of the eternal and, nevertheless, oddly enough [*singulièrement*], it *is* intrinsically.

> Ontology is what highlighted in language the use of the copula, isolating it as a signifier. To dwell on the verb 'to be'—a verb that is not even, in the complete field of the diversity of languages, employed in a way we could qualify universal—to produce it as such is a highly risky enterprise. In order to *exorcise* it, it might perhaps suffice to suggest that when we say about anything whatsoever that it is what it is, nothing in any way obliges us to isolate the verb 'to be'. That is pronounced 'it is what it is' [*c'est ce que c'est*], and it could just as well be written, 'idizwadidiz' [*seskecé*]. In this use of the copula, we would see nothing at all. We would see nothing whatsoever if a discourse, the discourse of the master, *m'être*, didn't emphasize the verb 'to be' [*être*]. (Lacan 1998, p. 40, p. 31 [my emphases])

In other words, the signifier *is* utterly contingent, and its true contingency—which is far from being reducible to the linguistic criterion of arbitrariness[5]—its *para*-ontological status, can only emerge, beneath the discourse of mastery epitomised by traditional ontology (i.e. the fundamental fantasy of Western thought), as the domain of the material letter.

---

2. Ibid., p. 152.

3. Ibid., p. 63.

4. Lacan 1998, p. 44.

5. Lacan would relate linguistic arbitrariness to the domain of the *automaton*, that is, probabilistic chance within the network of signifiers, as opposed to the field of *tyche*, the absolute contingency of the void of structure to be understood as its material cause (that is, as the cause of the very network of signifiers). I have developed this argument in 'Hyperstructuralism's Necessity of Contingency' (Chiesa 2010a, pp. 159-177).

Lacan also phrases this same argument in more conventional philosophical parlance when, in a succinct but original reading of Aristotle, he distinguishes para-ontological quiddity from ontological being:[6] the former as a factical 'what that is', or 'that which *it* is' [*ce que ça est*] cannot be confined to the latter as a 'what would have been produced if that which *must have been tout-court* had come into Being' [*ce qui se serait produit si était venu à être, tout-court, ce qui était à être*], that is, to a linguistic dimension of being, or better a hegemonic *dit*-mension, which always by necessity—by definition—involves the (failed) submission of contingency to the order of the Master ('it's quite simply *being* at someone's heel, *being* at someone's beck and call').[7] And yet, obviously, rendering the 'idizwadidiz' [*seskecé*] in the guise of quiddity runs itself the risk of turning para-ontology again into some form of necessary ontology, the ontology of the necessity of literal contingency, whereby the anti-philosophical 'exorcism' of the letter might after all prove insufficient. Lacan is well aware of this risk, for instance when, in Seminar XVII, he reminds us that 'from every academic statement by any philosophy whatsoever, even by a philosophy that strictly speaking could be pointed to as being the most opposed to it—namely, if it were philosophy, Lacan's discourse—the I-cracy emerges, irreducibly'.[8] However, he is nonetheless equally aware of the fact that he cannot avoid it (or, similarly, that he cannot completely dispel the impression that his psychoanalytic discourse remains also, on some level, a discourse of *Ur*-mastery).

To sum up, we should first of all learn to read philosophical ontology as a discourse of the *m'être*, which ultimately always presupposes a thwarted attempt to master the uni-verse as One,[9] and then to detect beside it, or rather at *its* side—an 'other' side of being that runs parallel to philosophical ontology—a para-being [*être à côté*] whose conjugation we should put into psychoanalytical practice ('I par-am, you par-are, he par-is, we par-are, and so on and so forth'[10]). Yet, most importantly, we also have to acknowledge that while 'language proves to be a field much richer in resources than if it were merely the field in which philosophical discourse has inscribed itself over the course of time', there persist nonetheless 'certain reference points [that] have been enunciated by that discourse that are difficult to completely eliminate from any use of language'.[11] The traditional ontology of mastery sustained by philosophy is to some extent unsurpassable. *Para*-ontology, as its name clearly indicates, does not overcome, or sublate philosophical ontology, not even in the guise of an eliminative move that would render the latter purely immanent to itself, and thus meaningless (this would be a very

---

6. Here, it is not important to establish whether Lacan's interpretation of Aristotle is exegetically tenable. What matters is the fact that he recovers a para-ontological (and repressed) element in the very work of the initiator of the traditional ontology of mastery. For him, ontology and para-ontology have always been inextricable.

7. Lacan 1998, p. 31 (translation modified) (my emphases). Or, to put it the other way round, the ontology of mastery necessitates the *impossibility* of complying with the master's order 'Be!', or better, 'Be one!'

8. Lacan 2006, p. 63 (translation modified).

9. 'Je suis *m'être*, je progresse dans la *m'êtrise*, je suis *m'être* de moi comme de l'univers. C'est bien là ce dont je parlais tout à l'heure, le *con-vaincu*. L'uni-vers, c'est un fleur de rhétorique' (Lacan 1975, p. 53).

10. Lacan 1998, p. 45.

11. Ibid., pp. 30-31.

reductive interpretation of the 'idizwadidiz'). By *siding* against it, para-ontology rather dialecticises (or unsutures) philosophical ontology's desire for totalisation and, pointing the finger at the contingency and materiality of the letter, uncovers its *envers*.[12] This is Lacan's precious legacy to future discourses on being, which, in various ways, the present collection tries to articulate.

Let me restate and clarify my argument one more time from a slightly different angle. The 'other reading' [*autre lecture*] of being advanced by Lacan recovers in the signifiers that are enunciated something else than what they signify,[13] both in the sense of locating the literal *m'être* that accompanies any traditional ontological discourse *qua* discourse of mastery and of debunking the latter's inevitable structuration of the verb 'to be' into a unitary worldview [*conception du monde*], by now amply disqualified by science.[14] Such an operation, revolving around the provisional psychoanalytic axiom 'we are dealing with something other than *a* world',[15] brings with it the danger of turning this very axiom into a continuation of traditional ontology—whereby the unmasking of the idealised discourse of the *maître* (of the necessary One) as the literal discourse of the *m'être* (of the contingent not-one that makes itself into One) would function as the ultimate master signifier. The only materialist way in which a new—para-ontologically psychoanalytic—discourse can coexist with this danger without remaining paralysed by it is, on the one hand, by insisting, in spite of their seeming proximity, on the irreducibility of the *par-être* to a further version of the *paraître*—that is, of 'the "appearing", as the phenomenon has always been called, that beyond which there is supposedly that thing, the noumenon'[16]—which would reinstate the split between immanence and transcendence within immanence itself, and, on the other, by leaving open the option that the a priori of the non-totalisable and hence acausal universe ('we are dealing with something other than *a* world') may not refute what Lacan calls the 'God hypothesis' ('As long as somebody will say something, the God hypothesis will persist'[17]). To put it bluntly, the signifier cannot simply be referred to as random matter, for otherwise the appearance of its literal dimension would concomitantly turn into *linguistic revelation tout court*; the signifier is contingently material *and*, at the same time, *besides* that, as such an improbable but nevertheless possible manifestation of a misleading transcendence. These are the meta-critical and agnostic poles of Lacan's materialist dialectics.[18] He struggles to articulate this specific point when, precisely in the lessons of Seminar XX

---

12. This would be the most succinct way of reading *l'envers* of Seminar XVII together with *l'être à côté* of Seminar XX.

13. See Lacan 1998, p. 37.

14. 'The world, the world is in [a state of] decomposition, thank God. We see that the world no longer stands up, because even in scientific discourse it is clear that there isn't the slightest world. As soon as you can add something called a "quark" to atoms and have that become the true thread of scientific discourse, you must realize that we are dealing with something other than a world' (Lacan 1998, p. 36). As I will show shortly, 'thank God' is not a simple interjection; it needs to be taken seriously together with 'we are dealing with something other than a world'.

15. Ibid. (my emphasis).

16. Ibid., pp. 44-45.

17. Ibid., p. 45 (translation modified).

18. I have started to develop a 'meta-critical realism' that takes its cue from Lacan, but also goes beyond his work, in 'Notes Towards a Manifesto for Meta-critical Realism' (Chiesa 2010b, pp. 23-37).

in which he confronts the uni-versal discourse of the *maître/m'être*—of a worldview which is by now in 'decomposition'—with his *autre lecture*, his para-ontology,[19] he surprisingly claims the following:

> To make myself understood, I will take a reference you read in the great book of the world. Consider the flight of a bee. A bee goes from flower to flower gathering nectar. What you discover is that, at the tip of its feet, the bee transports pollen from one flower onto the pistil of another flower. That is what you read in the flight of the bee. In the flight of a bird that flies close to the ground—you call that a flight, but in reality it is a group at a certain level—you read that there is going to be a storm. *But do they read?* Does the bee read that it serves a function in the reproduction of phanerogamic plants? Does the bird read the portent of fortune, as people used to say—in other words, the tempest? *That is the whole question. It cannot be ruled out, after all, that a swallow reads the tempest, but it is not terribly certain either* [Toute la question est là. Ce n'est pas exclu, après tout, que l'hirondelle lise la tempête, mais ce n'est pas sûr non plus]. (Lacan 1998, p. 37 [my emphases])

Lacan's other reading, founded as it is on the 'we are dealing with something other than *a* world', cannot after all rule out that the world which is not one may in the end be one *as* not-one, a world *mastered* by a *deceiving* God—Lacan's debt to Descartes would also need to be investigated in this regard. In the name of materialism, we cannot, and should not, exclude the eventuality that the equation of the not-one with the one—and of truth with contradiction—is what the (scientifically informed) axiom of the not-one, the a-causal universe conceals. The least we can say is that, contrary to recent debates on the necessity of contingency supposedly aimed at fighting the return of religious obscurantism, this reading does not institute itself as a *straightforward* theology, namely, as the absolutisation of non-totalisation, the turning of the not-one into *a* (not-one). At the edge of Lacan's anti-philosophical para-ontology stands the foretelling admonition that the contingent materiality of the letter (and of mathematics with it) should not ever be surreptitiously transvaluated into the hyper-necessity of being.

III

I believe that the topicality of Lacan's para-ontology is particularly evident with regard to current debates which, in attempting to overcome the spurious divide between continental and analytic philosophy as well as between the human, social and natural sciences, have been thoroughly rethinking the notions of realism and materialism along with their implications for aesthetics, ethics, politics, and theology. More or less explicitly, all the essays included in the present volume tackle such a complex speculative articulation by focusing on the way in which a Lacanian approach can shed new light on traditional concepts of Western metaphysics, if not rehabilitate them. In the case of the first two essays, the main topic at stake is precisely that of realism and the real. Alenka Zupančič's contribution shows how a psychoanalytically informed consideration of ontological questions based on an appreciation of the path-breaking work Lacan and

19. Jacques-Alain Miller has rightly entitled one of the sections of Lesson IV of Seminar XX, 'The end of the world and para-being'.

Freud carried out on phantasy and negation allows philosophy to go beyond the alleged dichotomy between the naturalisation of the discursive and the discursiveness of nature—two positions she identifies with, respectively, Catherine Malabou's scientifically mediated research on plasticity and Quentin Meillassoux's so-called 'speculative-realist' system. On the one hand, she reminds the former that, from a truly materialist standpoint, materialism cannot be guaranteed by any primordial matter which is not theorised through negativity (the letter 'does not represent sensible nature', but literally replaces it); in other words, an excessive reliance on the empirical sciences and their endeavour to totalise knowledge prevents us from conceiving the real dialectically. On the other hand, she warns the latter that the 'great outside' supposedly obfuscated by Kant's transcendental philosophy ultimately amounts to a phantasmatic scenario that veils the real that is 'already right here'. However, following Lacan, the real qua 'already right here' (or, also, 'nature continuing to stay there where it has always been') should not be considered as a substantial being, but rather as the *limit* of being. As we have already remarked with reference to para-ontology and the letter, the real is that which needs to be put aside for traditional ontology to be able to speak of 'being qua being', and consequently any discourse on being qua being is in the end made possible only by its very opposite, namely, by the fact that 'that which it is', Lacan's idizwadidiz, 'can only *be*'—to use Zupančič's highly convincing formulation—'by being something else than it is', i.e. *contingently*. Such a reflection on the utter contingency of ontology and of being qua being puts her in a position to denounce what she rightly calls Meillassoux's 'God of atheists', that is, 'a God guaranteeing that there is no God', the absolutisation of the absent cause which we defined earlier as '*a* (not-one)'. But while I prefer to associate Lacan's standpoint with an innovative form of para-ontological agnosticism, Zupančič chooses to understand her psychoanalytic realism as a 'Lacanian atheism'.

On his part, Felix Ensslin develops the connection between Lacan and theology arguing that the real identified by psychoanalytic experience can only truly be 'accessed' by philosophy if it is measured against the background of the monotheistic tradition, especially Luther's doctrine of predestination. For Lacan, the subject of psychoanalysis is heir to both the emergence of modern science, its algebraic ability to have concrete quantifiable effects in the world without this being in any way related to an intrinsic meaning of the cosmos, and, in parallel, to the Reformation's revival of god as a 'designified signifier' which, similarly, sustains signification only at the price of exhibiting unpredictably 'ferocious passions'. Ensslin emphasises that while both the Galilean-Cartesian and the Protestant revolutions thus bear on the materiality of the letter as a real remainder of the incompleteness of symbolic articulation, it is only the latter that—at least in its initial moments—truly manages to overcome a pre-existing discourse (i.e. Scholasticism) and establish a new symbolisation thanks to its full assumption of the nonsensical dimension of knowledge. Recent attempts, such as Badiou's, at formulating a mathematical formalised ontology that relegates god to the 'dustbin of history' should therefore not hurriedly be conflated with psychoanalytic realism. Rather, these efforts should be complicated by means of a thorough assessment of the epistemological and ethical implications of the resentment caused by acknowledging the death of god. Luther's ultimate theological lesson in 'wild analysis' is that the only possible relation to the absolute, which partially realises it beyond any distinction between the noumenal and the phenomenal while also disposing of the idea of divine viciousness, can be achieved through subtraction: the subject takes his position in the hole of the symbolic order and in doing so it becomes his responsibility to articulate his place in the Other without recourse to knowledge (of the absolute, of what the Other wants from him). In this context, Ensslin also extensively dialogues with Zupančič and agrees with her in proposing an updating of Kant's speculation on freedom as an act—of saying—that subjectively chooses contingency—the non-totalisability of language—*qua* what has always already been necessary (a topic that is further explored, from contrasting perspectives, in Moati's and Feltham's contributions to this volume).

Such a debate on the importance of a Lacanian resumption of transcendental philosophy from a materialist perspective is further enriched by Adrian Johnston's article, which focuses on the notion of history. Like Ensslin and Zupančič, Johnston opposes any simplistic equation of the real with an 'archaic' time that would precede, or follow, in a variation of the same argument, the correlation between subject and object. Yet unlike Ensslin, he denounces Lacan's own reflection about origins as excessively reliant on the Judeo-Christian tradition (most blatantly, in the case of his repeated notorious invocation that 'In the beginning was the Word'). In other words, it is not sufficient to condemn the theological drift of a speculative realist mathematical ontology oriented towards the direct attainment of the 'great outdoors', the absolute outside, if, conversely, we do not also criticise the frequent Lacanian veto on any ontogenetic or phylogenetic enquiry beyond the mediation of the symbolic order. Ultimately, the work of the French psychoanalyst presents us on this point, that of pre-history, with an unsurpassable tension, for he nonetheless comes to admit after all that some narratives about anthropogenesis are possibly 'less false' than others. In the name of this Lacan, of his anti-ideolinguistic insistence on the materiality of the signifier, we should therefore establish a constructive negotiation with science that neither circumvents the question concerning the emergence of language and the 'nature of nature' nor commits Meillassoux's mistake of numerically reifying acausality and non-totalisability (in this regard, I am myself tempted to label the speculative realists as post-Cantorian and post-Gödelian Pythagoreans). Johnston identifies here an unexpected interlocutor in Daniel Lord Smail and his concept of 'deep history', of 'a seamless narrative that acknowledges the full chronology of the human past', one that does not restrict itself to considering what came after the 'emergence of metal technology, writing, and cities some 5,500 years ago' but rather, to use Stephen Jay Gould's favourite phrase, takes into account the entirety of *homo sapiens'* 'natural history' (as the late Lacan himself concedes, in this light, our very DNA could be regarded as a series of material letters witnessing to the existence of innumerable generations of equally 'deep historical' and biological Others). Most importantly, Johnston stresses that although this novel idea of history is clearly informed by a 'quasi-naturalist', 'bio-materialist' approach, it should in no way remain confined to continuism: discontinuities, such as first and foremost the fact that, to the best of our knowledge, *homo sapiens* is the only species endowed with language, can themselves be dialectically integrated into such a unified narrative *whilst* also irrevocably disrupting it—this is all the more the case, I would add, once we better grasp the implications of the retroactive temporality with which psychoanalysis has always worked and which science has only of late started to benefit from in its empirical research.

The question of genesis is also the main concern of Michael Lewis's essay. His central claims strongly echo Johnston's in multiple ways: first, there are two strands of thought about the man/animal relationship and anthropogenesis in Lacan, which can be defined as, respectively, oppositional and continuist (or also, structural and genetic, synchronic and diachronic, transcendental and empirical). Second, both perspectives are necessary and should always be conceived of together. Third, it is the continuist/genetic approach that distinguishes the contribution of Lacanian psychoanalysis to twenty-first century philosophy insofar as it attempts to supersede the divide between the human and natural sciences, that is, to resume the dialogue between physics and metaphysics, without however abandoning 'what has been gained in the transcendental inflection which this separation took on with Kant' (Lewis is thus yet another author who feels the urgency to deploy a materialist rescue plan to save what is saveable in correlationalism against its fashionable detractors). In this sense, Derrida's contention that Lacan would be 'too much at home with philosophy'—or too 'phallogocentric'—falls short and can be easily retorted back at Derrida himself. Lewis shows how the bottom line of Lacan's anti-philosophical strategy is to appeal for help to the empirical *independently* of any cogitation on the (non-eliminable) dichotomy between structure and genesis, nurture and nature. On the contrary, deconstruction—including Derrida's late work on the animal—resorts to the life sciences only after having posited a priori a possible way out of structure from *within* the openness of structure itself. In this way, unlike Lacan, Derrida fails to account for the genesis of structure, the phylogenetic prehistory of the symbolic order, that is to say, the contingency of anthropogenesis which, in founding logical necessity, could not be deduced by a philosophical logic. For Lewis, the methodological advantage of psychoanalysis over deconstruction becomes adamant in Lacan's theory of writing, where the material letter is both structurally 'the fantasy of a prehistory of the signifier'—i.e. against Derrida's denunciation of Lacan's supposed philosopheme about man as a different lacking animal, this difference is ultimately in his view just a retroactive myth—and, at the same time, genetically 'a real trace of such a prehistory'. Or, on a more general—para-ontological—level, as Lacan conclusively put it, 'asymmetry in nature is neither symmetrical nor asymmetrical'; language in nature is neither non-linguistic nor linguistic.

While Lewis finishes his article by implicitly evoking a close link between deconstruction and the hysterical discourse—and thus distances the former from psychoanalysis—since they both limit their scope to 'reveal[ing] the impossibility of suturing the impotent master' (the incompleteness of the symbolic order), Matteo Bonazzi moves from the opposite presupposition that Lacan's innovative ontology *qua* 'onto-graphy' should be firmly grounded in Derrida's and, in the last resort, Heidegger's thinking of the event of the sign. The real of the written letter is therefore to be theorised as the 'eventual One' that precedes the unattainable 'metaphysical One', namely, the traditional 'ontology of the *Krisis*' exiling the split subject into the differentiality of language. Psychoanalysis indeed recovers a different mode of the speaking being, based on *jouissance*, or better on an affective writing that could reverse our symbolic alienation and return us to a pre-metaphysical dimension of 'decision, act, awakening, and encounter', in brief, to an event of the sign that suspends the gap between the sign and its event, the letter and its taking place. Although Bonazzi unravels onto-graphy as an ontology of the not-whole, dwelling on the attack Lacan launches against philosophy as a discourse of mastery (of the *m'être*) which I have myself discussed in the opening to the present introduction, it is undeniable that his self-professed preference for *pre*-ontology makes his article largely depart from the *para*-ontological inferences brought to light, to different degrees, by all the previous contributors. He in fact explicitly rejects dialectic as outdated, leaves aside the relationship between psychoanalysis and science (endorsing in passing Heidegger's suggestion that science is inextricable from metaphysics) and seems at times even to insert the very materiality of the letter into a vitalist framework—for instance, in this vein, he asserts that 'in thinking man as a sign, Lacan has also loved that which is the liveliest [*Lebendiste*]'.

Guillaume Collett takes a completely different approach to the signifier/letter and, by unfolding its logic, traces a genealogy that links Lacan to Frege and Kant. If, on the one hand, Frege's theory of number fails to get rid of the transcendental subject yet succeeds in uncovering its lack of self-identity, which is repressed in Kant's genetic account of the formation of ideal concepts out of a material set of sensations, on the other hand, Lacan's logic of the signifier pushes the 'deforming character' of the Fregean count-as-one to its limit. The most remarkable result of this Lacanian lesson on arithmetical logic, Collett argues, is that it manages to save Frege from Russell's paradox inasmuch as it fully assumes that numbers (or letters) are not identical with themselves and cannot logically denote objects in states of affairs. Rather, signifiers always denote the object *a*, the objectification of the subject which is the logical referent of every proposition. As a consequence, logic as such rests on a contradiction: to put it simply, the root of the logical is nothing else than the illogical turned into an object. Collett highlights in this way how Lacan radicalises transcendental philosophy by overlapping the Fregean attempt to found modern logic and a logical basis for arithmetic on a purely non-psychological account of number with the Freudian discovery that the psychoanalytic unconscious (the logic of the signifier *qua* logic of fantasy) does not abide by the principle of non-contradiction. Not only does his piece develop the formalising path to the real hinted at by Ensslin but, more generally, functions as an unashamedly post-Kantian bridge between the para-ontological focus prevalent in the first half of this volume and the increasing attention the second pays to ethical and political issues revolving around Lacan's theory of the subject.

Moati's article and mine scrutinise Lacan's own pronouncements on freedom and the closely related notions of alienation and separation. According to Moati, in spite of their apparent proximity, Lacanian psychoanalysis should in this context be opposed to both Althusser's notion of ideological interpellation and Butler's and Žižek's post-Althusserian elaborations on this theme. While there is no doubt that Althusser was deeply influenced by the psychoanalytic model of the subject's unconscious subjection to the symbolic Law, the imperative of the latter has always entailed for Lacan, even in his early seminars, a subjective taking up or reduplication of the instituting order of the Other. The hegemonic status of the interpellating alienation is then further reduced starting from Seminar XI by means of what Lacan calls 'separation', a subjective destitution which he conceptualises as central to his understanding of the end of analysis. Against Butler, Moati maintains that this liberating moment should in no way be limited to the American philosopher's defence of the irreducibility of the subject's being to its identity, which allows her to think emancipation in terms of a performative 'reforming and resignifying the identity interpellation assigns'. For Lacan, this very unsurpassable gap—between the 'I' and the 'ego', the subject of the enunciation and that of the statement—is nothing else than alienation *tout-court*, and performativity ultimately amounts to 'the complete accomplishment of the operation of interpellation'. On the contrary, the end of psychoanalysis brings about 'the subject's ability to separate itself from its interpellated identity' in the guise of a subject of negativity, or freedom, that overthrows the symbolic order as such. Moati acknowledges that, unlike Butler, Žižek appreciates the extreme character of separation but reproaches him for associating it with psychotic regression, that is, a suspension of alienation, rather than with a *subjective subscription* to the choice of alienation, which necessarily coincides with its extinction [...] The subject is no longer subjected to the symbolic Other, insofar as it fully assumes this subjection as coming from *itself*'.

While in my contribution I fully subscribe to the idea that separation—in the ontogenesis of the subject as well as at the end of psychoanalysis—should somehow be conceived as a repetition of alienation through which what was a forced choice is thereby subjectivised retrospectively, I do not in the least believe that for Lacan this act coincides with an extinction of alienation. As detailed in the last few pages of the essay and in a long footnote in which I compare and contrast my stance with Moati's, far from establishing a 'subject of freedom' that reduces the import of the Marxist concept of alienation within psychoanalysis, separation rather amounts to Lacan's endeavour to dialectically develop the coincidence between dis-alienation and re-alienation: separation as liberation from alienation goes together with repression. Clinically, this is what is at stake in the logic of fantasy and in the interminability of its traversal. From this standpoint, although I do not explicitly discuss Žižek, I am more sympathetic than Moati towards his equation of freedom with madness, which is often made by Lacan himself. Instead of coining the oxymoron 'subject of freedom' we should rather speak of the 'virtual point of freedom', an absolute difference that can be *subjectively* attained thanks to psychoanalysis, yet manifests itself only retroactively by means of a new *subjection* to the signifier. This Lacanian dialectic of emancipation becomes especially convincing when we dwell on its aesthetical aspects—which I investigate in dialogue with Pasolini's considerations on the role of the cinematic author and spectator, Freud's concept of *Vorstellungsrepräsentanz*, and Velasquez's *Las Meninas*—as well as on its onto-logical effects. As I write, separation as the *creation* of a new fantasy can more precisely be understood as the 'covering of the *non-meaning* of meaning (the senselessness of the signifying Other) with *being* as non-meaning (the disappearing of the failed, psychotic subject who chooses being over meaning as *subjectively* experienced in retrospect by the non-psychotic subject at the moment of the encounter with the Other's desire)'.

Justin Clemens continues this debate on alienation and freedom by examining the figure of the slave as 'an integral part of Lacan's psychoanalysis from first to last'. In opposition to Kojève's resolution of the Hegelian dialectic of mastery/slavery in an end of history characterised by a paradoxical reconciliation of humanity with animality, Clemens insists on the fact that, according to the Lacanian emphasis on the interminability of psychoanalysis, 'slavery will always be with us' (a stance that resonates not only with my reading of separation but also with Zupančič's denunciation of the fantasy of the 'great outdoors', and Johnston's and Lewis's 'deep-historical' preoccupations). Man is enslaved to the signifier, speaking equates with coercion, not liberty, and free association is ultimately impossible, even and above all *after* we overcome the discourse of the master, that is to say, de-totalise it when we identify the master with a '*slave*-master'. In line with my own main argument, what Lacan's psychoanalysis would nonetheless gain from this desolate scenario are, according to Clemens, 'inventions of freedom within discourse'; in other words, it is precisely the 'loopiness of revolutions', not the *telos* of history, that can effectively 'transform the world'. This is the case because, like the slave, psychoanalysis comes to terms and works with the 'truth of matter', or better the irremediably material nature of discourse (and of power with it), which prevents its totalisation into knowledge (or sovereignty). Philosophy—first and foremost Hegelianism—thus appears as both a fellow traveller of psychoanalysis, in that it 'orients us towards the proper object and terms of study', and an enemy to be combated, since it 'falsifies their import', that is, it sutures truth to knowledge. Psychoanalysis exacerbates philosophy as long as it occupies an anti-systemic 'position of weakness' wherein the knowledge it accumulates goes hand in hand with the awareness of its own inevitable failure as a closed discourse.

Oliver Feltham expands precisely on the ethical and political consequences of psychoanalysis as a discourse that has done with the mastery of knowledge sought for by philosophy. If such a predicament inescapably declares the end of any tenable idea of macrocosm and even of *polis*, what is then the space for action after Lacan? While the desire of philosophy has always been that of acting for a school, which involves, first and foremost, transmitting knowledge so as to prepare someone else to act correctly, what can be said in this regard about the anti-philosophical desire of the analyst and his act (which, as Moati already anticipated in his article, is always an act of separation)? Dwelling on Seminar XV

L'acte psychanalytique and a number of later texts dedicated to the technical notion of the so-called pass, Feltham detects a constructive hesitation in Lacan's teachings: on the one hand, they are clearly themselves a *propaedeutics* for action, for 'giving a backbone to the action of young analysts', that is, forming a school, on the other, they also indicate how psychoanalysis is irreducible to the transmission of knowledge and rather institutes itself as isolated instances that are *exemplars* of action. From the latter perspective, 'each act is its own school', the school must be founded again and again, and truly becoming an analyst entails inventing analysis anew. Standing between these two apparently opposite alternatives, the technique of the pass devised by Lacan is meant to establish whether the blind leap that an act ultimately consists of (as well as the objectification of the subject into a detritus that is thus carried out—here Feltham, like Ensslin, evokes Luther) can give way to directives for others that are not rigidified as norms. Following a remark made by Moati, we could therefore advance that psychoanalysis teaches philosophy how acting amounts to transforming the *alleged* causes of a universe that is not one into *logical reasons*. As Feltham points out, resonating with an argument that is also central to my contribution, the successful pass is in the last resort a 'formalization of testimony' that guarantees the transmission of previous actions, that is, inscribes in the symbolic order the contingency of the signifiers that have emerged at the end of the treatment. Yet it exclusively achieves this to the extent that 'the psychoanalytic act takes the place of saying and changes it', erecting new (master) signifiers. The ethico-political as well as ontological repercussions of this operation are vast: if the acephalous act is retrospectively constituted during the pass only through a formalisation of its consequences that depends on a 'speaking *well*', then psychoanalysis exacerbates nothing else than the *contingency of being*.

In the final essay, Alvise Sforza Tarabochia deepens the investigation of Lacan's theory of the subject contained in the second half of this volume by comparing it with Franco Basaglia's. He identifies in both the French psychoanalyst and the Italian psychiatrist a common insistence on conceiving subjectivity as entwined with otherness in terms of an active assumption of lack. This he opposes to Foucault's lacking subject, a subject for whom there would be no possible liberation from a condition of subjection to power, especially where psychiatry is concerned. Sforza Tarabochia does not underestimate the influence that Foucault had on Basaglia's more openly anti-institutional work, which aimed at the 'destruction of the psychiatric hospital' and culminated with the approval of a law that sanctioned the abolishment of mental hospitals in Italy. However, he deems that Basaglia's socio-political engagement can be appropriately approached only by paying attention to the way in which the entirety of his oeuvre is characterised by an understanding of the 'psychic' as an 'interhuman dimension' based on language. In Sforza Tarabochia's view, such a stance can be profitably compared with Lacan's refusal of the so-called 'total personality' as well as, conversely, the emphasis he puts on the unconscious as a 'discourse of the Other' and the onto-genetic agency of the signifier. Lacan and Basaglia would converge most evidently on two related issues. Firstly, the fact that alienation in the other is necessary in order to achieve a separation from him. Secondly, the definition of psychosis as a failure to come to terms with otherness, or, more precisely, as a foreclosure of 'symbolic mediation', a loss of the distance from the other that precipitates the subject into the other.

IV

The 'new' in the 'new generation' that gives the title to the present collection of articles is far from rhetorical. All the authors included are under fifty years of age, and several are under forty. Without exception, they have, however, already secured a prominent position in debates concerning the relation between philosophy and psychoanalysis, or are in the process of doing so. Zupančič, Johnston, Lewis, Bonazzi, Clemens and I have written monographs and edited collections on Lacan; Ensslin, Collett, and Sforza Tarabochia consecrated their doctoral theses to his work; Moati and Feltham have produced several articles on the remarkable influence the French psychoanalyst has had on indispensable contemporary thinkers such as Slavoj Žižek and Alain Badiou. The other contiguous novelty of this volume that marks a major shift from previous attempts at presenting Lacan in dialogue *avec les philosophes* is its markedly international dimension. Contributors reside and work in seven different countries, which are, moreover, not always their countries of origin. As I hope the reader will be able to confirm by taking into consideration the respectful intensity of the many cross-references present in these essays—which should be taken as a very partial sedimentation of exchanges of ideas and collaborative projects that, in some cases, have been ongoing for more than a decade—geographical distance appears to have been beneficial to the overcoming of Lacan's confinement to the supposed orthodoxy of specific—provincial—schools and their pathetic fratricidal wars, whilst in parallel enhancing intellectual rigour. These pieces rethink philosophically through Lacan, with as little jargon as possible, in this order, realism, god, history, genesis and structure, writing, logic, freedom, the master and slave dialectic, the act, and the subject.

BIBLIOGRAPHY

Lacan, J., *Le séminaire. Livre XX. Encore,* Paris: Seuil, 1975
—— *The Seminar of Jacques Lacan. Book XX. Encore,* New York—London: Norton, 1998
—— *The Seminar of Jacques Lacan. Book XVII. The Other Side of Psychoanalysis,* New York—London: Norton, 2006
Chiesa, L., 'Hyperstructuralism's Necessity of Contingency', in *S,* volume 3, 2010a
——'Notes Towards a Manifesto for Meta-critical Realism', in *Beyond Potentialities? Politics between the Possible and the Impossible,* ed. by M. Potocnik, F. Ruda, J. Völker, Berlin: Diaphanes, 2010b

Realism in Psychoanalysis

Alenka Zupančič

Many recent philosophical discussions have been marked, in one way or another, by the rather stunning re-launching of the question of realism, triggered by Quentin Meillassoux's book *Après la finitude* (2006), and followed by a broader, albeit less homogeneous, movement of 'speculative realism'. Indeed it seems that we are witnessing a powerful revival of the issue of realism, with new conceptualizations or definitions of the latter, as well as of its adversary ('correlationism' in the place of nominalism). I propose to take this opportunity to raise the question of whether or not the conceptual field of Lacanian psychoanalysis is concerned by this debate, and if so, how. With the Real being one of the central concepts of Lacanian theory, the question arises as to the status of this Real, especially since Lacan relates it to the impossible. What could this rather strange realism that identifies the Real with the impossible amount to?

By way of a quick general mapping of the space of this discussion let me just very briefly recall Meillassoux's basic argument. It consists in showing how post-Cartesian philosophy (starting with Kant) rejected or disqualified the possibility for us to have any access to being outside of its correlation to thinking. Not only are we never dealing with an object in itself, separately from its relationship to the subject, but there is also no subject that is not always-already in a relationship with an object. The relation thus precedes any object or subject, the relation is prior to the terms it relates, and becomes itself the principal object of philosophical investigation. Contemporary (post-Cartesian) philosophies are all different philosophies of correlation. As Meillassoux puts it:

> Generally speaking, the modern philosopher's 'two-step' consists in this belief in the primacy of the relation over the related terms; a belief in the constitutive power of reciprocal relation. The 'co-' (of co-givenness, of co-relation, of the co-originary, of co-presence, etc.) is the grammatical particle that dominates modern philosophy, its veritable 'chemical formula'. Thus, one could say that up until Kant, one of the principal problems of philosophy was to think substance, while ever since Kant, it has consisted in trying to think the correlation. Prior to the advent of transcendentalism, one of the questions that divided rival philosophers most decisively

was 'Who grasps the true nature of substance? He who thinks the Idea, the individual, the atom, the God? Which God?' But ever since Kant, to discover what divides rival philosophers is no longer to ask who has grasped the true nature of substantiality, but rather to ask who has grasped the true nature of correlation: is it the thinker of the subject-object correlation, the noetico-noematic correlation, or the language-referent correlation? (Meillassoux 2008, pp. 5-6)

The insufficiency of this position is revealed, according to Meillassoux, when confronted with 'ancestral statements' or 'arche-fossils': statements produced today by experimental science concerning events that occurred prior to the emergence of life and of consciousness (say: 'The earth was formed 4.56 billion years ago'). They raise a simple and, still according to Meillassoux, insoluble problem for a correlationist: How are we to grasp the meaning of scientific statements bearing explicitly upon a manifestation of the world that is posited as anterior to the emergence of thought and even of life—posited, that is, as anterior to every form of human *relation* to that world? From the correlationist point of view these statements are strictly speaking meaningless.

One of the great merits of Meillassoux's book is that it has (re)opened, not so much the question of the relationship between philosophy and science, as the question of *whether they are speaking about the same world*. Alain Badiou has recently raised or, rather, answered a similar question in the context of politics: 'There is only one world'. Yet this question is also pertinent to the issue of epistemology's, or science's, relation to ontology. It may seem in fact as if science and philosophy have been developing for some time now in parallel worlds: in one it is possible to speak of the real in itself, independently of its relation to the subject, whereas in the other this kind of discourse is strictly speaking meaningless. So, what do we get if we apply the axiom 'There is only one world' to this situation? Instead of taking the—on the side of philosophy—more common path, criticizing science for its lack of reflection upon its own discourse, Meillassoux takes another path: the fact that certain scientific statements escape philosophy's 'horizon of sense' indicates that there is something wrong with it. It indicates that, in order to ensure its own survival as a discursive practice (one could also say: in order to ensure the continuation of metaphysics by other means) it has sacrificed far too much, namely the real in its absolute sense.

One should perhaps stress, nevertheless, that this less common path is becoming a kind of trend in contemporary philosophy, and Meillassoux shares it with several authors, very different in their inspiration. Let us just mention Catherine Malabou and her philosophical materialism, which aims to develop a new theory of subjectivity based on cognitive sciences. In her polemics with Freudian and Lacanian psychoanalysis she opposes to the 'libidinal unconscious', as always already discursively mediated, the 'cerebral unconscious' (the auto-affection of the brain) as the true, materialist unconscious.[1] Yet, if Malabou's materialism moves in the direction of a 'naturalization of the discursive' or, more precisely, if it represents an attempt to reduce the gap between the organic and the

---

1. Malabou 2007.

subject in the direction of finding the organic causes of the subject,[2] Meillassoux takes the same path in the opposite direction, namely, in that of the discursiveness of nature, although he does not go all the way. His realist ontology, differentiating between primary and secondary qualities of being, does not claim that being is inherently mathematical; it claims that it is absolute, that it is independent of any relation to the subject, although only in the segment which can be mathematically formulated. Meillassoux thus preserves a certain gap or leap (between being and its mathematisation), without addressing it. The possibility of certain qualities to be mathematically formulated is the guarantee of their absolute character (of their being real in the strong sense of the term). Meillassoux's realism is thus not a realism of the universals, but—paradoxically—a realism of the *correlate* of the universals, which he also calls the referent:

> Generally speaking, statements are ideal insofar as their reality is one with signification. But their referents, for their part, are not necessarily ideal (the cat on the mat is real, although the statement 'the cat is on the mat' is ideal). In this particular instance, it would be necessary to specify: the *referents* of the statements about dates, volumes etc., existed 4.56 billion years ago, as described by these statements—but not these statements themselves, which are contemporaneous with us. (Meillassoux 2008, p. 12)

There seems to be no way around the fact that the criterion of the absolute is nothing else but its correlation with mathematics. Not that this implies something necessarily subjective or subjectively mediated, but it surely implies something discursive. And here we come to the core problem of Meillassoux's conceptualizations, which is at the same time what is most interesting about them. I emphasize this as opposed to another dimension of his gesture, a dimension enthusiastically embraced by our *Zeitgeist*, even though it has little philosophical (or scientific) value, and is based on free associations related to some more or less obscure feelings of the present *Unbehagen in der Kultur*. Let us call it its psychological dimension, which can be summed up by the following story: After Descartes we have lost the *great outdoors*, the absolute outside, the Real, and have become prisoners of our own subjective or *discursive cage*. The only outside we are dealing with is the outside posited or constituted by ourselves or different discursive practices. And there is a growing discomfort, claustrophobia in this imprisonment, this constant obsession with ourselves, this impossibility to ever get out of the external inside that we have thus constructed. There is also a political discomfort that is put into play here, that feeling of frustrating impotence, of the impossibility of really changing anything, of soaking in small and big disappointments of recent and not so recent history. Hence a certain additional redemptive charm of a project that promises again to break out into the great Outside, to reinstitute the Real in its absolute dimension, and to ontologically ground the possibility of radical change.

---

2. Which is why Slavoj Žižek is right in pointing out that the cost of this kind of materialism might well be a re-spiritualisation of matter (see Žižek 2010, p. 303). Needless to say, however, that our cursory reference to Malabou here fails to do justice to her argument in its entirety, as well as to some most valuable points that she makes in presenting it.

One should insist, however, that the crucial aspect of Meillassoux lies entirely elsewhere than in this story which has found in him (perhaps not all together without his complicity) the support of a certain fantasy, namely and precisely the fantasy of the 'great Outside' which will save us—from what, finally? From that little, yet annoying bit of the outside which is at work, here and now, persistently nagging, preventing any kind of 'discursive cage' from safely closing upon itself. In other words, to say that the great Outside is a fantasy does not imply that it is a fantasy of a Real that does not really exist; rather, it implies that it is a fantasy in the strict psychoanalytic sense: a screen that covers up the fact that the discursive reality is itself leaking, contradictory, and entangled with the Real as its irreducible other side. That is to say: the great Outside is the fantasy that covers up the Real that is already right here.

The core of Meillassoux's project does not consist in opposing the real to the discursive, and dreaming of the break-through beyond the discursive; on the contrary, the core of his project is their joint articulation, which would escape the logic of transcendental constitution and hence their co-dependence. This joint articulation relies on two fundamental claims: the already mentioned thesis about the possible mathematisation of primary qualities, and the thesis about the absolute necessity of the contingent. Needless to say, both of these theses are philosophical, and aim at laying the foundations for what modern science seems to simply presuppose, namely, and precisely, a shared articulation of the discursive and the real. It would thus seem that they try to adjust the naïve realism of science, replacing it with a reflective, philosophically grounded 'speculative' realism.

Yet, the first really interesting question already appears here, namely: what is in fact the status of the realism which science's operations presuppose? Is it simply a form of naïve realism, a straightforward belief that the nature which it describes is absolute and exists out there independently of us? Meillassoux's inaugural presupposition indeed seems to be that science operates in the right way, yet lacks its own ontological theory that would correspond to its praxis. Considering the framework of his project, it is in fact rather astonishing how little time Meillassoux devotes to the discussion of modern science, its fundamental or inaugural gesture, its presuppositions and consequences—that is to say to the discussion of what science is actually doing. Contrary to this, we can say that Lacan has an extraordinarily well elaborated theory of modern science and of its inaugural gesture (to some extent this theory is part of a broader structuralist theory of science), in relation to which he situates his own psychoanalytic discourse. And this is where one needs to start. The relationship between psychoanalytic discourse and science is a crucial question for Lacan throughout his oeuvre, albeit it is far from simple. For, on the one hand, it presupposes their absolute kinship and co-temporality (marked by countless explicit statements like 'the subject of the unconscious is the subject of modern science', 'psychoanalysis is only possible after the same break that inaugurates modern science'...). On the other hand, there is also the no less remarkable difference and dissonance between psychoanalysis and science, with the concept of truth as its most salient marker, which involves the difference in their respective 'objects'. In short: the common ground shared by psychoanalysis and science is nothing else than the real in its absolute dimension, but they have different ways of pursuing this real.

What is the Lacanian theory of science? In the context of a similar debate and relying on Jean-Claude Milner, this question has been recently reopened, and given all its significance, by Lorenzo Chiesa,[3] to whom I owe this entry into the discussion. According to this theory, Galileanism replaced the ancient notion of nature with the modern notion according to which nature is nothing else than the empirical object of science. The formal precondition of this change lies in the complete mathematisation of science. In other words, after Galileo, 'nature does not have any other sensible substance than that which is necessary to the right functioning of science's mathematical formulas'.[4] Even more strongly put: the revolution of the Galilean science consists in producing its object ('nature') as its own *objective* correlate. In Lacan we find a whole series of such, very strong statements, for example: 'Energy is not a substance…, it's a numerical constant that a physicist has to find in his calculations, so as to be able to work'.[5] The fact that science speaks about this or that law of nature and about the universe does not mean that it preserves the perspective of the great Outside (as not discursively constituted in any way), rather the opposite is the case. Modern science starts when it produces its object. This is not to be understood in the Kantian sense of the transcendental constitution of phenomena, but in a slightly different, and stronger sense.

Modern science literally creates a new real(ity); it is not that the object of science is 'mediated' by its formulas, rather, it is indistinguishable from them; it does not exist outside them, *yet it is real*. It has real consequences or consequences in the real. More precisely: the new real that emerges with the Galilean scientific revolution (the complete mathematisation of science) is a real in which—and this is decisive—(the scientific) *discourse has consequences*. Such as, for example, landing on the moon. For, the fact that this discourse has consequences in the real does not hold for nature in the broad and lax sense of the word, it only holds for nature as physics or for physical nature. But of course there is always, says Lacan,

> the realist argument. We cannot resist the idea that nature is always there, whether we are there or not, we and our science, as if science were indeed ours and we weren't determined by it. Of course I won't dispute this. Nature is there. But what distinguishes it from physics is that it is worth saying something about physics, and that discourse has consequences in it, whereas everybody knows that no discourse has any consequences in nature, which is why we tend to love it so much. To be a philosopher of nature has never been considered as a proof of materialism, nor of scientific quality. (Lacan 2006a, p. 33)

Three things are crucial in this dense and decisive quote. 1) The shift of the accent from a discursive study of the real to the consequences of discourse in the real; related to this 2) the definition of the newly emerged reality; and 3) the prob-

---

3. Chiesa 2010, pp. 159-177.
4. Milner 2008, pp. 287-288.
5. Lacan 1990, p. 18.

lem of materialism. Let us first briefly stop at the third point, which we have already touched upon in passing with the question of the 'cerebral unconscious'. At stake is a key dimension of a possible definition of materialism, which one could formulate as follows: *materialism is not guaranteed by any matter.* It is not the reference to matter as the ultimate substance from which all emerges (and which, in this conceptual perspective, is often highly spiritualized) that leads to true materialism. The true materialism, which—as Lacan puts it with a stunning directness in another significant passage—can only be a dialectical materialism,[6] is not grounded in the primacy of matter nor in matter as first principle, but in the notion of conflict, of split, and of the 'parallax of the real' produced in it. In other words, the fundamental axiom of materialism is not 'matter is all' or 'matter is primary', but relates rather to the primacy of a cut. And, of course, this is not without consequences for the kind of realism that pertains to this materialism.

This brings us to the points 1) and 2) of the above quote, which we can take together since they refer to two aspects of this new, 'dialectically materialist' realism. The distinction between nature and physics established by Lacan does not follow the logic of distinguishing between nature as inaccessible thing in itself and physics as transcendentally structured nature, accessible to our knowledge. The thesis is different and somehow more radical. Modern science, which is, after all, a historically assignable event, creates a new space of the real or the real as a new dimension of ('natural') space. Physics does not 'cover' nature (or reduplicate it symbolically), but is added to it, with nature continuing to stay there where it has always been. 'Physics is not something extending, like God's goodness, across all nature'.[7] Nature keeps standing there not as an impenetrable Real in itself, but as the Imaginary, which we can see, like and love, but which is, at the same time, rather irrelevant. There is an amusing story about how some of Hegel's friends dragged him to the Alps, in order for him to become aware of, and to admire the stunning beauty of the nature there. All Hegel said about the sublime spectacle that was revealed to him is reported to have been: *Es ist so.* Lacan would have appreciated this a lot. *Es ist so,* no more to say about the mountains. This is not because we cannot really understand them, but because there is nothing to understand. (If we say that the stone we see is of this or that age, we are talking about another reality—one in which consequences of discourse exist.)

Lacan's definition of this difference is indeed extremely concise and precise. What is at stake is not that nature as scientific object (that is as physics) is only an effect of discourse, its consequence—and that in this sense physics does not actually deal with the real, but only with its own constructions. What is at stake is rather

---

6. 'If I am anything, it is clear that I'm not a nominalist. I mean that my starting point is not that the name is something that one sticks, like this, on the real. And one must choose. If we are nominalists, we must completely renounce dialectical materialism, so that, in short, the nominalist tradition, which is strictly speaking the only danger of idealism that can occur in a discourse like mine, is quite obviously ruled out. This is not about being realist in the sense one was realist in the Middle Ages, that is in the sense of the realism of the universals; what is at stake is to mark off the fact that our discourse, our scientific discourse, only finds the real in that it depends on the function of the semblance' (Lacan 2006b, p. 28).

7. Ibid., p. 34.

that the discourse of science creates, opens up a space in which this discourse has (real) consequences. And this is far from being the same thing. We are dealing with something that most literally, and from the inside, splits the world in two.

The fact that the discourse of science creates, opens up a space in which this *discourse has (real) consequences* also means that it can produce something that not only becomes a part of reality, but that can also change it. 'Scientific discourse was able to bring about the moon landing, where thought becomes witness to an eruption of a real, and with mathematics using no apparatus other than a form of language'.[8] To this Lacan adds that the aforementioned eruption of a real took place 'without the philosopher caring about it'. Perhaps we can see in this remark a problematisation of a certain aspect of modern philosophy, which tends to miss a crucial dimension of science at precisely this point of the real, and keeps reducing it to the logic of 'instrumental reason', 'technicism', and so on. We could also see in it a hint at the contemporary coupling of philosophy with the 'university discourse', the minimal definition of which would be precisely: the social link in which discourse has no consequences.

To return to the starting point of this digression: in regards to the question of realism in science, Lacan's diagnosis could be summed up in the following way. Although it may be that naïve realism constitutes the spontaneous ideology of many scientists, it is utterly irrelevant for the constitution of scientific discourse, its efficiency and its mode of operation. As we have already seen, this means: modern science did not arrive at the absolute character of its referent by relying on the presuppositions of naïve realism, that is, by naively assuming the existence of its referent 'in nature', but by reducing it to a letter, which alone opens up the space of real consequences of (scientific) discourse. And the word 'reducing' is not to be taken in the sense of reducing the richness of sensible qualities to an absolute minimum, yet a minimum in which we would be dealing with the continuation of the same substance; it should be taken in the sense of a *cut*, and of substitution. What is at stake is also not the classical logic of representation: the letter does not represent some aspect of sensible nature, but literally replaces it. It replaces it with something that belongs to discourse (to the semblance), yet something that can be—precisely because it belongs to discourse—formulated in the direction of the real. Which brings us again to the point formulated earlier: 'It is not worth talking about anything else than the real in which discourse itself has consequences'.[9] This is not an argument about the real only being the effect of discourse. The link between discursivity and the real (which is, after all, also what Meillassoux tackles in his polemics with contemporary obscurantism[10]) finds here a much firmer foundation than in the case of simply stating that the referent (a 'natural object') is absolute in, and only in, its mathematizable aspect. Meillassoux does not see the mathematization of science as a cut into reality that (only) produces the dimension of the real, but as the furthest point of a continuum, of a continuous sharp-

---

8. Lacan 1990, p. 36.

9. Lacan 2006a, p. 31.

10. His argument in this respect is that correlationist philosophy, precisely since it claims that we can know nothing about things in themselves, forces us to admit, at least as possible, even the most irrational obscurantist nonsense said about things in themselves.

ening of the ways in which scientists speak about reality; in his case, the real refers to the purely formal/formalizable segment of a thing remaining in the end
in the net of this sharpened form of scientific speech. Let us recall: '...the referents of the statements about dates, volumes etc., existed 4.56 billion years ago, as
described by these statements—but not these statements themselves, which are
contemporaneous with us'. The ideal character of a scientific formula catches
in its net, here and now, a fragment of the thing that is in itself absolute (that is
to say which existed as such and independently of this net 4.5 billion years ago).
Or, put in another way: the real is that portion of a substance that does not slide
through the net of mathematizable science, but remains caught in it. Lacan's
metaphor, and with it his entire perspective, is quite different in this respect: the
real is not guaranteed by the consistency of numbers (or letters), but by the impossible, that is by the limit of their consistency. This is why science does not operate by catching in its net the real as an absolute object, but rather touches upon
the real by means of the coincidence of the holes in its net and the holes in reality.
If it is not worth talking about the real or Nature outside of discourse, the reason
is that we necessarily stay on the level of semblance, which means that we can say
whatever we like. The real, on the other hand, is indicated by the fact that not all
is possible. Here enters the other crucial component of the Lacanian real, binding the realism of consequences to the modality of the impossible. Together they
could be articulated as follows: something has consequences if it cannot be anything (that is, if it is impossible in one of its own segments).

> The articulation, and I mean algebraic articulation, of the semblance—
> which, as such, only involves letters—and its effects, this is the only ap-
> paratus by means of which we designate what is real. What is real is what
> makes/constitutes a hole [*fait trou*] in this semblance, in this articulated
> semblance that is scientific discourse. Scientific discourse advances with-
> out even worrying whether it is a semblance or not. What is at stake is sim-
> ply that its network, its net, its *lattice*, as one says, makes the right holes
> appear in the right place. It has no other reference but the impossible to
> which its deductions arrive. This impossible is the real. In physics we only
> aim at something which is the real by means of a discursive apparatus, in-
> sofar as the latter, in its very rigor, encounters the limits of its consistency.
> But what interests *us*, is the field of truth. (Lacan 2006b, p. 28)

The absolutely crucial point of this 'psychoanalytic realism' is that the real
is not a substance or *being*, but precisely its limit. That is to say, the real is that
which traditional ontology had to cut off in order to be able to speak of 'being
qua being'. We only arrive at being qua being by subtracting something from
it—and this something is precisely the '*hole*', that which it lacks in order to be fully constituted as being; the zone of the real is the interval within being itself, on
account of which no being is 'being qua being', but can only *be* by being something else than it is. One can ask, of course, how can it matter if one cuts off
something that is not there to begin with? It matters very much not only because
it becomes something when it is cut off, but also since the something it becomes
is the very object of psychoanalysis.

In order to situate this in relation to the previous discussion, we could say: the curving of the space that constitutes the dimension of the real has a cause, and a consequence. Its cause is the emergence of a pure signifier, and its consequence is the emergence of a new kind of object. Yet this is also to say that there is no such thing as a pure signifier, because the purer, or the clearer its cut, the more palpable and irreducible—or simply real—the object it produces. This, for example, is the fundamental lesson of the psychoanalytic notion of *Verneinung*, negation.

Freud's short essay with that title is one of his most interesting and complex; it deals with a signifier par excellence, 'no', or negation. And if, as Freud is reported to have said once, 'sometimes a cigar is just a cigar', the point of this article is that 'no' is never just 'no', and that the more 'instrumental' its use (that is the more it functions as a pure signifier), the likelier it is that something else will get stuck onto it. Freud's most famous example is of course: 'You ask who this person in the dream can be. It's *not* my mother [Die Mutter ist es *nicht*]'. In which case, adds Freud, the question is settled, we can be sure that it is indeed her. Yet, what becomes more and more obvious as we follow Freud's arguments further, is that what is introduced by this negation is precisely something else besides the alternative: 'It is my mother' / 'It isn't my mother'. So let us take this step by step. Without being asked who played a part in his dream, the patient rushes forward and volunteers the word mother, accompanied by negation. It is as if he *has to* say it, but at the same time cannot, it is imperative and impossible at the same time. The result is that the word is uttered as denied, the repression coexists with the thing being consciously spoken of. The first mistake to avoid here is to read this in terms of what this person really saw in his dream, and then, because of a conscious censorship, lied about in the account he gave to the analyst. For—and this is crucial not only for the understanding of *Verneinung*, but also of the Freudian unconscious as such—what is unconscious in the given case is first and foremost the *censorship*, and not simply its object, 'mother'. The latter is fully present in the statement, and introduced by the subject himself, who could have also not mentioned her at all. The unconscious sticks here to the distortion itself (the negation), and is not hidden in what the subject supposedly really saw in his dream. It could well be that another, known or unknown person actually appeared in the dream, yet the story of the unconscious that is of interest to psychoanalysis begins with this '*not* my mother' that takes place in the account of the dream. But things become even more interesting, for Freud goes on to say that even though in analysis we can bring this person to withdraw the 'not' and accept the (content of the) repressed, 'the repressive process itself is not yet removed by this'.[11] The repression, the symptoms persist after the analysand has become conscious of the repressed, which could also be formulated as follows: we can accept the (repressed) content, eliminate it, but we cannot eliminate the structure of the gap, or crack that generates it. We could also claim that what the patient wanted to say is precisely what he said: that is, neither that it was some other person than the mother, nor that it was the mother, but that it was the not-mother or the mother-not.

---

11. Freud (1925h), p. 236.

An excellent joke from Ernest Lubitsch's *Ninotchka* can help us here to get a better grip on the singular object 'mother-not' that we are talking about:

> A guy goes into a restaurant and says to the waiter: 'Coffee without cream, please'. The waiter replies: 'I am sorry sir, but we are out of cream. Could it be without milk?'

This joke carries a certain real, even a certain truth about the real, which has to do precisely with the singular negativity introduced or discovered by psychoanalysis. A negation of something is not pure absence or pure nothing, or simply the complementary of what it negates. The moment it is spoken, there remains a trace of that which it is not. This is a dimension introduced (and made possible) by the signifier, yet irreducible to it. It has (or can have) a positive, albeit spectral quality, which can be formulated in the precise terms of '*with without* (cream)' as irreducible to both alternatives (cream/no cream).

When mother thus appears in this singular composition with negation, that is, when she appears as 'not-mother', it looks as if both terms irredeemably contaminate each other. As if the 'not' marks the mother with the stamp of unconscious desire ('like made in Germany stamped on the object', as Freud puts it), and 'mother' no less contaminates the formal purity of the negation with—as we sometimes read on the packaging of certain kinds of food—some 'traces of elements'. But we should be even more precise and say that the mother we start with (just before the negation hits her) is not the same as the object-mother produced through this negation, via the *work* of the unconscious. It is another mother, a mother—why not put it this way?—with consequences, not a mother as an element of Nature. Which is precisely why admitting to the analyst that it has been your mother, after all, does not help in the least, and why in spite of this admission the essence of the repression persists. For what we get in this way is of no use to us, it refers only to mother as something factual, as an 'element of nature', and it does not bring us any closer to the dimension of the real.

This brings us back to the core of our discussion, to the question of realism and of the real that psychoanalysis shares with science, and this is how one could sum up the main point of this discussion. If the subject of the unconscious is the subject of (modern) science, this is precisely in so far as it is essentially linked to the field in which discourse has consequences. Without the latter there is no subject, and certainly no subject of the unconscious. This is how one should understand Lacan's statement that the subject is the 'answer of the real', *la réponse du réel*. Which is something else than to say that it is an effect of discourse or discursively constituted. The subject, or the unconscious, are not effects of language, let alone linguistic entities, they belong to the field of the real, that is to the field that only emerges with language, but which is not itself language, nor is reducible to it (say as its performative creation); the real is defined by the fact that language has consequences in it. And we could perhaps say: if science creates and operates in the field where discourse has consequences, psychoanalysis is the science of this singular field, of the surprising ways in which these consequences work, and of the peculiar ontological status of the objects of this field.

It would not be appropriate, however, to conclude without accepting the challenge of Meillassoux's initial question in its estimable directness and simplicity. That is: what does the Lacanian realism of consequences, combined with the impossible, imply for the status of so-called ancestral statements? Does the statement 'the earth was formed 4.5 billion years ago' make any sense independently of us, that is: does it refer to a specific *object* which did in fact (although according to our way of counting and based on radiometric dating) exist 4.5 billion years ago?

Why not venture an answer? In order to formulate it I will draw on a very fascinating story, which revolves precisely around fossils and which—if taken in *its* speculative dimension—can give to the notion of arche-fossil a very intriguing Lacanian twist. In his book Meillassoux does in fact at some point hint at this story—but this remains an utterly cursory hint, serving only as a rhetorical argument for mocking the absurdities that correlationism would seem to be compatible with, and it entirely misses the true speculative potential of the story in question.

In one of his superb essays, entitled 'Adam's Navel', Stephen Jay Gould draws our attention to a most astonishing, 'ridiculous' yet extremely elegant theory suggested by the important British naturalist Philip Henry Goss.[12] Goss was Darwin's contemporary and he published the work that interests us (*Omphalos*) in 1857, that is only two years before Darwin's *On The Origin of Species*. He was a most passionate naturalist, and one of his greatest passions was fossils, which he studied and described with particular devotion. At that time the nascent science of geology had already gathered evidence for the earth's enormous antiquity, which bluntly contradicted its age according to Genesis (6000 years). And this was Goss's principal dilemma—for he was not only a dedicated naturalist, but also a deeply religious man. The core of his theory thus consisted of an attempt to resolve the contradiction between the (relatively recent) creation *ab nihilo*, and the real existence of fossils of a much more respectable age. He came up with a rather ingenious theory according to which God did indeed create the earth about 6000 years ago, but he did not create it only for the time to come, for the future, but also retroactively, 'for the past'—at the moment of creating the earth he also put the fossils in it. One should not miss the beauty of this self-effacing gesture: God creates the world by effacing the traces of his creation, and hence of his own existence, to the benefit of scientific exploration. And it is probably no coincidence that the theological world rejected this theory even more passionately than the scientific world did. Immediately, the consensus appeared that God could not have 'written on the rocks one enormous and superfluous lie'. According to Gould, modern American creationists also mostly and vehemently reject this theory for 'imputing a dubious moral character to God'.

The interest of Goss's theory for our discussion consists above all in pointing to the insufficiency of a simply linear theory of time in respect to the question of the real. Also, the patina of bizarreness that surrounds Goss's story should not blind us to the fact that structurally speaking his dilemma is exactly Meillassoux's. It suffices to replace God's creation with human creation (nature as sub-

---

12. Gould 1985.

jectively/discursively constituted), and we get a stunningly similar question: does science only study something which we have ourselves constituted as such, posited (as external), or is this exteriority independent of us and has existed exactly as it is long before we did? The Lacanian answer would be: it is independent, yet it only *becomes* such at the very moment of 'creation'. That is to say: with the emergence—*ex nihilo*, why not?—of the pure signifier and with it of the reality in which discourse has consequences, we get a physical reality independent of ourselves. (Which, to be sure, is not to say that we do not have any influence on it.) And of course this independence is also gained for the time 'before us'. The reality of arche-fossils or objects of ancestral statements is not different from the reality of objects contemporary with us—and this is because neither the former nor the latter are correlates of our thinking, but are instead *objective correlates of the emergence of a break in reality as homogeneous continuum* (which is precisely the break of modern science, as well as the break of the emergence of the signifier as such). This is the very reason why Lacan's theory is indeed 'dialectically-materialist': the break implies nothing else but a speculative identity of the absolute and of becoming. They are not opposed, but need to be thought together. Something can (in time) *become absolute* (that is timeless). The absolute is at the same time necessary and contingent: there is no absolute without a break in which it is constituted as absolute (that is to say as 'necessarily necessary'—whereby this redoubling is precisely the space in which discourse has consequences), yet this break is contingent.

Contrary to this, Meillassoux's gesture of absolutizing contingency as the only necessity ultimately succumbs, not to speculativity, but to idealism: all is contingent, all but the necessity of this contingency. By claiming this Meillassoux actually absolutizes the *absent cause* (the cause which, if present, would ground the necessity of the laws such as they are). His argument in this respect is well known: there is no higher cause on account of which natural laws are such as they are, no higher necessity. Therefore they can change at any moment—contingently, without any reason, which is to say *ex nihilo* (he does not back down from this notion here). But we can see what happens here: we get an atheistic structure which cannot do without the absolutization of the absent Cause, which thus guarantees the contingency of all laws. We are dealing with something like a 'God of atheists', a God guaranteeing that there is no God. In the conception that we are drawing up here with the help of Lacan the configuration is different. Lacanian atheism can only be the atheism of the absence of (any) guarantee or, more precisely, the absence of an external (or meta-) guarantee: the guarantee is included in, is part of what it guarantees. There is no independent guarantee, which is not to say that there is no guarantee (or no 'absolute'). This is what the notion of the not-all, as different from the notion of constitutive exception, aims at: that which can disprove one discursive theory, and confirm another, comes from within the discursive field. (In science this means that an experiment confirms or disqualifies a certain theoretical configuration *within the framework* in which it takes place; an experiment can only confirm or disprove a theory by being performed on its own grounds; there is nothing simply outside a theory with which the latter could be measured.) Instead of the logic of exception and of the meta-level which total-izes some 'all' (all is contingent, all but the necessity of this contingency), we are thus dealing with the logic of not-all. Lacan's axiom, which could be written as 'the necessary is not-all' does not absolutize contingency, but posits it as the point of *truth* of the absolute necessity in its becoming such (at some point in time).

And in the end this also brings us to the one important point of difference that nonetheless exists between psychoanalysis and science, and which Lacan keeps relating to the question of truth. In a few words: what science does not see, or does not want to know anything about, is the fact that one of the consequenc-es of discourse is also the dimension of truth. Truth as an objective dimension of discourse. Not the truth *about* a given configuration, but truth as an irreducible *el-ement* of this configuration, as an essential by-product of the cleavage of the imma-nence which makes the latter not-all, that is to say which makes it include with-in itself its own criterion of the real. As element of a given configuration—that is as *element of the real*—truth can only speak in the first person—which is where Lacan's idea of the prosopopoeia of truth comes from: 'I, the truth, am speak-ing'. And insofar as this field of truth is what interests psychoanalysis, this is the point where another story starts, another chapter of its realism, and where a cer-tain distance in respect to science steps in. It would not be all together wrong to call this distance a political one, for with the dimension of truth there necessarily enters the dimension of conflict.[13]

BIBLIOGRAPHY

Chiesa, L., 'Hyperstructuralism's Necessity of Contingency', in *S: Journal of the Jan van Eyck Circle for Lacanian Ideology Critique*, 3, 2010

Freud, S., (1925h), 'Negation', in *SE, 19*

Gould, S. J., 'Adam's Navel', in *Flamingo's Smile*, Harmondsworth: Penguin Books, 1985

Lacan, J., *Television. A Challenge to the Psychoanalytic Establishement*, New York & London: Norton & Company, 1990

—— *Le séminaire, livre XVI. D'un autre à l'Autre*, Paris: Seuil, 2006a

—— *Le séminaire, livre XVIII. D'un discours qui ne serait pas du semblant*, Paris: Seuil, 2006b

Malabou, C., *Les nouveaux blessés*, Paris: Bayard, 2007

Meillassoux, Q., *After Finitude*, London: Continuum, 2008

Milner, J.-C., *Le périple structural*, Lagrasse: Verdier, 2008

Žižek, S., *Living in the End Times*, London & New York: Verso, 2010

---

13. See Lacan 2006a, p. 38.

Accesses to the Real:
Lacan, Monotheism, and Predestination

Felix Ensslin

> This is why those who try to make the world and life sacred
> again are just as impious as those who despair about profana-
> tion. This is why Protestant theology, which clearly separates
> the profane world from the divine, is both wrong and right:
> right because the world has been consigned irrevocably by
> revelation (by language) to the profane sphere; wrong because
> it will be saved precisely insofar as it is profane.
> (Agamben, *The Coming Community*)

I. INTRODUCTION

In this paper I will investigate the relationship between two competing claims
on where to find the subject of psychoanalysis. The reason why this is important
for psychoanalysis can be considered to be obvious; the reason why this is important for philosophy lies in the fact that, as, among others, Alain Badiou has
pointed out, there can be no philosophy after Lacan unless it has undergone the
trial of Lacanian 'anti-philosophy'.[1] What are then these two competing claims
on how to think the subject of psychoanalysis? On the one hand, we have Jacques
Lacan's repeated claim that the 'subject of psychoanalysis is the subject of modern science' or, to put it differently, that 'the subject of psychoanalysis is the Cartesian subject'.[2] On the other hand, we have his claim, more implicit but no less
clear, that the subject of psychoanalysis is heir to the monotheistic implementa-
tion of a symbolic master-signifier as an act of speech producing in this act the
real *reste*; of a master signifier representing a subject for other signifiers as a master that 'does not know about sexual knowledge', but paradoxically knows a lot
about 'ferocious passion', about 'love, hatred and ignorance'.[3] This happens be-

---

1. See, for instance, Badiou's theory of the subject as presented in Badiou 2005.

2. Lacan 2006, pp. 726-745. Jean-Claude Milner has discussed this claim in his book *L'Œuvre claire: Lacan, la science et la philosophie* (Milner 1995) by, among other things, developing the different place of mathematics in the ancient *episteme* of Euclid and his successors, on the one hand, and in modern sci-ence, on the other.

3. Lacan 2007, p. 136. 'In interpellating this chosen people, it is characteristic of Yaweh, when he announces himself, that he is ferociously ignorant of everything that exists of certain religious practic-

cause such a monotheistic god does not present himself alongside his goddess as part and parcel of the eternal return of the same cycle of destruction and regeneration, but as a signifier that calls for another signifier: 'the people'.[4] 'Love, hatred, and ignorance' are thus the remnants of the impossibility of *le rapport sexuel*, which is literally covered up by the covenant that produces 'the people' as S_2 in respect to YHWE's S_1.[5] The focus of both the claims in question can in the last resort be brought to bear on the real of the 'letter/litter'.[6] In the case of modern mathematics this happens through algebra and its ability to inscribe infinite functions without giving them symbolic existence on the level of meaning, i.e. without tying them to what one could call a full ontology. The same goes with Lacan's working through of Descartes' dictum *cogito ergo sum*: 'Either I am not or I think not' is one of Lacan's formulations for the fact that the 'I think: "therefore I am"' does not contain two 'I' on the same level; in fact, they are one (in the place where the real, the imaginary and the symbolic are tied together, as a kind of proper name) and split on the level of symbolic existence (the 'therefore I am') and of the excluded being of the subject.[7] In the case of monotheism the real appears through the fact that the signifier is spelled by letters—or, better, each signifier (symbolic) that engenders a subject also produces with it the necessary step of giving meaning to this subject (imaginary) and the impossibility to sustain this meaning as full or sufficient (real). This condition splits the signifier into its literal elements. They are not phonemes—as the smallest 'meaningful units'—but

---

es that were rife at the time, and that are founded on a certain type of knowledge—sexual knowledge' (ibid.).

4. Ibid., p. 140.

5. This is not the place to recount in detail the development of this idea in Lacan's work. Suffice it to say that in Seminar XVII Lacan can speak of the 'Oedipus complex' as 'Freud's dream' (Lacan 2007, p. 117 and p. 137) and replace it with the observation that it is at the beginning of the prophetic tradition with Hosea—i.e. at the moment when, according to Freud's *Moses and Monotheism*, the latency of the repressed monotheistic religion instituted by Moses the Egyptian breaks open again—that we find the hallmark of what monotheism means, namely, the replacement of the representation of the sexual knowledge of destruction and regeneration with the institution of an S_1 that defines his S_2 (and vice versa). In a striking moment of Seminar XVII—a kind of scansion within the Seminar—the discourse of the university shifts into the discourse of the analyst: the scholar of religion Monsieur Chaquot comes out with a discourse of knowledge (S_2) that seems to finally give shape to what Lacan has been looking for, without knowing it, which in turn allows Lacan to shift it into the register of a S_1 (understood here as the *Deutung* of the analyst). 'Chaquot: There are at times *several* traits by which Israel is described as a goddess. But that has never been said. Lacan: That's very important. Ultimately something of what I was beginning to announce before hinges on that. *You hadn't indicated that to me at all* [my emphasis]. Chaquot: One has the impression that the prophetic religion replaces the goddess with Israel. This would be the case with Hosea—it replaces her with the people. Lacan: Given the hour, I think we can leave it there' (ibid., p. 140). With this interruption, or scansion, Lacan produces the new S_1: monotheism creates the conditions of interpellation, which in turn produce the conditions of universality and the real as 'effects of language' (ibid., p. 135).

6. 'A letter, a litter', a quote from *Finnegans Wake*, is used by Lacan in his 'Seminar on "The Purloined Letter"', contained in *Écrits* (Lacan 2006, p. 18). Here and in other places, Lacan then plays with it, producing, among other terms, *litura, liturarius, rature, terre, littoral, littéral*, etc. It is a good example of a new S_1 being produced after the 'letter/litter' of the (originally imaginarized) signifier becomes reconstituted as designified.

7. See for example Lacan 2007, pp. 154-155. I cannot discuss this in detail here but would like to call attention to the issue of deferred action (*Nachträglichkeit*) that should be taken into consideration in this context: the real subject which carries the symbolic is a *nachträglicher* effect of the symbolic Other in the first place.

simply *restes*, nothing else than letters/litters, and the real appears not as impossible, but as the possible object-cause of a new symbolization.

In what follows I want to sustain this second heritage[8] of the subject of psychoanalysis by means of some notes on the notion of god as a *designified signifier*, which will allow me to return to Lacan's claim that the *analytic discourse* emerges in any shift between discourses, and that such shifts produce 'love' as their sign. My claim will be that this is so because 'love' needs to be understood here in terms of a new S1, as it appears in the analytic discourse. By looking at the analogy between *eros*, *phallus* and S1, I will then discuss the relation of Kantian moral *Gesinnung* with love/*eros* as both being just such a new S1. All the above will also function as a propaedeutic to investigate Alenka Zupančič's critique of the Kantian 'postulates of practical reason'—the existence of god and the immortality of the soul—and her presentation of the possible different subjects that the split between law and subject—made necessary by the demand for a moral *Gesinnung*—can produce. In the final two sections, I will then discuss the break between macrocosm and microcosm in which the subject of psychoanalysis appears, and ask the question concerning why it is necessary to preserve both the mathematical and the monotheist heritages in the attempt to link psychoanalytic and philosophical discourse after Lacan. The answer to this question, I claim, lies in the fact that one can get to the truly contingent real of the letter (in mathematical ontology) only after losing the resentment against the lack of determinate objects, i.e. by working through the fantasy of the imaginary father.

The following reflections are meant as a contribution to the discussion of the relationship between mathematical ontology and Lacanian psychoanalysis. While I see the advantages of their alliance, I also think that—contrary for example to Alain Badiou's claim in his essay 'God is dead'[9]—it is not possible to leave the signifier 'god' in the dustbin of history. Nor is it indeed possible to do this since, as Alenka Zupančič put it, god 'knows that he is dead'.[10] On the contrary, since the prohibition of *jouissance* always issues from the imaginary place of full *jouissance* (from the imaginary father who in this sense is the father of the real of *jouissance*) and not just from prohibition as a symbolic mandate (i.e. from the real father in the ordinary sense of the word, the really existing father with his more or less sad and dumb holding the place of the symbolic, through which he institutes castration), the path of the subject in which the 'subject chooses herself as subject and not as (psychological) "ego"' necessarily has to move *through the loss of*

---

8. Derrida asks in *Specters of Marx*: 'Can one conceive of an atheological heritage of the Messianic?' (Derrida 1994, p. 168). Maybe what I have defined here as the heritage of monotheism comes close to this 'atheological heritage' as long as the *a*-theological is also meant to contain the object *a* that can sustain an act, not just its deferral. Presumably, for Derrida, the point of a Messianic that is 'atheological' is something of the order of the *avenir*, the to-come, i.e. the deferral of any possible affirmation or order. The *a*-theological heritage of monotheism in psychoanalysis points to both sides: the deferral—since no symbolic can ever be sustained that completes an order (the theological)—but also the object *a* as object-cause of a symbolization (or 'naming'), i.e. of an affirmation that does sustain a (new) order (for the subject).

9. Badiou 2006.

10. '"Highbrow relativism" (we have too much knowledge and historic experience to take anything as absolute) may well be regrettable, but it is nevertheless real. By attacking it directly and lamenting it, we will not change much. The fact is that not only do we know that "God is dead" (that the Other does not exist), He knows it too' (Zupančič 2000, p. 255).

this image of (full) *jouissance* and utter prohibition.[11] In order to work with the possibilities that an algebraic reading of the real gives us, we need to work through the real that is left from symbolic castration and repeats it, namely, the fantasy of *jouissance* in the Other, which makes him an other to the subject, the other that robs and deprives (*priver*) the subject of *jouissance*.

II. DESIGNIFIED SIGNIFIERS AND THE BAN OF SOVEREIGNTY

'God' is a *designified signifier*—this is the lesson Eric Santner developed in his seminal *On the Psychotheology of Everyday Life*.[12] Such a signifier no longer 'means' anything to 'us'. It does not denote[13] anything in particular and has no moorings in anything like an 'ethical substance' (in a Hegelian sense) or the practices or habits that make it thus (in a Scholastic or Neo-Aristotelian sense); nevertheless it still has the capacity to address us. It does so in the manner of a haunting interpellation, a manner maybe best described by Shakespeare, whose Hamlet knows that the Other is speaking to him and also knows that this Other knows that it is dead, but cannot derive from it a certain identity within this world or a particular and definitive duty in the next. If this is so, we need to keep in mind an immediate doubling of the designified signifier: while it is such, it *appears* in a way that seemingly contains a very specific address as an imaginary apparition. Thus, for the designified signifier to be able to be assumed as truly designified, it is not enough that the signified 'knows' it is no longer present under the signifier; the apparitions that such knowledge of the Other engenders in the subject needs to be if not eradicated—a work of mourning that is impossible to conclude, as Derrida has shown—at least laid to rest or dried up, split up in the establishment of a new subject or a new S1 carried out by a partial object-cause. Designification leads to the *Other* appearing to the subject as *other*, as an other on the imaginary axis a-a'.[14] The imaginary father appears because it is impossible to immediately move from the experience of the impotence of the real father (as the guarantor of a symbolic universe that would truly sustain and guarantee the objects of the subject's drives) to a positive construction of alternative partial realizations of subjective truths without passing through the resentment against the imaginary father as the agent who is supposedly responsible for this mess by keeping all the *jouissance* stolen from the subject (the imaginary whole of real *jouissance*) stored away for himself in an all inclusive reservoir. Only out of a confrontation with this imaginary father (that is, as we shall see, a confrontation with the ideal-ego) can something that is—*literally*—left over from this confrontation become the object-cause of a new articulation, which this time fol-

---

11. Ibid., p. 32. A more technical way to argue this would be the following: as there is in each neurosis the core of a psychosis (the mythical moment at which a subject produces his/her *Neurosenwahl*) so there is in each castration the fundamental dimension of privation. See Lacan 2007, p. 124 and Lacan 1994.

12. Santner develops this idea with reference to Gershom Scholem, Walter Benjamin, Franz Rosenzweig, Sigmund Freud, and Jean Laplanche. See Santner 2001, p. 44.

13. The term 'denote' is meant here to designate a kind of extensional scope of a predicate that shows the 'relation between language and the world' (Lohnstein 1996, p. 65 ['Die Beziehung zwischen Sprache und Welt bezeichnen wirr demzufolge als Denotation']).

14. This is exactly what happens in Lacan with the imaginary father as the 'agent of privation'—I shall return to this soon.

lows the logic of the *pas-tout* and no longer the imaginarized phallic logic of the whole. The same double movement holds for the designified signifier: it can become for the subject what it is only after it has been ripped from the image that appears as an apparition in order to cover its designification. Designification, like trauma and human sexuality, can realize itself only in *Zweizeitigkeit*, in the temporal structure of a repetition producing its own cause. The designified signifier confronts us with the very dimension of a signifier that makes it different from any sign or code: it exists as a signifier independently of the meaning it has for someone or the information that is stored in it. Referring to the differentiation between 'validity' and 'meaning' that Gershom Scholem develops apropos the question of the status of revelation at the beginning of the 20th century, Santner sums up the nature of a designified signifier in the following way: 'The word signifies, *but not for us*, even though we continue, in some sense, to be addressed by it, to live, as Scholem so powerfully phrased it, within the space of its validity beyond and in excess of its meaning'.[15]

It was Giorgio Agamben who made the point that the Scholemian terminology of validity and meaning conveys an important reference in contemporary political theory.[16] He uses it to describe the double nature of sovereignty and its effects: not only does sovereignty constitute subjects (like Althusser's notion of interpellation), but it produces an excess with regard to the purely instrumental function of subjectivation, that is, obedience and order.[17] It does so since the collapse of *potestas* and *auctoritas* into the establishment of the new dimension of *imperium* in the Roman Empire produced a *nomos empsychos* that functions like S1 in relation to S2 (the other of sovereignty and of the *nomos empsychos*): this (non-)relation or impossible relation generates a surplus, like any discourse of the master. This excess of sovereignty has to do with the groundless ground of authority, which becomes addressable (or readable, or visible, or noticeable…) only at the moment of a crisis, such as the crisis of metaphysics or the problem of legitimacy in modernity. That is to say, it becomes readable or visible only at the moment in which the S1 that has been instituted shows itself as designified—by the production of its spectral imaginary double. This excess is analogous to an excess of validity over meaning, which is usually repressed by any positive law or constituted power. It only becomes obvious when the problem of constitutive power and its double (i.e. divine power or pure violence) surfaces. If constitutive power as a *state of exception* is, for instance according to Carl Schmitt, a kind of whole or abso-

---

15. Santner 2001, p. 44.

16. See, for instance, Agamben 2005, p. 35: 'Being outside yet belonging to it, this is the topological structure of the state of exception'. Here we also find the history of the creation of the *nomos empsychos* as the embodiment of the collapse of *auctoritas* and *potestas* into a new S1, which is precisely more (and less) than the literal embodiment of power; of course, the *nomos empsychos* as an individual body is less than 'power'—for who could sustain power only in an through himself? Yet it is also more than power, for who, or what, would be only an effect of power or of its exercise? (For the second option one should remember Heidegger's analysis of Nietzsche's 'will to power' as a form of subjectivity.) So, by occupying all knowledge of power with the image, name and representation of a living body or his *flesh*, the collapse of *auctoritas* and *potestas* into the *nomos empsychos* shows the spectral occupation of the other or objective knowledge (S2) by a sovereign (S1).

17. It is obvious that such a structure then makes operable what, in Seminar XVII, Lacan calls the *discourse of the master*.

lute ground of sovereignty, then divine power or pure violence is its truly designified double.[18] There is then a dimension of sovereignty that is no longer exert-
ed in order to establish (preserve or reaffirm) order, but is simply identical with
itself. It is no longer an imaginarized real—like the fantasy of the imaginary father—but simply real. For Agamben—as for Santner in his appropriation of this
logic—there is an ambiguity in the excess of validity over meaning: while it allows for an exodus or escape from the logic of means (of instrumentality, or order, or being, which are all tied to what has already been thought and done), it
also opens up a subjective dimension of excess. The subjects who try to get their
bearings in a world in which such sovereignty is experienced are exposed to what
Agamben tries to capture with the Italian terms *bando* and *abbandono*, ban and
abandonment, precisely because they are in the thrall of the double nature of designification: imaginary ban and real abandonment. Santner puts forward this
association when he introduces the notion of a designified signifier (and of 'God'
as a designified signifier):

> We are always within the 'ban' of such signifiers by virtue of the historici-
> ty of meaning. We are, that is, always haunted, surrounded by the remain-
> ders of lost forms of life, by concepts and signs that had meaning within a
> form of life that is now gone and so persists, to use Lacan's telling formula-
> tion, as 'hieroglyphs in the desert.' (Santner 2001, p. 44)

It is thus precisely through the loss of 'life-forms, concepts and signs' as potentially meaningful that the dimension of the designified signifier shows up,
including its double possibility of producing either a subject that is motionless
under its imaginary ban or left to itself in the real abandonment that is necessary to produce a new S1 from the debris of its encounter with the dimension of
designification.

III. CHANGING DISCOURSES: THE EMERGENCE OF THE ANALYTIC DISCOURSE

In 1973 Lacan returns to the four discourses that he had developed in Seminar
XVII, *The Other Side of Psychoanalysis*, a few years earlier. In the context of his
discussion as to why 'the fact that I say (*mon dire*) that the unconscious is structured like a language is not part and parcel of the field of linguistics',[19] Lacan
develops the following idea: whenever there is a shift in what counts as reason
and reasons, i.e. whenever there is a shift in discourse, there always emerges a
kind of break or break-up of the significations that counted as knowledge in the
previous discourse and were held up by it. Lacan, who had originally turned
to linguistics (as many of his contemporaries) not least because it seemed to offer an approach to the real of the object of science without having recourse to
a psychological or transcendental subject,[20] speaks of the 'fact of saying' in or-

---

18. This conclusion is obviously indebted to Agamben's reconstruction of Walter Benjamin's 'Critique
of Violence' and his dialogue with Carl Schmitt (see for instance Agamben 1998, p. 35). For a more detailed discussion, see also my 'Potentiality in Agamben' (Ensslin 2010, pp. 121-136).

19. Lacan 2007, p. 14.

20. See the entirety of session XI of Lacan's Seminar XVII, which has been given the title 'Furrows
in the alethosphere' by the editor. In it Lacan speaks about the topic in question: the relationship be-

der to demonstrate that psychoanalysis always has to start from the split between the level of the statement and that of enunciation. While the first is the object of linguistics and in this sense objective (nobody makes up the elements from which language produces what can count as phonetic elements within its linguistic structure), the second is not. Lacan pays attention to this level by reference to *mon dire*, i.e. to his 'act of saying'.[21] While *what is said* on the level of the enunciated is dependent on 'what is determined in advance'—because it 'can only use the given signifiers, the (shifter) I is determined *retroactively*'[22]—the *mon* of *mon dire*, as it were, retroactively becomes an S1 that ties together the levels of the symbolic, the imaginary and the real, rather than simply the levels accessible to linguistics. It 'becomes a signification, engendered at the level of the statement, of what it produces at the level of the enunciation'.[23] What the subject is—*is* in a fundamental, ethical sense—can only be revealed through what *what is said*/the level of the enunciated means to the *jouissance* of the subject that is produced (retroactively) by the act of *saying*/the level of enunciation. Furthermore, what that enjoyment will have been can only be ascertained retroactively. In Zupančič's words: 'It is at this level that we must situate the ethical subject: at the level of something which becomes what "it is" only in the act (here a "speech act") engendered, so to speak, by another subject' (Zupančič 2000, p. 103). This 'other subject' is none other than the Other as the place of differences, where the 'given signifiers' are always already operative—and are operative as if they had 'meaning' and not just 'validity'. In Seminar XX, Lacan wants to point out that this process of subjectivization of the act of saying depends on the possibility of the signifiers first becoming 'designified' and thus literalized, for then it is possible to reconfigure them in a way that produces a new/different discourse, despite the fact that on the level of *what is said* there is only an engagement with the *given signifiers*. In order to illustrate the designification necessary in the shift of levels, Lacan uses a very specific image of destruction, namely that of the destruction of an arrange-

tween the readable real of modern science and the effects of language. Lack becomes readable in science as object *a*/algebra. But 'the effects of language are retroactive, precisely in that it is as language develops that it manifests what it is qua want-to-be' (ibid., p. 155). This 'qua want-to-be' is the name of the lack presented by *mathematics*/real science in algebraic form. This is, contrary to what is often argued, not a development that is only proper to the later Lacan. See, for instance, the discussion about the real in Seminar IV, where it is said that 'in the real there is present already something marked by signifierness', i.e. the *Es* (Lacan 1994, p. 37). Lorenzo Chiesa has recently discussed the relationship between the S1 and the mark of the real (the unary trait) in his article 'Count-as-one, Forming-into-one, Unary Trait, S1' (Chiesa 2006, pp. 68-92). If I understand him correctly, his argument takes the opposite direction of mine: while I want to insist on the necessity to think the monotheistic creationist heritage alongside the mathematico-ontological structure of the subject, he seems to be thinking of an evolution from the 'mark of the hunter' to the master-signifier (ibid., pp. 76 ff). While I am very fascinated by this narrative (and the references to Lacan's unpublished Seminar IX, *L'identification*, from 1961-1962, that make it possible), I would simply point out what Lacan never tires of saying: 'Our first rule is never to seek the origins of language, if only because they are demonstrated well enough through their effects' (Lacan 2007, p. 155). He also points out that the *Urvater*—and with him the function of the imaginary father—is a 'Darwinian buffoonery' of Freud (ibid., p. 112) which precisely makes it necessary to locate the emergence of the S1 in creationist monotheism.

21. Lacan 2007, p. 16.
22. Zupančič 2000, p. 103.
23. Lacan 1998, p. 138.

ment in the life-world, of now littered elements that previously meant what they
meant as a matter of fact:

> Yet, it is in the consequences of what is said that the act of saying is judged.
> For one can do all kinds of things with it, like one does with furniture
> when, for example, one is undergoing a siege or a bombardment. (Lacan
> 1999, pp. 15-16)

If, at the moment T1 (i.e. on the level of *what is said*, of the enunciated) the arrangement of the elements seems a matter of fact,[24] then, at the moment T2, the
elements become visible as such: the previously given arrangement shows itself
as, indeed, having been always already *designified*.[25] The elements that then show
themselves as litter or letters of the previous arrangement are open to a new construction or articulation. This, however, does not happen in a simple way. For
the destruction of the order produces the guilt of somehow having been responsible for it and of having been punished accordingly, although the order could
never have lasted anyway, because it had been, from the start, badly built. The
latter is then only one of the subjective ways in which the elements of a situation
are again brought together into the image of a whole: through imaginarization.
Only if this image is itself broken, if the fundamental meaninglessness of the appearance of the elements out of the old order is accepted, can the elements then
function as an object-cause of a new articulation.

Let me restate this point: as soon as some traumatic excess of or within a giv-
en arrangement of the life-world appears, that which seems to have made the level of the enunciated be whole and make sense crumbles. Now, in destruction and
destitution, it becomes apparent that it did not make sense of its own, but because
the subject of another level (i.e. of enunciation) had decided to hold it together.
From the broken elements of the old level of *what is said*, a new subject can appear
in a new *act of saying*: this is Lacan's point in Seminar XX. It follows that in the
precise moment of the shift towards a new retroactively constituted subject, the
very split between enunciation and what is enunciated, while only becoming apparent in this process, also disappears in this very *act of saying*.

Lacan unfolds this issue by famously saying that while the four discourses are not to be read as stages of a historical development in the manner of a
Geschichtsphilosophie, there is 'some emergence of psychoanalytic discourse whenever there is a movement from one discourse to another'.[26] For such a shift between the discourses to take place, there needs to be a subject that is objectified in the signifiers that structure the new discourse—this is what Lacan means
when he says that at the place of the 'product' of the analyst discourse there is the
sign of a master-signifier: S1. In fact the *only* discourse that allows for this process
is the analytic discourse, which produces in the position of the product a new S1,

---

24. That is, one might say, the condition of a functioning repression; or of the *discourse of the master*—
which is, of course, also the discourse of repression. On the level of *what is said*, S1-S2, it seems as if S
or *a* could never intervene. But, once there is a shift in discourse, *a*-S, i.e. the *analytic discourse*, necessarily appears.

25. One should remember here also Lacan's dictum that, if god is dead, this means he was always already dead. See Lacan 1997, pp. 126-127.

26. Lacan 1999, p. 16.

a new master-signifier. *Such a signifier appears in all shifts of discourses,* but is immediately denied again or foreclosed, as happens in the discourse of the hysteric or in that of the university.

Before moving, in the next section, to a more historical discussion of the break implied in the destructive imagery of siege and bombardment—a discussion that will revolve around the subject of modern science and the event of the Reformation—I want to return to the designified signifier and its link to love (*Eros*) by explaining a seemingly enigmatic statement that Lacan makes in this context: 'I am not saying anything else when I say that love is the sign that one is changing discourses'.[27] On the one hand, there is the emergence of the analytic discourse; on the other, there is love as the sign 'that one is changing discourses'. Transference-love is what first comes to mind when trying to understand this. Or, in the register of the phenomenology of the life-world, the observation that when a once stable symptom, built on the discourse of repression (the master-discourse), becomes unstable, falling in love is a possible outcome—as an attempt to regain the stability lost by the now dysfunctional symptom. Both are special cases of what, in Seminar XVII, Lacan calls the function of *Eros*: the 'making present of lack'.[28] These are special cases because, as defensive mechanisms, they make present the lack precisely by denying it. However, what if the love that Lacan speaks of as a sign of shifting discourses has also the function of making the lack present *as lack*? If this were the case, there would essentially be two further options. One could read 'love' as a sign of the fact that, in the shift between discourses, the analytic discourse makes manifest the latent truth that the object which is supposed to fill in the lack will never be reached; or, also, as a sign that *all* that can ever be done is to fill in the lost object with metonymic instantiations, while being oriented in an asymptotic approach towards the presence of lack in the impossible object of desire. So the subject created here would be a subject that attempts to realize what it knows it cannot realize fully: as a sign of his/her ethical orientation towards the love that has emerged in the shift between discourses.

Already in the attempt to formulate this orientation we notice that we have entered the field of ethics. We started with the question of how 'love' emerges as a sign of the shift in discourses, and in order to explain this, we had to think about ethics. In a Kantian language, we can unravel this as follows: it becomes necessary to speak about ethics insofar as the only way in which we know anything about love emerging as a sign of changing discourses is because of a subject orienting itself towards it as if it had been incorporated into the 'maxims of his will', into the *Triebfeder* (incentives) of his behavior: either by only *seemingly* doing this (i.e. by upholding the pathological—in Kantian terms—current state of affairs by filling in the lack opened up by a shift in discourses with an imaginary object of love) or by *actually* doing this. This act-ually doing it, however, presupposes the complete designification of the S1/phallus that makes the lack present in love. We can then see why the emergence of 'love as a sign' and of the analytic discourse coincide with the break from a formerly functioning discourse: it is because in the

27. Ibid.
28. Lacan 2007, p. 77.

analytic discourse a new 'S1' emerges. It is no longer the S1 of the master's discourse that is imaginarized as if it were the support of being; nor is it the S1 of the
hysteric's discourse, i.e. the object of questioning; nor is it the hidden truth of the
command 'Know!' as is the case in the discourse of the university. Rather, in the
analytic discourse, the S1 is in the place of the object, vis-à-vis the S2, which occupies the place of truth, a truth that upholds the impossibility of knowledge and
'master-signifier' ever coinciding or combining into one: the truth of the unconscious. The S2 here knows of the unconscious and of the hole in being, whereas
the S1 is in the place of the product, i.e. it is a new 'constructed' orientation for
the subject that—once it knows itself—*will have (always already) been* the subject of
this new signifier. This is the case because the new signifier structures not only
the future, but also the past.

IV. *GESINNUNG*, EROS, PHALLUS: S1

In Kantian terms, we can say that the product of the analytic discourse—S1—is
the result of a shift in law/*Gesinnung*; a new/different S1 must be incorporated as
Triebfeder into the maxims of the will.

At first sight, this might appear to be dangerously close to the standard liberal reading of Kant's ethics: while it is impossible to make oneself the subject
of a holy will, i.e. a will that conforms fully to the moral law, the moral subject
is nevertheless oriented towards that goal as an asymptotic guiding post. Alenka Zupančič has convincingly shown why this is not the best (and only) way to
read Kant.[29] In short, her argument consists of six steps and distinguishes three
options (of which only two are really options dealing with the ethical problem
of the split between the subject of the enunciated and the subject of enunciation.
The first option, as we will see, simply does away with the necessity of working
through this split):

1. Kant needs the postulates of practical reason concerning the existence of
   god and the immortality of the soul in order to provide a vantage point
   from which the asymptotic approach towards the impossible holy will can
   be judged.
2. The postulates are the equivalent of Lacan's famous dictum according to
   which the problem of judging whether one has given up on one's desire
   implies necessarily the assumption of the position of a Last Judgment.[30]
3. Since the object of desire and the moral law both do not exist in the sense of
   a definable 'highest good' but only as a 'form', realizing one's desire, or, having a holy will is impossible (except as a doubling of the 'form' in the 'material', i.e. in the form of the incorporation of a symbolic element in the real).
4. This is so, since the very relation to the unconditional object of desire/
   the moral law splits the subject in willing/desiring and willing the will/
   desiring desire. This is then the form that the doubling of the form takes:
   the will does not will something—it wills itself as willing (the moral law,
   which is a form).

29. Zupančič 2000.
30. See Lacan 1997, pp. 313-314.

5. Thus, this structure keeps the subject in either an impossible position—suffering/enjoying the *jouissance* of attempting to realize this very impossibility (of the holy will)—or it incinerates it in a ball of fire, realizing the impossible by way of negation, which is the case of Antigone: by not realizing any of the other possible objects of her life, she realizes the one unconditional object. 'To sum up: "wanting *jouissance*" maintains us on the side of desire, whereas "realizing desire" transposes us to the side of the *jouissance*'.[31]

6. Against these two possibilities, which either put *jouissance* and the law/ *Gesinnung* aside through the act (Option a), or keep the subject in an eternal metonymic shifts, never realizing any of his/her desire, but orienting it to some 'highest good', some unconditional desire (Option b), Zupančič argues that there needs to be a reading of Kant in which the subject is split between the law/*Gesinnung*, on the one hand, and *jouissance*, on the other; yet there is a moment when their impossible relationship is broken into pieces—the letter/litter—thus making the realization of some of the real of the unconditional possible out of the impossible (Option c).

I want to show in the rest of this paper where I differ from Zupančič's excellent work. If I understand her correctly, she takes Options b) and c) to be mutually exclusive, the former being close to the Lacan of Seminar VII and of 'Kant avec Sade', while the latter being similar to the *subject of truth* as it is elaborated in the philosophy of Alain Badiou and in the later Lacan (of Seminar XX and XXIII). Against this, I would insist that *Option c) can only be realized as the loss of Option b)*,[32] and claim that this is equivalent to realizing the designification of the signifier by *passing through* its imaginarization.

Before taking a closer look at the issue of *Gesinnung* as the Kantian name for what S1 means in the analytic discourse, let me return for a moment to where we left Lacan, who maintained that love, or rather *Eros*, is 'the making present of lack'.

> The question is to elaborate the nature of this phallic exclusion in the great human game of our tradition, which is that of desire. Desire has no immediately proximate relationship with this field. Our tradition states it for what it is, Eros, the making present of lack. (Lacan 2007, p. 77)

'Phallic exclusion'—the exteriority of the phallus with regard to any functioning narrative of being, power, or knowledge—is the condition of desire, here understood as the 'game' of *Eros*, the 'making present of lack'. Yet, there are two fundamental ways in which this phallic exclusion functions. Either it works as a master-signifier in a discourse that structures repression. In this case, it is an S1 that intervenes in the 'already constituted field of the other signifiers, insofar as they are already articulated with one another as such'.[33] These other signifi-

---

31. Zupančič 2000, p. 255.

32. This has great implications, particularly for appraising the relation between Lacan and Badiou. See my essay 'Resurrection without Death? Notes on Negativity and Truth in Luther's and Badiou's Interpretations of Paul' (Ensslin 2008, pp. 99-111).

33. Lacan 2007, p. 15 (see also p. 17: 'How is this fundamental form to be situated? Without any further ado we are, if you will, going to write this form in a new way this year. Last year I wrote it as the ex-

ers are the field of S2, of knowledge, that becomes structured by a signifier that takes first place—and thus destroys the possibility of any other signifier taking this position. 'Phallic exclusion' then stands for a *lien social*—the discourse of the master—in which the phallus/S1 is excluded as a hierarchically prior place of 'order', in the double sense of the word: the place which holds the order together like a key-stone, but also the place from which orders are issued (thus indicating the very lack that the order as S1 in the form of *nomos enpsychos* is supposed to cover up).

This exclusion produces both $\mathcal{S}$ and object *a*: it produces the 'split' or 'castrated' subject, since as a command, i.e. an act of speech, it betrays the lack at the place from which this order issues forth. The S1 covering this truth becomes the object of love (of identification) for the elements of the *lien social* structured by this discourse. But this same operation also produces the object *a*: the surplus *jouissance* given to the phallus/S1 as *prestige* and experienced by knowledge/the slave as the know-how (*savoir-faire*) of the life-world. Thus, in the order of exchange it is given to the S1 (filling the lack that it covers with the products of the labor of the slave); in the order of production it is experienced as the enjoyment of the 'knowhow' of the slave.

Yet, there is a second possibility for S1 to appear as 'phallic exclusion', one that knows itself as an impossibility, namely the impossibility to totalize the *lien social* as the discourse of the master and—differently—the discourse of the university attempt to do. This S1 of exclusion is in the place not of the 'agent', as in the discourse of the master, but of the 'product', as in the discourse of the analyst. Here we see that these two discourses are related to each other like on a Moebius strip. The S1 of the master-discourse *is both aligned with (is the* envers *of) and is interrupted by* the *a* that enables the shift of discourses, i.e. that enables the 'emergence of the analytic discourse'. If the interruption dominates, and object *a* is not successfully pacified by being imaginarized and thus made a part and parcel of a functioning discourse of repression/neurosis, then this in turn may produce a new S1, and so on. The object *a* functions here (in the discourse of the analyst) as the *cause* of desire for a subject already alienated into language, already split; and in the process, S1—a phallic exclusion from the permanent and seemingly coherent discourse of the Other, that is the super-ego—emerges (or is 'constructed').

The difference between the S1 in the first and second discourse is that in the first it has a supposedly unquestioned meaning—god, king, father, I/Ego, etc.—whereas in the second it does not: after going through the imaginarization of the super-ego, S1 appears only in its validity, striped of all meaning. S1 does not appear as the truth about the dreams, fantasies or the desire of the subject, but as that which makes 'present the lack' and *mi-dit*, half-says, the truth. It does so *as lack*, i.e. as a knowledge[34] about the split in the subject and the possibility to say

---

teriority of the signifier S1—the one that is the point of departure for the definition of discourse that we will emphasize at this first step—with respect to a circle marked with the sign A, that is the field of the big Other').

34. Knowing in the sense of S2 in the place of truth in the analyst's discourse: it is a knowledge that at first might be the knowledge of the Other (the super-ego), but which essentially is the knowledge about the unconscious—and its designified elements: letter/litter.

the truth about desire only as an act of *mi-dire*, half-saying. But also as a knowl-edge that the *act of saying* itself is precisely an (ethical) act: it collapses, as we have seen, the split in the subject. So here we have a split of the subject between itself and its new law, its new S1—and we have this split not as the relation to the ever receding or deferred impossible, but as the realization of something (the *letter/lit-ter*) of the real, of the truth: of something of the object-cause (for which the ana-lyst is the stand-in).

A more general way to formulate this would be to say that S1 in the analyst discourse is the production of a new *Gesinnung* and its doubling into and of the real (into nature itself), the doubling of (ethical/creationist) form into (pathologi-cal/evolutionary) form as the condition of effecting the real: without ever becom-ing identical with it or realizing it fully. For Kant, *Gesinnung* is the 'inner princi-ple of the maxims of the will':[35] it produces something like ethical consistency. It does so either by producing negative unity/wholeness through the asymptotic model (Option b), or by realizing some of that *Gesinnung* but only in the manner of non-all (Option c). The maxims themselves are the *formulations* which are ca-pable of becoming subjective *Triebfedern* of action.[36] *Gesinnung*, Kant says, can only be 'one and relates generally to the totality of the use of freedom'.[37] It is rooted in the non-sensible, it is a *virtus noumenon*, and can also be thought of as the formu-lation of an idea of reason (*Vernunftsidee*). Like such an idea (that of world for in-stance), it allows for movement from the series of always conditioned elements— the concrete acts of an empirical I or subject—to the unconditioned: it is, like the transcendental ideas of the *Critique of Pure Reason*, a formulation of totality. Based as they are on the pure concepts of the understanding (categories), the ideas of reason are related specifically to the categories of relation; in the case of *Gesinnung* one would have to say, more precisely, that it is related to the category of relation between cause and effect and to the 'hypothetical synthesis of the elements of a series'.[38] And it is this *Gesinnung* that is, in the words of Alenka Zupančič, the 'ul-timate foundation of the incorporation of incentives into maxims',[39] i.e. of mak-ing what the formulation of the *Gesinnung* contains—a formulation which is nev-er phenomenally accessible in its totality, but that can only be 'half-said', which means that *it is unconscious*—into *Triebfedern* for the maxims, which govern each and every action of a human being.

---

35. Kant 1977, p. 670.

36. See Charles and Webb 1926, p. 95: 'The origin of this use of the word is to be explained as follows. Every properly human—that is deliberately willed—act is done for some reason, subsumed as it were, under some syllogism, under some major premise or *major propositio*. That to which any individual act is ultimately referred is thus the ultimate major premise, *maxima propositio* or *maxim*'. What is, of course, im-portant here, is that maxims are symbolic—and that their real are thus letter(s)/litter able to produce new maxims.

37. Kant 1977, p. 672.

38. See Kant 2003, B 380. That is, it is a 'totality' as opposed to an 'unconditioned in the categorical synthesis within a subject' (substance/soul) or the 'disjunctive synthesis of parts within a system' (uncon-ditioned/god, i.e. the existence of an unconditioned being which guarantees the unity of elements not re-lated by a rule—which is therefore disjunctive within an ordered system). Maybe one way of summing up what I am arguing here is that, as designified signifier, god moves from the category of the uncondi-tioned to the category of totality—as a totality *pas-tout*.

39. Zupančič 2000, p. 33.

If maxims are the subjective ground for particular actions, then *Gesinnung* is the subjectively necessary ground for the formulation of maxims. This is not only true because of the subjective need for totality or unity, i.e. for some kind of semi-empirical moral correspondence to the epistemological "'I think", that must be able to accompany all my representations'. Normally it is thought that the latter simply stands in for the completely noumenal 'thing that thinks' in transcendental apperception. But, for Zupančič, the 'I think' becomes a limit case hovering over the very split between the *noumenal* and the *phenomenal*. She is right in saying that achieving 'unity' through the ideas of reason, i.e. the idea of the immortality of the soul and of the existence of god, simply retains the problem of maxims—and thus of ethics—within the realm of fantasy (since the unconditioned is never and can never be an object of experience). Thus today, when the immortality of the soul and the existence of god are nothing other than designified signifiers, the position of judgment about the subject can no longer simply be that of a Last Judgment. However, this may still retain the problem of *Gesinnung* as the subjective ground of maxims, which are the subjective ground of acts: namely by thinking of *Gesinnung*—in its analogy to the ideas of reason—as an unconditioned totality, but as an unconditioned totality that is *pas-tout*. How would this be possible?

Luckily, there still is a relation of *Gesinnung* to totality. Not to the unity of the soul as a stand in for the 'thing that thinks', but to the totality of the *elements of the thinking thing*. Thus, there is a relation to the elements of *Gesinnung* as a totality: this is true because *Gesinnung* is, as it were, the reservoir of the stuff of which maxims are made: formulations, discourse, ultimately letters. The *Triebfedern* are necessary precisely because that literal stuff is the stuff they are made of, and somehow that stuff needs to enter—in Zupančič's words: needs to be 'incorporated'[40]—into the field of nature, i.e. of causality itself, and not just into its imaginary subjective totality/unity through the ideas of reason.[41]

1) The Danger of 'Dialectical Illusion'

There is, however, an analogy to the ideas of pure reason when the *Gesinnung* in moral philosophy takes the place of the 'totality of the infinite series of approximations', which empirical acts constitute in relation to the moral law. Like the world, it is then simply the idea of the totality of an infinite series of empirical events. This is how it appears in the discussion of 'Religion Within the Limits of Reason Alone'. So this term of approximation is tied solely to one possible reading of the place of morality (as opposed to legality) within the Kantian system, namely the idea that, since it is impossible for embodied rational beings like us to fully assume the *noumenal* virtue, the only thing left for us is an asymptotic approach to morality in a series of empirical, one could say reformatory, steps (Op-

40. Ibid.

41. See Kant 1960, p. 19 (quoted in Zupančič 2000, p. 33): 'The freedom of the will (*Willkür*) is of a wholly unique nature in that an incentive (*Triebfeder*) can determine the will to an action only so far as the individual has incorporated it into his maxims (has made it the general rule in accordance with which he will conduct himself); only thus can an incentive, whatever it may be, co-exist with the absolute spontaneity of the will (i.e. freedom)'. See also Zupančič 2000, p. 33.

tion b above). In this reading the *dialektischer Schein*, the dialectical illusion, which according to Kant is the product of any idea of reason that is not properly put in its transcendental place, is avoided by realizing that the subjective necessity—the principle—of unity of these acts, i.e. of the totality of the series of events, does not legitimize the conclusion—the *Schluss*—of affirming its objective necessity, i.e. its existence as totality for us (as a possible object of cognition). We keep it out of the range of knowledge and at the same time keep it in the place of impossibility: the object then becomes a sublime object of desire.

2) The Real of an Illusion

However, as Alenka Zupančič has beautifully shown, this is only one reading of the place of the moral law and its subjective principle, the *gute Gesinnung* or good disposition.

There is another reading (Option c), which rests on the clear separation of the 'thing that thinks' and the 'I of transcendental apperception'. One, the 'thing that thinks', is *noumenal*—the subject in Lacanian terms—whereas the empirical I/Ego is *phenomenal*; yet, the third option rests on the 'I of transcendental apperception' and is neither *noumenal* nor *phenomenal*; rather, it is the separation of the two (or also: it is the subject of the *act of saying*, of the unconscious). It is not the place here to reconstruct the whole argument, but this shows how the split subject of Kant cannot be thought simply as being split between the *phenomenal* and the *noumenal*, but between the *phenomenal*, i.e. between causality, and the very split between causality and freedom.[42]

Thus, from the perspective of the analogy of *Gesinnung* with the ideas of reason the seeming totality of the empirical series of acts of a subject is nothing but *dialektischer Schein*. But that illusion gains something real if we realize that to incorporate an *incentive*—i.e. a subjective drive for action—into a *maxim*—i.e. a subjective rule of action—it needs to be governed by a subjective *necessity*, a subjective principle, a *Gesinnung*. It becomes the 'Real of an Illusion' as the title of Zupančič's book in its German translation makes clear. Why is it real? Because it is neither *noumenal*—that is, the *thing that thinks*—nor *phenomenal*—that is, the actions themselves, or even the maxims, which one can elucidate from them. But it resides on the limit of that split and thus allows for the conceptualization in Kantian terms of how practical freedom can be brought into relation with theoretical—or natural—necessity.

3) The Subject and Causality: the Pas-Tout of Conditions

Gesinnung was introduced by Kant as the transcendentally ideal formulation of the totality of the empirical series of actions by an individual. As such it is synthetic, for it expresses a relation, namely that of conditions to the unconditioned. Within the realm of causality—i.e. in the world of nature, where man is a *Naturding* among other *Naturdinge*—all actions are conditioned. Yet, in order for this conditioning to be subjectively at work (to work 'itself through', as it were), this causality itself needs to be chosen in an 'act of saying'. Let us imagine an indi-

42. See Zupančič (2000) particularly Chapter 2, 'The Subject of Freedom', pp. 21-41.

vidual (maybe a less articulate version of Hannibal Lecter) before a court of law stating: 'I couldn't help it, it was like an instinct or a force I couldn't resist, I had to kill and eat those victims'. From the perspective of what I have outlined here, the answer would have to be: 'Well, all of this might be true, and probably is true. However, before you experienced this heterogeneous force as inescapable necessity, you made an unconscious choice to view yourself only as an object of nature, as *Naturding*. This causality may very well be existent; however, what you ignore is that on some level you chose yourself as the subject of this causality (you chose to subject yourself to this causality). In doing so you not only denied the *noumenal* realm, but also the limit between the *noumenal* and the *phenomenal* (regardless of whether it is structural or only an effect of finitude). By denying this limit, you made it impossible for you to experience that no determination through causality is ever a totality: since no totality can ever be the object of experience, but only a subjective necessity (i.e. it rests on the split whose limit you deny). Thus, being under the conditions of necessity, you denied that there is a condition of conditions: namely that they are never complete on the level of phenomena/nature'.

In this example one can see why Kantian freedom is not simply the freedom of arbitrariness or liberal choice. On the contrary, it is the choice of necessity which allows us to have access to the realm of freedom. In the words of Alenka Zupančič, to whom goes all the credit of having worked this out:

> So this freedom cannot be founded upon the arbitrariness of our actions but, on the contrary, only upon law and necessity themselves: *one has to discover the point where the subject itself plays an (active) part in lawful, causal necessity*, the point where the subject itself is already inscribed in advance in what appear to be laws of causality independent of the subject. (Zupančič 2000, p. 33)

V. THE BREAK BETWEEN MACROCOSM AND MICROCOSM: REPEATING THE LOSS OF THE IMAGINARY PHALLUS

If we recall for a moment the above discussion of the designified signifier, we might be able to connect it to the problem of *Gesinnung* in the following manner. The designified signifier makes its presence felt as its very opposite: it approaches us as a signifier that is so full of meaning that it eclipses all other possible meanings—and thus eclipses meaning itself, which depends on contingency, i.e. on the ability to be different. Here we can see why the designified signifier carries with it the dimension of the *ban*. While it is true that it does not have a meaning *per se*, which might place it within a structured whole, as it would if it were a functioning S1 in the discourse of the master, it still interpellates a subject by means of precisely claiming jurisdiction over the whole subject. It can do this because the symbolic phallus, whose function I described above, is imaginarized, holds sway over the subject as *Ideal-Ich*.

How does it do it? We might be able to elucidate this easily if we look at Lacan's dictum from the beginning of Seminar XVII that 'knowledge is the *jou-*

issance of the Other'.[43] In relation to the *Gesinnung* of a subject that is still in its (Kantian) pathological state, this simply means that the unconscious discourse of the Other is imaginarized as supposedly forming a whole: as a discourse of the super-ego. Or, to put it the other way around, that the subject holds on to his/her pathological *Gesinnung* because it allows the continuation of the idea (very much in the pathologized sense of a Kantian idea of reason) that there is a totality in the sense of a whole. If the hysteric's discourse produces knowledge, then it is because it is the other knowledge of this Other knowledge (which is *jouissance*, the truth of the hysteric's discourse). It is the knowledge that S1 cannot maintain its imaginarized mastery—in the discourse of the master—because the unconscious is 'structured like a language' (and with it the literal *reservoir of Gesinnung*). This means that knowledge, which is the Other's *jouissance*—the discourse of the super-ego as imaginarized, i.e. as holding the images of the ideal-ego and of the supposed place of total *jouissance*—is destroyed and its elements can be reconfigured.[44] However, not in a new whole, but in the S1 of the analytic discourse, in a new *Gesinnung* (a totality *pas-tout* of the subjective principle) which keeps open the split and does not seek to orient itself towards the impossible ideal of a *realization* of the S1.

In Seminar VII, Lacan states very clearly that this confrontation of the subject with the ideal-ego is in fact a kind of self-relation. It is the place where the subject encounters itself as the subject of privation (*privée*):

> We will now define the ego ideal of the subject as representing the power to do good, which then opens up within itself the beyond that concerns us today. How is it that as soon as everything is organized around the power to do good, something completely enigmatic appears and returns to us again and again from our own actions—like the ever-growing threat within us of a powerful demand whose consequences are unknown? As for the ideal ego, which is the imaginary other who faces us at the same level, it represents by itself the one who deprives us. (Lacan 1997, p. 234)[45]

The translation here is not completely felicitous, as it does not make entirely clear what the 'deprived' (*privée*) means in this context. In Seminar IV, Lacan introduces the dialectic of castration, frustration, and privation. Along with it he introduces for each of these productions of lack a specific 'agent'. It is clear that the idea behind the term agent is not sovereign *energeia*, but rather of something being employed by the subject, being the instrument of the subject's process.[46] In this sense, Lacan introduces as the *agent of privation* the imaginary father, whom Lacan in Seminar VII calls the 'basis of the providential image of God'.[47] Thus, *privée* must be understood here as 'being robbed'. Privation is defined as the 'real lack of a symbolic object'.[48] From the above we can say that the object that is lacking

---

43. Lacan 2007, p. 14 (Lacan's reference here is to Seminar XVI, *From an Other to an other*).
44. Remember here the imagery of a siege and bombardment that Lacan uses in Seminar XX quoted above.
45. Earlier on in the same passage, Lacan makes it clear—by using the German term—that the ego-ideal is the *Urbild* of the ego.
46. This is not only true of Seminar IV, but also of Seminar XVII (see p. 169).
47. Lacan 1997, p. 308.
48. This definition occurs throughout Seminar IV.

is the phallus as that 'which makes lack present'.[49] Privation thus lacks the (presenting of a) lack.

We are here at the heart of the modern problem of *resentment*. What the image of the providential god is supposed to provide is an object for the hatred of the subject. The affect of hatred is owed to the fact that there is no real symbolic phallus in being (or Phallus of Being), i.e. that there is no world-order which is structured in such a way that there are guaranteed objects for the subject's drives. All realizations have to go through the symbolic and through a symbolic that simply has validity, but no meaning in relation to a whole, precisely because it lacks the ability to denote those objects. Thus, the imaginary father only appears once the regulative ideas of reason such as the existence of god or of the immortality of the soul have ceased to be convincing—i.e. once they have actually been reduced to the status of 'regulative ideas' devoid of any anchor in ethical substance; once they have disappeared from the Other.[50] Thus the attempt of the subject to regain a unitary being through relating itself to an ideal-ego stalls in the utter darkness of impossibility and in the hatred for the one who produced this impasse. By attempting to make itself into the ego that the ideal-ego seems to be (thus confusing the split between the *phenomenal* and the *noumenal* with the program of *phenomenalizing* the *noumenal*—i.e. Option b), the subject in fact only confronts this impossibility, and is thus confronted with the 'one that deprives' it and the affect that this produces:

> It is the imaginary father and not the real one which is the basis of the providential image of God. And the function of the superego in the end, from its final point of view, is hatred of God, the reproach that God had handled things so badly. (Lacan 1997, p. 308)

In the same Seminar, Lacan refers to Martin Luther in a passage where he essentially defines drives as different from instincts. They are different because there are no guaranteed objects of drives (contrary to the knowledge of the super-ego, which claims to bring the subject in contact with these guaranteed objects).

> It is obvious that the libido with its paradoxical, archaic, so-called pregenital characteristics, with its eternal polymorphism, with its world of images that are linked to the different sets of drives [...] that whole microcosm has absolutely nothing to do with the macrocosm; only in fantasy does it engender the world. (Ibid., p. 92)

Martin Luther, Lacan continues, is a thinker that leads us 'to the ultimate consequence from the form of exile in which man finds himself relative to any good in the world whatsoever'.[51] Luther, Lacan argues here—opposing *avant la lettre* the Foucauldian idea that the modern ego was invented by the Discourse of Man around 1800—already spells out the consequences of what it means to have an ego-ideal come down, as it were, from the level of the Other to that of

---

49. Lacan 2007, p. 77.
50. The inevitable conclusion here is that, of course, precisely as regulative ideas, they always already have 'disappeared from the Other'.
51. Lacan 1997, p. 93.

the other as an ideal-ego. In Seminar XVII we get a more structural account of the same process:

> *D'un Autre à l'autre*, From an Other to an other, I called it. This other, this little other, with its famous 'the', was what at this level, which is the level of algebra, of signifying structure, we designate as the object *a*. (Lacan 2007, p. 14)

If in Seminar VII Luther is thought of as a precursor of the analytic discourse because he claims that we are 'shit falling from the devil's anus',[52] here, over ten years later, that 'essentially digestive and excremental schema'[53] is re-introduced at the level of 'algebra'.

Jean-Claude Milner has spelled out clearly why Lacan has always insisted on the fact that the subject of psychoanalysis is the subject of modern science.[54] To recount this succinctly: while ancient science was also related to mathematics, the latter used to have a function that is different from the one it has in modern science. As an element in a science that described the eternal recurrence of the same in an eternal cosmos, mathematics was simply a language to describe, on the symbolic level, what truly is. In modern science, however, the literalized mathematics of calculus, algebra, and later set theory is precisely an instrument to move beyond intuition and its symbolic inscription.[55] In modern science, the letter of mathematics serves as an infinite function of calculating and manipulating the real in contrast to 'seeing' in an intuitive manner the arche-tectonics of a closed and eternal cosmos.[56]

We only have to note that the break between macrocosm and microcosm happens in both modern science (and its Cartesian subject) and in Luther's identification with the excrement through the designification of what appears in the Other. The object *a* appears in both cases, because in both cases there is a movement from the Other to the other—and back in the case of algebraic science and the production of a new S1. Of course, the bodily image of the excrement is a kind of imaginarized real—the exact equivalent of the imaginarized symbolic, which is the image of the providential god. The mathematical inscription of the object *a* as letter/litter, on the other hand, moves itself to the limit of the image, of *the-*

---

52. So Lacan claims. While the idea is certainly present in the very core of Luther's thought, I have been unable to find the sentence quoted by Lacan in Luther's *Tischgespräche*.

53. Lacan 1997, p. 93.

54. See Milner 1995; see also Lacan 2007, p. 158: 'Science [in the sense of modern science] emerged from what was embryonic in the Euclidean demonstrations'.

55. In Seminar XVII, Lacan returns to this difference between ancient mathematics and modern science —and the latter's relation to psychoanalysis. 'This wisdom, this episteme, created with every recourse to every dichotomy, led only to knowledge that can be designated by the term that Aristotle himself used to characterize the master's knowledge—theoretical knowledge. Not in the weak sense that we give this word, but in the emphatic sense that the word "theoria" has in Aristotle. A singular mistake. I will come back to this, since for my discourse this is the crucial point, the pivotal point—it was only when, by a movement of renunciation of this wrongly acquired knowledge, so to speak, someone, for the first time as such, extracted the function of the subject from the strict relationship between S1 and S2—I named Descartes, whose work I believe I am able to spell out, not without agreement with at least a significant number of those who have discussed it—that science was born' (Lacan 2007, p. 23).

56. For Lacan, one of the most influential voices for this point of view was certainly Alexandre Koyré. See Koyré 1957 and Koyré 1973.

oria in the Aristotelian sense: as letter it is a fragment of the 'knowledge that is the *jouissance* of the Other' and can become the object-cause of a new signifier, which is now truly devoid of any guarantee and meaning; it simply stands as a product of a subjective act that partially realizes what has come out of the symbolic, of its fragments—the reservoir of *Gesinnung*. So now it seems that the first case—which is still tied to the image—and the second—which is tied to holding open the split between the real and the symbolic, but nevertheless establishes a link where there was previously only an impossibility—are analogous to Option b) and Option c) as previously outlined by reference to Zupančič. Identifying with the excremental real would in fact be a masochistic manipulation of the Other, seeking *jouissance* by realizing it. On the other hand, the algebraic, mathematical version could be linked to an ontology à la Badiou, one that washes its hands of any excremental *reste*. But what if one can get to Option c) only by subtracting intuition/*theoria*, i.e. the idea of a phallus/S_1 that guarantees a cosmos, from Option b)? What if it is necessary to go through the privation of the absolute in Option b) for Option c)—a partial realization of S_1 as it appears in the working-through of analysis—to take hold?

VI. THE DOCTRINE OF PREDESTINATION: A FORM OF WILD ANALYSIS

In this final section I intend to dwell on Lacan and Luther and investigate an aspect of the latter's quarrel with Erasmus: the issue of predestination. One of the background philosophical questions that structured the conflict between Erasmus and Luther concerned the question of God's freedom vis-à-vis creation (and, of course, also vice versa). I will not recall the entire history of this problem, but only point out one particular terminological conceptual invention of scholasticism that aimed at diffusing the issues associated with it, namely the distinction between god's two powers: the *potentia dei absoluta* (or absolute power of god) and the *potentia dei ordinata* (or the power of god as it regards his accomplished creation). Succinctly put: once it became apparent that creationism implied a dynamism that could not easily be squared with the ontological model of an eternal cosmos, philosophers wanted to solve the issue by dividing the world into two by dividing god's power into two. There would be one world and god that allowed for creationism (the absolute), and one that allowed for ontological consistency and necessity (the established order). It is true, it could be argued, that the cosmos is not eternal, but created. But the 'return of the same' is still guaranteed by god's benevolence or contractualism.[57] According to the *potentia dei ordinata* (the established/created order), we can describe things in the world in a reliable fashion, either via Ockham's *notitia intuitiva* (the bedrock of early nominalist 'empiricism') or in an epistemologically different, but metaphysically equivalent fashion, through revelation. Thus an attempt was made to actually avert the anxieties that might have been produced by introducing a creator-god (who is a 'debtor to

---

57. There were different schools that emphasized this in different ways. See Oakley 1987, pp. 231-245; Oakley 1984; Moonan 1994.

no-one'[58]) into a metaphysically understood *kosmos* with its fixed teleological causality of *generation and corruption* (Aristotle). The tool to attempt at containing the
fall-out of the tension between the god of philosophers and the god of monotheism was the introduction of this distinction. Now, it seemed, man did not have to
be anxiety ridden because, according to the *potentia dei absoluta* (the absolute order), the established order was merely contingent and could also look differently,
function with different laws or commandments for salvation, if god had so chosen.[59] The introduction of the two powers—particularly of the absolute power—
was originally meant to contain the tension by making that power of god which
was not immediately accessible through either sensation, reason, or revelation at
least subject to a kind of secondary cognition. By *knowing* there were these two
powers, the ontological uncertainty seemed to be contained—exactly by means
of this knowledge.

However, in this way, a split between the 'options initially open to god'[60] in
the realm of possibility, on the one hand, and the realm of actuality (and thus of
second order necessity) in the actually created world, on the other, was created.
When Erasmus attacked Luther's doctrine of the bondage of the will, he used this
distinction. While god according to his *potentia dei absoluta* might know everything
with foreknowledge, this does not mean that in the realm of phenomena—in the
world according to the *potentia dei ordinata*—man is not free to choose his behavior according to the old doctrine of *facere quod in se est*, to do what is in him[61]—and
thus to become justified through his actions, albeit with the help of grace.[62]

---

58. As Ockham noted. He thought that for god it is impossible to do what he is not allowed to do, as it
is the case that god is in fact not obliged to anyone. This is Ockham's version of the *potentia dei absoluta*.
See II dist. 19 H of his *Commentary on Sentences*: 'Deus autem nuli tenetur nec obligatur tanquam debitor;
et ideo non potest facere quod non debet facere: nec potest non facere quod debet facere' (Ockham 1990).

59. In an older tradition of the history of philosophy and of science, one associated in France with the
names of Etienne Gilson and Paul Vignaux, this anxiety has in fact been assessed thoroughly. Hans Blu-
menberg is a later version of the same conviction that the nominalist stress on the *absoluta* in fact created
extreme epistemological anxiety, since it seemed to erect impossibly high hurdles for scientific certainty: after all, who can see in the mind of god? But I will show with reference to Martin Luther that there
was another possible solution: namely, to accept the absolute as inaccessible, but in the fashion of a subtraction from what is accessible, thus opening the space for the subject that would also become the subject of psychoanalysis.

60. The 'absolute' power of god is according to one interpretation described as 'the total possibilities *initially* open to God, some of which were realized by creating the "established order" with "the unrealized
possibilities" [. . .] [being] [. . .] now only hypothetically possible' (Courtenay 1974, p. 39).

61. *Facere quod in se est* is the formula by means of which scholastic moral philosophy designated the duty
of man to do 'what was in him' in order to fulfill the commandments of god, thus participating in his salvation even after the fall and with the aid of his fallen nature. It is, among other things, this principle that
Luther most radically fights against (and the Aristotelian philosophy of virtue that was its inspiration).

62. Erasmus actually introduced the distinction by differentiating between *necessitas consequentiae* and
necessitas consequentis (see Erasmus 2001, pp. 102-104). The *necessitas consequentiae* (the necessity of what produces the consequence) is necessity pure and simple, which means of course in this context: god in his
eternal being, since this is the only truly necessarily existing thing. Now, if through his will god creates
something, then any action of this something as secondary cause is not necessary in itself, i.e. according
to the *necessitas consequentiae*, but only factually necessary by having been done. For this reason, man, as
created, has free will, since what he does or does not do is not necessary according to the *necessitas consequentiae*, but only *consequentis*. Luther makes short shrift of this logic by saying that all this playing around
with concepts is simply expressing that 'everything happens with necessity, but not everything that happens is god' (Luther 1883 ff., Vol. 18, p. 617. All quotes are taken from the definitive 'Weimarer Ausgabe'

Luther has nothing but scorn for this line of argument. For him, it is clear that all we have is revelation, that is, we can know only what has been revealed to us by the signifier, as it were. There is no knowledge of the real unless it is as a *reste* of the signifier. However, in his most radical position, Luther does not interpret this to mean that what is offered through the *deus revelatus* is literally *all*. Rather *absoluta* and *ordinata* are related to each other on the same plane, like on a Moebius strip. They are not two elements that together make a whole, as Ockham and the other scholastic thinkers that employ the distinction, all the way up to Erasmus, had it; they are the impossible coincidence that breaks the plane of this world into a plane that is out of joint. Such a plane is what is accessible to the subject, but not as a whole or as all, but as non-all. One of the clearest formulations of this position is—maybe unsurprisingly—Luther's interpretation of Mary in his translation and interpretation of the *Magnificat*.[63] There Mary is no longer understood as an exemplary case of a Christian-Aristotelian virtue-ethics, particularly of the virtue of 'humility', as the *via moderna* had often seen her. Rather, the confrontation with the gaze of god who 'looked upon her nothingness'—rather than her 'humility'—as Luther translates the famous text, is a confrontation with a hole in the world of the *potentia dei ordinata*. The absolute power of god— as absent from the world of the *ordinata*—appears *as this absence* and at the same time as an interruption of the normal realization of Mary's powers of the soul, of her cognition, memory or willing. Mary, then, without being aware of this being an act of herself ('unbewusst', or unconsciously, as Luther states), can hold onto this experience through the production of a new S1 or, rather, a symbolization of faith that runs counter to the situation which was interrupted by this experience.

Yet this relation of non-all to the signifier does not offer itself immediately, but only as the loss of the image of a seemingly totalized symbolic, in which the subject would have its place as S2 relating to S1. To indicate this, Luther translates the scholastic virtue of *humilitas* not as humility, but as '*Nichtigkeit*', that is, 'nothingness'.[64] He thus moves the subject from the position of the slave/S2 to that of object *a*. Similarly, the passages of the *Bondage of the Will*[65] where Luther describes how he despaired with anxiety, because he felt God enjoyed putting him in a position where he was given the knowledge of what he should do (the Law) but not the ability to do it, are some of the most moving in his entire *oeuvre*. Luther describes how he thought that God actually enjoyed (*quasi delectur*[66]) his sins and his eternal damnation, giving us a clear instance of the phantasy of the imaginary father. And he gets very close to the wish Lacan associated with Oedipus' wish when he was at Colonus, namely to *mae phynei*,[67] to never have been brought into existence.

or Weimar edition (WA) of Luther's works. The references are henceforth given as WA, followed by the number of the volume and the number of the page).

63. Luther 1883 ff., WA 7, pp. 544-604.
64. Ibid., pp. 559-561.
65. Luther 1883 ff., WA 18, pp. 600-787.
66. Ibid., p. 719.
67. Lacan 1997, p. 313. Alenka Zupančič points out that this phrase is in fact uttered by the chorus, not by Oedipus himself (Zupančič 2000, pp. 178 ff.).

For centuries many a great man has taken offense with this and have been to the deepest abyss of despair [*ad profundam et abyssum desperationis*]—until I [sic] even desired to never have been created a human being.[68] (Luther 1883 ff., WA 18, p. 719)

It is obvious that we find here the phenomenon described by Lacan when he says that the imaginary father is the image of the providential god. What leads Luther to despair? The fantasy that god-father actually enjoys his impotence to fulfill the commandment. Yet, in this fantasy, Luther encounters god-father not as god—as Other—but as the small other, who has been moved to the level of an imaginarized object *a*. Luther often says about his opponents that they do not 'let god be god'—and in this despair he experiences the affective consequences of this failure. Here he is engaged on the level where the subject as *moi/ego* encounters god as an *ideal ego* (on the imaginary axis: a-a'), and no longer as the place of a partial identification with an *ego-ideal*.[69] Luther hates god, because he 'handled things so badly'.[70] But Luther then makes the discovery that grace is exactly adjacent to this experience (i.e. grace consists in moving the signifier back up into the Other, reconfiguring it from the letter/litter of the wrong *Gesinnung*): 'This was before I knew, how healing despair can be and how adjacent it is to grace'.[71]

If the imaginary father Luther describes becomes the agent of privation, then it is clear why *grace* is close to *despair*: because in privation all that is left is *nothing*, designified elements which can and need to be reconstituted into a new S1 without reference to any guarantee. While the scholastic speculation about the absolute power of god and his ordained power or established order essentially served to make a whole out of two halves—i.e. to combine the Jewish creative god with the eternal cosmos of Greek philosophy—Luther realized that the only way to deal with what cannot be known within the register of the symbolic (i.e. the real according to the absolute) is to relate to it (the absolute) as a *subtraction* ('*Nichtigkeit*/nothingness') from what is given to the subject by way of the symbolic. Another way of saying this is: when the subject is oriented towards the Other as the place where it meets the signifiers that make it a subject, these are not thought of as complete, as being structured by an imaginarized S1. Here, the subject does not even take up the position of a Last Judgment (of what in Kant is the regulative idea of immortality of the soul and of the existence of god). Rather, as in the discussion of *Gesinnung* above, the subject takes its position vis-à-vis the reservoir of the symbolic from the position of the real / the lack in and of the symbolic. For if it did take up these other positions as if they were positions of knowledge this would constitute an imaginarization that would lead to the movement

---

68. Note the sudden change into the first person singular.

69. There is no room here to discuss in detail the difference between the (symbolic) ego-ideal and the (imaginary) ideal-ego that Lacan finds in Freud. For our purposes the difference is obvious. If the Other (as barred and thus as the place of speech) is conceived in my own image as the other who has all the *jouissance* and power—i.e. as an ideal ego—then I have no longer any distance from him. The only choice is despair and a *passage à l'acte*, or a genuine act in order to traverse that phantasy. However, if I encounter the other in the place of the Other as a bearer of a partial trait of identification, then this can function as an ego-ideal, regulating my relation to *jouissance*.

70. Lacan 1997, p. 308. See above.

71. Ibid.

from an Other to an other. (This is what Luther means when he says that those who speculate on salvation and *facere quod in se est* do not 'let god be god'.[72]) As an image, the imaginarized phallus would again institute a notion of the providential imaginary father as a place where *jouissance* is in fact accessible. It would again institute an image as the ideal-ego that can never be reached. Subtracting the absolute and thus giving up the notion of a supposed whole of enjoyment that happens some other place and thus deprives/robs (*priver*) the subject of it, opens up the possibility of realizing *some* of the real through a new signifier: in the mode of non-all. To 'let god be god' does not mean thinking of god as the place of total knowledge that is in some way unified (and unifies, through the Last Judgment). Rather, it means accepting that the signifier is accessible only in the Other and that there is fundamentally a signifier without meaning, a designified (de-imaginarized) signifier. Here, we can see that this notion is twofold; the designified signifier shows itself in the ghosts of modernity[73] but also in the structure of the analytic discourse: as a truly designified signifier, freed even of its imaginary content. Letting go of the 'knowledge that is the *jouissance* of the Other', i.e. of the superego pressure, in which the subject ultimately only meets itself—'deprives itself'—, and letting the absence of the absolute, its subtraction from the symbolic, be the object-cause that carries with it the truth of revelation, i.e. of the signifier. I would claim that this is where Luther actually brings back the Jewish heritage into the universality of the address (the *per me* of Pauline Christianity, where this *me* stands for the universality of the singular speech acts anchored by the *je*, not for the imaginary fullness—and anxiety—of the *moi*[74]). While it is clear that the 'Other' wants something from me, I cannot ever know what that is, for in order to really know it, I would need to be able to access the absolute, not just the contingent ordinary world of the *ordinata*, the world of phenomena. But I can access the absolute only as a hole—a subtraction—in the symbolic structure of the Other, never as a symbolic chain, of which I could decipher the meaning. Here

72. See the 'Disputatio contram Scholasticam': '*Non potest homo naturaliter velle deum esse deum, immo vellet se esse deum et deum non esse deum*'. This could also be read as: 'Left to the function of the ideal-ego which appears as a place-holder to supposedly naturalize the pathological state of affairs, the subject is unable to reconfigure its *Gesinnung*'. Thus, in Luther's theological terms, the subject is unable to let 'god be god' and let itself be structured by a new S1. If the subject were able to 'let god be god' it would stand—according to Luther—in a relation of faith to this process of articulating the new S1. The subject would accept that it has access to this S1, not as part of a totalizing knowledge, but by having first access to a real that makes such a knowledge impossible, yet which functions as the *cause* of the process of symbolization of the new S1; it would also have to accept that such symbolization could ever only be a *mi-dire*, a half-saying. It would not succeed in totalizing the signifier to which the subject has become subjected, i.e. the new S1.

73. 'As by a ghost of a faith once alive our lives are haunted by the thought of "professionalism/professional duty"' (Weber 2000, p. 38).

74. 'This means that Judaism in forcing us to face the abyss of the Other's desire (in the guise of the impenetrable God), in refusing to cover up this abyss with a determinate fantasmatic scenario (articulated in the obscene initiatic myth), confronts us for the first time with the paradox of human freedom. There is no freedom outside the traumatic encounter with the opacity of the Other's desire—I am, as it were, thrown into my freedom when I confront this opacity as such, deprived of the fantasmatic cover that tells me what the Other wants from me. In this difficult predicament, full of anxiety, when I know *that* the Other wants something from me, without knowing *what* this desire is, I am thrown back into myself, compelled to assume that risk of freely determining the coordinates of my desire' (Žižek 2003, p. 129).

we are confronted with the dimension of the signifier that is *designified*—of the signifier as that which is carried by the object-cause, not as its fulfillment, but simply as its support. Max Weber observed that Luther forbade any speculation on the majesty of god's will, while Calvin incessantly tried to pry into the secrets of the Other. Weber thought this was due to the fact that Calvin had only intellectual access to the issue, while Luther spoke from the abyss of his own experience.[75] The difference in their doctrines of predestination derives from this difference: whereas for Calvin it was a question of the certainty to 'know' that one was chosen, for Luther it was the exact opposite. Since one could not know, one had to take responsibility for the signifiers that one produces as the S_1 that carries one from the abyss—while always knowing that it can only be non-all.[76] So the doctrine of predestination coupled with the prohibition to speculate about the Other / about god's majesty / about the absolute functions like the object-cause in the analytic discourse. Or, to put it less sensationally, in Martin Luther's Reformation there is an *emergence of the analytic discourse*. From the structure of this emergence we can discern that the immediate access to the algebraic real that is a product of the necessary relation between S_1 and S_2, i.e. to object a, is not possible. The object a falls from the image of the imaginary father, and appears most fundamentally in privation. From there it can structure itself in the articulation of a new S_1—a structure which might indeed best be described by a mathematical ontology.

Thus, we could sum up by saying that the (Lutheran) doctrine of predestination with its subtraction of the absolute from the accessible face of the signifier is a case of wild psychoanalysis. It structures the subject in a permanent split, while offering a possibility to realize some of the absolute, precisely by taking it up as a subtraction from the symbolic. In its most radical dimension, it reaffirms the monotheistic fundamental insight: since

a. I am structured by the Other, and
b. I have no access to the Other, and
c. I can only exist in the Other, it is
d. fully my responsibility to articulate my place in the Other without recourse to knowledge (of the absolute, of what the Other wants from me).

I hope I have made it clear why I think this heritage of the subject of psychoanalysis is just as important as its alliance with modern science and the writing of mathematics. Only a confrontation with the designified signifier and its ghostly productions allows for a new subject to emerge in the process of working through by taking up a truly designifed signifer from the rubble of the reservoir of the Other. A mathematical ontology does not account for this process. For mathematical ontology the apparition of the imaginary father—of the agent of privation—is simply obscure. On the other hand, for the monotheistic tradi-

---

75. Weber 2000, pp. 60-66; see also Luther 1883ff, WA 58 I, p. 139.

76. This is not the place to further trace the development of Luther's thought. Suffice it to say that if, in his most radical moment, he conceptualized a subject that was produced by the subtraction of the absolute from the established order, in his most reactionary phase, later in life, he considered the interpellation into a calling as being complete and without *reste*. His later theory then adheres more clearly to the discourse of the university than to that of the analyst.

tion, the struggle between an Other that enters into conflict with the subject as an other and an Other that can truly be the place where a signifier is articulated as *pas-tout*, non-all, is the consequence of the structure of revelation. Psychoanalysis may not be able to move beyond this, as it possibly is the heir of this tradition. The idea of psychoanalysis' keeping faith, as it were, to this monotheisitic tradition was spelled out clearly by Lacan when he demonstrated that the importance of the signifier was not due to some transcendental structure called 'Oedipus complex', but was rather based on the prophetic tradition which instituted a signifier in the proper sense of the word by opposing it to 'sexual knowledge'. Contrary to polytheistic religion with its claims to knowledge about sex, reproduction, fertility and the cycle of being, this tradition founded religion on a god who was ignorant of such things, as Lacan pointed out. Thus any alternative to the monotheistic tradition's twinning with modern mathematics in the production of the subject of psychoanalysis—and of anti-philosophy—would always imply a return to an imaginary world saturated with the knowledge of *jouissance*—a world that is perhaps similar to the one promoted by consumerist culture or New Age philosophies. This would be the world of the imaginary father, grimacing at the subject while enjoining it to *enjoy!*, and cursing it for its inevitable failure (since, of course, all the *jouissance* rests with him). Against this, the structure of monotheism holds up the structure of what it means to sustain a truth, a truth that has come to the subject as an interruption of the normal state of affairs. Monotheism, by instituting a place—the Other—as the place of articulation of this truth, and by organizing this place as not being the place where the coupling of the *rapport sexuel* takes place, has thus given psychoanalysis its subject—just as much as science has. It is the subject of truth, but of half-saying it, of *mi-dire*. It is the subject that produces truth by constructing a new S1 in the encounter with the real, and by holding—in theological terms 'faithfully'—onto the process of its articulation. And it is the subject that—because it is open to the unconscious, to another knowledge—does not try to totalize the new S1, but rather knows this articulation necessarily follows the logic of *pas-tout*, of non-all. A monotheism that understands itself as 'all' is much closer to the imaginary father, and thus to our social condition, than to a return to fundamental principles. Monotheism in fact has given psychoanalysis a heritage: the heritage of the subject that half-says the truth.

BIBLIOGRAPHY

Agamben, G., *Homo Sacer. Sovereign Power and Bare Life*, Stanford: Stanford University Press, 1998
—— *State of Exception*, Chicago: Chicago University Press, 2005
Badiou, A., *Being and Event*, London: Continuum 2005
—— 'God is Dead', in *Briefings on Existence. A Short Treatise on Transitory Ontology*, Albany NY: SUNY Press, 2006
Charles, C., and Webb, J., *Kant's Philosophy of Religion*, Wotton-under-Edge: Clarendon Press, 1926
Chiesa, L., 'Count-as-one, Forming-into-one, Unary Trait, S1', in: *Cosmos and*

History. The Journal of Natural and Social Philosophy 2: 1-2, 2006

Courtenay, W. J., 'Nominalism and Late Medieval Religion', in *The Pursuit of Holiness in Late Medieval and Renaissance Religion*, Charles Trinkaus and Heiko A. Obermann (eds.), Leiden: Brill, 1974

Derrida, J., *Specters of Marx. The State of the Dead, the Work of Mourning, and the New International*, New York: Routledge, 1994

Ensslin, F., 'Resurrection without Death? Notes on Negativity and Truth in Luther's and Badiou's Interpretations of Paul', in: *umbr(a)* (Utopia), 2008

—— 'Potentiality in Agamben', in *Beyond Potentiality*, Frank Ruda, Jan Völker, and Mark Potocnik (eds.), Berlin: Diaphanes, 2010

Erasmus von Rotterdam: Ausgewählte Schriften. Lateinisch und Deutsch, Vol. 4, Werner Welzig (Ed.), Darmstadt: Wissenschaftliche Buchgesellschaft, 2001

Kant, I., *Religion within the Limits of Reason alone*, New York: Harper Torchbooks, 1960

—— 'Religion innerhalb der Grenzen der bloßen Vernunft', in *Werke in zwölf Bänden*, Vol. 8, Wilhelm Weischedel (ed.), Frankfurt am Main: Suhrkamp, 1977

——*Critique of Pure Reason*, Basingstoke: Palgrave Macmillan, 2003

Koyré, A., *From the Closed World to the Infinite Universe*, Baltimore: John Hopkins Press, 1957

—— *The Astronomical Revolution. Copernicus, Kepler, Borelli*, London: Methuen, 1973

Lacan, J., *Le Séminaire. Livre IV. La relation d'objét. 1956-57*, Paris: Seuil, 1994

—— *The Seminar. Book VII. The Ethics of Psychoanalysis*, New York: Norton, 1997

—— *The Seminar. Book XI. The Four Fundamental Concepts of Psychoanalysis*, New York: Norton, 1998

—— *The Seminar. Book XX. Encore. On Feminine Sexuality. The Limits of Love and Knowledge*, New York: Norton, 1999

—— *Écrits*, New York: Norton, 2006

—— *The Seminar of Jacques Lacan. Book XVII. The Other Side of Psychoanalysis*, New York: Norton, 2007

Lohnstein, H., *Formale Semantik und Natürliche Sprache*, Wiesbaden: Verlag für Sozialwissenschaften, 1996

Luther, M., *Kritische Gesamtausgabe*, Weimar: Verlag Hermann Böhlaus Nachfolger, 1883 ff.

Milner, J-C., *L'Œuvre claire: Lacan, la science et la philosophie*, Paris: Seuil, 1995

Moonan, L., *Divine Power. The Medieval Power Distinction up to its Adoption by Albert, Bonaventure, and Aquinas*, Oxford: Clarendon Press, 1994

Oakley, F., *Omnipotence, Covenant and Order. An Excursion in the History of Ideas from Abelard to Leibniz*, Ithaca: Cornell University Press, 1984

—— 'Lovejoy's Unexplored Option', in *Journal of the History of Ideas*, 48:2, 1987

Ockham, W., *Philosophical Writings*, ed. Philotheus Boehner, Indianapolis: Hackett, 1990

Santner, E. L., *On the Psychotheology of Everyday Life. Reflections on Freud and Rosenzweig*, Chicago: Chicago University Press, 2001

Weber, M., *Die Protestantische Ethik und der 'Geist' des Kapitalismus*, Klaus Lichtblau

and Johannes Weiß (Eds.), Weinheim: Beltz Athenäum, 2000
Zupančič, A., *Ethics of the Real. Kant. Lacan,* London: Verso, 2000
Žižek, S., *The Puppet and the Dwarf,* Cambridge MA/London: MIT Press, 2003

On Deep History and Lacan

Adrian Johnston

I. TRAVERSING THE PHYLOGENETIC FANTASY: REVISITING THE ARCHAIC IN PSYCHOANALYSIS

Starting with Freud, the topic of phylogeny has remained a vexed, troubling matter for psychoanalysis. Freud's ambivalence with respect to this issue is rather evident.[1] On the one hand, especially in his later works, he repeatedly appeals to a phylogenetic 'archaic heritage' both as a subject of metapsychological speculation and as an explanatory device at the level of clinical practice.[2] Freud not infrequently goes so far as to echo the theory of recapitulation à la Ernst Haeckel's famous statement asserting that 'ontogeny recapitulates phylogeny'[3] (before proceeding further, it must be noted that 'phylogeny' and 'ontogeny' are employed here throughout primarily in their Freudian analytic senses, as opposed to their contemporary scientific meanings; as Daniel Lord Smail clarifies, 'natural selection allows organisms infinite room for variation—but the variation is infinite within a set of phylogenetic constraints that evolved upstream... There's a subtle but crucial distinction... between a phylogenetic constraint and what Freud called "archaic heritage". The former determines what you can't be; the latter determines part of what you are'[4]).

On the other hand, Freud's reservations regarding phylogenetic hypotheses are testified to not only by textual evidence—the fact that he refrains from publishing his metapsychological paper focused on such hypotheses (entitled 'Overview of the Transference Neuroses'[5]) bears witness to his hesitancy (a copy of this lost paper was discovered by Ilse Grubrich-Simitis in 1983 amongst Sándor Ferenczi's belongings, with Ferenczi himself having avidly indulged in musings

1. I would like to thank, to begin with, Daniel Lord Smail for his substantial and encouraging critical feedback on an earlier draft version of this text. In addition, I was prompted to address the topics treated herein by a series of very thoughtful questions put to me by Nathan Brown, Tracy McNulty, and Knox Peden. Finally, I appreciate the suggestions for revision of this piece kindly offered to me by Jean Wyatt.

2. Freud 1916-1917, p. 371; Freud 1918b, p. 97, pp. 119-120; Freud 1940a, p. 167, p. 188, pp. 206-207.

3. Freud 1916-1917, p. 199; Freud 1916-1917, p. 354; Freud 1924d, p. 174; Freud 1925e, pp. 220-221; Freud 1939a, p. 99.

4. Daniel Lord Smail, personal communication with the author via e-mail, May 27th, 2010.

5. Freud 1987, pp. 5-20.

about phylogeny). In a brief letter to Ferenczi (dated July 28th, 1915) accompanying this draft manuscript, Freud tells him, 'You can throw it away or keep it'.[6] If Ferenczi hadn't kept it, this text would have been lost forever.

In print, the negative side of Freud's ambivalence *vis-à-vis* phylogeny comes through on a couple of occasions. The case study of the Wolf Man, although containing an instance of recourse to the claim that a reservoir of ancient, collective human experiences provides stock material for 'primal phantasies' springing into operation when the individual's ontogenetic life history fails to furnish the psyche with such material,[7] harbors a moment of wavering with implications for his phylogenetic theories. Therein, Freud expresses this skepticism in a footnote:

> I admit that this is the most delicate question in the whole domain of psycho-analysis. I did not require the contributions of Adler or Jung to induce me to consider the matter with a critical eye, and to bear in mind the possibility that what analysis puts forward as being forgotten experiences of childhood (and of an improbably early childhood) may on the contrary be based upon phantasies created on occasions occurring late in life. According to this view, wherever we seemed in analyses to see traces of the after-effects of an infantile impression of the kind in question, we should rather have to assume that we were faced by the manifestation of some constitutional factor or of some disposition that had been phylogenetically maintained. On the contrary, no doubt has troubled me more; no other uncertainty has been more decisive in holding me back from publishing my conclusions. I was the first—a point to which none of my opponents have referred—to recognize both the part played by phantasies in symptom-formation and also the 'retrospective phantasying' of late impressions into childhood and their sexualization after the event... If, in spite of this, I have held to the more difficult and more improbable view, it has been as a result of arguments such as are forced upon the investigator by the case described in these pages or by any other infantile neurosis—arguments which I once again lay before my readers for their decision. (Freud 1918b, p. 103)

Later, in *The Ego and the Id* (1923), he very quickly performs a sort of intellectual *fort-da* game with phylogeny, remarking:

> With the mention of phylogenesis, however, fresh problems arise, from which one is tempted to draw cautiously back. But there is no help for it, the attempt must be made—in spite of the fear that it will lay bare the inadequacy of our whole effort. (Freud 1923b, pp. 37-38)

Of course, in the longer of these two passages from 1918's 'From the History of an Infantile Neurosis', the thesis positing the effective existence of a deeply buried, hard-wired archaic phylogenetic heritage is not itself directly in question; indeed, it's spoken of as established ('we should rather have to assume that we were faced by the manifestation of some constitutional factor or of some disposition that had been phylogenetically maintained'). Instead, the supposition of the actual, factual historical reality of early infantile/childhood episodes as

---

6. Grubrich-Simitis 1987, p. xvi.

7. Freud 1918b, p. 97; Johnston 2005, pp. 220-221.

the concrete ontogenetic basis of fundamental fantasies is manifestly what's explicitly at stake.

However, considering that Freud elsewhere concedes a reciprocity between phylogeny and ontogeny such that the former is reversed-engineered out of the latter—this indicates that factors pertaining to the ontogenetic dimension can and do entail implications for the phylogenetic dimension[8]—Freud's worries circling here around retroactive deferred action (i.e., *Nachträglichkeit, après-coup*) ought to apply to the phylogenetic as much as to the ontogenetic. That is to say, not only is a healthy skepticism warranted when analytically confronting the traces of unconscious fantasies apparently originating in very early life events, namely, in the singular subject's prehistory—serious doubts should be entertained in reaction to narrative tableaus purporting accurately to depict the shared ordeals of humanity transpiring long, long ago, namely, in the trans-individual group's prehistory. In short, Freud has no reason to abstain from raising the same reservations in connection with phylogeny that he raises in connection with ontogeny (also, it's worth observing that these reservations regarding retroaction in ontogeny surface only a few pages after a seemingly quite confident deployment of the notion of archaic heritage in the same text—maybe a displacement of uncertainty is at work on this occasion).

Jacques Lacan cuts the knot of Freud's ambivalent *rapport* with things phylogenetic by more or less jettisoning them. Unlike Freud, he has no sympathy whatsoever for the idea of the ontogenetic recapitulating the phylogenetic.[9] He mocks Ferenczi's wild imaginings in these Freudian veins.[10] For a thinker committed to a conception of both individual and collective histories as essentially staccato movements, as propelled and marked by sharp breaks and ruptures thwarting consistency through repeatedly introducing irreparable discontinuities,[11] Lacan detects the suspect assumption of too much substantial, underlying temporal continuity dwelling at the heart of the ontogenetic-phylogenetic couplet—a couplet he sees as indissociable from a problematic, non-psychoanalytic developmental psychology of well-ordered, sequential stages organically flourishing out of a preordained (perhaps 'natural') program.[12] At one point, he compares the recapitulationist version of the ontogeny-phylogeny link to the proto-rationalist Socratic-Platonic doctrine of reminiscence, an epistemological doctrine resting on an ontological theory of a unified soul (*psuchê, âme*) harmoniously enmeshed with the organic *polis*, the enveloping cosmos, and the timeless heaven of pure forms[13] (needless to say, for Lacan, Freudian analysis, with its split subject [$], irreversibly shatters this ancient vision of ultimate, seamless unity).

The agenda of this intervention is, in essence, simple: to challenge the Lacanian prohibition of phylogenetic speculations in psychoanalytic metapsychology (this includes Lacan's recurrently pronounced ban on asking after the origins

---

8. Freud 1939a, p. 100.
9. Lacan 2005a, p. 32.
10. Lacan 2004, p. 377.
11. Lacan 2005b, p. 117, pp. 120-121; Lacan 2007a, p. 65; Johnston 2009a, pp. 149-150.
12. Lacan 1977, pp. 63-64.
13. Lacan 1967.

of language). As will be seen, doing so doesn't mean thoughtlessly endorsing the shakiest, most dubitable versions of such speculations as articulated by Freud; it's not as though the concept-term phylogeny is inherently and necessarily wedded to a Haeckel-style recapitulationism automatically entailing the continuity and consistency of a fundamental, macrocosmic totality, a grand One-All as 'the great chain of being'. What's more, given relatively recent advances in relevant fields (biology and its offshoots first and foremost), Lacan's now somewhat dated arguments (primarily of an epistemological variety) against investigations into archaic origins and sources are much less convincing than they once were. They arguably might not hold water anymore. Harvard historian Daniel Lord Smail's important and intriguing 2008 book *On Deep History and the Brain* will play a key role in this critical reassessment of phylogeny in relation to Lacanian theory.

II. 'IN THE BEGINNING WAS THE WORD': LACAN'S SACRED HISTORY

Lacan periodically identifies himself as a materialist, hinting that he's inclined in the direction of Marxist-inspired historical and dialectical materialisms in particular.[14] Moreover, he indicates that one of the remaining crucial tasks bequeathed to contemporary materialists is the surprisingly incomplete and difficult struggle exhaustively to secularize materialism, to purge it of camouflaged residues of religiosity hiding within its ostensibly godless confines.[15] The author of the present piece elsewhere has argued at length that carrying out the mission of forging a fully atheistic and materialist Lacanian theoretical apparatus requires, among other things, forcing psychoanalysis and the life sciences dialectically to interpenetrate each other.[16] Thus far, these efforts to meet this requirement have been centered on constructing scientifically-informed-yet-non-reductive/eliminative accounts of various aspects of ontogenetic subject-formation. But, insofar as these ontogenetic accounts take for granted the established framework of trans-individual socio-linguistic scaffoldings pre-existing the being of the living entity thrown into processes of subjectification, the question of whether these collective historico-representational structures (i.e., Lacanian big Others) themselves are amenable to and ought to be brought into the orbit of (quasi-)naturalist, bio-materialist strategies of explanation remains open. In other words, for an ontogenetic theory of subject-formation elaborated at the intersection of Freudian-Lacanian psychoanalysis and the life sciences not to presuppose tacitly, in the phylogenetic background, the enigmatic, impossible-to-see-behind 'Holy Spirit'[17] of a mysteriously always-already given big Other *qua* symbolic order—such a presupposition hardly becomes any position purporting to be anti-idealist, immanentist, and atheist—scientifically guided investigations into the early emergence of the properly socio-representational dimensions of humanity

---

14. Lacan 1977; Lacan 2006a, p. 194; Lacan 1990, p. 112.

15. Johnston 2008a, pp. 166-188.

16. Johnston 2008b, pp. 167-176, pp. 203-209, pp. 269-287; Malabou and Johnston 2013; Johnston 2007, pp. 3-20; Johnston 2008a, pp. 166-188; Johnston 2008c, pp. 27-49; Johnston 2011a; Johnston 2012a; Johnston 2012b.

17. Lacan 1994, pp. 41-58; Johnston 2011a.

(i.e., inquiries into phylogeny) must be pursued and integrated into analytic theory. This short essay is a first, rough-and-preliminary gesture in this direction.

In the third seminar, Lacan bluntly admits that, 'I'm not interested in prehistory'[18] (the full significance of this admission will become glaringly apparent in the third section of this essay). Later, in the ninth seminar, he makes clear that, in line with a very standard view amongst historians themselves, he privileges the invention of writing as demarcating the boundary between prehistory and history proper.[19] Even later, in 'L'étourdit', Lacan speaks of 'the misery of historians' as their being confined to investigating 'documents of signification' (i.e., writings of which they can make sense, in relation to which they can establish a *connaissance* and/or *méconnaissance*).[20]

One of Lacan's invariant principles affirmed regularly across the lengthy span of his intellectual itinerary is that the constellations of his register of the Symbolic must be treated as always-already given, established realities pre-existing any and every particular subject.[21] He describes the 'symbolic dimension'[22] as 'the whole symbolic, original order—an environment'[23]—as an 'environment', this 'dimension' entirely envelops those living beings delivered into subjectivity, not only surrounding them, but making their forms of life possible to begin with. Appealing to the authority of Heidegger (someone incarnating anything but a Marx-inspired historical/dialectical materialism indebted to the physical, experimental sciences of modernity), Lacan maintains that 'language is there before man, which is evident. Not only is man born in language, exactly as he is born into the world, but he is born by language'.[24] As mentioned above, Lacan, while tending to defend his interdict of queries probing the origins of language on epistemological grounds, sometimes blurs together epistemological and ontological strata of reflection without explicit explanation and justification.[25] In these just-quoted assertions, the ontological emphasis (under Heideggerian influence) is to the fore, with the human being *qua parlêtre* (speaking being) owing his/her very existence to the eternally prior Symbolic big Other into which he/she is thrown. Similarly, Lacan elsewhere claims that, 'the best anthropology can go no further than making of man the speaking being'.[26] As François Balmès insightfully remarks in a study focusing on the Heidegger-Lacan relationship, 'at the very moment where he solemnly proclaims not to have an ontology, Lacan forges the term *parlêtre*'.[27] The fact that Lacan doesn't consistently restrict himself to a Kantian/Wittgensteinian-style epistemology in which the prison-house of language (to borrow a phrase from Frederic Jameson) sets limits rendering the non/extra-linguistic inaccessible to linguistically constituted and mediated knowledge is on display in declarations

---

18. Lacan 1993, p. 306.
19. Lacan 1961.
20. Lacan 2001a, p. 480.
21. Lacan 1993, pp. 147-149; Lacan 1958.
22. Lacan 1993, p. 81.
23. Ibid., p. 120.
24. Lacan 2005b, p. 39.
25. Lacan 1998a, pp. 307-311, p. 317; Johnston 2011a.
26. Lacan 1990, p. 114.
27. Balmès 1999, p. 3.

like 'reality is *at the outset* marked by symbolic nihilation'[28] (*'la réalité est marquée d'emblée de la néantisation symbolique'*[29]) and 'the symbolic universe exists first, and the real universe comes to settle itself down in its interior'.[30]

Similarly, in what one might suspect is a less-than-secular bend of his knee to the Bible, Lacan again and again redeploys as one of his axioms the appropriated announcement, 'In the beginning was the Word'.[31] He insists that 'it's an enigmatic beginning'.[32] No wonder, then, that he earlier, in a session of the fourth seminar entitled by Jacques-Alain Miller 'The Signifier and the Holy Spirit', proclaims that 'The Holy Spirit is the entrance of the signifier into the world'.[33] But, why must the genesis of *'le Verbe'* (i.e., the *Logos* of socio-symbolic orders as signifiers and linguistic-institutional systems) be left shrouded in (sacred) mystery? How does Lacan justify this insistence on the emergence of language (or, at least, language-like structures) as a timeless enigma?

One line of argumentation insinuated by Lacan quietly trades on Freud's premise that one is able to move back-and-forth between ontogeny and phylogeny such that findings at one level can be applied to the other level (i.e., there's a reciprocity in which ontogenetic phenomena reveal aspects of phylogenetic sequences and vice versa). Throughout the course of his teachings, Lacan contends that, ontogenetically speaking, the 'preverbal', as what comes before the acquisition of language by the young, nascent subject-to-be, is capable of being (mis)recognized exclusively through *après-coup* retrojections arising from and conditioned by the 'verbal'; speaking beings seeking to apprehend what they were prior to socio-linguistic subjectification are doomed to project backwards the verbal onto the preverbal,[34] to be stuck straining in vain to reach an inherently inaccessible transcendence.[35] Along these lines, in a 1956 paper co-authored with Wladimir Granoff, Lacan straightforwardly states:

> ...we must first recall that psychoanalysis, which permits us to see farther into the psyche of children than any other science, was discovered by Freud through the observation of adults—more precisely, by listening to them or, rather, to their speech. Indeed, psychoanalysis is a 'talking cure'. (Lacan and Granoff 1956, p. 266)

Lacan and Granoff continue:

> To recall such generally accepted truths may at first seem an imposition; upon reflection, it is not. It is only a reminder of an essential methodological point of reference. For, unless we are to deny the very essence of psychoanalysis, we must make use of language as our guide through the study of the so-called pre-verbal structures. (Ibid., pp. 266-267)

---

28. Lacan 1993, p. 148.
29. Ibid., p. 168.
30. Lacan 2007, p. 75.
31. Lacan 1992, pp. 213-214; Lacan 2001b, p. 12; Lacan 2001a, p. 135; Lacan 2007b, p. 60; Lacan 2005a, pp. 89-91.
32. Lacan 2005a, p. 90.
33. Lacan 1994, p. 48; Johnston 2011a.
34. Lacan, Seminar XXIV. *L'insu que sait de l'une bévue s'aile à mourre* (unpublished), lesson of 18/1/1977.
35. Lacan 1998a, p. 329.

This 'methodological' constraint bearing upon ontogeny *qua* the temporally elongated emergence of the *parlêtre* also gets applied by Lacan to matters pertaining to phylogeny. In particular, the problem of the ancient creation of languages is handled by him exactly as is the preverbal in the life history of singular speaking subjects. One of the ironies in the current context is that this move partially assumes and accepts the mutually mirroring parallelism between the phylogenetic and the ontogenetic proposed by Freud, a proposal Lacan, as pointed out above, dismisses as analytically wrong-headed. More generally, as the engagement with Smail's work below will show, the presumed equivalence between speechless infants and archaic human beings has become extremely contentious and debatable.

Exemplary instances of Lacan's unwavering stance *vis-à-vis* the question of the origin of language are to be found both relatively early and quite late in his corpus. Relatively early, at the very start of the second seminar, he says:

> When something comes to light, something which we are forced to consider as new, when another structural order emerges, well then, it creates its own perspective within the past, and we say—*This can never not have been there, this has existed from the beginning.* Besides, isn't that a property which our own experience demonstrates? (Lacan 1988b, p. 5)

As seen, Lacan himself recurrently expresses the view, as regards language, that, '*This can never not have been there, this has existed from the beginning*'. Hence, a plausible interpretation of this passage is that, in tension with his stronger ontological claims about the primordial, ground-zero originarity of 'the Word', he's on this occasion content to rest with a weaker epistemological claim to the effect that the initial advent of the 'structural order' of the Symbolic big Other engenders a Kantian-type necessary/transcendental illusion, a mirage in which this order appears as always-already present. Immediately following the preceding quotation, Lacan turns to the topic of language's root-source:

> Think about the origins of language. We imagine that there must have been a time when people on this earth began to speak. So we admit of an emergence. But from the moment that the specific structure of this emergence is grasped, we find it absolutely impossible to speculate on what preceded it other than by symbols which were always applicable. What appears to be new thus always seems to extend itself indefinitely into perpetuity, prior to itself. We cannot, through thought, abolish a new order. This applies to anything whatsoever, including the origin of the world. (Lacan 1988b, p. 5)

Human history prior to the surfacing of language-as-speech is, for Lacan, Real *qua* impossible. This archaic phylogenetic *an sich*, although admitted to exist, if only as a spectral pre-existence outside the domain of acknowledged existence proper (i.e., the being of existence as constituted by the *Logos* of an onto-*logy*) is an epistemologically out-of-bounds, off-limits time before time, a Real beyond the Imaginary-Symbolic realities of speaking beings.

Moreover, following closely in Kant's footsteps, Lacan alleges that illegitimate speculative attempts to overstep the linguistically demarcated border between the prehistorical-as-prelinguistic and the historical-as-linguistic generate fictions and phantasms.[36] As he has it, efforts symbolically to comprehend the pre/non-symbolic inevitably result in the production of mere confabulations (i.e., 'organized deliriums'):

> Well understood, the question of the origin of language is one of those subjects which best lends itself to organized deliriums, collective or individual. This is not what we have to do with. Language is there. It's an emergent. Now that it has emerged, we will never again know when or how it commenced, nor how things were before it was. (Lacan 2005c, p. 27)

Although the first occurrence of 'we' in this quotation ('This is not what we have to do with') almost certainly refers to 'we analysts', the second occurrence of 'we' ('we will never again know') has a much wider semantic scope, referring to all agents of knowing. That is to say, while Lacan starts with what initially sounds like a stipulation holding strictly for analytic clinical practitioners (i.e., a methodological principle, in the spirit of what is said in the earlier-quoted paragraphs from the 'Fetishism' essay co-authored with Granoff), he quickly jumps to the broadest of theoretical levels stretching well beyond psychoanalysis alone. One reasonably might wonder what, if anything, licenses this abrupt leap across the span of many wide chasms. But, for the time being, attention should be paid to the absolutism of the final sentence of these lines. Therein, Lacan emphasizes the ineliminable permanence ('never') of this fantasy-inducing ignorance.

Well after the 1950s, in the seventeenth, eighteenth, and nineteenth seminars, Lacan once again underscores what he puts forward as a theoretically fundamental law against raising the question of origins with respect to the symbolic order. In the seventeenth seminar, he comments, 'we all know that to structure knowledge correctly one needs to abandon the question of origins', specifically 'the origins of language'.[37] In the eighteenth seminar, Lacan attributes the historical progress made by linguistics to this discipline's abandonment, in the nineteenth century, of the problem of the primordial historical sources of languages; it thereby bids farewell to a 'period of genetic mythification'.[38] In the nineteenth seminar, Lacan adamantly endorses this prohibition.[39] Knowledge gets nowhere if it wastes its precious time getting entangled in the semblances of hallucinations, imaginings, and rantings.

Returning to the highlighted issue of Lacan's unqualified absolutism (à la the 'never' in 'we will never again know') he subtly introduces qualifications on other occasions. For instance, subsequently in the second seminar, he speaks of a conceptual grasp of the birth of language in a conditional mode ('if') and replaces 'never' with 'for a long time' ('if we had an idea of how language is born—something which we must renounce any knowledge of for a long time'[40]). In the seventeenth seminar, he hints that insights into the origins of language can be in-

36. Lacan 1994, p. 50; Johnston 2011a.
37. Lacan 2007a, p. 19.
38. Lacan 2007c, p. 61.
39. Lacan 2011a, pp. 68-69.
40. Lacan 1988b, p. 189.

ferred retroactively from within and out of language itself.[41] And, in 1967, Lacan rearticulates himself thus:

> Do not imagine that man invented language. You're not sure of it, you have no proof, and you've not seen any human animal become before you *Homo sapiens* like that. When he is *Homo sapiens*, he already has language. When one, and especially a certain Helmholtz, wanted to interest oneself in it in linguistics, one refused to raise the question of origins. That was a wise decision. It does not mean that this is a prohibition it would be necessary to maintain forever, but it is wise not to tell fabricated tales, and one always tells fabricated tales at the level of origins. (Lacan 2005b, pp. 46-47)

In the section dealing with Smail to follow shortly, Lacan's appeal to ignorance ('you have no proof') will be submitted to harsh interrogation. Additionally, whether strictures productive for certain domains (for example, linguistics and/or psychoanalysis) are applicable and conducive to other domains is highly questionable. Related to this and at an intra-psychoanalytic level, whether a (methodological/epistemological) limit appropriate to clinical analysis (in which ontogeny predominates) directly and as a matter of course holds for analytic metapsychology is also vulnerable to fierce dispute. However, the preceding quotation is especially curious for its last sentence: 'It does not mean that this is a prohibition it would be necessary to maintain forever, but it is wise not to tell fabricated tales, and one always tells fabricated tales at the level of origins.' It contains a tension, if not an outright contradiction. On the one hand, Lacan concedes that the interdict forbidding inquiry into the origins of linguistic-symbolic configurations, an interdict he unflinchingly upholds, need not be taken as eternally unbreakable. On the other hand, he goes on to postulate, in the very same sentence and in accordance with his own orthodoxy, that any and every eventual breaking of this taboo inevitably ('always') gives rise to confabulations, fantasies, fictions, illusions, etc. ('fabricated tales'). Is this to suggest that, some day in the indeterminate future, people ought to resume constructing stories of phylogenetic origins, even if the products of these activities amount to nothing more than that, namely, just-so stories? Does this indicate that Lacan believes some tales yet to be told have the chance to be less false and misleading than the tales told thus far in and about human history (in the same manner in which Christianity is, for him, 'the one true religion'[42] *qua* the least false of all religions[43])? Are certain artificial, contrived narratives of phylogeny somehow (potentially) preferable or superior to others? These unanswered (and, perhaps, unanswerable) questions aside, this intervention is interested in gambling on the hypothesis that the moment Lacan casts into a hazy, distant, not-guaranteed-to-arrive future (i.e., the 'long time' of the not 'forever'[44]) has, indeed, finally arrived—and this maybe sooner than expected (at least for Lacan and most Lacanians).

41. Lacan 2007a, p. 155.
42. Lacan 2005a, pp. 79, 81-82; Johnston 2008a, pp. 185-187.
43. Chiesa and Toscano 2005, p. 10; Chiesa and Toscano 2007, p. 118.
44. Lacan 1988b; Lacan 2005b.

III. THE DAMNING WITNESS OF MATERIAL SIGNIFIERS: TOWARD A LACANIAN DEEP HISTORY

Daniel Lord Smail's 2008 *On Deep History and the Brain*, a book using the neurosciences to dismantle firmly entrenched, long-standing perceptions regarding prehistory as distinct from history proper, not only is incredibly relevant to the topic of phylogeny (as archaic heritage) in Freudian-Lacanian psychoanalysis—this compact text deserves careful attention from today's philosophers and theorists concerned with novel varieties of materialism and realism. Before examining *On Deep History and the Brain* in light of the preceding analyses of Lacan, Smail's position should be situated with respect to Quentin Meillassoux's realist 'speculative materialism' in particular. Smail unearths a zone neglected by partisans of various versions of 'speculative realism' (a movement spawned by Meillassoux's 2006 programmatic treatise *After Finitude: An Essay on the Necessity of Contingency*).

Without providing a synopsis of *After Finitude*—this clear, concise book has been summarized thoroughly in other contexts[45]—suffice it to say that Meillassoux's focus on 'ancestrality'[46] in his assault on idealist 'correlationism'[47] obviously is fixated upon the labor of thinking a time before thought (i.e., an 'ancestral' real[ity] prior to the coming-into-existence of sentient and, eventually, sapient beings). One of Ray Brassier's supplements to Meillassoux's critique of correlationist idealism consists in foregrounding a future after both sentience and sapience (i.e., 'life after humans' as well as all other forms of [self-]aware existence, up to and including the death-by-dissipation of the physical universe itself) in addition to a past before any and every consciousness.[48] What's more, as Alain Badiou and Jean Laplanche, among others, already indicate well before the recent birth of speculative realism as an orientation,[49] Meillassoux and Brassier undoubtedly likewise would identify the Lacan discussed in the preceding section as a structural linguistic correlationist for whom the pre-Symbolic (or, for Brassier, post-Symbolic as well) Real exists solely in and through a (co-)constituting correlation with the Symbolic.

And yet, what Lacan's 'idealinguistic' correlationism obfuscates specifically with regard to the psychoanalytic problem of phylogeny, and what Smail renders palpably visible, is neither Meillassoux's ancestral time of the 'arche-fossil'[50] nor Brassier's post-apocalyptic future of extinction. Smail too presents arguments against what could be labeled a certain sort of correlationism prevalent amongst historians and, as demonstrated at length earlier, shared by Lacan (especially when he addresses the question of the origin of language). However, what this correlationist creed denies is a real(ity) neither prior nor

45. Brassier 2007, pp. 49-94; Harman 2007, pp. 104-117; Hallward 2008, pp. 51-57; Žižek 'An Answer to Two Questions', in Johnston 2009a, pp. 214-230; Hägglund 2011; Johnston 2009b, pp. 73-99; Johnston 2011b.

46. Meillassoux 2008, pp. 10-22, pp. 26-28.

47. Ibid., pp. 5-11, pp. 14-21, pp. 35-45.

48. Brassier 2007, pp. 228-230, p. 238.

49. Badiou 2009, p. 188; Laplanche 1987, p. 134; Johnston 2009a, pp. 120-123.

50. Meillassoux 2008, p. 10, p. 14, pp. 16-18, pp. 20-23, pp. 26-27, p. 34.

posterior to awareness/sentience, but, rather, a time of sentience, and probably even sapience, anterior to the currently remaining testimony of socio-symbolic written documents as, so to speak, linguistic fossils; Smail isolates not past or future times entirely external to human beings, as do Meillassoux and Brassier, but, instead, he pinpoints, in Lacanese, a time that's 'extimate' in relation to humanity, an 'arche', as it were, in history more than history itself. This time is casually labeled 'prehistory' by both professional historians and the habits of everyday discourse. Smail convincingly contends that this is a loaded word implying that, before the invention of writing and related technical, practical, and ideational forms, humanity presumably dwelt in an unchanging natural stasis as opposed to the changing cultural kinesis supposedly ushering into being exclusively thanks to a socio-symbolic revolution inexplicably irrupting almost *ex nihilo*.[51] At the beginning of his text, Smail contrasts 'prehistory' with 'deep history'—'historians, for all intents and purposes, still regard deep history as prehistory, the time before history.'[52]

How, exactly, does Smail define deep history in his precise sense? Right up front, he offers this preliminary definition:

> A deep history of humankind is any history that straddles this buffer zone, bundling the Paleolithic and the Neolithic together with the Postlithic— that is, with everything that has happened since the emergence of metal technology, writing, and cities some 5,500 years ago. The result is a seamless narrative that acknowledges the full chronology of the human past. (Smail 2008, pp. 2-3)

In Smail's view, the 'full chronology' is, according to his deep historical ambitions, the long as opposed to the short chronology. For him, Lacan definitely would count as a proponent of the short chronology, that is, as an opponent of deep history (Freud, by contrast, would count as an advocate of a deep history, i.e., phylogeny as archaic heritage, constructed with the combined help of clinical analyses and Darwinian speculations—instead of, as in Smail's position, with the help of neurobiology). This truncated timeline, unlike the much vaster one favored by deep history, treats everything older than four- to five-thousand years as prehistory, not history per se.

One of the catchiest refrains in Smail's book is his assertion that the shallow history of the short chronology is a symptom of a lingering Judeo-Christian hangover.[53] Despite the nineteenth-century 'time revolution' brought about by geological discoveries, an event in which the Biblical account of creation and all its fruit rapidly were uprooted empirically,[54] Smail shows how historical consciousness (that of both historians and laypersons) lagged behind this revolution (in the well-known Lacanian terms of Octave Mannoni, unconscious fidelity to Judeo-Christianity results in historical consciousness resorting to a fetishistic 'disavowal' [*Verleugnung*] of the 'castrating' blow of the geology-driv-

---

51. Smail 2008, pp. 33-34, pp. 40-47, pp. 50-52, p. 75.
52. Ibid., p. 2.
53. Ibid., pp. 9-10, pp. 13-14.
54. Ibid., p. 1.

en time revolution, leading to variations of the line '*je sais bien, mais quand même...*'[55]). To greater or lesser extents, this consciousness continues failing completely to digest the revolutionary implications flowing from revelations of 'deep time' brought about via such domains as geology and astrophysics (Meillassoux and Brassier similarly draw attention to failures by philosophers and quotidian individuals to confront the consequences of a time whose depth and breadth exceeds the finitude of humanity itself). Smail blames religiously inculcated habits of thought, engrained over the course of many, many centuries, for the absence of and resistance to an honest, thorough reckoning with deep time:

> Of all the obstacles to a deep history, the most serious may well prove to be simple inertia. For several thousand years, historians writing in the Judeo-Christian tradition were accustomed to framing history according to the short chronology of sacred, or Mosaic, history, the chronology that frames the story recounted in Genesis. The time revolution brought an end to the short chronology as a matter of historical fact. Yet the historical narrative that emerged in U.S. history curricula and textbooks between the late nineteenth century and the 1940s did not actually abandon the six thousand years of sacred history. Instead, the sacred was deftly translated into a secular key: the Garden of Eden became the irrigated fields of Mesopotamia, and the creation of man was reconfigured as the rise of civilization. Prehistory came to be an essential part of the story of Western Civ, but the era was cantilevered outside the narrative buttresses that sustain the edifice of Western Civilization. Its purpose was to illustrate what we are no longer. In this way the short chronology persisted under the guise of a secular human history. (Smail 2008, pp. 3-4)

Smail provides helpful reiterations of this powerful thesis further on in his book. Addressing short chronological treatments of such 'catalyzing events' as the invention of writing, he observes:

> The catalyzing events described in these accounts are secular. Nevertheless, they function in the narrative in a fashion identical to the infusion of God's grace. I make no claim, would in fact resist the claim, that the authors of these accounts were crypto-creationists. The problem lies in the grip of the narrative itself, whose rhythms and patterns were left essentially unchanged as the sacred was translated into the secular. (Ibid., p. 35)

In the paragraph summing up the chapter in which the above quotation is situated, Smail writes:

> By the early twentieth century, most professional historians had abandoned sacred history. Yet the chronogeography of sacred history and its attendant narrative of rupture has proved to be remarkably resilient. History still cleaves to its short chronology. The otherwise meaningless date of 4000 B.C. continues to echo in our histories. Authors still use the narrative device of rupture to create an artificial point of origin, reducing the Paleolithic to the status of a prologue to history, humanity's 'apprenticeship,' and history's point of origin is still Mesopotamian, or even more recent than

---

55. Mannoni 1969, pp. 9-33.

that, given how the myth of the medieval origins of the modern world has embedded itself in the historical community. (Ibid., p. 39)

Smail's lucid writing requires little by way of accompanying clarifications. So, circumnavigating promptly back to Lacan on phylogeny, one can make the claim, relying upon Smail, that Lacan himself (however wittingly or unwittingly) inhabits the prison of sacred history. To be more exact, even if Lacan's avowed psychoanalytic atheism guarantees that the contents of his theorizations regarding the ontogenetic and the phylogenetic are secular, Smail's insights compel an acknowledgement that crucial formal features of these same theorizations are far from secular, ultimately amounting to disguised vestiges of a traditional, conservative theology.

Here, Lacan falls victim to a trap he himself dissects better than anyone else: atheists who noisily trumpet the ostensible death of God usually tend to ignore the fashions in which, as Lacan puts it, 'God is unconscious';[56] from the standpoint of psychoanalysis, the less one consciously believes oneself to believe, the more likely is it that one's beliefs will persist precisely by remaining unconscious and unanalyzed.[57] An analysis of Lacan, as atheistic in the ways in which Lacan insists any genuine analysis worthy of the name must be,[58] demands flushing out and liquidating his own conscious and unconscious stubborn investments in the theological and religious. That is to say, if Lacan is sincere in his rallying cry for the pursuit of the arduous, far-from-finished endeavor of secularizing materialism,[59] then faithfulness to this Lacan dictates submitting to merciless criticism those other Lacans who deviate from this uphill path.

Related to the notion of materialism, Smail sees sacred history as an outgrowth of an onto-theology. Specifically, he links it to an idealist ontological dualism epitomized by, of course, Descartes:

> ...the short chronology of the standard historical narrative of the twentieth century was built on a rigid Cartesian distinction between mind and body: the body may be old, but the mind, for all intents and purposes, is young. This is why the standard historical chronology used in cultures influenced by Judeo-Christianity, beginning as it did around 4000 B.C., could afford to ignore humanity's deep history. (Smail 2008, p. 112)

One easily could substitute '*parlêtre*' for 'mind' here to produce an accurate rephrasing of certain of Lacan's anti-phylogeny sentiments. As seen, Lacan concedes that humans as biological organisms (i.e., as bodies) have existed for longer than the comparatively shorter stretch of recorded history (i.e., short/sacred history as based solely upon socio-linguistic remains). But, he plunges these bodies into the dark noumenal abyss of an impossible *qua* inaccessible Real forever after obscured and obliterated by the genesis of 'mind' as symbolically mediated subjectivity. As noted previously, this author, on other occasions, has elaborated in

---

56. Lacan 1977, p. 59; Lacan 2007a, pp. 119-120.

57. Johnston 2009c, pp. 178-181.

58. Lacan 2004, pp. 357-358; Lacan 2006b, pp. 280-281; Lacan 2007a, p. 119; Johnston 2008a, pp. 170-171.

59. Johnston 2008a, pp. 166-188.

detail how a properly materialist and secular Lacanianism can and must articulate a theoretical account of ontogenetic subject formation grounded, in part, on
the life sciences (primarily the neurosciences and evolutionary theory[60]). But, in
order to go to the end, to finish the job thoroughly, the same sort of articulation
has to be spelled out for the phylogenetic formation of the collective 'objective
spirit' (in Hegelian parlance) of Lacan's Symbolic big Other(s). Again, fidelity to
the truly atheist Lacan forces a betrayal of the Lacan who categorically forbids
phylogenetic inquiries.

In addition to the 'inertia' of unconscious beliefs in sacred history, beliefs
borne witness to by the forms (rather than the contents) of historical narratives,
Smail draws attention to explicit epistemological objections underpinning resistance to the acceptance of deep history. Although *On Deep History and the Brain*
unsurprisingly involves no engagement with Lacan (there is, however, a passing mention of 'poststructuralism' therein[61]), Lacan's critiques of phylogenetic
reasoning on the grounds of epistemology are, as should come as no shock by
now, precisely the same objections made by the historians described in Smail's
book who cling to the not-so-secular short chronology. Just as Lacan insists that
history must begin with 'the Word' (i.e. the 'Holy Spirit' of the big Other *qua*
symbolic order[62]), if only due to the epistemological finitude/limitations of historically conscious subjects as speaking beings always-already ensconced in socio-linguistic constellations, so too do resistors rejecting Smailian deep history
insist that 'documents', conceived of as socio-linguistic records and remnants,
are the sole basis for the (re)construction of any and every plausible, defensible
history.[63] As Smail elegantly encapsulates this line of resistance, 'that speechless
past: no other phrase could capture so well the skeptical attitude toward the possibility of studying time beyond the veil.'[64] This sentence could be applied directly to Lacan himself. Through mobilization of the explanatory strategies and resources of the life sciences, Smail demonstrates that investigators can and should
tear aside this veil and cross the threshold beyond the shallowness of the sacred.

The crux of Smail's rebuttals of the epistemological objections raised against
deep history is his distinction between 'documents' and 'traces'.[65] Succinctly stated, documents are the written records, composed in natural languages, which
partisans of the short chronology insist upon as the only reliable and valid foundations upon which to erect historical narratives. By contrast, traces, as defined
by Smail, can be documents, but further encompass a much broader range of
materials, including remnants left from before the time of history as recorded by
written, linguistic documents as per the short chronological definition of these
sources. Smail's examples of traces are 'artifacts, fossils, vegetable remains, pho-

---

60. Johnston 2008b, pp. 167-176, pp. 203-209, pp. 269-287; Malabou and Johnston 2013; Johnston
2007, pp. 3-20; Johnston 2008a, pp. 166-188; Johnston 2008c, pp. 27-49; Johnston 2011a; Johnston 2012a;
Johnston 2012b.
    61. Smail 2008, p. 124.
    62. Johnston 2011a.
    63. Smail 2008, pp. 4-6, pp. 49-50.
    64. Ibid., p. 44.
    65. Ibid., pp. 5-6, 53-56.

nemes, and various forms of modern DNA'[66] as well as 'cave paintings', 'graves and grave goods'.[67] Obviously, only vegetable remains and DNA are evidently troubling instances for Lacan, Smail's other examples of traces fitting Lacan's criteria for signifying elements of structural-symbolic systems. Lacan's short history wouldn't be quite as restrictive as those of historians who turn up their noses at anything other than written, linguistic documents.

What's more, other Lacans are able to be rendered amenable to things close to the deep historical traces appealed to by Smail. Several times, Lacan grants that DNA can be construed as a series of 'letters' *qua* material signifiers, as signifying traces subsisting in the Real.[68] In the eleventh seminar, Lacan, anticipating cutting-edge scientific research into the dynamics shaping both genetics and epigenetics (research that takes off after his death), rightly hypothesizes that the persistent, enduring socio-symbolic mediation of Lévi-Straussian 'elementary structures of kinship' in humans' patterns of mating and family formation across innumerable generations means that human DNA itself testifies, as a sequence of traces, to various historical Others.[69] Smail concurs with this hypothesis,[70] a hypothesis which points to the now well-established life scientific deconstruction of the nature-nurture dichotomy; and, with the implosion of this opposition, the partitioning of natural prehistory and cultural history proper (a partition Lacan-the-phylogenetic-skeptic maintains) collapses too. Plus, apart from the later Lacan's increasing emphasis on the materiality of signifiers (an emphasis facilitating a *rapprochement* between Lacanian signifiers and Smailian traces), his expansion of Saussurian structuralism beyond the disciplinary confines of linguistics alone—this expansion informs his teachings from start to finish—indicates that the status of counting as a signifier has more to do with form than content. In other words, a Lacanian signifier isn't always and necessarily a component (i.e., a word, phrase, sentence, etc.) of a given language *qua une langue* (i.e., a 'tongue'); non-linguistic contents (such as sensory-perceptual mnemic materials and/or Smailian traces) qualify as signifiers too if they entertain determinative differential relations with various other contents bound together in organized, cross-resonating arrangements.[71] The Lacanian protests against a phylogenetic deep history scrutinized in the previous section of this intervention are contestable even on the basis of Lacanian principles.

But, what, if anything, might Lacan add to Smail? To cut a long story short, the fifth and final chapter of *On Deep History and the Brain*, entitled 'Civilization and Psychotropy', employs a dialectical blend of history and neuroscience[72] to chart a deep historical thread running its winding way through time under the influence of human brains' modes of achieving enjoyment-producing self-stim-

66. Ibid., p. 6.
67. Ibid., p. 55.
68. Lacan 1990, p. 112; Lacan 1998b, p. 17; Lacan, Seminar XXV. *Le moment de conclure* (unpublished), lesson of 15/11/1977; Miller 2001, p. 21.
69. Lacan 1977, pp. 150-151.
70. Smail 2008, pp. 114-119, pp. 124-126, pp. 130-131, p. 133, pp. 136-138, p. 144, pp. 154-155.
71. Johnston 2005, pp. 300-315.
72. Smail 2008, pp. 201-202.

ulation.[73] To briefly and merely suggest a potential trajectory of future investigation bringing together Smailian deep history (itself having already begun to bring together the so-called 'hard' and 'soft' sciences) and Lacanian psychoanalytic metapsychology (in this particular instance, drive theory), Lacan's complex, sustained reflections on libidinal economies indicate that history is as much driven along by continual struggles to cope with failures to enjoy as it is by techniques and technologies of pleasure, gratification, etc. (as per Smail's narrative).[74] The historical present provides perhaps the best evidence, the key case-in-point, for this: contemporary consumer (late-)capitalism propels itself forward in historically fateful directions partially on the basis of how it continually and frenetically (re)produces dissatisfaction and lack.[75] Moreover, Lacanian sensibilities push for keeping in mind, even at the evolutionary and neuroscientific levels, the constitutive disharmony and dysfunctionality of human being, right down to the barebones, raw-flesh fundaments of these beings' physiologies—namely, the barred corpo-Real[76] of the kludge-like[77] anatomies of creatures internally generated out of a lone immanent-material plane of contingencies devoid of solid, underlying necessities, meanings, and/or teleologies. Biology itself has reached a juncture at which it unveils what Lacan, in 1955, characterizes as 'the dehiscence from natural harmony, required by Hegel to serve as the fruitful illness, life's happy fault, in which man, distinguishing himself from his essence, discovers his existence.'[78] Hence, an existential materialism positioned at the intersection of science and psychoanalysis, a materialism in which science too lends true credence to the postulated precedence of existence over essence, is a real possibility nowadays.[79]

In Lacan's mind, the phylogenetic perspectives he repudiates are associated with evolutionism. The latter is in turn associated for him with a temporalized, spontaneous substance metaphysics stressing smoothness, gradualness, continuity, and teleological directedness[80] (hence the association between Haeckelian recapitulationism, which Lacan erroneously takes to be the one-and-only version of the phylogenetic, and evolution). The name 'Stephen Jay Gould' (not to mention many other names) stands for the empirical, intra-biological demolition of this wholly false image of evolution in (post-)Darwinian evolutionary theory, a demolition that clears space for alternate dialectical reconceptualizations of phylogeny in which discontinuities immanently arise out of a background of bio-ma-

73. Ibid., pp. 127-128, pp. 157-189.

74. Johnston 2005, pp. 253-255, pp. 328-332, pp. 340-341.

75. Johnston 2009a, pp. 98-101.

76. Johnston 2004a, pp. 227-228; Johnston 2004b, pp. 250-251; Johnston 2005, p. xxxvii, p. 264, p. 266, p. 270, p. 341; Johnston 2006, pp. 34-55; Johnston 2008b, p. xxiii, p. 60, p. 63, p. 65, pp. 79-81, p. 113, p. 284, p. 286; Johnston 2009a, p. 79; Johnston 2011a; Johnston 2012a; Chiesa 2007, p. 123, p. 183, p. 187.

77. Linden 2007, pp. 2-3, pp. 5-7, pp. 21-24, p. 26, pp. 245-246; Marcus 2008, pp. 6-16, pp. 161-163; Malabou and Johnston 2013; Johnston 2012a.

78. Lacan 2006a, p. 286.

79. Johnston 2008c, pp. 27-44; Johnston 2012a; Johnston 2012b.

80. Lacan 1988a, p. 128; Lacan 1988b, p. 24; Lacan 1992, pp. 126-127, pp. 213-214, pp. 223-224; Lacan 2001b, pp. 120-122; Lacan 2011a, p. 78; Lacan 2011b, p. 24; Lacan, Seminar XII. *Problèmes cruciaux pour la psychanalyse* (unpublished), lesson of 16/12/1964; Lacan, Seminar XIII. *L'objet de la psychanalyse* (unpublished), lesson of 19/1/1966.

terial bases[81] (given his guiding intention to break down the barriers separating prehistory from history, Smail understandably emphasizes continuity against discontinuity—but, both psychoanalytic and scientific considerations cry out for a dialectics in which discontinuities of various kinds remain part of the historical picture). A series of remarks by Smail waves in this same general direction: 'with phylogeny, there is no blueprint';[82] 'Darwinian natural selection... has a fundamentally *anti*-essentialist epistemology. That is the whole point. Species, according to Darwin, are not fixed entities with natural essences imbued in them by the Creator';[83] and, apropos the 'futile quest to identify "human nature"'... Here, as in so many areas, biology and cultural studies are fundamentally congruent'.[84]

Contra Lacan's famous counterintuitive thesis in the renowned seventh seminar according to which the originally Christian notion of creation *ex nihilo* is more authentically atheistic than ostensibly atheist Darwinian evolutionary theory[85]—this has everything to do with his problematic assumption that believing in evolution logically requires being committed to a fundamentally seamless monistic ontology allowing for no radical breaks or ruptures—an atheism inspired by analysis need not be left languishing in the spirituality-sustaining mystical void of the anti-scientific 'out of nowhere'. Near the end of his teaching, in the twenty-fifth seminar, Lacan, after asking what the definition of 'the nature of nature' might be, shifts away from his 1960 thesis apropos the *ex nihilo*; here, in 1977, instead of 'creationist raving' being superior to 'evolutionist raving', they are said to be equivalent, the former no longer being deemed better than the latter.[86] They're both hypothetical.[87] But, since the 1960s and 1970s, a great deal has happened in the life sciences. The balance of the scales between these two hypotheses rapidly has tipped ever more decisively in favor of Darwin's legacy. If Lacanianism is to achieve the task of transforming itself into a soundly secular theoretical framework integrated with the historical and dialectical materialisms first delineated by Marx and Engels,[88] it must make its peace with neurosciences and evolutionary theories dramatically different nowadays from what Lacan himself had before him.

Enough enigmas! Down with veils! Holy Spirits be gone! It's high time for more profanation, more desacralization! As Smail declares, 'all that remains for us to shake off is the grip of sacred history'.[89] To conclude with an enthusiastic call-to-arms that's simultaneously a warning of the danger of the return of old (un)holy ghosts ('*Dieu, à en reprendre de la force, finirait-il par ex-sister, ça ne présage rien de meilleur qu'un retour de son passé funeste*'[90]): the future of the past awaits.

---

81. Johnston 2008b, pp. 269-287; Johnston 2007, pp. 3-20; Johnston 2012a.

82. Smail 2008, p. 79.

83. Ibid., p. 124.

84. Ibid., p. 125.

85. Lacan 1992, pp. 213-214; Chiesa and Toscano 2005, pp. 10-11, p. 14; Chiesa and Toscano 2007, p. 118; Johnston 2008a, pp. 185-187.

86. Lacan, Seminar XXV. *L'acte psychanalytique* (unpublished), lesson of 15/11/1977.

87. Ibid.

88. Engels 1940, pp. 279-296; Levins and Lewontin 1985, pp. 1-5, pp. 45-46, pp. 69-70, p. 89, p. 99.

89. Smail 2008, p. 55.

90. Lacan 1973, p. 54.

BIBLIOGRAPHY

Badiou, A., *Theory of the Subject*, London: Continuum, 2009

Balmès, F., *Ce que Lacan dit de l'être (1953-1960)*, Paris: Presses Universitaires de France, 1999

Brassier, R., *Nihil Unbound: Enlightenment and Extinction*, Basingstoke: Palgrave Macmillan, 2007

Chiesa, L., *Subjectivity and Otherness: A Philosophical Reading of Lacan*. Cambridge MA: MIT Press, 2007

Chiesa, L., and Toscano, A., 'Ethics and Capital, *Ex Nihilo*', in *Umbr(a): A Journal of the Unconscious—The Dark God*, Buffalo: State University of New York at Buffalo, 2005

—— '*Agape* and the Anonymous Religion of Atheism', *Angelaki: Journal of the Theoretical Humanities*, vol. 12, no. 1, April 2007

Engels, F., 'The Part Played by Labour in the Transition from Ape to Man', in *Dialectics of Nature*, New York: International Publishers, 1940

Freud, S., (1916-1917), 'Introductory Lectures on Psychoanalysis, Part II. Dreams', in *SE, 15*

—— (1916-1917), 'Introductory Lectures on Psychoanalysis, Part III. General Theory of the Neuroses', in *SE, 16*

—— (1918b), 'From the History of an Infantile Neuroses', in *SE, 17*

—— (1923b), 'The Ego and the Id', in *SE, 19*

—— (1924d), 'The Dissolution of the Oedipus Complex', in *SE, 19*

—— (1925e), 'The Resistances to Psycho-Analysis', in *SE, 19*

—— (1939a), 'Moses and Monotheism: Three Essays', in *SE, 23*

—— (1940a), 'An Outline of Psycho-Analysis', in *SE, 23*

—— 'Overview of the Transference Neuroses', in *A Phylogenetic Fantasy: Overview of the Transference Neuroses* [ed. Ilse Grubrich-Simitis], Cambridge MA: Harvard University Press, 1987

Grubrich-Simitis, I., 'Preface to the Original Edition', in *A Phylogenetic Fantasy*, Cambridge MA: Harvard University Press, 1987

Hägglund, M., 'Radical Atheist Materialism: A Critique of Meillassoux', in *The Speculative Turn: Continental Materialism and Realism* [ed. Levi Bryant, Graham Harman, and Nick Srnicek], Melbourne: Re.press, 2011

Hallward, P., 'Anything is possible', *Radical Philosophy*, no. 152, November/December 2008

Harman, G., 'Quentin Meillassoux: A New French Philosopher', *Philosophy Today*, vol. 51, no. 1, Spring 2007

Johnston, A., 'Revulsion is not without its subject: Kant, Lacan, Žižek, and the Symptom of Subjectivity', *Pli: The Warwick Journal of Philosophy*, no. 14, Spring 2004a

—— 'Against Embodiment: The Material Ground of the Immaterial Subject', *Journal for Lacanian Studies*, vol. 2, no. 2, December 2004b

—— *Time Driven: Metapsychology and the Splitting of the Drive*, Evanston: Northwestern University Press, 2005

—— 'Ghosts of Substance Past: Schelling, Lacan, and the Denaturalization of

Nature', in *Lacan: The Silent Partners* [ed. Slavoj Žižek], London: Verso, 2006

—— 'Slavoj Žižek's Hegelian Reformation: Giving a Hearing to *The Parallax View*', *Diacritics*, vol. 37, no. 1, Spring 2007

—— 'Conflicted Matter: Jacques Lacan and the Challenge of Secularizing Materialism', *Pli: The Warwick Journal of Philosophy*, no. 19, Spring 2008a

—— *Žižek's Ontology: A Transcendental Materialist Theory of Subjectivity*, Evanston: Northwestern University Press, 2008b

—— 'What Matter(s) in Ontology: Alain Badiou, the Hebb-Event, and Materialism Split from Within', *Angelaki: Journal of the Theoretical Humanities*, vol. 13, no. 1, April 2008c

—— *Badiou, Žižek, and Political Transformations: The Cadence of Change*, Evanston: Northwestern University Press, 2009a

—— 'The World Before Worlds: Quentin Meillassoux and Alain Badiou's Anti-Kantian Transcendentalism', *Contemporary French Civilization*, vol. 33, no. 1, Winter/Spring 2009b

—— 'Life Terminable and Interminable: The Undead and the Afterlife of the Afterlife—A Friendly Disagreement with Martin Hägglund', *The New Centennial Review*, vol. 9, no. 1, Spring 2009c

—— 'The Weakness of Nature: Hegel, Freud, Lacan, and Negativity Materialized', in *Hegel and the Infinite: Religion, Politics and the Dialectic* [ed. Clayton Crockett, Creston Davis, and Slavoj Žižek], New York: Columbia University Press, 2011a

—— 'Hume's Revenge: À Dieu, Meillassoux?', in *The Speculative Turn: Continental Materialism and Realism* [ed. Levi Bryant, Graham Harman, and Nick Srnicek], Melbourne: Re.press, 2011b

—— '"Naturalism or anti-naturalism? No, thanks—both are worse!": Science, Materialism, and Slavoj Žižek', *Revue Internationale de Philosophie*, 2012a

—— 'Turning the Sciences Inside Out: Revisiting Lacan's "Science and Truth"', in *Concept and Form: The Cahiers pour l'Analyse and Contemporary French Thought* [ed. Peter Hallward and Knox Peden], London: Verso Books, 2012b

Lacan, J., *Télévision*, Paris: Seuil, 1973

—— *The Seminar of Jacques Lacan, Book XI: The Four Fundamental Concepts of Psychoanalysis, 1964*, New York: W.W. Norton and Company, 1977

—— *The Seminar of Jacques Lacan, Book I: Freud's Papers on Technique, 1953-1954*, New York: W.W. Norton and Company, 1988a

—— *The Seminar of Jacques Lacan, Book II: The Ego in Freud's Theory and in the Technique of Psychoanalysis, 1954-1955*, New York: W.W. Norton and Company, 1988b

—— 'Responses to Students of Philosophy Concerning the Object of Psychoanalysis', in *Television/A Challenge to the Psychoanalytic Establishment* [ed. Joan Copjec], New York: W.W. Norton and Company, 1990

—— *The Seminar of Jacques Lacan, Book VII: The Ethics of Psychoanalysis, 1959-1960*, New York: W.W. Norton and Company, 1992

—— *The Seminar of Jacques Lacan, Book III: The Psychoses, 1955-1956*, New York: W.W. Norton and Company, 1993

—— *Le Séminaire de Jacques Lacan, Livre IV: La relation d'objet, 1956-1957*, Paris: Seuil, 1994

—— *Le Séminaire de Jacques Lacan, Livre V: Les formations de l'inconscient, 1957-1958*, Paris: Seuil, 1998a

—— *The Seminar of Jacques Lacan, Book XX: Encore, 1972-1973*, New York: W.W. Norton and Company, 1998b

—— *Autres écrits* [ed. Jacques-Alain Miller], Paris: Seuil, 2001a

—— *Le Séminaire de Jacques Lacan, Livre VIII: Le transfert, 1960-1961*, Paris: Seuil, 2001b [seconde édition corrigée]

—— *Le Séminaire de Jacques Lacan, Livre X: L'angoisse, 1962-1963*, Paris: Seuil, 2004

—— *Le triomphe de la religion, précédé de Discours aux catholiques* [ed. Jacques-Alain Miller], Paris: Seuil, 2005a

—— *Mon enseignement*, Paris: Seuil, 2005b

—— *Des noms-du-père* [ed. Jacques-Alain Miller], Paris: Seuil, 2005c

—— *Écrits: The First Complete Edition in English*, New York: W.W. Norton and Company, 2006a

—— *Le Séminaire de Jacques Lacan, Livre XVI: D'un Autre à l'autre, 1968-1969*, Paris: Seuil, 2006b

—— *The Seminar of Jacques Lacan, Book XVII: The Other Side of Psychoanalysis, 1969-1970*, New York: W.W. Norton and Company, 2007a

—— *Le mythe individuel du névrosé, ou poésie et vérité dans la névrose* [ed. Jacques-Alain Miller], Paris: Seuil, 2007b

—— *Le Séminaire de Jacques Lacan, Livre XVIII: D'un discours qui ne serait pas du semblant, 1971* [ed. Jacques-Alain Miller]. Paris: Éditions du Seuil, 2007c

—— *Le Séminaire de Jacques Lacan, Livre XIX: ...ou pire, 1971-1972* [ed. Jacques-Alain Miller]. Paris: Éditions du Seuil, 2011a

—— *Je parle aux murs. Entretiens de la chapelle de Sainte-Anne.* Paris: Éditions du Seuil, 2011b

Lacan, J., and Granoff, W., 'Fetishism: The Symbolic, the Imaginary and the Real', in *Perversions: Psychodynamics and Therapy* [ed. Sandor Lorand], New York: Gramercy Books, 1956

Laplanche, J., *Problématiques V: Le baquet—Transcendance du transfert*, Paris: Presses Universitaires de France, 1987

Levins, R., and Lewontin, R., *The Dialectical Biologist*, Cambridge MA: Harvard University Press, 1985

Linden, D. J., *The Accidental Mind: How Brain Evolution Has Given Us Love, Memory, Dreams, and God*, Cambridge MA: Harvard University Press, 2007

Malabou, C., and Johnston, A., *Self and Emotional Life: Philosophy, Psychoanalysis, and Neuroscience*, New York: Columbia University Press 2013

Mannoni, O., 'Je sais bien, mais quand même...', in *Clefs pour l'Imaginaire, ou l'Autre Scène*, Paris: Seuil, 1969

Marcus, G., *Kludge: The Haphazard Evolution of the Human Mind*, New York: Houghton Mifflin Harcourt Publishing Company, 2008

Meillassoux, Q., *After Finitude: An Essay on the Necessity of Contingency*, London: Continuum, 2008

Miller, J.-A., 'The Symptom and the Body Event', *Lacanian Ink*, no. 19, Fall 2001

Smail, D. L., *On Deep History and the Brain*, Berkeley: University of California Press, 2008

Structure and Genesis in Derrida and Lacan: Animality and the Empirical Sciences

Michael Lewis

If metaphysics and physics definitively separated with Galileo and Newton, it is relatively quickly becoming a significant concern of philosophers (particularly those who have come to wonder about the completion and end of metaphysics) to put an end to this, without sacrificing what has been gained in the transcendental inflection which this separation took on with Kant.[1] This apparent isolation of continental philosophy from the insights of the exact and the natural sciences, particularly in the phenomenological tradition, has come to be regarded by some as a narcissistic self-regard, which ends up seeing itself everywhere, and thus failing to acknowledge its inherent openness to those discourses and events which lie beyond its disciplinary borders. Derrida perhaps most of all was concerned with such narcissism—on the part of *any* totality— and his ultimate intent was to open philosophy to other disciplines, or rather to show that it is despite itself always already infiltrated: the most totalising of all sciences is, like all totalities, an open totality, an incomplete whole. For various reasons, it is generally understood that the other disciplines to which Derrida is considered to have angled philosophy have tended to be human sciences, if not simply the 'literary'. But, in his later work in particular, and indeed right at the very beginning, defining as it were another, more encompassing boundary to his thought, it also means the exact and the natural sciences: in *Of Grammatology* and *Positions*, and *Dissemination* at least, his references to mathematics ('undecidability', *mathesis universalis*) and biology (the inscriptions of the genetic code) are prominent. At the same time, perhaps very slightly later than the very beginning (with Derrida's work on Husserl and genesis and structure), deconstruction's closest ally was psychoanalysis. But in a way that Derrida never quite came to grips with, Lacanian psychoanalysis entertained from the very beginning another relation to the natural sciences—perhaps one that his ear-

---

1. The substance of this essay was first presented at the Jan van Eyck Academy, Maastricht, on Wednesday 26th May 2010. I wish to thank all of the participants there for their incisive comments, some of which I have been able to incorporate here.

lier love for phenomenology and Husserl prevented him from seeing. Similarly to the case of deconstruction itself, it is far from accurate to think of the Lacanian rethinking of Freudian categories as referring simply to the human sciences of anthropology and linguistics, as Derrida seems to when he thinks of Lacanianism early on, and as is so perhaps the most common association. It is as if for Lacan, philosophy is not always and essentially narcissistic but *becomes* so, like all structured totalities. This then may be the difference between Derrida and Lacan in this context: for Derrida, we must begin to think from within the structure(s) in which we find ourselves, and we are afforded a way out by the inherent openness of the structure; for Lacan, this openness can itself be explained by an attention to the genesis of structure itself.

The current essay confines itself to the—admittedly enormous—question of the relation between (philosophical) theory and empirical science. For Derrida, philosophy, an apparently closed structure, needs to work away at itself in order to prise apart an already implicit opening in which the heterogeneous insights of science might find a place and be incorporated by philosophy; for Lacan, one can explain the openness of structure precisely by means of a reference to the empirical sciences, which, at the other end of the process, also help to explain how this openness is—at least temporarily—closed, rendering the symbolic order, the order of structure, to speak broadly, autonomous from the real whence it emerged, 'sutured' to use Jacques-Alain Miller's term.

Thus we are reviving the old question of structure and genesis. Derrida's own work began here, with this question of genesis, and he explicitly refers back to this beginning in one of his later works, which is also one of his most personal (or 'autobiographical'), *The Animal That Therefore I Am*, from 1997. Here, as elsewhere in his works on 'the animal', Derrida is at his most insistent that philosophers need to open themselves to the insights of the natural sciences, to usurp the philosopheme which would state that man stands opposed in splendid isolation from every other member of the animal kingdom. Despite the important references to the exact sciences, it might be argued that Derrida devoted more pages (the 'critical' or 'negative' preparatory part of his work, designed precisely to open up a supposed totality to novelty and otherness) to the human sciences in their structuralist form, demonstrating as he did the necessary openness of any finite structure. This openness precisely showed that a totality of any kind could not be self-founding and called for a genetic explanation of its very nature and existence ('"Genesis and Structure" and Phenomenology' along with the other early works on Husserl) and indeed a historical one ('Violence and Metaphysics'). Indeed, it is this openness which explains why there *is* such a thing as 'genesis' and 'history'. Up to a point, the majority of Derrida's works can be said to engage primarily in the 'negative' gesture of finding these openings, without themselves dealing at length with the nature of these geneses. But in his works on the *animal*, the natural sciences hove into view. It seems to be here most of all and most often that Derrida insists on the need for philosophy actually to *refer* to empirical scientific work, and for this reason it is here that we shall stage a brief encounter between Derrida and Lacan on the question of science.

In general, one can quite easily see why an encounter between philosophy and psychoanalysis might be particularly pertinent to this question, since the latter is a highly sophisticated theory that has never shirked empirical work and indeed has always insisted on the necessity of actual experiences with particular cases in the very formation of concepts, particularly the pathological cases, which precisely put in question a traditional pre-psychoanalytic conceptuality.

I. THE TWO DIRECTIONS OF LACAN'S THINKING

I should like to begin with a hypothesis: there are two basic strands in Lacan's work when it comes to the question of the relation between man and animal: these map onto this distinction between the structural and the genetic; the synchronic and the diachronic; the 'transcendental' and the 'empirical'. (For now, let us simply define genesis as any process of development, temporal or historical, which conditions a certain entity in a non-transcendental way, which is to say in a way that is not logical or synchronic, the latter comprising necessary conditions of possibility which can be *philosophically* deduced, which is to say, logically, or *a priori*.)

The two strands may be described, roughly, as follows:

1. A structuralistic, transcendental derivation of the conditions of possibility of man, understood as the subject of the signifier, divided between consciousness and the unconscious thanks to the imposition of a supernatural Law that dictates the self-distantiation which is ultimately explained by the nature of the signifier—the conditions of possibility of man are thus also the conditions of possibility of the signifying order. On this view, man and animal are opposed to one another: the human being must be accorded a number of characteristics which uniquely differentiate him from all of the other animal species: these include language *stricto sensu*, culture, law, prohibition, desire, and death drive: and most of all, the unconscious itself.

2. An attention to the chronological genesis of man, ontogenetically and phylogenetically, the latter including most crucially the prehistory of the symbolic order: in this respect, Lacan seems to produce a developmental, naturalistic account. On this account, by definition, man and animal must exist on something like a continuum, at least initially, and are not separated by any radical discontinuity or heterogeneity; all of those features of man which are supposed to be uniquely his own, 'cultural' as opposed to 'natural', may be found *in embryo* in nature itself, in the phenomena—revealed by *empirical* work—of animal techniques and animal languages.

So, in Lacan's work, we can isolate two understandings of the relation between man and animal that *coexist*: the oppositional and the continuist,[2] two ways of relating to our animal 'past', one of which deduces *logically* those events which *must have* happened in order for such a being as 'man' to come about, the necessary conditions of such a thing as a signifier, and an unconscious: in other words, a retrospective or transcendental account, while the other attends to the sciences

---

2. I take this pair of terms from Derrida, where they name precisely the two extreme positions which he wishes to avoid (cf. Derrida 2009, pp. 15-16, and Derrida 2008a, pp. 47-48).

that actually study the contingent genesis of the *anthropos* and the material qualities that this 'species' happens to share. The latter is the scientific and the former the philosophical: 'philosophical' precisely because its statements aspire to an apodictic necessity that can result only from a logical, *a priori* deduction. In this context—while admitting that I had previously invoked a broader definition which included the exact sciences of mathematics among other *non*-empirical forms of 'science'—I shall take 'science' simply to mean those activities which aspire to intersubjectively verifiable results which may be falsified just as much as they may be, provisionally, verified by experimental work, or which at least attempt to incorporate such an empiricism, even if certain philosophical prejudices are admitted to their 'basic concepts'.

One reason for the missed encounter between Derrida and Lacan, on Derrida's part, is that in this regard he focuses almost exclusively on the first strand, the transcendental-philosophical, and treats Lacan as if he had a tendency to become part of the history of philosophy or 'metaphysics', 'too much at home *with the philosophers*'.[3]

Nevertheless, it is my contention that *both* of these tendencies are equally essential to the project of psychoanalysis: we cannot simply understand man to be an animal cut off entirely from the rest of the animal kingdom by its dependence on the symbolic, because this dependence can only be *explained* by an attention to our continuity with the other animals, our faulty 'evolution'. And to go even further, without an attention to the genesis of the symbolic order, we cannot properly understand why certain symbolic regimes carry out the particular transcendental deductions that they do with regard to their own conditions of possibility: in the end, these will take the form of the fantasy (fantasy is always a fantasy of origin, the replacement of a naturalistic explanation of the continuous emergence of a symbolic-cultural order with the story of an event that initiates a discontinuous leap from real to symbolic, which are in this mythical context understood as 'nature' and 'culture'). If we believe that these deductions are purely logical, and can be exhaustively explained by means of the machinations of the signifier, then we are being duped by the fantasy. My hypothesis will be that it is *fantasy*, and in general the *imaginary* elements which help to totalise an incomplete symbolic order, that Derrida cannot do justice to. To do so, he would need to have examined the *chronological* generation of the symbolic, and this he ultimately does not, or at least relegates its delineation to a logically *secondary* position with respect to his 'deconstructive' labour.[4]

---

3. Derrida 1998, p. 56.

4. Since this entire work is something like an impossible attempt to complete my *Derrida and Lacan: Another Writing* (cf. Lewis 2009) impossible because no finite structure can be completed, everything I say here might be considered as footnotes to that work, or as the expansion of two notes that already exist, on p. 266 n. 43, and pp. 264-265 n. 34. These were added only towards the very end of the construction of the book and in fact begin to undermine it from within. It is only their relegation to the subliminal and half-invisible space of endnotes that allows the book's structure to hold up at all. This attempt to complete, as Derrida has shown, in fact results in an ever greater incompleteness, and perhaps in the collapse of the entire structure. The latter footnote, on the possibilities of writing a prehistory of writing, will be addressed elsewhere. It is noticeable that an attention to these questions did increase in Derrida's later works, particularly when it comes to the animal—one thinks, for instance, of his occasional late

So ultimately, the thesis of the present work will be as follows: while Derrida accuses Lacan of being 'too much at home with the philosophers' — one might say, 'too cosy' — in fact it is Derrida who is too wary to venture very far and very often beyond the threshold of the house which he *remained* largely content with undermining from within. This will be demonstrated by the fact that Derrida's thought, like Lacan's, *also* places in question the simple opposition between structure and genesis, but *without in the first place* appealing to science for help.

Thus it should be clear that the question of structure and genesis bears on the question of philosophy's relation to the natural or rather the empirical sciences: our somewhat brutal hypothesis has it that Lacan incorporates certain insights from these sciences from the very *beginning*, while for Derrida the relationship to science comes about only at the very *end*: indeed, this is what Derrida begins to do towards the very end of his life, in his later work on the animal: here, the very purpose of the deconstruction is to *open* philosophical thought to the insights into animality that are provided by zoology, ethology, and primatology. However, although this amounts to a positive, and perhaps a genuinely new development in Derrida's work, we shall suggest that it remains caught within too abstract a relation and even risks putting philosophy in a position all too similar to that of the *a priori* foundation of the 'regional', empirical sciences.

II. PSYCHOANALYSIS BETWEEN NATURE AND CULTURE

Let us begin with psychoanalysis.

According to a common understanding, psychoanalysis would primarily be concerned with the repressions of sexual and lethal desire that result from the inhibiting strictures of human culture and the belated appearance of the evidence for these repressed desires in the form of neurotic and psychotic symptoms: in this sense, it would be a discourse that protests against the damage inflicted upon the animal when it is submitted to a certain non-physical, non-natural law. While it might not be simply a nostalgia for the pastoral, pre-cultural paradise, it at least addresses the problems that demonstrably arise *as a result of* the hominisation process, in order that its patients find themselves in the end better able to cope with their entrapment within the symbolic machine, a wild animal locked in a cage.

The specific difficulty of understanding man is that he *cannot* be considered in a purely structural, synchronic way, without reference to this *process* of ensnarement. As if he could once and for all find himself at home there, and forget his animal past. For his very predicament is to be constantly *in the process* of being assimilated by culture, and always in a way that is more or less unsuccessful. The *animality* of man is not simply sublated in his *humanity*. Thus, psychoanalysis bears witness to a persistence of the animal in man, the discontented animal in culture, and the persistence of a reference *from* man to his animal past in the form of a memory which civilisation encourages us to forget.

---

adoption of the word 'hominisation' (anthropogenesis) (cf. Derrida 2008a, p. 61). One might even speculate that he was by this time feeling the increasingly weighty influence of that most pertinacious thinker of the relation of philosophy and anthropology, Bernard Stiegler.

What is clear is that there is something about the nature of man and his unconscious which *cannot* be explained unless we take into account the *process* of his immersion into the symbolic order, resulting in his division from himself, and the unconscious which forever invents new ways to resist its repression. So, in order to do justice to man we must capture him as he is *in motion,* as if man were nothing more than this process of *becoming*-man, an always incomplete transition between the natural and the cultural, the memory of the natural *within* the cultural. We already have a science that has, since its rudiments were laid down by Rousseau, studied just this process: anthropology. In addition to this, particularly in the structuralist form given to it by Lévi-Strauss, Lacan also finds it necessary to invoke neurology, animal ethology, and other related sciences, particularly with respect to the mirror stage, which one finds at the very beginning of his life's work, and at the beginning of each human life. Here Lacan brings to bear a related set of facts concerning human neurology, animal ethology and biology, all of which identify a certain *lack* or deficit which can be shown to characterise man when compared with the other animals. As a result of this, Lacan *then* finds it necessary to appeal to anthropology and linguistics, in order to demonstrate how this lack is *compensated* for by means of the unnatural supplements of *technē*, law, and language.

III. THE GENETIC STORY: FROM IMAGINARY DEFICIT TO SYMBOLIC EXCESS

With the aid of insights into man's physiology and the differences between his sexual behaviour and those of certain other animals, insights derived from certain of the natural sciences, Lacan describes the genesis of the human subject. Lacan's description of the evolution of subjectivity begins from the animal imaginary and leads to the human symbolic.[5] This description appears to present itself as a *scientifically* accurate, 'objective' description of the 'evolution' that runs from non-human animals to man, and bases itself ultimately on a certain biological fact about man, without which the discourse loses its motivation (his 'premature birth' and consequent neoteny, which unfold into a certain de-calibrated relation between man and his environment, and which ultimately derives from certain of man's neurological features). What is crucial to note is that, here, at the very beginning, Lacan appeals to a scientific insight into the nature of man and *grounds* his theory upon it; or at the very least, one strand of his thought departs from this insight.

This crucial biological fact is, then, what Lacan, in his early work on the 'mirror stage' and indeed later on describes as a 'specific prematurity of birth',[6] which leads to an underdeveloped motor coordination on the part of the human infant, resulting in a generalised 'neoteny' of the human animal, the persistence of childhood or quasi-animal traits into human adulthood. This underdevelopment of the brain at birth also results in man's 'disordered imagination',

---

5. To save time, I am here identifying the symbolic order with human culture and human language. I suspect, as I indicated earlier, that this identification is largely made in the context of phantasmatic myths of origination, and so in this context constitutes a Lévi-Straussian reference.

6. Lacan 2006, p. 78.

the specific, free and fantastic form which 'the imaginary' takes in him. 'The imaginary' is constituted by the set of images or schemata which allow an animal to identify the biologically useful features of its environment. These images or perceptual schemata, which are supposed in non-human animals to allow a perfect, 'instinctive' adaptation of the animal to its environment, are lacking in man: his instincts fail to drive him towards biologically advantageous objects. Unlike the animal world in which only a limited number of features are 'significant' to the animal, in the human world, it is as if everything and nothing has 'significance'.

The immediate question to be raised is why this deficit, this lack of adaptation, does not lead to extinction, which it surely would if the survival of the fittest or the best-adapted were the rule. The answer is that, in man, again as a result of certain (other) contingent material features, this lack of natural, instinctual adaptation is compensated for. This compensation takes the form of the symbolic order. But, it does not simply compensate in the way of bringing man's ability to survive in his environment up to the level of the animal's; it tips the balance in the other direction, and increasingly so—it seems—as history progresses. It manages to transform a deficit into a surplus, an excess.

Largely by virtue of various skeletal and postural features, man in this state of deficit finds himself able to open up and exploit the virtualities of things, their implicit possibilities for utilisation, and thus to use them as primitive 'tools'. He is thus *naturally* able to use *technical* apparatuses in order to counteract his natural deficiency. Eventually, as a simple *technē* becomes modern industrial *technology*—if we are justified in drawing such a distinction—his defective adaptation to his environment is compensated so well that another kind of imbalance between man and his environment is established, an opposite kind: from a destitute vulnerability to its environment, man assumes an unheard of control of his surroundings. This is manifest in the destruction we have been witnessing for several hundred of years now with regard to ecology, for man not only over-exploits his own environment, but even expands this 'environment' beyond its previous boundaries, if such things existed. He is allowed to do so precisely because such boundaries were questionable as to their exactness: it is even questionable whether man, in either his natural or technical state can be said to have an 'environment' in the strict sense (which Lacan derives from Jakob von Uexküll's studies of animals). Strictly speaking man does not have an environment of his own, as the animals do, so we can indeed speak of '*the* environment' in his case, one characterised by a certain infinity, in contrast to the finite categories of ('significant') objects that the animal is able to experience.

The most crucial deficit, with respect to the survival of the species, is the lack of a properly functioning sexual instinct, summarised later on by Lacan with the slogan, 'there is no sexual relationship [*il n'y a pas de rapport sexuel*]'.[7] In order for

---

7. Cf. Lacan 1999, p. 9. Given the prehistory of this phrase, I think we should recognise the limits of 'sexual relation' as a translation of '*le rapport sexuel*' because the sense of 'proportion' and 'ratio' connoted by *rapport* predominates here, particularly if we are correct in believing that the origin of the failure is the lack of imaginary tessellation between the inner world of needs and the outer world of objects which might satisfy them, the lack of an instinctual ability to find a suitable partner with whom to form a 'cou-

mating to be successful, which is to say to result in a product that ensures the species' survival, certain *un*natural rules must be put in place. This is perhaps the most basic form of the symbolic supplement to man's defective imagination. It takes the form of purely symbolic rules and conventions, which guide human needs towards the object that will satisfy them, which, following Lévi-Strauss, Lacan describes in terms of marriage rules or kinship structures. *Naturally*, there is no sexual relationship from the beginning, no adequate sexual instinct, and as a result successful mating can only be brought about by means of a cultural, symbolic intervention, which is sometimes summarised in terms of the prohibition of incest, which Freud rewrote at the ontogenetic level in terms of the Oedipus complex.

Thus we have a simple chronological tale, a straight line of evolution that would lead from animal to man, nature to culture, empirically specified, with its ultimate foundation in the contingency of empirical facts that are specified by the natural and (as we pass into the symbolic) the human sciences. The crucial point to bear in mind here is that, as contingencies, these facts could *not* have been deduced by a philosophical logic, nor have the necessity and consequent certainty that this logic demands.

We should also note that this continuist, 'evolutionary' understanding of the symbolic does not mean that the symbolic is fundamentally *homogeneous* with the imaginary. Phenomena *within* human culture are precisely not hereby susceptible of naturalistic explanation. This explanation precisely explains *how such a thing as the novel event of human-symbolic culture could have arisen from the natural order.* The novelty of this culture, where it makes a certain infinite, qualitative leap with regard to nature and its animals, may be inferred from two features of this account:

1. the *contingency* involved in both the imaginary corruption of man and the evolution of features that allowed him to use tools—contingency allows the possibility of an event that could not have been deduced from prior conditions; necessity does not;

2. the fact that a deficit is *reversed* into a surplus: this absolute *opposition* (+ and – ['plus' and 'minus']) seems to me difficult to explain if one remains on the level of a homogeneous continuum.

Thus we already have a slackening of the strict opposition between the continuist and the oppositionalist explanations of 'man', since Lacan appears to begin from a position that presupposes nothing except a kind of ontological 'univocity', the continuum, and yet from precisely this starting point derives an explanation for the *generation* of such a thing as the 'opposition'. If a 'structure' is defined by a series of ordered sets of oppositions, we thus have the rudimentary outline of Lacan's account of the *genesis* of *structure*.

IV. DERRIDA'S RELATION TO TRANSCENDENTAL PHILOSOPHY AND GENESIS

Thus we have at least a sketch of psychoanalysis's approach to the question of

---

ple'. Naturally there are sexual relationships, but are they 'suitable'...?

genesis and structure. We shall come back to it at much greater length, but we are now in a position to ask how, by contrast, discourses such as *philosophy* might claim to do justice to man *without* attending to the empirical sciences of genesis which psychoanalysis invokes.

We invoke Derrida as a representative of philosophy, in the sense that interests us, since we believe that he carries transcendental philosophy to the very limits of its possibility, where in fact it discovers the necessity to open onto something besides itself. The basic thrust of Derrida's work carries him *from* this philosophical starting point *to* the outer limits of philosophy, but, at least as far as the natural sciences are concerned, not beyond it. This will become clearer as we go along, but for now we can at least indicate that it is for this reason that we shall speak of Derrida here, where we might also have said 'philosophy'.

At one level, deconstruction *is* a form of philosophy, it does not claim to go beyond philosophy, but dedicates itself to bringing out and dwelling upon the aporias of transcendental thought, and perhaps of philosophy as such, the 'contradictions' into which it falls precisely as a result of its attempt to suture itself, and assert its own totality and independence from other discourses. Deconstruction finds itself more or less confined to the task of opening philosophy to an other (that would not be *'its* other'[8]) which its narcissism would like to exclude, but it goes no further.[9]

It is, however, in his writings on animality that Derrida comes closest to *actually invoking* the non-philosophical sciences. He suggests that when it comes to the animal, it is more urgent than ever to criticise the dogmatic presuppositions of philosophy *in order* to open philosophy to the insights of the natural sciences.

Derrida's writings on animality almost always have two principal targets: Heidegger and Lacan. Here we must leave Heidegger aside and focus on Lacan: according to a trope which recurs in *all* of Derrida's writings on Lacan, with respect to animality, Lacan always introduces something new with respect to traditional philosophical discourses on the animal, usually in a way that at least appears to be inspired by the empirical sciences, but in the end he always betrays it by reintroducing a certain *philosophical* prejudice.

In 'Heidegger's Hand', from 1987, Derrida makes the following striking statement: 'the manner, lateral or central, in which a thinker or scientist speaks of so-called animality constitutes a decisive symptom regarding the essential axiomatic of the given discourse'.[10] We shall take him at his word and ask after what *he* says of animals and animality. In our pursuit of this question, we shall for the most part focus upon certain very late texts by Derrida, which very often focus on the question of life, animal in particular. His very last seminar was entitled *The Beast*

---

8. Cf. Derrida 1982, x-xii.

9. At least this is the case with the natural sciences; less so with literature and poetry perhaps, and even the human sciences of linguistics and anthropology, as *Of Grammatology* might attest. Although even here the importance of Gödelian undecidability and Leibnizian writing suggests that mathematical science is given a privileged place in deconstruction. In spite of all this, in his discussions of animality, where the natural sciences are insisted upon with the greatest force, the logical order for Derrida begins with philosophy and the necessity of bringing to light its self-undermining, *with a view* to opening philosophy to the insights of science.

10. Derrida 2008b, p. 40.

and the Sovereign (*La Bête et le Souverain*) (2001–3), and one of his most autobiographical pieces, the 1997 text, *The Animal That Therefore I Am*, deals at length not only
with the animal, but on this very terrain stages Derrida's most prolonged engagement with Lacan after 'Le facteur de la vérité' from 1975.[11]

V. THE METAPHYSICAL OPPOSITION OF MAN AND ANIMAL

Derrida states that deconstruction itself *begins* with a troubling of the absolute oppositional separation of 'nature' and 'culture'.[12] The title of one Part of *Of Grammatology* adds to this pair the third and unplaceable term, 'writing'. In his works
on animality, Derrida focuses on this opposition in the specific form of the relation between 'man' and 'animal'. For him, the traditional philosophical attitude
posits an absolute opposition between them, citing a distinctive feature that sets
man apart from all of the other animals.

   As is always the case with Derrida, the opposition is not criticised in order to reduce the field of entities which it divides to a qualitative homogeneity
or continuum, but to establish *another* difference, or rather a plurality of differences, some of which allow entities to cross the limit that had previously separated them, some of which do not. In the case of man and the animal, Derrida
shows that this limit takes at least two (related) forms: the possession of language (or reason, *logos*), and the 'as such'—the 'as' structure (*Als-Struktur*) of experience as identified by Heidegger in his early work, according to which man
alone can experience things absolutely, 'in themselves' rather than in relation
to a particular project: the animal is confined to experiencing things within a
certain limited horizon of possibilities, ultimately centred around its own survival. In this respect, man is on the side of possession, animals on the side of
deprivation.[13]

   Derrida thus wishes to open philosophy to the fact that 'the animal' is in
fact a fragmented plurality which is only ever unified by man, when he wishes to define *himself* in contrast to it, and thus as unique with respect to the en-

---

11. Although given that five years later Derrida will *reread* the chapter on Lacan almost verbatim in
his seminar, and given that this seminar contains certain other theses about Lacan, *The Beast and the Sovereign* might itself deserve this honour. (The latter part of the fourth session of this seminar (2001-2) is a
more or less unchanged reading of Chapter 3 of *The Animal That Therefore I Am*, 'And Say the Animal Re-
sponded?' (to Jacques Lacan)' (cf. Derrida 2009, p. 111ff)). In an almost constantly surprising and delight-
ful book, it is only the formal structure of the response to Lacan which might remind one of a certain me-
chanical refrain. One could be forgiven for believing that one has heard this kind of thing before. And
indeed, one will hear it again, as if when it came to Lacan, an uncharitable reader might consider Derrida's writings to be akin to a 'broken record'.

   12. Derrida 2002a, p. 235.

   13. Curiously, in relation to Lacan, the polarity is reversed and initially, according to what is perhaps an even older philosopheme, man is situated on the side of lack. Nevertheless, as Derrida always
insists, a simple reversal solves nothing and above all does not alter the underlying logic of a position;
only a 'generalisation' or 'displacement' of a certain kind will do that (cf. Derrida 2002b, p. 41f; Derrida 1982, p. 329). Nevertheless, compared with his other deconstructions, there is a curious difference in
Derrida's procedure with respect to animality: here that which is to be generalised is not a positive feature but a lack, the lack of the 'as such', with respect to which all of animal, man, and god are deprived.
In the case of many other deconstructions, it is indeed the 'minor' half of the opposition that is shown to
underlie and thus problematise the opposition itself, that half which has less 'being', less presence, it is a
degeneration, but rarely is it a downright absence.

tire animal realm: it is only this opposition, and thus only an activity of man's, that allows the realm of 'the animal' to be totalised at all. When deconstruction reveals to philosophy its narcissistic anthropocentrism, this opposition must be complexified. As a result, philosophy will then be able to attend to 'the innumerable structural differences that separate one "species" from another [which] should make us vigilant about any discourse on animality or bestiality *in general*'.[14] And Derrida generally attributes the responsibility for *revealing* these differences—and at the very least, for classifying them—to the natural sciences.

What would these differences actually be? In fact, but perhaps for essential reasons, it is relatively difficult to unearth positive examples of these differences in Derrida's work. Our provisional explanation for this is related to our general characterisation of deconstruction as a journey towards the outer limit of philosophy, to the point at which it opens onto other discourse, but which does not itself topple over this crumbling border. Derrida seems to understand its task as the merely negative one of clearing a *space* for these insights within philosophy, while precisely relinquishing the right to believe that one's own (philosophical) discourse is capable of—responsibly—making positive statements about them. And perhaps this positivity is precisely what is to be supplied by the positive *sciences*. Nevertheless, Derrida does indeed, briefly supply certain examples of how one might divide up 'the animal' in a way that does not respect the simply binary opposition between man and every other animal: he lists the differences between the sexed and non-sexed, mammals and non-mammals, and no doubt we might add to this the differentiated kinds of 'tool use' that we find in primates and other 'lower' animals: such might be inferred from his references to 'the enormous progress that has been made in primatological and ethological knowledge in general'. [15]

What is crucial here is the logical order: for Derrida, this begins with deconstruction and only subsequently comes to the positive insights of the sciences; it seems that empirical science itself has no input into the actual deconstruction, although it might just possibly be a desire to open to this other that *motivates* it. Derrida's concern is to problematise these purely philosophical statements *in order then* to open philosophy to the empirical insights. These insights do not affect the deconstructive procedure itself.[16]

It seems that Derrida must believe that there is an inherent tendency in metaphysical thinking to *misinterpret* what it hears from science, as if whatever this other of philosophy tells it, philosophy can only insert it into its own categorial

---

14. Derrida 1993, pp. 75-76.

15. Derrida 2008a, p. 59. Derrida refers to his own time as a student of ethnology and 'zoological anthropology', the discipline that concerns the analogies between anthropoid apes and men (Derrida 2009, p. 283).

16. Derrida states explicitly that his new way of defining language, as mark, trace, archi-writing, which would no longer confine it to man (and hence commit us to an oppositional determination), is what would *let* us take account of scientific knowledge regarding animal language, genetic coding and so on (Derrida 1995, p. 286). But it seems as if science itself is not able by means of its own force to break into philosophy and carve out a space for itself: philosophy must inflict a certain damage on itself, tear itself open at the seams, act upon *itself*, in order to open up to an other, to affect itself with heterogeneity, it must auto-affect in order to become genuinely hetero-affectible.

framework, it can only filter it through its own conceptual sieve.[17] Thus it is necessary to dismantle the oppositional apparatus, to tear a wider rent in it, to allow entry to an other *in* its true otherness.

Now, to turn to Lacan, the advance which Lacan is said to make on the philosophical tradition is that he *does* take into account a certain number of differences within the animal kingdom, which cut across the simple opposition between man and animal. Lacan finds it necessary to attend to a difference other than the mere possession or non-possession of language, and he does this by way of certain insights drawn from the natural sciences; this is particularly apparent with respect to the 'mirror stage' and the sexuality of animals; and yet in the end, even when Derrida is at his most charitable—in the 1997 text—Lacan still slips up. The step advanced is yet taken back, for there is a philosophical reappropriation. Perhaps Derrida's lesson is a cautionary one, warning against the dangers of taking *positive* account of scientific data rather than simply making a space for it, a space which one must jealously protect, as one shelters a guest, but without presuming to understand any of it.

VI. DERRIDA'S EARLIER CRITIQUES OF LACAN

Derrida's critique of Lacan is more or less consistent throughout his work, although one might well think that the former's periodic returns to the latter throughout his life suggest that he was never wholly satisfied, as if the encounter had never quite properly been staged. To demonstrate this, let us look briefly at Derrida's early criticisms of Lacan, to be found in their most extensive form in *Positions* (1972). In effect, they also revolve around the imaginary, the space that man shares with the animals, and the beginnings of a novel invocation of scientific insight that in truth ends up falling under the sway of a philosophical prejudice. It is always the justification for the tripartition of imaginary, symbolic and real that Derrida cannot see, and the imaginary in particular.[18]

To recapitulate, the imaginary is the field which man shares with all of the other animals: not so much the capacity to make images as to experience and recognise them in their Gestalt totality.[19]

We have seen Derrida demanding that when it comes to the animal, scientific knowledge must eventually be consulted, and this scientific insight is *precisely* what Lacan takes into account in his theory of the imaginary, from the very

---

17. Cf. Derrida 1982, p. xii.

18. The real will for the most part be elided from our discussion since Derrida focuses largely on the symbolic/imaginary articulation, which he identifies, correctly, as isomorphic with the human/animal opposition. In the end, we are not suggesting that Derrida ignores the real: this, in the form which Lacan finally gives to it, is precisely what Derrida means by 'the other': the unnameable singularity of a real entity. It is the imaginary understood as the scientifically identified realm of the perceptual Gestalt on the part of organic life that Derrida excludes, and that we shall find to be lacking in another way: for him, the narcissism of philosophy is a consequence of the nature of the signifier, and can be explained exclusively in symbolic terms.

19. The word 'image' is used to name anything that any of the animal senses can comprehend as a totality, and not just the visual images that are particularly important for *man* due to the contingent superiority of his sense of vision in relation to all of his other senses: the word is used by Lacan because it appears to be the most intuitive way in which we, men, can understand what it is to comprehend something in its totality or Gestalt.

beginning, so it seems. Lacan simply did not begin his career as a philosopher; he was a medical practitioner, and it may well be said that his very early work—where the notion of the imaginary predominates—was not chiefly influenced by philosophy, its conceptual tropes and oppositional structures. Lacan's work delineates what is in effect a naturalistic, scientific story—which we have already briefly recounted—and it is *this* narrative which *justifies* the tripartition of imaginary, symbolic, and real.

The important point for our purposes is that in his *early* work on Lacan, Derrida seems to assume that this threefold distinction is a *'conceptual* tripartition'.[20] This might be taken to mean that it constitutes a formal framework which is simply imposed on various phenomena in order to make them intelligible—a transcendental move, one might say—and in *this* form, Derrida finds himself unable to countenance it: it thus shows itself to be a *philosophical* presupposition.

Now, here we might propose a rather cruel hypothesis: Derrida has elsewhere admitted he is in fact more or less *incompetent* when it comes to the natural sciences,[21] and we are already, in the background, entertaining the suggestion that science has only a belated and abstract relation to his work; could we risk the suggestion that Derridean deconstruction is only capable of criticising a work insofar as it is based upon *philosophical* presuppositions, *not* on scientific insights? This would explain why, in his early work, Derrida approaches Lacan's tripartition *as if it were philosophy*.

VII. THE DECONSTRUCTION OF THE IMAGINARY

It was to be expected that, of the triad of imaginary, symbolic, and real, the imaginary would be the place chosen to begin the deconstructive hollowing out: it involves a certain harmony, fullness, a perfection on the part of the animal, and for deconstruction any moment of full presence is ripe for colonisation by a gesture which hollows it out and provides a space for otherness. Derrida describes the imaginary as the space of a narcissistic relation to the other, which treats that other as if he, she, or it were akin to oneself. In this sense, an imaginary relation to the other would characterise the whole of philosophy: to demonstrate this is the very first task of a deconstruction. Thus, with regard to any positive thesis that might issue from a (negative) deconstruction, the imaginary *has* to be eliminated. To summarise, the imaginary must be deconstructed if we are to achieve a more 'proper' relation with a genuinely heterogeneous other.

In the second phase of his work, when the symbolic order had begun to capture his attention, Lacan himself seemed to believe that the imaginary relation was to be surpassed and the genuinely other reached by means of the 'Big Other' that is the symbolic order, originally represented by the well-adjusted adult in the anonymous form of the analyst. Symbolic laws would prohibit the most problematic form of an imaginary relation, the incestuous couple, and *thereby* compel the

---

20. Derrida 2002b, p. 84.

21. 'But nothing can justify the limits of my scientific knowledge, which I admit with both regret and humility' (Derrida 2005, p. 120).

subject to seek a non-consanguineous other. This would begin to open the subject to an experience of genuine heterogeneity. So the symbolic order of the big Other would involve a certain distance and legal prohibition that are introduced to break up the fusion that supposedly takes place at the level of nature, life, and the imaginary: the 'perfect world of the animals', the place of the successful sexual relationship.

So, Lacan, at least in a certain phase of his work, to be precise from the inception of his seminars at St. Anne's Hospital in Paris in the 1950's, like Derrida, considered the symbolic to be a solution to the 'problem' of the imaginary, and to supplant it. Nevertheless, Derrida's problem with Lacan here is that this *chronological* way of expressing the relation between the imaginary and the symbolic presupposes that, at one time, there really *was* a purely imaginary relation, in the non-human animal, and *only later* did this presence come to be undermined by the distance and difference introduced by the symbolic order. For him, the very idea of a fully present, harmonious and balanced natural state without prohibition is a *mirage* created *by* the symbolic order itself. Hence it can only be posited retrospectively, and cannot play a part in any genuinely naturalistic, chronological explanation of the emergence of the symbolic order.

This is crucial, for it is at precisely this moment that Derrida rules out the possibility of a real, presuppositionless, chronological account of the genesis of the symbolic such as Lacan provides.[22]

This in outline is Derrida's objection to a clear distinction between imaginary, symbolic, and real.

Nevertheless, from near to the very beginning, a frequent trope in Derrida's writings on Lacan is the acknowledgement that *later on* Lacan modified his position with respect to this strict demarcation of the three realms.[23] This 'later on' is crucial since it allows Derrida to confine his critique to the early work while upholding its accuracy there, and postpone a genuine engagement with Lacan's less easily assimilable phase. However, as I shall go on to show, I believe that we could even demonstrate that the slackening of the rigid boundaries of the tripartition was happening from the very start in Lacan's work, and precisely *as a result of* the naturalistic strain that predominates there.

To do justice to Derrida, we must now examine his later works on Lacan to see how he did indeed make good on his continually reiterated promises to write a full

---

22. Although strictly speaking, we might say that a deeper reading of Derrida might suggest that it precisely makes such an account possible, precisely by pointing out the philosophical presuppositions which normally undermine it, which in general involve the *petitio principii*, presupposing that which it wished to explain; and yet this reading might also excavate the insight that in fact this account of genesis is both demanded *and* rendered impossible, since any such genesis may *only* be sought from the standpoint of that *of which* it is the genesis: in fact, this seems to be precisely what Derrida's *Of Grammatology* is concerned to show: the impossibility (and necessity?) of grammatology in its usual form, which is that of a prehistory of writing (cf. Derrida 1974, p. 3, pp. 74-88, which I briefly discuss in Lewis 2008, pp. 264-265 n.34.)

23. *Inter alia*, 'I shall have to leave in suspense the question of whether, in later texts or in certain seminars (published or unpublished, accessible or inaccessible), the armature of this logic came to be explicitly reexamined. Especially since Lacan seems progressively to abandon, if not to repudiate, the oppositional distinction between imaginary and symbolic that forms the very axiomatics of this discourse on the animal' (Derrida 2008a, p. 132).

Michael Lewis   99

engagement with Lacan, and at the same time, whether this engagement ever managed to grapple with the later Lacan and everything that changed there.

VIII. DERRIDA'S LATER APPROACH TO LACAN

When Derrida returns to Lacan, in 1997, it is on the topic of animality, and the animality of man, the persistence of a certain imaginarity in the symbolic world. It is as if he realised that the very nature of Lacanian psychoanalysis forbade an absolute distinction between the imaginary and the symbolic.

Here, Derrida takes a slightly different tack to that of a simple deconstruction of the notion of the imaginary understood as simply philosophical: he wants to show that despite everything good and progressive in Lacan's account, including its scientific attention to a plurality of differences traversing the animal realm, there is a moment at which it becomes 'philosophical', and it is here that Derrida identifies a certain philosophical trope as having certain fundamental features in common with myth, and this is Lacan's persistent description of man as *lacking*, as suffering from a fundamental defect in comparison with the other animals.

The positive advances which Lacan makes over the philosophical tradition are as follows: he identifies certain differentiations within the category of 'the animal' that frequently cut across the simple oppositional limit that separates those which possess language from those which do not, differentiations which Derrida acknowledges result from a regard for ethology and primatology.[24] These include the difference between sexual and non-sexual animals, and the division between those capable of recognising their own reflected image and those which are not. However, these advances are betrayed by a certain return of the philosophical, which Derrida identifies in terms of the difference Lacan seems to institute between animal codes and human languages, which—as Derrida shows—implies the difference between leaving tracks and effacing their traces, pretending and pretending to pretend. It is in other words a reinstitution of the difference between the imaginary-animal and the symbolic-human. For Derrida, Lacan once again posits—dogmatically and without scientific justification—an opposition between man and animals: animals can pretend, but only man can *pretend* to pretend, to lie by telling the truth.[25] This ability is a direct result of the fact that man alone is in possession of the signifier, the symbolic, *as opposed to* the animal code. In the former, the bi-univocal relation of sign and signalled is removed and a plurality of different signifiers immediately proliferates to infinity in the attempt to isolate a unique signified. This is precisely the same difference that we have already encountered with regard to the animal's relation to its *Umwelt* and man's disordered imagination. The imaginary-gestaltic sign in the environment signals to the animal and the animal makes a pre-programmed or automatic response.

---

24. Derrida 2008a, p. 59.

25. Apparently without critical, deconstructive reservations, Žižek frequently refers to the Jewish story which Lacan takes from Freud, in which one Jew exclaims to an other, 'Why are you telling me you're going to Krakow when you are *really* going to Krakow!' The ultimate point of the story for our purposes seems to be that the one who is attempting to deceive (by telling the truth) must be taking into account (and must be able to take account of) the other's attitude towards him in making his statement: he assumes that he, the other, will take him to be lying, when in fact he is not.

Because the signifier is no longer a univocal sign, it could just as well refer to a certain signified as not: in other words, it can be used to actually refer to a certain signified (and 'tell the truth') while also appearing *not* to ('to tell the truth while appearing to deceive').

Why speak of 'effacement'? For the animal, there is a univocal reference between 'signifier' and 'signified'; in man this may be trampled over with a multiplicity of tracks, that may lead to the same place, or may lead elsewhere. Thus a diffraction of reference occurs in which the univocal reference between sign and designated, stimulus and response, is split into a multiplicity of possible meanings, opening up the possibility of irony, in which even an explicit avowal can mean the opposite of what it says. Thus effacement could here be understood as an erasure of the original unambiguous reference, or, in the precise context of leaving tracks, the disguising of the individuality of the one particular animal which has here left its own unique trace or scent, to be replaced by the universality of a signifying mark which could designate *anyone*.[26]

IX. THE PHILOSOPHICAL REAPPROPRIATION IN LACAN

This explains why the animal is unable to pretend to pretend, to tell the truth *in order* to deceive. It seems as if Derrida wants to say that either an animal *simply* leaves behind an unequivocal sign of its former presence, *or* if it does cover its tracks then it will never do so without leaving *another* trace of itself. Thus in the animal world, there is never a pure erasure, no entirely effective cloak of anonymity; that is provided only by the signifier. What the animal *cannot* do is simply to leave its tracks as a double bluff, designed to make the predator believe that the tracks were left there with the intention of deceiving him into thinking that they were a '*single* bluff' and that his quarry had gone another way. This cannot be done because for the animal no ambiguity can enter into the reference, and consequently there can be no finesse in the interpretation of the sign. The animal cannot lie by telling the truth; it can only ever tell the truth by telling the truth. No animal will ever be able to say 'why is this sign pointing towards Krakow when in fact Krakow really *is* in that direction?' (Or rather, 'these tracks run in that direction, but they are meant to deceive me that my prey is really *not* lying somewhere in that direction; which means that he is'.)

Only the signifier proper introduces this possibility. Thus, for Derrida, in this opposition between pretence and a pretended pretence we are returned to an oppositional understanding of the relation between man and animal, a typical 'Cartesian' opposition which Derrida also describes in terms of reaction and response, or mechanism and spontaneity, the machinic and the living. Thus, Lacan's initially promising, scientifically grounded identification of a plurality of differences traversing the animal kingdom has superimposed upon it the traditional philosophical distinction between the rigidity of a fixed, hard-wired, in-

---

26. That would be the traditional, metaphysical understanding of erasure—and indeed Derrida attributes it to Lacan, the great traditionalist, the one so cosy with his philosophers. The deconstructive understanding is almost exactly the reverse, and it would be one in which the very semblance of an original univocal reference and a fully present meaning is the *result* of an erasure: the erasure and idealisation of an infinite set of material marks—'archi-writing', to move quickly.

stinctual, bi-univocal stimulus-response system, and the infinite differentiality of a free, arbitrarily assigned signifier.

X. DECONSTRUCTION OF THE OPPOSITION

Let us now very briefly reconstruct Derrida's deconstruction of the opposition between pretence and pretended pretence, which recalls his deconstruction of the tripartition invoked earlier.

Pretence, which the animal *is* indeed capable of on traditional accounts, already takes the other into account, and for Derrida this means that in addition it could already be a *pretence* of pretence: it takes into account the reaction of the other, and the way in which it will take the sign, and that is all that is required for the trick of deceiving by telling the truth, since for Derrida, it seems, all that is really required for that is that a sign not be left behind naively, without thought as to how an other will interpret it: as soon as one covers tracks, one shows that one *is* responsive to the possible reading of that sign on the part of the other.[27]

If there is parade and ritual in animal encounters, sexual and bellicose, the partner in these dances must 'understand' that what is being performed is not a gesture that carries a real threat of action, but is precisely imaginary, a mere act. And neither would initiate the parade if it did not *expect* that the other would take the gesture in that way. Once the expectation takes on this duality in which the other's attitudes are already anticipated, we are in a situation that cannot be simply opposed to the human position in which one can deceive by taking advantage of just such an anticipation of the other's perception (which is to say, that I am deceiving).

XI. DERRIDA ON THE MYTH OF THE MAN WITHOUT QUALITIES

What Derrida isolates here is therefore the imposition of a traditional philosophical structure upon a set of scientific data. For Derrida, Lacan fails to justify the postulation of a difference between man and animals, and it remains therefore a dogmatic assertion which falls back into traditional philosophical presuppositions.

How can Lacan evade this criticism? It seems like an opposition has been imposed where in truth a plurality of scientific differentiations should have prevailed, or at least a deconstruction of the opposition between man and animal.

One Lacanian response might take the following form, which we shall come back to in more detail: the opposition is not an unjustified philosopheme, but a myth, and moreover, a myth that is necessarily produced by the symbolic order when it looks back upon its own origins. However, Derrida agrees here: the philosophical opposition of man and animal, particularly as Lacan understands it *is* a myth. Therefore, to gauge the full force of Lacan's retort in detail, we need to understand more of Derrida's relation to myth.

Derrida identifies the philosophical opposition as a 'myth' (specifically, Christian and Greek-Promethean), but a myth in the very precise sense of a mirage, an image projected by the symbolic order, which depicts something that is supposed

---

27. Cf. Derrida 2008a, pp. 127-136.

to lie beyond its horizon. The very form of Derrida's discourse in *This Animal that Therefore I Am* suggests that one of his ultimate goals is to do away with all such myths.[28] And yet, as we shall see, Lacan has a thing or two to say about myths as well, under the heading of the 'fantasy'.

For Derrida, philosophy has always thought of man in the way of the Epimetheus myth (in philosophical discourse this first appears in Plato's *Protagoras*, but is also to be found 'before' philosophy in Hesiod's *Works and Days* and the *Theogony*) and the Christian myth of Adam's nomination of the animals in the Garden of Eden. Epimetheus, the brother of fellow-Titan, Prometheus, charged with distributing positive characteristics among the animals, forgets to save any qualities for man, who follows after the other animals. This impels his more ingenious brother to steal fire (and by extension *technē*) from the gods as a compensatory gift for man, with the mixed results that constitute the fate of the human race and his 'environment'.

For Derrida, any discourse that attributes to man a *lack*, be it in the form of fall, sin, or even a 'disordered imagination', is—whatever it may say—mythical. These discourses institute an oppositional relation of lack and plenitude into the man-animal relation, whichever way around it ultimately goes. Man lacks happiness but makes up for it with language, technology, and the domination that comes along with naming and an advanced capacity to manipulate.

Derrida begins his 1997 work with the avowal of a desire to escape the mythical, biblical and Greek understandings of the animal, and later on quite clearly identifies Lacan as belonging to that 'Adamic and Promethean' tradition.[29]

Derrida does recognise that it is an inevitable feature of the symbolic order that it produce myths of origin—this is the specific narcissism of the symbolic—but he also thinks that Lacan himself presents a certain myth as objectively *true*. To demonstrate this he isolates a passage in Lacan which distinguishes between the *Oedipus* complex and the *castration* complex and identifies the former as mythical, but the latter as scientific: there is an 'original fault, [...] an original sin that finds its mythical relay in the story of Oedipus, then its nonmythic relay, its scientific relay, in the "castration complex"'.[30] Here, the castration complex is *explicitly* related to the human being's specific prematurity of birth, and we have already identified this as the fundamental *natural scientific* reference in Lacan's work, the beginning of a naturalistic story which justifies the tripartition of imaginary, symbolic, and real.

Let us interrogate Derrida's reading here. There is certainly a great deal of evidence to support his postulation of the mythical status of the Oedipus com-

---

28. Indeed, he suggests that he wishes to escape the entire history of fall and redemption, of sin and eschatological judgement, within which time animals are seen both as lacking (language, mastery, immediate proximity to God, but also, therefore, sin) and (as a result) perfect, innocent. Thus to escape the opposition and its fruitless reversals. In this context he appeals to the second telling of the myth of Eden in which Adam names the animals before Eve is created and before nakedness and shame, a process which is overseen by god, but in which god does not intervene. In the first narrative, man and woman are brought into being at the same time, and both are commanded to command animal, but not yet to name them (Derrida 2008a, p. 15ff).

29. Derrida 2008a, pp. 129-130.

30. Ibid., p. 139.

plex. It is for Lacan, particularly in his second, 'structuralist' phase, the result of a purely transcendental deduction, and Lacan states quite explicitly that it could not have been discovered by a naturalistic or empirical investigation: 'there is no possible means, starting from the natural plane, of deducing the formation of this elementary structure called the preferential order'.[31] 'There is no biological reason, and in particular no genetic one, to account for exogamy'.[32]

Nevertheless, the castration complex, which is supposed to result from the imaginary lack which afflicts the human infant, since ultimately the imaginary lack is understood by the child as the lack of a phallus possessed by the castrating father, is *not* mythical. It is here therefore, that, for Derrida, Lacan reintroduces the mythical understanding of man as lacking, while presenting it as non-mythical, the insight of an empirical science. Derrida cites a passage from Lacan which states quite clearly that Lacan's whole edifice depends upon this insight and its scientificity.[33]

XII. LACAN'S MYTHOPOIESIS: THE GENERATION OF OPPOSITIONS

In truth, I think there is something more subtle going on in Lacan's oppositional statements involving positivity and lack. Simply put, to begin with, what we have in Lacan is something like a theory of mythopoiesis. But more basically, we have a *genetic* theory of how such a thing as an opposition comes about, and hence an explanation of how the possibility of *positing* an opposition comes about—an opposition such as the mythical pairing of man and beast. We find more evidence of this in the first half of Lacan's career, particularly in the first five Seminars, but also in Seminar IX and here in particular. What this theory amounts to is an identification of the *precursors* of the symbolic opposition *in* the real, in nature itself, and in primitive man and his proto-technical 'erections'. In this way we can reconstruct a prehistory of the symbol, and its oppositionality, as it gradually takes shape.

In this way, we shall see that as the exits by which one might quit the symbolic order are gradually closed off, it becomes harder and harder for man to experience and speak of things in non-oppositional terms, and in particular, the very relation between the symbolic order and its outside. This would mean that as soon as man starts to speak and to name, he can only understand his relation to the outside—and to the *animal*—as an *oppositional* relation.

In the course of the generation of oppositions and their progressive systematisation, the structures of the signifier come to infect the whole field of man's experience, and this can lead to the impression that the signifier is infinitely extensive in time: 'there's a mirage whereby language, namely all your little o's and 1's, is there from all eternity, independently of us. [...] [W]ithin a certain perspective, we can only see them as being there since the beginning of time'.[34]

---

31. Lacan 1988b, p. 29.
32. Ibid.
33. Derrida 2008a, p. 139.
34. Lacan 1988b, p. 292.

This progressive colonisation also leads to the impression that what lies beyond the world of the signifier is strictly *opposed* to it: this would be the ultimate colonisation, as Derrida has shown: to assimilate the very *relation* between the signifier and its other *to* the signifier. It is this opposite that we find in the idyllic vision of a perfect harmony in the animal world, the possibility of a fully and perfectly satisfied desire (which is to say a desire that would assume the form of need alone).

In the early 1950's, Lacan describes our view of the animal kingdom as follows: 'There is a convergence, a crystallisation, here which gives us the *feeling*, however sceptical we may be, of a pre-established harmony [...] an animal recognises its brother, its fellow being, its sexual partner. [...] The animal fits into its environment'.[35] And in 1969, he clearly states that such a vision can only be a mirage: 'Once the human being is speaking, it's stuffed, it's the end of this perfection, this harmony, in copulation—which in any case is *impossible to find anywhere in nature*'.[36] Therefore, such idyllic perceptions of the world of the animal would in fact be a *retrospective—mythical—projection* and not an objectively true statement about the nature of the animal world.

As if to remove any ambiguity, since a 'mirage' *stricto sensu* does after all reflect something real, albeit transporting that real from *beyond* the horizon and placing it *within* the horizon in the form of an image, Lacan describes this projection not merely as a mirage but as an *'error'*: he refers to, 'the error of believing that what science constitutes by the intervention of the symbolic function has always been there, that it is given'.[37] This error is the result of a forgetting, a foreclosure of the actual genesis of the symbolic order itself: 'This error exists in all knowledge, in as much as it is only a crystallisation of the symbolic activity, and once constituted there is a dimension of error, which is the forgetting of the creative function of truth in its nascent form'.[38] Lacan goes on to specify that an attention *to* this genesis, the very birth of the signifier, is precisely what psychoanalysis must *not* neglect: 'But we analysts, we can't forget it, we who work in the dimension of this truth in its nascent state'.[39] In other words, the statements produced by the analysand, the very symbolic order itself, and indeed Lacan's own work, cannot be understood without an attention to the developmental process that lies behind them.[40]

Let us then draw together Lacan's somewhat brief allusions to this process in

---

35. Ibid., p. 86.

36. Lacan 2007, p. 33.

37. Lacan 1988b, p. 19.

38. Ibid.

39. Ibid. Cf. also p. 5.

40. This would explain certain of Lacan's gestures in 'Raison d'un échec' which imply that the static moments of the *Écrits*, the 'public' form which Lacan imparts to his thought, cannot capture the truth that is developed in the *process* of the 'private' seminars, as if that truth were not in the result but in the becoming, and perhaps even the very following of the seminars *by* its participants, as if something could be generated in the relation between the listeners and a transferential figure in a private room, as in an analytic session, that would not so simply be present in the relation between an *absent* writer and the reader who could at the time be absent to the writer. I suspect that this is where we would need to open an interpretation of the notions of 'writing' and 'publication' (qua *'poubellication'*) in Lacan's thought.

order to sketch out a prehistory of the symbolic order. In this way we shall fill in a gap in our previous recounting of the story: the hiatus between the imaginary deficit and the symbolic compensation. How exactly do we move from the imaginary to the symbolic, really?

XIII. STAGE 1 OF THE PREHISTORY OF THE SYMBOLIC— 'NATURAL SYMBOLS'

Lacan identifies various elements of nature which *resemble* symbols: proto-signifiers. What we discover in these paired elements is something *like* an opposition which is nevertheless not a genuine symbolic opposition, an opposition *stricto sensu*, but merely an *imaginary quasi*-opposition. This latter will eventually prove to be the foundation of the former.

Lacan speaks of these quasi-oppositions as 'natural symbols'[41] which exhibit 'pseudo-significance',[42] an anticipation of the binary signifier-signified relationship. The phenomena which Lacan includes under this title are natural cycles in which there are clearly two or more distinct and rhythmically alternating phases: the circular passage of the constellations, the seasons, night and day, the tides, the moon, and one might add the various forms of organic generation and corruption—all more or less classic examples of the early Lacanian notion of 'the real' which 'always returns to its place'. These are not strictly speaking oppositions since each part is not defined *exclusively* by the absence of the other: it still has a positive (imaginary) content of its own which helps to individuate it without reference to the other. In other words, while a signifier in the strict sense signifies without relying on its imaginary content, in these proto-symbols, the imaginary form is relevant:

> The first symbols, natural symbols, stem from a certain number of prevailing images—the image of the human body, the image of a certain number of obvious objects like the sun, the moon, and some others. And that is what gives human language its weight, its resources, and its emotional vibration. (Lacan 1988b, p. 306)

Nature, in its capacity to take on the form of images, is thus the primal source of material which a properly symbolic opposition will eventually colonise:

> There are already in nature certain reservoirs and equally in the signified a certain number of elements which are given to experience as accidents of the body, but which are reworked [*repris*] in the signifier, and give it, if one can say this, its first armaments [*armes première*]. (Lacan 1994, p. 51)[43]

Nature provides—I must use the word—signifiers. (Lacan 1998a, p. 20)

What is crucial about these natural phenomena is that they involve a rhythmic pulsation, which Lacan identifies as anticipating the most fundamental form of the opposition, presence and non-presence or absence:

41. Lacan 1988b, p. 306.
42. Lacan 1988a, p. 38.
43. The reference here is to the erectness of the human body and of the standing stones which resemble it in a more enduring way, and to which we shall return in the second stage of our prehistory.

> Day and night are in no way something that can be defined by experience.
> All experience is able to indicate is a series of modulations and transforma-
> tions, even a pulsation, an alternation, of light and dark, with all its tran-
> sitions. Language begins at the opposition—day and night. (Lacan 1993,
> p. 167)

We are then able to name and experience these alternating lightnesses and
darknesses *as* the diurnal and the nocturnal: 'Very early on, day and night are
signifying codes, not experiences. They are connotations, and the empirical and
concrete day only comes forth as an imaginary correlative, originally, very early on'.[44]

These alternating processes are defined by the peculiarity that each of their
phases is already beginning to stretch out beyond itself towards the *other* phases.
It is as if it *points* towards it. These phenomena thus involve something like a *natural* relation of *reference*, from the one to the other.

Sometimes, Lacan speaks of this phase-quality of natural phenomena in
terms of symmetry:

> We have, of course, to take the formal side of nature into account [the im-
> aginary side], in the sense in which I qualified it as possessing pseudo-sig-
> nificant asymmetry [*asymétrie pseudo-significative*], because that is what man
> embraces in order to produce his fundamental symbols. The important
> thing is what gives the forms of nature *symbolic* value and function, what
> makes them function in *relation* to one another.[45] (Lacan 1988b, p. 38, em-
> phases added)[46]

It is the relation *between* the imaginary phases that is crucial here, for it
amounts to the beginning of symbolicity, an incipient reference.

These natural symbols are not signifiers, but they *resemble* signifiers. Resemblance is an imaginary relation. Thus, what is essential in these natural elements
is their imaginary form. Ultimately, this fact will be crucial in Lacan's genetic explanation of the symbolic: the real is not an inert immanence that remains
merely what it is: it has the capacity to produce *images*, to produce something of
an order other than itself.[47]

---

44. Ibid., p. 149.

45. The English translation has 'symmetry' for 'asymmetry', a difficult transcription which is not
borne out by every transcript of this particular seminar.

46. Nevertheless, Lacan immediately goes on to say, 'it is man who introduces the notion of asymmetry. Asymmetry in nature is neither symmetrical, nor asymmetrical—it is what it is'. The trope 'it is
what it is' always refers to the real in Lacan's work. One might however ask whether this ceases to hold
when one considers the imaginary qualities of the real: could asymmetry not genuinely exist there in the
real, when thought of in this way? Indeed later on, Lacan determines the real when understood from
the imaginary point of view—as 'object *a*'—in *terms* of asymmetry, whereby a certain lack of symmetry between right and left cannot be reflected in the symmetrising of the specular reflection (cf. Seminar
IX. *L'identification* (unpublished), lesson of 30/5/62; Lacan 2005, p. 121; Seminar XIV. *La logique du fantasme* (unpublished), lesson of 19/4/67). Nevertheless, in this context Lacan's remark testifies to the retrospective nature of the imposition. In other words, even when we address the genesis of the symbol, it
is a genesis that presupposes the symbol, since we must know that it exists and what it is in order to seek
its actual genesis.

47. Or at the very least, as soon as organic life evolves, the capacity emerges to recognise things *as*
images. There is some ambiguity here, since Lacan does at a certain point refer to the origin of consciousness in the form of a lake on an *uninhabited* planet which produces images by means of reflection:

Thus we witness in a rhythmic alternation of phases in the natural cycle, the earliest beginnings of signification. These are the anticipations of the symbol in nature. The next stage in our prehistory has to do with their presence in primitive prehistoric 'culture', in other words, the seizure of such rhythmic alternations in artificial, proto-human productions. Here, Lacan focuses the best part of his attention on primitive buildings or erections. In other words, phallic monuments, the raised megaliths of the Stone Age.

XIV. STAGE 2—THE PHALLIC FORM AS ARTIFICIAL ANTICIPATION OF THE FORM OF THE SYMBOL

The crucial thing to remember about the phallus is its erection, but also what erection implies: the possibility of non-erection. What can be erected may also be demolished. Thus in the form of an erection we have an alternation between two seemingly opposed states, a *plus* and a *minus* (+&−), a 1 and a 0. Presence and absence, but not in a disparate, abstract juxtaposition, but rather synthesised, such that the presence of the phallus *implies* the (possible, future or past) *absence* of the phallus, while its absence suggests the possibility of presence.

Here we have more than is to be found in the natural symbol, since here we go beyond an unsynthesised opposition to something like an anticipation and a remembrance—the manipulated stone is always a memorial, raised in order to *counter* the passing of time, just as the upright adult retains traits and even a memory of the stooping man or the child. In order to erect a stone, or to view it *as* erected, there must have been in advance some sort of conscious synthesis of its erect state with its flaccid or reclining state, thus binding one state and its opposite.

Lacan's chief example in this case is the standing stone,[48] one of the earliest forms of artificial construction, which mimics the upright stance of the human body and was perhaps raised to the deity, as man himself is. This deity was in all likelihood also manifest in or consubstantial with the 'natural symbols' we identified in the first stage of our itinerary, those meteoric phenomena to which sacrifices were offered and monuments set up, to ensure that their cycle always returned, lest man come to ruin.

So we now have two stages: the natural symbols, which are phased or periodic alternations in the real, constituting proto-references; and then the proto-technical phallic images, which are parts of the *real* but also *images* of the *symbolic*, constituting a proto-opposition.

What would the complete version of this prehistory of the signifier need to encompass?

XV. STAGE 3—TOTALITY AND INFINITY, THE EVACUATION OF IMAGINARY CONTENT

We have not yet finished our transition between the imaginary quasi-opposition and the opposition properly speaking. Lacan's explicit statements suggest that two

'consciousness is linked to something entirely contingent, just as contingent as the surface of a lake in an uninhabited world' (Lacan 1988b, p. 48).
48. Cf. Lacan 1994, p. 51.

things are missing in the anticipatory resemblances of the signifier in pre-histo-ry: *totality* and *infinity*. These are the two definitively *novel* features of the signifier, which finally put in question any attempt to assert the existence of a continuum between nature and symbolic culture.

> In the human order, we are dealing with the complete emergence of a new function, encompassing the whole order in its entirety. The symbolic func-tion is not new as a function, it has its beginnings elsewhere than in the human order, but they are only beginnings. [...] [W]e must start with the idea that this order constitutes a *totality*. In the symbolic order the totality is called a universe. The symbolic order from the first takes on its univer-sal character. [...] It isn't constituted bit by bit. As soon as the symbolic ar-rives, there is a universe of symbols. (Lacan 1988b, p. 29, emphasis added)

During the first two stages in the evolution of the symbolic, we have only iso-lated pairs, which can only constitute 'symbols' in Saussure's sense, iconic terms which have not evacuated themselves of imaginary content and generally refer to just one other thing, in a disconnected—and hence still imaginary—coupling. These symbols remind us of the enigmatic Stone Age monoliths in their scat-tered dispersion, as they stand today: they do not form a totality. The third stage in our prehistory will need to explain how this finite number of diffuse symbols cohere to form a totality, and one which is as it were so dense and so extensive that it will be infinite.

We shall then witness something like a leap into infinity in the constitution of the symbolic order in all of its novelty. Indeed, quite frequently, Lacan will in contrast assert the finitude of the animal world, the limited number of stimuli to which they have innate and differentiated responses.

It is the specificity of the imaginary form of the proto-signifier that locks it in an iconic relation with just one or at most a finite number of referents. If the symbol is to acquire the potentially infinite ambiguity of a true signifier, entirely unmotivated by its content, this imaginary form must be eradicated, or at least rendered inoperative with respect to its signifying function. This is what gradu-ally happens as the signifier extends its colonisation of the natural elements hos-pitable to it: this imaginary content is gradually evacuated, eventually allowing a pure reference relation to come about, in which each term is nothing over and above its negative relation to the other. In this context, the proto-signifier comes to be understood simply as a differential mark, a distinguishing characteristic that marks out one thing as different from another. The mark's actual imaginary quality is irrelevant: the only thing that matters is the possession or non-posses-sion of the mark, differentiating one half of an opposition from the other. Only when we have reached a stage at which all imaginary content has been eradicat-ed, which is to say when entities have no identity of their own outside their re-lation to others, we have a signifier, and we have a relation of opposition in the strict sense, if we define an opposition as a binary relation in which each half is defined as nothing but the absence of the other.

Here we might invoke Lacan's own attempt to construct a prehistory of *writ-ing*. This is inaugurated in Seminar IX, which is avowedly concerned to describe, 'the genesis, the birth, the emergence of the signifier itself [*la genèse, la naissance, l'émergence du signifiant lui-même*]', 'the attachment of language to the real'.[49]

That Lacan is interested here in an effacement of pictorial or imaginary content is testified by the stress which he lays on the *score-mark*. Lacan goes so far as to place the scratches etched into the primitive hunter's bone at the origin of writing itself, and precisely for the reason that they are produced chronologically much *later* in the prehistory of mankind than the ability to create pictograms. 'These strokes which only appear much later, several thousand years after men knew how to make objects of a realistic exactitude'.[50] In other words, writing as such begins with the occurrence of a break from all forms of imaginary singularity.

The hunter begins by recording his successful hunts pictorially, with each picture intended to depict the slaughtered ox in its singularity. This procedure finds its limits in the sheer *number* of kills. Once the pictures become too numerous, it becomes difficult and ultimately impossible to tell the oxen apart. From then on, the qualitative difference that distinguished them at the level of their representation becomes a merely *quantitative* difference, and is marked by the repetition of a single stroke or 'unary trait' (*le trait unaire*), 'the|which distinguishes each repetition in its absolute difference'.[51] Paradoxically, or so it seems at first, it is only this evaporation of imaginary content that allows each ox to be considered as absolutely different from any other. Pure or absolute difference can *only* be marked when all attempts at *qualitative* (imaginary) difference have been renounced: 'the signifying difference is distinct from anything that refers to qualitative difference'.[52]

The scoring is a mark that one thing absolutely possess, and the other absolutely does not, and hence it allows them to be opposed, each absolutely different from the other, separated by the sheer break represented by the empty space between marks, |||| : 'This | as such [...] marks pure difference'.[53]

However, this imaginary erasure notwithstanding, Lacan does find it important to stress the *unitary* nature of the stroke that forms the basis and essence of the signifier. Lacan describes this unary trait as a 'letter', speaking in hindsight from the point of view of the phonetic writing that is made possible by the erasure of 'ideograms'. These letters would indeed be the indivisible units that form the real material basis of the signifier.[54] And how are we to understand such unity and wholeness save in terms of the *imaginary?* It is as if the chronological origins of the signifier *in* the imaginary are preserved in the form of the wholeness

49. Seminar IX (unpublished), lesson of 20/12/1961, and lesson of 10/1/1962. From this point onwards, references to writing proliferate the more they are sought in Lacan's seminars. I believe a full engagement with this theory of writing would need to examine a great deal of Lacan's more complex mathematical work, his discourse on Frege, set theory, and the various kinds of mathematical writing, along with their relation to the status of writing in natural languages. For this reason, a more satisfying engagement must be postponed here.

50. Ibid., lesson of 6/12/1961.

51. Ibid., lesson of 14/3/1962.

52. Ibid., lesson of 6/12/1961.

53. Ibid.

54. It is around this point that the polemic of 'Le facteur de la vérité' (1975) turns. Nevertheless, I have contended elsewhere that a certain lack of attention to the imaginary causes Derrida to miss the sense of this indivisibility of the letter, which for him is always infinitely divisible, as is anything which comes within reach of the signifier (cf. Lewis 2008).

and unitarity of the trait, which assumes the guise of the letter in phonetic or alphabetic writing.

It will turn out that this retention of the imaginary in a minimal form will ultimately provide the signifier with another resource with which it might (temporarily) totalise itself: this suture will take the form of the *fantasy*, which always involves a *letter*, the letter 'a', the very *first* letter: the object *a* should not be understood simply as the real of the imaginary (that which is subtracted from the imaginary, that part of our self-image which the other subject retains), but also as the real of the symbolic (that which is subtracted from the symbolic), the material letter as distinct from the idealising signifier. The letter 'a' is both the fantasy of a prehistory of the signifier and—in its unitary and material form—a *real* trace of such a prehistory. To deploy Lacan's own image from Seminar XIII, it is both a picture of the view from the window placed over the window, but also the window itself, which is really there, and really opens onto the 'great outdoors' that is the real.[55]

XVI. HORIZONTAL EFFACEMENT: TOWARDS TOTALITY AND INFINITY

For our purposes, what seems crucial in the relation between the material letter and the signifier is the effacement that takes place between them. This is the moment, primaevally speaking, when the horizontal bar is drawn across a sequence of score-marks, both deleting them and grouping them together. Lacan identifies this as the moment at which the subject understood as divided (*barré*) is first formed, just as it is the moment at which a quasi-Saussurean bar is drawn between S and s, signifier and signified, a barrier which can then be crossed by the signifier in order to produce an effect of signification. In order to produce an ideal meaning (the signified) from a real signifier, a bar must be drawn, an excision made, and this is precisely the erasure of the material letter. It should be noted that the score-marks exist in a certain degree of isolation: the drawing of the bar in a *different* direction, at right angles to the vertical marks, groups a certain number of them together (generally five, although the number of vertical strokes is four, since the horizontal bar itself counts as the fifth—although we cannot enter into it here, this horizontal bar might be understood as the *subject* of the signifier). This crossing-out, I would contend, is the beginning of the *totalisation* of the signifier. It might also be said to be the origin of the signifier's infinity. The horizontal erasure could be identified with the definitive erasure of the relevance of the pictorial content and consequent individuality of the letters. On the assumption that there are only a finite number of ways in which to depict the singularity of an entity, there are only a finite number of possible pictures. Replacing this qualitative differentiation with a pure, identical mark, and thus enabling the quantitative differentiation of counting, opens up the possibility for an *infinite number* of marks or signifiers.

At the same time, when all imagistic individuality has been erased, the identity of a signifier can only be picked out by differentiating it from *all* of the other signifiers, and this ultimately amounts to an *infinite* number, an infinite *totali-*

55. Cf. Seminar XIII (unpublished), lesson of 30/3/1966.

ty. Thus the two distinctively novel features of the signifier properly speaking are bound together here.

Thus, we have shown how the prehistory of writing completes our journey from the imaginary to the symbolic. What we have here are the rudiments of a genetic account of the development of opposition, which does not *presuppose* opposition, and hence avoids the mythical.

Now, why is this long story of the genesis of the symbolic necessary? Because it allows us to understand something about the way the fully formed structure operates that would *not* be obvious without it, and this is I think what Derrida misses. Everything here issues in the Lacanian notion of the fantasy. The Lacanian-mathematical representation of the fantasy is $S \lozenge a$. The subject facing the object a, the cause of the desirability of the object.[56] The object a is what remains missing from the imaginary, the non-specular object: it is that imaginary deficit which Lacan identified at the very beginning as the human being's defining trait in comparison with all of the other animals.

The symbolic is incomplete in the sense that there is an infinite number of signifiers determining the actual significance of any signifier in particular: the chain of references never comes to an end, and hence meaning becomes indeterminate. No signifier by itself can ever finally complete the symbolic system, precisely because it is *itself* a signifier and so itself refers to an infinite number of *other* signifiers, and so on *ad infinitum*. Derrida's work more or less stops there; but Lacan's goes further.

What *can* totalise the symbolic in a relatively effective, albeit temporary way is not a signifier, not a part of the symbolic, but a part of the *imaginary*: the fantasy. '[T]he true *imaginary* function [...] insofar as it intervenes at the level of desire, is a privileged relationship with *a*, object of desire, term of the fantasy'.[57]

The object *a*, the object of desire that is staged in the fantasy, is always, according to Lacan, an image of the phallus,[58] in the sense that it stands in a proto-contradictory position, both inside and outside the individual person: it is a part of us but is not in our possession. But, being strictly speaking subtracted from the symbolic, the object *a* does not exist on a level in which the law of non-contradiction actually has any purchase. The phallic form (the imaginary form of the phallus) does not *signify* the symbolic, it is an *image* of the symbolic: as we have seen in our description of the origin of the symbolic, the phallus *resembles* the symbol. Its very imaginary form involves a proto-symbolic opposition, a precursor of $+$ and $-$, presence and absence. As a result, the phallus resembles every single signifier that there could ever be. In this way, it totalises the signifier, but *not* in the

---

56. More precisely, the subject is related to the object *a* by a desire which is at bottom a drive that circulates around the rim of an abyss or hole. Lacan relates the void-circling structure of the drive to the lozenge in his eleventh Seminar (cf. Lacan 1998a, p. 209ff).

57. Seminar IX (unpublished), lesson of 13/6/1962, emphasis added.

58. 'The object *a* is something from which the subject, in order to constitute itself, has separated itself off as organ. This serves as a symbol of the lack, that is to say, of the phallus, not as such, but in so far as it is lacking' (Lacan 1998a, p. 103). Since in an indirect way, desire is always this desire for the totalisation of the signifier, which would allow me to say in a symbolic way just what I *am*, what the truth of my desire is, so whatever completes the totality, this phallic image, in whatever form it takes, is the object small *a*. And this object *a* as object(-cause) of desire is staged precisely in the *fantasy*: $S \lozenge a$.

way that a signifier would, which is to say *without* reducing its infinity to a finitude (which in any case is impossible).[59]

Had we not attended *beforehand* to the actual chronological genesis of the signifier, we would not have discovered the phallic image and would hence have no
inkling of a method that could totalise the symbolic without deploying yet another signifier, the latter method of necessity failing, since there is no 'signifier
of the signifier', that signifier is ultimately *mythical*. It is because he himself fails
to attend to this chronological genesis of the signifier that Derrida is only able to
understand *Lacan* as remaining at the level of *this* form of suture, the mythic nature of which he would remain oblivious to. But this only testifies to the impov-
erishment with which Derrida is left. The one who wanted to be without myths
is ultimately left without the fantasy. Deconstruction is then confined to pointing
out the impossibility of suturing the symbolic, save strategically and temporarily by means of a momentarily privileged term, which in the end only reveals itself to be an impotent master, who opens the finite system onto its own infinity.

In other words, my hypothesis would be that the way in which the incompleteness of the symbolic order is compensated for, and hence the way we attribute meaning to our lives, we animals caged in by language, can only properly be
explained by attending to the prehistory of the symbolic order as it emerges from
the non-symbolic, and in particular to the imaginary aspects of the real which
allow the symbolic order to take root in nature.

XVII. CONCLUSION

So ultimately, the basic difference between Derrida and Lacan on the topic of
structure and genesis is as follows: for Derrida, before we can ever speak of an actual genesis of any kind, we need to demonstrate that a supposedly stable structure is unstable and incomplete and may thus change in the future and must itself
be the result of a process of generation; for Lacan, on the other hand, it is only
an attention to genesis that can tell us *why* structure is necessary, why it is incomplete, and how that incompleteness is frequently patched up.

This difference is reflected in the two thinkers' respective attitudes to the
empirical sciences, in that, for Derrida, the first thing to be done is for a prior
deconstruction to undermine and open up philosophical discourse to science,
which seems only to illuminate philosophy after the fact, once its narcissistic
self-enclosure has been exposed to an outside; while, for Lacan, science must inform our conceptualisation from the very beginning.

And all of this is needed to explain how it is that we humans remain nevertheless animals.

---

59. Such a signifier would be the signifier of the signifier, Other of the Other, the name-of-the-father, a metalanguage, which would finitise and speak accurately of its object-language, without affect-
ing or being affected by it. Despite the fact that the catchword, 'There is no Other of the Other', begins
to proliferate in Lacan's writings from around Seminar V onwards, with his later works on writing, I believe that his position changes yet again, and we once again find that it is possible to gain some sort of
foothold and coign of vantage *outside* of the symbolic order. At the end of 'Lituraterre' (1971), Lacan says
that if the sexual relationship *is* possible (which would presuppose a completion of the symbolic order),
it is by means of the letter, by means of writing, and perhaps (avant-garde) literature, of the kind which
James Joyce created.

BIBLIOGRAPHY

Derrida, J., *Of Grammatology*, Baltimore: Johns Hopkins University Press, 1974
—— '"Genesis and Structure" and Phenomenology' in *Writing and Difference*, London/New York: Routledge, 1978
—— 'Violence and Metaphysics' in *Writing and Difference*, London/New York: Routledge, 1978
—— *Dissemination*, London/New York: Athlone, 1981
—— *Margins: Of Philosophy*, Brighton: Harvester Press, 1982
—— 'Le Facteur de la Vérité' in *The Postcard: From Socrates to Freud and Beyond*, Chicago: University of Chicago Press, 1987
—— *Aporias*, Stanford, CA: Stanford UP, 1993
—— *Points... Interviews 1974-1994*. Ed. Elisabeth Weber, Stanford, CA: Stanford University Press, 1995
—— *Resistances of Psychoanalysis*, Stanford CA: Stanford UP, 1998
—— 'Force of Law: The "Mystical Foundation of Authority"', London/New York: Routledge, 2002a
—— *Positions*, London/New York: Continuum, 2002b
—— *Paper Machine*, Stanford, CA: Stanford UP, 2005
—— *The Animal That Therefore I Am*. Ed. Marie-Louise Mallet, New York: Fordham UP, 2008a
—— 'Heidegger's Hand (*Geschlecht* II)', in *Psyche: Inventions of the Other, Volume II*. Ed. Peggy Kamuf and Elizabeth Rottenberg, Stanford, CA: Stanford UP, 2008b
—— *The Beast and The Sovereign, Volume I* (2001-2). Ed. Michel Lisse, Marie-Louise Mallet, Ginette Michaud, Chicago: University of Chicago Press, 2009
Lacan, J., *Seminar Book I: Freud's Papers on Technique, 1953–1954*. Ed. Jacques-Alain Miller, Cambridge: Cambridge UP, 1988a
—— *Seminar Book II: The Ego in Freud's Theory and in the Technique of Psychoanalysis, 1954–1955*. Ed. Jacques-Alain Miller, Cambridge: Cambridge UP, 1988b
—— *Le Séminaire livre VIII: Le Transfert, 1960–1961*. Ed. Jacques-Alain Miller, Paris: Seuil, 1991
—— *Seminar Book VII: The Ethics of Psychoanalysis, 1959–1960*. Ed. Jacques-Alain Miller, London/New York: Routledge, 1992
—— *Seminar Book III: The Psychoses, 1955–1956*. Ed. Jacques-Alain Miller, London/New York: Routledge, 1993
—— *Le séminaire livre IV: la relation d'objet, 1956–1957*. Ed. Jacques-Alain Miller, Paris: Seuil, 1994
—— *Seminar Book XI: Four Fundamental Concepts of Psychoanalysis [1964]*. Ed. Jacques-Alain Miller, New York/London: Vintage, 1998a
—— *Le séminaire livre V: les formations de l'inconscient, 1957–1958*. Ed. Jacques-Alain Miller, Paris: Seuil, 1998b
—— 'Lituraterre', in *Autres écrits*, Paris: Seuil, 2001
—— *Ecrits*, New York/London: W. W. Norton, 2006
—— *Seminar Book XVII: The Other Side of Psychoanalysis [1969–1970]*. Ed. Jacques-Alain Miller, New York/London: W. W. Norton, 2007
Lewis, M., *Derrida and Lacan. Another Writing*, Edinburgh: Edinburgh UP, 2009

Jacques Lacan's Onto-Graphy

Matteo Bonazzi

The *Trieb* can in no way be limited to a psychological notion.
It is an absolutely fundamental ontological notion.
(Lacan, Seminar VII)

I. A LACANIAN ONTOLOGY?

Is there a Lacanian ontology? The immediate answer should be no, if one bears in mind the countless times Lacan attacks philosophy as ontology, stressing its totalising dimension and reducing it to a sort of *ontototology*.[1] Yet a subtle, constant, and reiterated attention towards the fundamental enquiries of metaphysics and the question of being persists in his teaching, like an underground river, almost as if it were a musical theme. Especially with regard to the enjoying substance, which emerges as an atopic place only towards the end of Lacan's teaching, an unexplored place, which is to a large extent yet to be thought. Hence, if we try to re-read the itinerary of his teaching keeping in mind this finishing line, we might well have the chance to speak of a Lacanian ontology, although it is crucial to stress outright that, if there is such thing as a Lacanian ontology, it has nothing to do with being and the *logos* as such. I would argue that it is precisely the 'as such' that is suspended by the ethical and singular dimension of Lacan's reflection, and propose to structure this inquiry into the question of being in Lacan around a new signifier, which I call *onto-graphy*: a form of writing that takes the place of being and *its* logic.

Let us begin with Heidegger, because this is Lacan's main reference, not only in relation to *existential analysis* but also, and especially one might say, in respect to the structure of the *Kehre* 'Sein: Dasein'. We know that Heidegger questioned classical and modern ontology in that he performed a fundamental shift, which, in brief, has forced us to rethink being independently of its reduction to any entity. He also affirmed that contemporary philosophy, having arrived at its end and fulfillment, had to think, beyond metaphysics and science, first of all, the sign

---

1. 'Mais l'artifice des canaux par où la jouissance vient à causer ce qui se lit comme le monde, voilà, l'on conviendra, ce qui vaut que ce qui s'en lit, évite l'onto—, Toto prend note, l'onto—, voire l'ontotau-tologie, l'ontototologie' (Lacan 1973, p. 312). [Translator's note: the Postface to Seminar XI to which the author refers here has not been included in the English edition.]

with its event (*Ereignis*). Therefore, it is by all means a question of being before the entity, but also and especially of the event before being and, I would add, of the event *of* the sign—which, after all, also means the event *of* the *logos*, and therefore the evental [*evenemenziale*] dimension that enables the entire *onto-theo-logical* path of the Western metaphysical tradition. Let us try to use different words or, better still, let poetry say it, as Heidegger himself does, and read Hölderlin:

> Ein Zeichen sind wir, deutungslos
> Schmerzlos sind wir und haben fast
> Die Sprache in der Fremde verloren.[2]

I believe that the coded presence of an ontology in Lacan's teaching should be placed in the track left by Heidegger in the wake of Hölderlin's poetic thought. We have to rethink, starting from the unavoidability of the function of the sign, the relationship between the particular entity that interrogates itself about the meaning of being and the being which 'epochalises' itself [*si epocalizza*] in the care (*Sorge*) of that very entity. However Lacan might have rethought ontology, we cannot draw anything significant from it if we do not keep in mind that, all things considered, in Lacanian psychoanalysis, man is, first of all, a sign. From this perspective, which draws Lacan's teaching near to the late Heidegger, we can say that the French psychoanalyst has indeed thought that which is the deepest (*das Tiefste*), the event of the sign, but not without pain. Now, this dimension of pain, of suffering—or, to use a French term, with all the semantic richness that Jacques Derrida ascribed it, of *souffrance* (suffering, support, instrument, succubus, lying down)[3]—is pivotal. Man is certainly a sign, but not without *souffrance*: not without pain, not without suffering, not without that fundamental subtraction (the event of the sign) that opens the question of singularity and repression (which maybe 'calls for a new logic of the repressed'[4]). For this reason, we could say that, in thinking man as a sign, Lacan has also loved that which is the liveliest (*Lebendiste*). The subjective split, the *Spaltung* that Lacan identifies as the most specific feature of Freud's discovery of the unconscious, leads us back to the insurmountable split between sign and event. The Freudian/Lacanian subject is caught up in this split. Ontology is therefore to be rethought starting from this fundamental fracture.

If there is such thing as a Lacanian ontology, it is, first of all, an ontology of the *Krisis*, of the original split (*Verurteilung*[5])—it is therefore an ontology of exile, but also of decision, of the act, of the awakening, and of the encounter. As subjects, we are, first of all, subjected *to* language, that is, to the sign. Hence we are lost and confused subjects: this is what being exiled means.[6] Furthermore, we are

2. 'A sign we are, without meaning/Without pain we are and have nearly/Lost our language in foreign lands' (F. Hölderlin 1984, p. 116).

3. See Derrida 1998a, p. 84.

4. Derrida 1988, p. 108.

5. In Lacan's words, it is 'the condemnation that it [*Verurteilung*] designates as equivalent to (*Ersatz*) repression, whose very "no" must be taken as a hallmark, as a certificate of origin comparable to "made in Germany" stamped on an object' (Lacan 2006, p. 754).

6. With regard to the *ontology of exile*, I refer the reader to my paper 'Alemán tra Lacan e Heidegger. Lo statuto ontologico della pulsione' (Bonazzi 2009, pp. 5-42).

subjected to a fundamental 'per-diction' [*per-dizione*], the term by means of which Lacan translates, in a very original manner, Freud's *Versagung*:

> *Versagung* [...] becomes what the structure of the word implies: *Versagen*, the refusal that concerns what is said. If I wanted to mislead you in order to find the best translation, I would say *per-diction*. All that is condition becomes 'per-diction'.[7] (Lacan 1994, lesson of 17/5/1961)

If the sign is the precondition of the subject, it is also its fundamental 'per-diction'. We are confused, lost, exiled in language: as Lacan will say during the last phase of his teaching:

> How is it possible that we do not all sense that the words on which we depend are somehow imposed on us? This is indeed where a so-called sick person sometimes goes further than a man who is defined as healthy. The issue is rather one of knowing why a so-called 'normal' man is not aware that the word is a parasite, a coating, that the word is a form of cancer that afflicts the human being. (Lacan 2005)

We are therefore dealing with an *ontology of exile*, but also, *the other way round* and following a movement that dialectics could never thematise, with an ontology of the act, of the decision and, we might even say, of the event. And this is so since Lacan has thought the sign with pain—the sign and the letter that is *en souffrance* in the sign: it lies beneath the sign, conceals and masks itself in it. Hence, we could say that exile and the promised land go together. But this neither means nor points in the direction of a return to the fatherland (*Heimat*). Rather, it is a courageous bet on what lies beyond it. The Lacanian subject is confused and lost in the exile of language. But it is precisely here, among signs, and nowhere else, that at times the possibility of an unforeseeable, new, and unprecedented adventure opens up between the 'two Walls of the impossible':[8] this is the event of singularity, of the *not-born* that, although it was impossible, all of a sudden, breaks into the scene, completely unexpected. Lost in language, exiled, puzzled as we are, we are finally awakened to embark in the adventure of *lalangue*, enter the *dit-mension*: 'another mode of the speaking being in language',[9] another relation between man and the sign, between man and that place of fundamental suffering we call being. I call *onto-graphy* this new dimension of the subject, of *logos* and of being.

Before discussing in detail this supposed Lacanian ontology we should pause for a moment to observe its preconditions. If Lacan talks about philosophy it is because, to a certain extent, he acknowledges its status as a discourse, its status as a *specific* discourse. Lacan traces the discourse of philosophy (in brief, that of ontology) back to the discourse of the master. In the swift but dense genealogy that he advances in his seminar XVII of 1969, we discover that knowledge, that is, philosophy's knowledge, was born from an original theft: the master's theft of the *savoir-faire*, the know-how, of the slave, of a slave who was not yet dialectically

---

7. [Translator's note: *Per-diction* in French is pronounced as *perdition*, which has in French the same meaning it has in English. The addition of the hyphen and the change of spelling emphasise the word *diction*, which means 'enunciation', 'pronunciation' or 'elocution'.]

8. Lacan 1998, p. 167.

9. Lacan 1973, p. 252.

tied to the knowledge of the *maître*. Lacan asks: 'What does philosophy designate over its entire evolution?' And answers: 'It's this—theft, abduction, stealing slavery of its knowledge, through the maneuvers of the Master'. This theft, so to say, inscribes the fundamental pragmatics that rests at the bottom of any concrete practice into a codifiable field, that of language. But 'how did the philosopher manage to inspire the master with the desire to know?'[10] Lacan presses. This is philosophy's cunning and audacity: following the signifying chain '*Maître, M'être, M'essére*',[11] its gesture is in the end traced back to the desire of *être*, which always becomes the desire of a *maître*, a desire of *mastery*.

Having said this, we still have to ask, radically: *where* is Lacan speaking *from*? Because, if his genealogical gesture is not inscribed into one of the four discourses (it is not by chance that there are four—and only four—discourses according to Lacan) we still have to ask what the place of Lacan's enunciation and interrogation is: it is not philosophy's, or psychoanalysis', and certainly not that of the hysteric or of the University. I think that this place signals [*fa segno*] an ontological possibility that remains to be thought; an *onto-graphy* that lives up to the logic of the *not-whole* from which Lacan takes the floor, because he does not speak simply in the name of the psychoanalytical experience. As he himself repeatedly re-marked in his Seminars, he occupies a place from which he takes the floor. This is not the analyst's place, because Lacan's teaching is not immediately a psychoanalytical experience. It is a different place. Lacan often repeats it: he speaks from the perspective of a logic of the *not-whole*. Onto-graphy, if there is such a thing, must, first of all, be brave enough to think the peculiar status of this place, beyond the opposition between the whole and the parts.

II. THE ONTOLOGY OF EXILE

The being about which metaphysics speaks is, according to Lacan, an imaginary or symbolic product. First of all, it is imaginary, in that it is a retroactive construction of the nostalgic and contemplative gaze of the philosopher: this being is a harmonious, compact, non-variegated universe; the Parmenidean being as a perfect sphere. All this should be traced back, Lacan says, to the phantasmatic and imaginary construction that is reality. Phantasy, covering the real hole of the non-origin of the origin, would delineate the perfection of the metaphysical being. In other words, reality would be structured according to a universal and cosmological order, a totalising vision, because *he who* watches it is the philosopher, with his desire for manifestation and totalising phenomenalisation. *Theorein*: this is the desire that directs the gaze of the philosopher—bringing to presence, *phenomenalising*, making visible, in order for being to be what it must be.

Yet, according to Lacan, being is also a symbolic construction. There is 'being' where there is a *maître* that reduces the experience of the world to the *One which is*, to the univocity of the signifier 'One' (*l'Un-signifiant*):

> Ontology is what highlighted in language the use of the copula, isolating
> it as a signifier. To dwell on the verb 'to be'—a verb that is not even, in the

---

10. Lacan 2007, p. 21, p. 24.
11. Lacan 1999, p. 31.

complete field of the diversity of languages, employed in a way we could qualify as universal—to produce it as such is a highly risky enterprise [...] In this use of the copula, we would see nothing at all. We would see nothing whatsoever if a discourse, the discourse of the master, *m'être*, didn't empha- sise the verb 'to be' (*être*). (Lacan 1999, p. 31)

When the copula is isolated as the index of being *as such*, the field of inves- tigation of ontology is opened. However, nothing forces us, Lacan maintains, to perform this transition from the copula to being *as such*, but the gaze of the mas- ter-philosopher who stresses this form of transition (or of transference) over oth- ers. Thus, without the discourse of the master there would not be any metaphysics of being. And, to look at it the other way round, being as such gives itself and be- comes substantial only within this discourse. Being, therefore, becomes the effect of a symbolic operation that is carried out in the field of language starting from what a master signifier orders to the subject. As Lacan puts it,

> Every dimension of being is produced in the wake of the master's dis- course—the discourse of he who, proffering the signifier, expects therefrom one of its link effects that must not be neglected, which is related to the fact that the signifier commands. The signifier is, first and foremost, impera- tive. (Ibid., p. 32)

In other words, to put this in a more radical way, we could say, with Lacan, that 'were it not for the verb to be, there would be no being at all'.[12] By focusing on the reduction of being to its signifier, Lacan is targeting a metaphysical concep- tion of reality as an organic, harmonious whole, subjected, that is, to the prima- cy of the signifier 'One' (*l'Un-signifiant*). The whole of the universe, the universe's being as a whole, or, better still, the being of the totalising universe of discourse is that in which everything *runs smoothly, succeeds*. In this perfect world, everything succeeds, which means that it returns to the sender following a circular economy, the economy of the symbolic proper. Yet everything succeeds only when it has been previously reduced to the 'said' (*le dit*). *Being-said* is also being successful, 'be- ing at someone's heel, being at someone's beck and call', 'what would have been'.[13] As Lacan says, commenting on Aristotle, 'the universe is the place where, due to the fact of speaking, everything succeeds (*de dire, tout réussit*)'.[14]

With regard to the universality of this imaginary and symbolic being, it should perhaps be said that something *suffers*: there is *perdition* (*Versagung*), *failure*. This suffering, this remainder *en souffrance* that lies beneath the *uni-versalising* grasp of the master signifier 'One', resists the symbolic, and insinuates itself into the network of the discursive machine; in turn, it says something and speaks of what is concealed within desire, under the phantasmatic squaring of metaphysics. The Parmenidean being is therefore derided, precisely like, in the *Symposium*, Aris- tophanes laughs at the image of the primordial sphere. The sphere is a laugh-

---

12. Lacan, Seminar XXI. *Les non-dupes errent* (unpublished), lesson of 15/1/1974.

13. Lacan 1999, p. 31. [Translator's note: 'What would have been' renders the French *allait être*, which, as Fink, the translator of Seminar XX, remarks, 'involves an imperfect tense, and Lacan often plays on the French imperfect, since it can mean what "was going to be", "was about to be", or "would have been if"' (ibid., pp. 31-32 note 19)].

14. Ibid., p. 56.

ing matter, as Lacan reminds us, quoting Léon Robin, one of the most important commentators of Plato: 'I do not want to dwell on the sphere; the important
thing is the cut'.[15] In the place of the sphere, Lacan puts the symbolic phallus or,
as he writes it, Φ: the barred, fractured, segmented sphere. The real cut is thus
perhaps more important than the imaginary/symbolic sphere. The writing of
this cut segments the symbolic image of metaphysical being.

The subject's unconscious desire—which, at the bottom of its phantasmatic
articulation, always conceals something real—emerges precisely there where, all
of a sudden, this imaginary sphere collapses. The radical question should therefore be posed as follows: *who speaks* in metaphysics? Which subject speaks behind
this conciliatory gaze? Who speaks on behalf of the master signifier?

> One senses that the ego is about to collapse any minute, when the sound of
> broken glass informs everyone that it is the large drawing-room mirror that
> has sustained the accident, the golem of narcissism, hastily invoked to assist
> the ego, having thereby made its entrance. (Lacan 2006, p. 343)

A completely different scene opens up in this symptomatic fall, in this falling together (*symptôma*) of the pieces of the mirror that kept the ego, the world
and the universe standing. The unconscious scene opens up following the failure of the phantasmatic picture: the subject meets something of his own desire
there where, to a certain extent, he fails. The real suffering of the split subject reveals itself in this failure, in *saying no* to the very signifier that allows him to speak.
Here we return again to Freud's *Versagung*: rather than a simple refusal, this *saying no* is an 'un-saying' (*disdire*), a saying that is also, at the same time, a way of con-
tradicting (*contra/dire*).

> An original *Versagung* beyond which there is both the way to neurosis and
> to normality, whereby one is not more worthy than the other with respect
> to what is, initially, the possibility of the *Versagung*. It is self-evident that this
> untranslatable *Versagung* is only possible in the register of a *sagen*, insofar as
> the *sagen* is not simply the operation of communication, but the saying (*le
> dire*), the emergence as such of the signifier in so far as it allows the subject
> to refuse himself. (Lacan 1994, lesson of 24/5/1961)

It is a matter of retrieving the subject's unconscious desire at the point of the
coupure, not in his 'said' but in his 'saying', not in his signified, but in the event of
his signified, there where the *Versagung*'s untranslatability resonates. This is because it is precisely in the gap that separates it from demand that desire evokes,
in an inverted form, the assertion that is produced around refusal: '*Je te demande
de refuser ce que je t'offre parce que ce n'est pas ça*'.[16] Understood as an interrogation of
the unconscious desire, psychoanalysis teaches us that the subject is a *want-to-be*
(*manque-à-être*): he is 'in the place from which "the universe is a flaw in the purity of Non-Being" is vociferated. [...] This place is called *Jouissance*, and it is *Jouissance* whose absence would render the universe vain'.[17]

---

15. Lacan 1994, lesson of 21/12/1960.

16. Lacan 1975, p. 142. [Translator's note: this citation from Seminar XX is given in French in the
original.]

17. Lacan 2006, p. 694.

Lacan puts *Jouissance*, the enjoying substance, which is neither being nor not-being, and belongs to the order of that which is 'unrealized', in the place of being—understood as a product of the theoretical, contemplative and nostalgic gaze, or of the master signifier; of the abstraction of being derived from the copula. In other words, *Jouissance* is not that which has been, the essence (*Wesen/Gewesen*), but that 'pre-ontological' dimension that Lacan assigns to the pulsating function of the unconscious:

> The gap of the unconscious may be said to be *pre-ontological*. I have stressed that all too often forgotten characteristic—forgotten in a way that is not without significance—of the first emergence of the unconscious, namely, that it does not lend itself to ontology. Indeed, what became apparent at first to Freud, to the discoverers, to those who made the first steps, and what still becomes apparent to anyone in analysis who spends some time observing what truly belongs to the order of the unconscious, is that it is neither being, nor non-being, but the unrealized. (Lacan 1998, pp. 29-30)

The *jouissance* to which we are referring is the object of neither intellection nor sensibility. Much like in the case of the atopic bottom of our affliction and suffering, it is a matter of a hybrid and anonymous place: that of the *pathetikón*, for which there is no appropriate essential attribute. I believe that what emerges in this way is the outline of a Thing that is, by and large, yet to be thought, and together with it, possibly, of a new ontology, an ontology of the drive.[18] We should therefore think, at the same time, that the Thing is nothing outside of the law (the symbolic law, that of the signifier) which makes it possible, and that, nonetheless, it is that which *suffers from* the signifier: we could call it, the pain *of* the sign. This substance is irreparably lost, since, by taking it over to speech, language kills it. But it is only in this way that it also persists, insists, and resists: as a remainder that targets us, stings us, and surprises us with its suffering, which is, all in all, our own. Not at the origin, but in every moment, as if for the first time.

According to this perspective, instead of resting, like metaphysics, on the imaginary construction of the original unity, Lacan's ontology of exile rests, the best it can, on this hybrid figure, which is drawn through the symbol of the symbolic: the symbolic phallus, the barred sphere, the non-origin of the origin. But if, as Derrida maintains, the Dyad is at the origin, it is because the principle of principles of Lacanian psychoanalysis is that *there is no relation*. The two partners never make one. This is what psychoanalytical practice proves on a daily basis, not as a psycho-logical knowledge, but as a *fundamental praxis* which Lacan names *erotology*.[19] In the beginning, according to psychoanalysis, there was neither the Word, nor Action: in the beginning there was Eros.[20] And Eros, as Derrida reminds us in *Résistances de la psychanalyse*, is to be understood, first and foremost, as *poleros*—a relationship of forces that irreducibly ties *eros* with *polemos*.[21]

---

18. See Alemán 2009.
19. See Lacan 2004.
20. See Lacan 1994.
21. See Derrida 1998b, p. 9.

Deconstruction shares with Lacanian psychoanalysis this critical distance from any origin, unity, or universality. Like deconstruction, Lacan's teaching re-opens the *chance* of adventure behind the project or the program that frames existence. When the subject begins to take note of his condition of exiled—first and foremost, from the sexual relationship—he breaks loose of the phantasmatic figures that nail him to the impression that a relationship might take place or took place. Here begins the adventure, in an eternal perdition, but not without a home: because home becomes precisely this in-finite transit that accompanies, as a shadow, the life of the subject. That which transits is also that which repeats itself. What remains is, so to speak, the trail left by the route of experience. In the fading of figures, in that transit that is truth in its becoming temporal, this trail leaves behind remnants, debris, details that are barely visible. But what we lose at every turn, what is left behind, what we discard at every crossroad returns, calls us, obsesses us, targets us and is lethal: *it is written.*[22] Hence, exile reveals the reversed figure of a promised land, that never was and never will be, and that, not having a past, approaches us at every moment as an absolute *to come* [*a venire*], free from any bond with the present, presence and, ultimately, being.

III. THE ONTOLOGY OF *KRISIS*

Lost, exiled, and split, the Lacanian subject dwells neither in the place of being, nor in that of non-being: as a pulsation, drive, fracture, the unconscious is in the order of pure difference. Here, the speculative question does not have the same hold that it might have with regard to the still metaphysical dream of 'a purely *heterological* thought [...] A pure thought of pure difference'.[23] Although difference can only be thought starting from non-difference, and for this reason it is never pure, as Derrida rightly reminds us when, drawing on Hegel, he deconstructs his mentor Lévinas, we should nevertheless say that, for what concerns the unconscious as the place of the original deferment of difference, it is not really a matter of thought, whether possible or impossible, but rather of acts. The act of the *coupure* happens before any thought we might construct about its status of difference. This is because, in the first place, the difference that operates at the level of the unconscious is *sexual difference*. The unconscious subject, having lost his home in being, dwells in the world in the modality of 'having'. The loss opens therefore the dimension of 'having', and 'having' structures itself around sexual difference. This is how we should interpret in Lacanian terms the originality of the non-origin, the Dyad, which Derrida understands as the *origin of the origin*.

The phallus, Φ, the symbol of the symbolic, is the barred sphere that, by deleting being, poses difference as originary. Behind any possible ontology and any possible direction of thought that aims at thinking being as such, Lacan poses the unavoidability of difference, not as an ontological difference between being [*essere*] and that which is [*essente*], but as sexual difference. The term 'sexual' is not to be understood in the sense of a hypothetic priority of the instinct over the *logos*. That which is sexual is, properly speaking, produced by the signifier,

---

22. See Lacan 2001, p. 20.
23. Derrida 2001, p. 189.

that is to say, by the fact that the human subject is such because, first of all, he speaks. And, as a speaking being, having irremediably lost his home in being, he has been handed over to the dimension of 'having'. Thus, the signifier is, properly speaking, that which produces this loss: the minimal pre-semantic component of the signifier is its function as a cut. The event of the symbolic inevitably inaugurates the dimension of sexuality that is therefore founded not on the instinct but on the drive, understood as that which the signifier produces beyond itself.

For this reason, we can claim that Lacan thought the 'deepest' (*das Tiefste*) but also the 'liveliest' (*Lebendiste*). The subject is such not only as subjected *to* the sign, but also, and chiefly, as subjected *to* the signifier. Hence, we need to grasp that, unlike the sign, the signifier is always the effect of the deferring of difference. In other words, there is no halting point in the chain of signifiers, as each of them is that which represents a subject for another signifier. Deprived of any referent, the minimum that signals the presence of a signifier is the presence of a spatial or temporal articulation: within/without, before/after. Sexual difference is therefore original because that which is at the origins is the cut of the signifier: man/woman.

The subject, in an eternal exile, is therefore thrown in the field of the Other by the event of the *coupure*, by the inaugural cut. The Principle of this ontology of *Krisis* is trauma. The advent of language is the trauma that produces the subject as an answer, and psychoanalysis—as the Argentinian psychoanalyst Jorge Alemán maintains—becomes the 'possibility of recovering from metaphysics',[24] that is to say, from the traumatic seizure operated by the language of ontology. The trauma of metaphysics is actually the trauma of language. Psychoanalysis presents itself as a cure because it somehow proposes a different, non-metaphysical way of being in language and meeting up with its inaugural trauma. 'An other mode of the speaker in language'.[25]

The cure passes through desire because we could say, with Lacan, that there would be no desire without a trauma. Hence, recovering from metaphysics means crossing the traumatic threshold of that speech which, leaving behind the imaginary and symbolic illusions that we have mentioned, enables a subjective transformation. This ethics of the subject that calls us to perform the fundamental shift from being subjected *to* language to being subjects *of* language, changes our way of relating to speech [*parola*] and hence also to that *essere di parola*[26] which is, as we have seen, the object of metaphysics. The subject of desire therefore replaces the subject of metaphysics, the subject of knowledge, his gaze, his *theorein*. The partial—and hence absolute, bondless—desiring gaze of desire takes the place of the panoramic gaze of the metaphysician. The ethical subject of this *onto-graphy* is born out of the *Krisis* that runs through it: he does not try to saturate the *Krisis* but takes note of it and turns it into the cause of his own actions. Having become one with his own act, he has emancipated himself from the myth of the origin

---

24. Alemán and Larriera 1989, p. 112.

25. Lacan 1973, p. 252.

26. [Translator's note: in Italian, *essere di parola* means 'keeping one's word'. There is no English translation that can maintain both the idiomatic meaning of *essere di parola* (keeping one's word) and its reference to being (*essere*) according to which the phrase literally means 'being of speech'.]

and has replaced it with the indestructibility of the *cause*. Where metaphysics saw the origin, the *parlêtre* encounters the cause that thrusts and renews, right on the spot, his own 'extimate' [*estimale*][27] desire. He no longer looks at what he is facing, as he is no longer subjected to noetic intentionality. His cypher is precluded to him; it is unconscious because it is always behind him. The cause thrusts him and there is no way to visualize it. One cannot *turn back*, because the difference that is produced here is precisely that between he who wants to see or know and he who no longer wants to say what cannot be said, because he has transformed it into the cause of his own saying.

The subject as subjected to language is a split, barred, deleted subject—thus, he is a subject who desires, but who, because he desires in language, does nothing but pass from one signifier to the other. Now, this subject who cures himself, in the sense of Heidegger's *Sorge*, from the phantasies of metaphysics is, at a closer inspection, not far from the Hegelian subject. The Lacanian subject is a split subject, in that he is affected by the signifier: having lost the supposed originary dimension of being, he is the subject who *wants-to-be* [*manca-a-essere*] and hence desires. The Hegelian subject is, in his own way, split as the effect of the originary split of judgment: the *Subjekt seines Urteils* is a de-substantialised subject, in that he is split between certitude and truth. Now, in both cases, we can find the radical point that lies in the background of this ontology of *Krisis*, namely, the metonymic character of desire or, in Hegelian terms, bad infinity as an effect of the signifying displacement.

Lacan's *onto-graphy* puts this question in a different perspective, turns around its general framework and, through a sort of emptying of the Other (*there is no Other of the Other*), allows to perform the 'quarter turn' that moves the subject from the scene of the symbolic unconscious to the adventure of the real unconscious. The remainders of the subject and of his ontology can be found only through a new writing, a writing of which we do not have to be the authors, a writing that is born out of the crisis that runs through the subject and humiliates his supposed position of mastery. This *onto-graphy* 'is a response to a crisis of consciousness that we are not necessarily obliged to identify, since we are living it'.[28]

IV. ONTO-GRAPHY

Even from an ontological perspective, the shift of the subject—from the field of the Other, the field of the unconscious structured like a language, to the plane of the real—is decisive. In fact, what is the substance (*substantia*) that lies at the basis of the metaphysical discourse if not, indeed, the subject (*subjectum*), the *hypokeimenon*, which Aristotle places at the foundation of our *onto-theo-logical* tradition? If the subject moves and changes his skin, this affects the entire ontological framework. Not only, then, the subject of knowledge, the modern subject. The transformation of the substance we are discussing immediately implies a general upheaval of the fundamental ontology. The exiled subject, subjected to the *Krisis* of

---

27. [Translator's note: *estimale* in Italian is a neologism, an adjective derived from the Lacanian term *extimité*, translated as *estimità* in Italian and as *extimacy* in English.]

28. Lacan 1992, p. 127.

judgment, is, properly speaking, the subject that undermines the foundation as such. De-substantialisation is not only an existential operation; it is, first of all, a gesture that unveils and unmasks the entire ontological project of metaphysics. If the subject no longer has a foundation, and is rather to be sought in the poem of signifiers that shapes his destiny, substance loses consistency and necessity: it is no longer its own necessary cause, but pure happening, mere contingency—it is no longer a *quidditas* but a *quodditas*.[29] This shift marks the opening of what I call an *onto-graphy*. But let us take one step at a time. First of all, what happens to the subject, to the *hypokeimenon*, at this stage of our reflection?

Scattered in the metonymic chain of signifiers, the subject is nonetheless not deprived of a halting point. Lacan call this full stop the *letter*, a hurdle that is not possible to elaborate further, a real bone. Thus, there is no subject without the signifier's hold on him, but also, there is no subject without this bouncing of the letter *en souffrance*. How should we now place the position of the letter? How should we understand the way in which the letter affects the subject enabling an interruption in the metonymic revival of desire as 'desire for something else'? Let us go back to what we said before concerning the function of the symbolic phallus.

The Parmenidean sphere of being is irreparably lost, in that it is cut off by Φ. But Φ, as the symbol of the symbolic, exceeds the field of the Other, because it is, at the same time, its condition of possibility. The event of the fissure—a *letter* that comes to vertically cut off the whole—is hence more originary than the *Krisis*, the original division. The taking place of the *coupure*, as the engraving of the letter, witnesses to the *One that there is*, as the condition of possibility of the Dyad. If the Dyad is what can be, the One—as real—is, rather, the impossible: that 'possibilitating' possibility [*possibilità possibilitante*] (*Ermöglichung*) which, in order to make the possible such, cannot but remain in the dimension of the impossible. 'There is something of the One. *Yad'lun*', as Lacan puts it, 'but we do not know where'.[30]

The One of the letter is not the One of metaphysics. If the latter is the One that *is*, the former is the One that *ek-sists*. For this reason, the One of the letter has no 'where', no place: as fissure and event, it happens continuously. The One of the *coupure* is in the place of the *Urvedrängung*, the primary repression that accompanies, in every instant, the taking place of the signifying articulation. The One is therefore the event of the Dyad: not the unconscious as 'said', but its 'Saying'. Not everything signifies, not everything is processed by the symbolic machine of the unconscious *qua* the Other. And also, not everything can be traced back to the Dyad. Something happens, which means that the One gives itself as an event and not as meaning. The One of the letter repeats itself in-finitely; it is that which subtracts itself in every signifying donation. This subtraction can never belong to the order of the one *like* the other [*dell'una come l'altra*]—it always and only belongs to the absolute order of the *one by one* [*dell'una per una*]. The One that there is, *Yad'lun* (as Lacan writes in his *lalangue*), belongs to the order of the pure occurrence [*acca-*

29. See J.-A. Miller, *Extimité* (unpublished seminar), lesson of 8/1/1986: '*C'est-à-dire qu'il y a, et c'est tout. L'ensemble de ce dont peut être qualifié l'objet est du registre de la quidditas [...]. Mais il y a autre chose qui s'isole et qui n'est précisément rien de plus qu'un 'il y a', qu'un 'il y a là', sans qu'on puisse dire ce que c'est [...] C'est précisément cela ce quod : que c'est, et non pas ce que c'est [...] L'objet a [...] c'est le quod*'.

30. Lacan 2005, lesson of 13/1/1976.

dimento], to the *quodditas* and no longer to the *quidditas*—it does not answer the Socratic question *ti esti*, because it is neither a thing, nor a sign of the thing, but an event that, between the one and the other, makes the world happen, and makes us happen in the world.

Now, the place of the evental One [*Uno evenemenziale*] is the letter. Yet the letter is no longer understood as a signifier. In fact, if the signifier is, by definition, always at least two signifiers—according to the well known Saussurean differential law that states that a signifier is what other signifiers make of it—the letter is, instead, an isolated signifier, separated from the symbolic chain, extracted from the Other. As such, the letter no longer *means* anything—it subtracts itself from the mechanism of the *Bedeutung*, of meaning and the reference to the Other. The letter no longer belongs to the register of language, but, rather, to that of writing. For this reason, here, we are speaking of an *onto-graphy*: at the level of the event, language no longer shows us the way. Writing operates where language is finally silent.

This shift achieves a torsion also at a temporal level. If time, in its signifying articulation, is a linear, chronological time, at the level of the letter we rather encounter the punctual and vertical rhythm of the drive: the unconscious is, for Lacan, 'this somehow pulsatile function', the 'beat of the fissure'. The drive, actually, pulsates without moving, opening up the now—that metaphysics has emptied—to a new dimension. The now, as it is known, is, since Aristotle, an empty point—a limit between past and future. Well, for Lacan, on the contrary, the instant has its own duration, its own thickness. The unconscious subject, the *je*, 'is isolated from the other—that is, from the relation of reciprocity—by a *logical beat* [*battement de temps*]'[31]—as Lacan maintains in 'Logical Time and the Assertion of Anticipated Certitude'. Like the Hegelian *Ein sich Entzweiendes*, the One of the letter, in an instant of beating, divides itself.

In the place of the Thing, killed by the signifier, the letter reveals the infinitesimal point of fundamental suffering. The *object a*, here understood as a letter, Lacan's original *invention*, is to be thought as a *páschein*, as a 'feeling that is a being hit from the outside'.[32] This fundamental and anonymous suffering is the axis around which the re-writing of substance that Lacan performs through the reversal of the metaphysical subject revolves. The enjoying substance [*sostanza godente*] that Lacan begins to mention towards the end of his teaching can no longer be thought as lying within the universe of the Aristotelian discourse—it is the substance that, with its fundamental suffering, leaves traces of itself on the crest that remains after the emptying of metaphysical ontology operated through the crisis of the subject. The drive thus assumes an ontological status—it is no longer a matter of instinct and of what thrusts a subject unbeknown to him. The *Trieb*, as Lacan maintains, discloses a new field of inquiry that reveals the un-thought space of the fundamental suffering at the bottom of which we recognize the possibility of an *ethics* of *aísthēsis* that should be thought beyond everything, or beyond the whole.

---

31. Lacan 2006, p. 170.
32. Ronchi 2008, p. 36.

But what *whole* is Lacan referring to? The whole of the Aristotelian universe of discourse. Here, as is known, the infinite is admitted only potentially, precisely in order to guarantee the framing of the world. According to Lacan, the object *a*, being the materiality of the letter, embodies the dimension of the actual infinite. It has to be placed at the infinite point of the metonymic line, where the orientation of the vector can be reversed and, all of a sudden, modify the way in which it affects the signifying chain. In this way, the subject happens to change the singular mode of his own enjoyment, and the metaphysical One eclipses itself to give space to the eventual One [*Uno evenemenziale*]. According to this (im)possible reversal, the experience of analysis can end. It can end because it does not reduce itself to the bad infinite of the signifying metonymy. Not everything signifies. The object *a*—absolute and unique to each one of us—is the contingent space of this end. It is a space that, although it happens in an instant, has its own duration and thickness—more than anything, it has its own rhythm, that of the drive.

V. A LOVE LETTER

In order to locate the place where and the way in which this reversal of the symbolic unconscious into the real unconscious, of ontology into *onto-graphy*, occurs, let us take into account the modal logic that Lacan develops starting from the 1970s. To fully understand this passage we have to read those pages of Seminar XX in which Lacan introduces the logic of sexuation. Sexuation is a matter of logic because it involves the operator Φ, the symbol of the symbolic which, as we have seen, structures the field of language and of semiotic enjoyment.

The universal affirmative, as Lacan transcribes it, reads: 'all x are Φ of x' ($\forall x \Phi x$). That is to say, there is only semiotic enjoyment, there is only an existence mediated by symbolic castration. As Lacan puts it, this is the relentless law of necessity: *something never stops writing itself*, or, more specifically, something writes itself always and only through the mediation of the phallic function. This obviously entails that *something also never stops not writing itself.* These are the two sides of phallic necessity. To say, with Lacan, that there is no *Other of the Other* means to affirm, at the same time, that *there is nothing but the Other*. Everything is mediated symbolically. And, beyond the whole there is nothing but the impossible, precisely *something that never stops not writing itself.* Yet this is not without consequences, at least because, in ascertaining the law of necessity, we put ourselves on the trail of its beyond, that is to say, of the impossible. It is here, however, that this issue becomes complicated. If the whole is not enough for itself, if the universal affirmative is true even when the universal negative is true, then it happens, at times, that the impossible turns into the contingent, that is to say, into what Lacan writes as follows: *something stops not writing itself.* Where the phallic mediation fails, where there is a stumbling, we meet something that exceeds castration, not from the outside but from the inside, as an *extimité*. The exception does not affect the enclosed totality of discourse from the outside, but, all in all, it is what sustains it and also continuously threatens it from the inside. Where is it that the universal affirmative, that sustains the logic of the whole because it is wholly mediated by Φ, is true along with the universal negative, the exception to the whole? In the case of the empty set, where there is no x. Only here, in the place of non-existence, in the place of *The woman*, the logic of the not-whole subtracts itself from the mediation that sustains the whole.

How does Lacan write at this point the universal negative? Moving negation from the copula to the quantifier: 'not all x are Φ of x' ($\overline{\forall x}$. Φx). In this way the logic of the *not-whole* opens up. The whole and the *not-whole* write themselves together at the place where the *displacement* of negation takes place, because negation is precisely this infinite displacement, reversal, this see-saw of the unary trait that divides insofar as it cuts, but also opens up the possibility of the encounter in its absolute contingency. 'All x are Φ of x and not all x are Φ of x' [($\forall x \Phi x$) $\wedge (\overline{\forall x}$. Φx)] is true where Lacan positions the place of woman, the place where, precisely, *The* woman does not exist as a universal. The empty set is the impossible set in which existence shows itself for what it is, that is to say, shows *that* it is and not *what* it is, *that* we say and not *what* we say. Here, the woman that does not exist *gives herself*; here, the universal leaves space to the infinitely particular, to that singularity that will no longer be able to be reduced to mediation, because it is incalculable and exceeds any phallic or semiotic grasp. The *not-whole* is a supplement and not a complement.

> The fact remains that if she [*woman*] is excluded by the nature of things, it is precisely in the following respect: being *not-whole*, she has a supplementary *jouissance* compared to what the phallic function designates by way of *jouissance*. You will notice that I said '*supplementary*'. If I had said '*complementary*' what a mess we'd be in! We would fall back into the whole. (Lacan 1999, p. 73)

The logic of the *not-whole* operates under the sign of *supplementarity* [*supplementarietà*] and not of complementarity. *Onto-graphy* is not an exception alongside *ontology*; rather, it is the whole supplementing [*in supplenza*] the excess, and the excess supplementing [*in supplenza*] the whole. It is not the one and the other; it is not the one that completes the other, following again an *ontototological* vision of the whole; but the one *in the place* of the other, always and no matter what.

The contingent exceptionality of the in-finite point that we indicate with the lower-case letter *a*, this location of the (im)possible, can be obtained by moving negation, as we have seen, and as Lacan remarks in saying that

> I incarnated contingency in the expression 'stops not being written'. For here there is nothing but encounter, the encounter in the partner of symptoms and affects, of everything that marks in each of us the trace of his exile—not as subject but as speaking—his exile from the sexual relationship. Isn't that tantamount to saying that it is owing only to the affect that results from this gap that something is encountered? [...] The displacement of the negation from the 'stops not being written' to the 'doesn't stop being written', in other words, from contingency to necessity—there lies the point of suspension to which all love is attached. (Ibid., p. 145)

The affect that *writes* the space of the *aísthēsis*, the *páschein*, is what the letter produces on the margin of the signifier. Literally, it *affects* the subject's enjoying substance and produces the creation of 'zones' of the drive, which, in turn, trace the division of the bodies in the *common* space. This literal affection fills the gap left by the subjective *béance*. The density and the rhythm of this filling rests in the hands of the encounter's contingency.

As is known, Lacan draws the dimension of the encounter from Aristotle. In *Physics* the latter says, in fact, that there are two forms of causation: αυτόματον (which Lacan translates as 'network of signifiers') and τύχη (which Lacan translates as 'encounter with the real').[33] Now, Lacan knows well that τύχη is precisely the point at which the Aristotelian *whole* collapses—the perfect whole, limited, finite, the one in which everything *runs smoothly*. Contingency shows, once again, the extimate place. Since, in principle and necessarily, there is no relationship and there is trauma, the (im)possibility of the encounter is also given—in the liminal trace of the exile which belongs to each and every one of us.

Having reached this point, we are no longer in the dimension of being nor in that of having: neither in the One nor in the Multiple—we happen in the event of the real fracture: we *ek-sist*. Lacan's *onto-graphy* produces a new subject, a subject who is not simply here (*da*), Heidegger's *Dasein*, precisely because he is always there (*fort*): this is how he can *really* love. The subject who says 'I love you', Lacan maintains, is not the same subject who says 'I am here'.[34] He is a subject who eclipses himself in becoming a *love letter*.[35]

To conclude, *onto-graphy* exceeds the history of the metaphysical onto-theo-logy precisely because it corresponds, first and foremost, to a new image of love, as Lacan claims in 1976:

> I allow myself to put forward that writing changes meaning, the mode of what is at stake, that is to say, the φιλία of wisdom. It is not so easy to support wisdom otherwise than by writing [...] So that in the end, excuse my infatuation, what I am doing [...] is nothing less than the first philosophy that might be holding up. (Lacan 2005, lesson of 11/5/1976)

Eros, that is, transference love, articulates our experience of the world through what Lacan calls here 'time-thought'. The primacy of thought in the existential temporality depends on the spell of transference. Lacan says that 'the φιλία is time *qua* thought. Time-thought is φιλία'.[36] Lacan understands 'time-thought' as a tight knot between *Wesen* and *Gewesen*, which leads to the well-known Hegelian statement: '*Wesen ist was gewesen ist*'.

Conversely, Lacan advances a writing that thinks *against* the signifier that structures the 'time-thought' inside the Other. In doing so, this writing exposes the re-written ego, the one made up of the *parlêtre*'s letters, to what Lacan calls the *apensée*.[37] To write is, therefore, to think offbeat, against time [*contro tempo*]. Here, to write means to bring into thought the letter, the object *a*, which *a-pense*. Clearly, one has to go behind the erotics that inflames the *aísthēsis* by articulating it

---

33. Lacan 1998, p. 52.
34. Lacan 2013, lesson of 19/11/1958.
35. See Lacan 1999, p. 78ff.
36. Ibid.
37. Ibid., lesson of 18/11/1975.

into the three forms of temporality. It is therefore a matter of grasping the *cause* of such a flame behind philosophical erotics.

Psychoanalytical disenchantment enables us to take a step that we deem crucial with regard to philosophical discourse or human desire in general. *Who does the philosopher love and how?* Lacan affirms that it is the love 'which is addressed to the father, in the name of the fact that the father is the carrier of castration'.[38] Hence, we could say, very briefly, that there is transference love because the Father comes to perform castration and thus produces the *want-to-be* that triggers the tension of desire. This is the love of truth, if by truth we mean the impotence about which Lacan speaks in Seminar XVII. We have therefore to reverse the impotence of truth into the impossible of writing.

The free play of the letter, that Lacan enigmatically calls 'punctuation without a text',[39] exposes us in this way to the exercise of writing that lies beneath (*en souffrance*) the symbolic order. The letter opens saying to the ethical responsibility of that act which, being a function of the cut, we incarnate every time we start speaking, feign a voice, and trace the three forms of time: the instant of the gaze, the time for understanding, and the moment for concluding—in one word, the erotics of the *aísthēsis*. What is, in the end, its ethics, its place? The *ethos* of this erotics dwells in a fourth time, that of the contingency of the encounter, the τύχη.

> The function of the *tuché*, of the real as encounter—the encounter in so far as it may be missed, in so far as it is essentially the missed encounter—first presented itself in the history of psychoanalysis in a form that was in itself already enough to arouse our attention, that of the trauma. [...] [The] accident, [...] the obstacle of the *tuché* [...] brings us back to the same point at which pre-Socratic philosophy sought to motivate the world itself. It required a *clinamen* [...] *Nothing, perhaps?—not perhaps nothing, but not nothing.* (Lacan 1998, p. 55, pp. 63-64)

Translated from the Italian by Alvise Sforza Tarabochia

BIBLIOGRAPHY

Alemán, J., and Larriera, S., *Lacan: Heidegger. El psicoanálisis en la tarea del pensar*, Madrid: Miguel Gómez Ediciones, 1989

Bonazzi, M., 'Alemán tra Lacan e Heidegger. Lo statuto ontologico della pulsione', in J. Alemán and S. Larriera, *L'inconscio e la voce. Esistenza e tempo tra Lacan e Heidegger*, Milan: et al/EDIZIONI, 2009

Derrida, J., 'Avoir l'oreille de la philosophie', in L. Finas (ed.), *Écarts. Quatre Essais à propos de Jacques Derrida*, Paris: Fayard, 1973, qt. in J. Derrida, *Limited Inc.*, trans. by Samuel Weber, Evanston: Northwestern University Press, 1988

—— *To Unsense the Subjectile*, trans. by Mary Ann Caws, in J. Derrida and P. Thévenin, *The Secret Art of Antonin Artaud*, Cambridge MA: MIT Press, 1998a

—— *Resistances of Psychoanalysis*, trans. by Peggy Kamuf, Pascale-Anne Brault

---

38. Ibid., lesson of 11/5/1976.
39. Lacan 2006, p. 324.

and Michael Naas, Stanford: Stanford University Press, 1998b

—— *Writing and Difference*, trans. by Alan Bass, London: Routledge, 2001

Hölderlin, F., *Mnemosyne* in *Hymns and Fragments*, trans. by Richard Sieburth, Princeton: Princeton University Press, 1984

Lacan, J., *Postface*, in *Le séminaire de Jacques Lacan. Livre XI. Les quatre concepts fondamentaux de la psychanalyse. 1963-1964*, Paris: Seuil, 1973

—— *Le séminaire de Jacques Lacan. Livre XX. Encore (1972-73)*, Paris: Seuil, 1975

—— *The Seminar of Jacques Lacan. Book VII. The Ethics of Psychoanalysis 1959–1960*, trans. by Dennis Porter, London: Routledge, 1992.

—— *Le séminaire de Jacques Lacan. Livre VIII. Le transfert (1960-61)*, Paris: Seuil, 1994

—— *The Seminar of Jacques Lacan. Book XI. The Four Fundamental Concepts of Psychoanalysis (1963-64)*, trans. by Alan Sheridan, London: W.W. Norton & Co., 1998

—— *The Seminar of Jacques Lacan. Book XX. On Feminine Sexuality. The Limits of Love and Knowledge (1972-73)*, trans. by Bruce Fink, London: W.W. Norton & Co., 1999

—— *Autres écrits*, Paris: Seuil, 2001

—— *Le séminaire de Jacques Lacan. Livre X. L'angoisse (1962-63)*, Paris: Seuil, 2004

—— *Le séminaire de Jacques Lacan. Livre XXIII. Le sinthome (1975-76)*, Paris: Seuil, 2005

—— *Écrits*, trans. by Bruce Fink, London: W. W. Norton & Co., 2006

—— *The Seminar of Jacques Lacan. Book XVII. The Other Side of Psychoanalysis (1969-70)*, trans. by Russell Grigg, London: W.W. Norton & Co., 2007

—— *Le séminaire. Livre VI. Le désir et son interprétation 1958-1959*. Paris: Éditions de La Martinière, 2013

Ronchi, R., *Filosofia della comunicazione. Il mondo come resto e come teogonia*, Turin: Bollati Boringhieri, 2008

The Subject of Logic:
The Object (Lacan with Kant and Frege)

Guillaume Collett

I. FREGE AND KANT

Gottlob Frege's *The Foundations of Arithmetic* (1960, [1884]) is an attempt to develop a purely logical account of cardinal numbers: what they are, how they succeed each other, how they quantify objects in a state of affairs.[1] The text seeks to found modern logic while simultaneously providing a logical basis for arithmetic. Moreover, in this text Frege wishes to develop an objective understanding of reference (the proposition's ability to designate objects in a state of affairs) and its relation to syntax, and to establish a propositional logic that is fully intertwined with an analysis of arithmetic.[2] Frege had already developed his 'context principle' before 1884, which holds that a word only has meaning in the context of a proposition,[3] and in *The Foundations* the logical proposition's syntax now becomes rigorously grounded in number, while at the same time number and its extensibility (1, 2, 3) are founded on a *linguistic* idea of syntax.[4]

In *The Foundations* Frege opposes the contemporary 'psychologistic' tendency to consider reality as *mental representation* or *image*, which he considers as an unreliable and 'subjective [...] blurred and undifferentiated fog'[5] which thus cannot possibly be shared by a community as a consistent concept. For Frege number is something completely objective, beyond doubt, intersubjectively shared, and which can pave the way for an objective description of the world free from subjectivist bias.

We can discern here the (post)-Kantian tenor of *The Foundations*: it is an attempt to circumvent the Copernican Revolution, Kant's discovery that knowl-

---

1. This article is intended as a Lacanian lesson on elements of arithmetical logic, culminating in a section on Lacan; one should always bear in mind the Lacanian context of the following pages on Frege and Kant, which form the core content of the article.

2. As Dummett makes clear, Frege's theory is a 'semantic theor[y] based on syntactic analys[is] after the pattern of mathematical logic' (Dummett 1991, p. 76).

3. See Frege 1960, p. xxii.

4. See Carl 1995, Ch. 3, and Dummett 1991, p. 76.

5. Frege 1960, p. xvii, p. xx.

edge of objects must be considered as *subjective* representation, although Kant's approach is not psychologistic in any simple sense. Kant's transcendental subject and its faculties, like Frege's number,[6] provide an intersubjectively shared principle of generating knowledge which is *a priori* and thus precedes the individual psychological subject and its subjectivist mental representations. It is above all with Kant, with the role of the transcendental subject as fundamental to knowledge, that Frege must contend: Frege's logical theory is aimed precisely at doing away with the subject, yet his project is post-Kantian in intention because he is well aware of the dangers of subjectivism[7] and essentially wishes to provide an alternate—syntactic—transcendental account of the generation of knowledge from perception.

Frege argues in *The Foundations* that while number does not exist objectively, in the sense that it is not the property of a sensible object, it is not subjective either. He gives number a special status, defining it as 'objective' but not 'handleable, or spatial, or actual'.[8] Two people will always agree whether or not there are five apples lying on a table even if they disagree about the apples' colour, shape, and so on. This is because for Frege any object insofar as it is one is a number, 1. There is no subjective colour and shape to debate if there are no objects in the first place. Number becomes the transcendental basis for perception, even if it is itself imperceptible. This is because *number* is always in a tripartite relation to *object* and *concept*; the traditional logical distinction between subject and predicate is replaced by concept and object: there is no subject of a proposition qualified by a predicate, say a cat sitting on a mat, there is only ever a chain of objects corresponding to numbers. A logical subject, say a cat, is only knowable insofar as it is an object, *one* object, the number one. All logical questions become reduced to the (always existential) quantification of objects.

Moreover, *number subtracts the state of affairs' materiality*: the cat must become an immaterial 1 in order to pass over into knowledge. Rather than repeat a fairly dominant view according to which Frege's understanding of number is Platonic or Leibnizian,[9] I would like to suggest that number's ideality in Frege can be considered as the result of a subtraction of materiality bearing resemblance to Kant.[10] In the *Critique of Pure Reason*, Kant (2007 [1787]) argues that knowledge of an object requires us to *combine* the faculty of *Sensibility*, which presents us with an intuition of the material world—the manifold of sensations—with the faculties of the *Imagination* and the *Understanding*, both of which are subject to the Ideas of *Reason*. As Gardner explains,[11] our intuition is sensible not intellectual, it is a *passive* ability to be affected by a manifold of unstructured sensations—what

6. See Currie 1982, p. 179.

7. Unlike Frege's explicit opposition to psychologism, Kant's Copernican Revolution was chiefly opposed to the radical empiricism of Hume and the idealism of Leibniz, but both Frege and Kant are concerned with founding a quasi-scientific connection to objects of knowledge, free from subjective bias or metaphysical speculation.

8. Frege 1960, p. 35.

9. See for example Sluga 2008.

10. Both Carl 1995, pp. 188-191, and Dummett 1991, p. 98, agree that Kant is Frege's preeminent philosophical influence.

11. Gardner 1999, p. 43, p. 58.

Kant calls 'receptivity'.[12] The other two faculties however only extend to the manifold *indirectly*, via the Sensibility. The Imagination subjects the matter—the manifold of sensations—offered to it by intuition to spatio-temporal schematisation; the Understanding subjects the Imagination's schematised products to conceptual categorisation. Reason subjects the Understanding's categorised products to the three Ideas: Self, World, and God.[13]

The first of these Ideas can be summed up with the equation 'Self=Self',[14] meaning that the products of the Understanding must be *re-cognised* by a subject who precedes psychological subjectivity. Through this transcendental subject, objects of contemplation—having been specifically shaped to be knowable by a subject—are merely identified with as objects, rather than as objects that have been produced by a subject. The object is apprehended as an end result, suppressing its previous stages all the way down to the Sensibility. The subject, being identified with the immaterial object rather than the material and immaterial stages, seals this process and its suppression of the preceding stages. The process described has the effect of transforming an initially material set of sensations into a set of ideal concepts, making the end result, the identification of the subject with the conceptualised object it has produced, completely *immaterial*: the materiality of the manifold has been hollowed out by the categories and identified with as a representation, even if the manifold was the initial raw material out of which the concepts and final object were sculpted. The object is thus ideal because it is the objectification of the subject. The subject is the faculties of material subtraction *plus* the recognition of this subtraction as the subject: the subject is both the faculties (which converge on the subtraction of materiality) and their redoubling at the level of pure ideality—the immaterial forms produced by the subject's faculties are identified with as the subject by the pure Idea of Self.

Self=Self comes down to the fact that in order for an object to be knowable it must be internally unified, it must be identical with itself, and so a unified subject is also needed. As Gardner explains, accompanying every object there must be 'a pure, original, unchangeable consciousness' of self.[15] If all representations were not identified as belonging to me then every representation of sense experience would be attributable to a different 'I'. What Kant calls the 'synthetic unity of apperception' is the fact that each of my representations appears familiar, i.e. as a *recognition*. In fact, Kant claims that the entire basis of the Understanding lies in submitting the Sensibility, via the Imagination, to the unity of apperception: 'The first pure knowledge of the understanding, therefore, on which all the rest of its use is founded [...] is this very principle of the synthetic unity of apperception [which] is therefore the highest point to which we must connect all use of the understanding, and even the whole of logic'.[16] For Kant, every object is one (1) insofar as it is identified with as a subject (Unity of apperception), and hence we have the equation Self=Self (1=1).

---

12. Kant 2007, p. 148.

13. See especially Kant's 'Transcendental Dialectic' (Kant 2007, pp. 285-570).

14. This equation is borrowed from Deleuze and Guattari 1994, pp. 56-57.

15. Gardner 1999, p. 122.

16. Kant 2007, p. 131, p. 127.

II. NUMBER IN *THE FOUNDATIONS*

If we take the example of the proposition 'There are eighty trees in this wood', Frege argues that we cannot know what 'eighty' refers to, nor what a 'tree' or a 'wood' are, outside of this propositional form. In fact the way he prefers to express it is 'The **number** of the **trees in this wood** is **eighty**':[17] number, concept, object(s). Although number for Frege is primary, since it is objective, it can only be established in relation to concepts and objects. Similarly, concepts can only denote objects for Frege within a logical proposition on the basis of number. Frege argues that in this particular proposition, the number eighty does not simply precede the concept (trees in this wood), nor the object/s (the individuated things in a state of affairs—eighty trees in this wood). *We must count eighty and only eighty things which share the same features, and be sure that these features are shared only by these eighty things and by nothing else in the wood, in order to establish simultaneously what a tree is, what 'eighty' is, and by extension, what 'this wood' is*. As Frege puts it: 'only a concept which isolates what falls under it in a definite manner, and which does not permit any arbitrary division of it into parts, can be a unit relative to a finite Number'.[18] For Dummett,[19] in Frege the subsumption of objects by concepts takes place first by comparing proto-relations between what are not yet objects ('this is darker/bigger/smoother than that'), then by differentiating the set of similarities-differences into a number of objects or identities.

Concept and object enter into a bi-univocal relationship based on the equinumerousness of concept and object. On the one hand, the concept determines what the object falling under it is: if the concept were 'number of branches' the trees would no longer exist as objects as they would no longer figure in the proposition, and similarly the number eighty would have to be greatly increased. On the other hand, the concept must be filled by objects in order to be realised as a concept, as a concept is nothing but a frame that limits quantity. This bi-univocal relation results in a number being assigned to—or formally redoubling—a realised concept, thus exteriorising the formal content of the concept onto the concept's exterior, marking it with an index and giving it the capacity to be re-applied to ever-increasing sets of objects. Like Kant's transcendental subject, number renders the object as pure form of identity rather than as individuating sensation; number is a redoubling of an identification.

Now, following Peano's axioms, Frege is required to define the three fundamental numbers: zero, one, and successor:

o—Frege defines the zero as 'that which is not identical to itself',[20] which

---

17. This is a modification of Dummett's example, Dummett 1991, p. 88.

18. Frege 1960, p. 66.

19. See Dummett 1991, pp. 162-163.

20. Frege 1960, p 88. Following Leibniz, Frege defines truth as that which is identical to itself. For Frege truth is a function of the proposition's being saturated or filled by the object it denotes. For example, the proposition 'The number of cats on this mat is two' is considered as true if such a corresponding state of affairs exists (see Carl 1995). Therefore any number greater than zero has a potential truth value: it can be 'saturated' by a corresponding state of affairs. In this regard, Badiou (2008, Ch. 3) considers Frege to be Leibnizian (and thus pre-Kantian). However, Frege's definition of truth as self-identity can equally be found in Kant, for whom knowledge of objects is founded on the equation 'Self=Self'.

Miller calls the 'zero-concept'.[21] There are no objects in the world that are not identical with themselves. However, unlike axiomatic set-theory which allows there to be an empty-set (subsuming no objects), in Frege's arithmetical logic the concept 'that which is not identical to itself' subsumes one object, the number zero itself (now considered as what Miller calls the 'zero-object'), and thus the number one is assigned to this concept.[22] The number one, assigned to the zero-concept, is the concept which subsumes the zero-object, thus generating the zero-object as *one* object: the one is one *zero*, and the zero is what there is *one* of.

1—The passage from 0 to 1 is a *counting-as-one* of the zero. From the number one we automatically have the concept of the number one. To the concept of the number one is assigned the number two, since the concept of the number one subsumes two objects: the zero-object and the number one (which we have seen is the number zero considered as one object, the zero-object). To the concept of the number two is assigned the number three, and so on. All numbers are thus composed solely of zeros, of *single* counts of the *zero*-object, and the number one is the conceptual operator of all bi-univocal relations (it presides over the one-to-one mapping of elements found in contiguous sets).

N + 1—We thus always have object (n-1), concept (n), number (n+1), in this ascending numerical sequence. The number three (+1) is assigned to the concept of the number two (here n=2) which subsumes three objects: the concept of the number one (1 object), the concept of the number zero (1 object), and the zero-object itself (which is not an object, -1). The number three is an excess (+1) of a number because it counts the zero-object as an object when it really is a number (making the zero-object a lack (-1) of what it was counted as). Therefore, if all objects are nested collections of collections (of zeros) there is no such thing as an object, only the counting-as-one of the zero-object.[23]

In order to illustrate the function of the zero-object as -1, let us take the example of the concept 'the number of Queens in this deck of playing cards'.[24] One would naturally assume that the number assigned to this concept should be four. But in order to establish what a 'Queen' is, we first need to know what a Queen *is not*. There is one object that stands outside the four Queens (or eighty trees) and counts them. If we are to establish what a Queen—and bi-univocally what 'four'—is, we need to find only four objects that share common features. Since there are four legs on a typical horse and on most chairs, as well as four Queens in most packs of playing cards which are not this one, it is necessary to limit the numerical extension of the concept to *this deck of cards* so that 'four' only refers to 'the number of Queens in this deck of playing cards'. The way to do this is via this concept, which limits the realm of objects whose extension is four only to this

---

21. Miller 1973.

22. Russell's paradox stems from this situation where the zero is considered as both an object and a number (see Ayer 1972, Ch. 2). Zermelo's axiom of separation attempted to save Frege from Russell's paradox by making objects belong to but no longer be *included* in (or subsumed by) their concepts, meaning that the zero-concept no longer subsumes one object and so it thus becomes an empty-set. This also changes the ontological status of the elements of a set and their relation to the subject or proposition (on both these points see Badiou 2008 and 2006b).

23. Duroux (1966) stresses the fact that the zero is a function of repetition.

24. This is an example Frege (1960, pp. 28-9) gives.

deck, cancelling out everything else whose extension is also four. In order for this to be achieved an additional object is required which cancels out all extension, rendering everything outside the concept undifferentiated, indifferent matter (Frege's 'illogical' realm).

This object is the zero. It forms a wall around the objects of the concept, rendering everything else in existence undifferentiated matter from the point of view of the concept at hand. Once we know what the Queen is not, namely everything else, which becomes cancelled, we can establish a bi-univocal correspondence between the number four and the concept 'the number of Queens in this deck of playing cards'. There are thus four objects that fall under this concept, that is to say really five: 0, 1, 2, 3, 4. The zero is the illogical realm counted as one and thus cancelled as such. By being made into the object of a concept, the illogical realm is kept at bay from logic. But the illogical, being reified as an object, also has the positive function of erecting a wall around the objects denoted by the concept, limiting the field to the playing cards in hand. The illogical is crucial for establishing the inner consistency of the logical realm and the referential power of the concept. The illogical, reified as the zero-object, is thus included in the series of whole numbers as a repeated and internal limit. What Frege calls the illogical, that which remains uncounted and outside the logical realm, is that which is not identical with itself, that which has not fallen under the influence of the concept. But Frege clearly contradicts himself by assigning the illogical a number, and thus making it into an object.

III. ZERO AS TRANSCENDENTAL SUBJECT

Frege's zero plays a double role: on the one hand it opens up the possibility of the illogical, of that which is not identical to itself, by providing this realm with a concept and by allowing there to exist a concept with no object. On the other hand, the zero-concept merely generates knowledge of its double—the zero-object—which dramatically reduces its opening towards the illogical to an object or reification that is itself the root of the logical. We see a similar movement in Kant's transcendental subject, whose faculty of sensibility opens it up to a rich manifold of sensations, but just as quickly reduces this field to conceptual forms pre-conditioned by the understanding. Kant is clear on this point: concepts are not formed out of the manifold of sensations, they are the condition of our ability to consciously apperceive the manifold, though never as it is given to the Sensibility.[25] Just as with the equation Self=Self, Frege's zero involves a zero-concept redoubling itself as a zero-object. The zero-object prevents the illogical manifold of unstructured sensations from contaminating the realm of logical objects. The manifold is always conveniently reduced to zero.[26]

---

25. For one, this can be seen in the architectonic ordering of the first *Critique*: the most important break in the primary section entitled 'Transcendental Doctrine of Elements' lies between the part devoted to the Sensibility on one hand ('Transcendental Aesthetic'), and the part devoted to the other two faculties plus Reason on the other ('Transcendental Logic'). In short, Kant emphatically bars the Sensibility from logic.

26. This contrasts sharply with axiomatic set-theory, arguably a truly non-Kantian theory, whose empty set contains no objects and where each set is the count-as-one of the 'inconsistent multiple' (see

Regarding the concept 'the number of Queens in this deck of playing cards', the only thing that does not fall under the concept is the illogical realm counted-as-one, thus we can hypothesise that the illogical has a parallel function to the Kantian manifold, since for Kant, the manifold is the excluded basis of objects of knowledge.[27] The one-manifold limits sensations to a circumscribed field that will be structured by the faculties. In other words, the erection of a barrier around the four Queens, such that everything else in existence is cancelled, is tantamount to turning the manifold of sensations into the *one* manifold that becomes structured as one object (composed of four sub-sets). All possible sensation, that is to say every possible object whose number is four, such as a horse's legs, etc., is cancelled and barred from the field circumscribed by the concept. The zero in Frege is the object that the objects of a set are not, and thus it is their common boundary or form. It is indeed the objects of the set themselves since the annulling function of the boundary eradicates everything in existence except for them.

In Kant, even before the manifold is intuited by the faculty of sensibility it must have been actively targeted so that the sensibility can be passively affected by it. It is targeted using what Kant calls the 'object=x',[28] which is the form of the object in general and which is projected onto the manifold by the faculty of the understanding prior to the sensibility's possible interaction with it.[29] The object=x is the objective corollary of what Kant calls the transcendental subject's function of 'originary apperception' or *Einheit* (meaning *unicity*),[30] which Badiou defines as the 'counting-as-one' of the manifold.[31] The object=x provides the transcendental form of the object in general, as distinct from all empirical objects, and this form is counted-as-one by synthetic apperception (the 'pure concept'[32] of the object=x), by the function of unicity, of the 1.

Badiou 2008; Badiou 2006a, p. 138)—roughly parallel to Frege's 'illogical' realm—rather than of the zero-object.

27. See Kant 2007, p. 104, p. 118.

28. See Gardner (1999, pp. 127-132), for a clear overview of the Kantian object=x. Kant himself describes this 'transcendental [...] non-empirical' object as 'an object corresponding to, and therefore also distinct from, our knowledge' (Kant 2007, p. 141, p. 135). Kant also claims that the object=x's 'elements must necessarily, in reference to this object, agree with each other, that is, possess that unity which constitutes the concept of an object' (p. 135), which directly accords with the zero in our example of the Four Queens. Kant reinforces this point later on, saying that only the 'pure concept' of the object=x 'can provide for all our empirical concepts in general a reference to an object, or objective reality' (p. 141), and 'the necessary unity of consciousness, and therefore also of the synthesis of the manifold [...] [is] combine[d] in one representation' (p. 142).

29. See Badiou 2006a, pp. 136-138.

30. See Gardner 1999. See also Lacan, Seminar IX. *L'identification* (unpublished), lesson of 21/2/1962.

31. Badiou 2006a, p. 136. Badiou argues that 'the existent-correlate [the object] of originary apperception conceived as non-existent operation of the counting-as-one is not, strictly speaking, the object, but rather the form of the object in general—which is to say, that absolutely indeterminate being from which the very fact that there is an object originates [...] And we also know that x is the pure or inconsistent multiple, and hence that the object, in so far as it is the correlate of the apparent binding, is devoid of being' (p. 138). This 'inconsistent multiple' would correspond to the annulled realm outside the manifold counted-as-one, which I referred to earlier, with the object=x functioning both as determination of the manifold counted-as-one, and, retroactively, as indeterminacy of everything which lies outside it, as we saw with our Four Queens example. Here we see all senses of the term *Einheit* simultaneously at work.

32. Kant 2007, p. 141.

Austin says in his translation of *The Foundations* that in Frege's usage, *Einheit* also covers unity and unit (synthesis), oneness and one, as well as indeterminacy (the unruly manifold).[33] While agreeing with Kant that number, which is always *Einheit*—the number one, is *a priori*, for Frege it is *analytic*,[34] which is to say intrinsic to the concept, and not *synthetic*, which requires a subject to mediate between one or more concepts. In *The Critique of Pure Reason*, Kant defines arithmetic truths as *a priori* and synthetic, not analytic, making arithmetic dependent on a subject capable of synthesis. But in *The Foundations* Frege reverses this in order to found arithmetic and logic on number itself. Frege explicitly contrasts his approach with Kant's in the introduction to *The Foundations*, and while he says it is only a minor quibble, and that otherwise he admires the philosopher's work, we can see that it in fact constitutes a direct attack on Kant's transcendental subject. For example, elsewhere in *The Foundations* Frege claims that 'the concept has the power of collecting together far superior to the unifying power of synthetic apperception'.[35] To illustrate the function of the *Einheit* in Frege, let us take the proposition 'two cats are sitting on this mat'. We do not count the first cat as such, we count it as a pure indeterminate form of the object whose only property is its unicity, since we do not yet know what a 'cat' is. The first cat is an *Einheit*, a zero counted as one. Since the concept 'cat' is only established simultaneously with our understanding of what 'two' refers to, in the proposition 'two cats are sitting on this mat', the first cat we count cannot be judged to be a cat, since we have not yet counted both cats, and so cannot know what either 'two', or 'cat', are. Only with the second cat can we know that the first one was a cat all along, and what 'two' and 'cat' refer to. With the first cat we are testing this object to see if it falls under the concept 'cat' to the power of two, that is if it is a cat to the same extent that the cat next to it is one, and if it is, then the first cat will have already been a cat, but only after the second cat is counted. Indeed every object is a zero counted as one. *We do not actually count the second cat as an object*, we merely extend the concept to the second cat.[36] The first cat, while not being a concept, only the form of the object in general—the object=x, the zero—is the only thing that is counted. We therefore have three objects: the first cat as object=x or zero; the second cat as one; the first cat as one, which appears retroactively, and simultaneously with the second cat.

If Frege wishes to establish an objective, anti-psychologistic arithmetical logic founded on number itself (essentially on the number one's conceptual bi-univocal relations with the zero), he needs to prove that the one, *Einheit*, does not depend on a subject. Yet, Russell's paradox, which ensues from the counting-as-one of the zero (namely the one's dependence on the zero), demonstrates that Frege does not succeed in logically grounding number. It is no coincidence that his entire theory founders on what we have shown to be the site of the transcendental subject, which his theory appears to fold into number itself—thus destabilising

33. Austin 1960, p. 39.
34. Frege 1960, p. 55, p. 5.
35. Ibid., p. 61.
36. Ibid., p. 63.

it—rather than eliminate. When considered as a (post-)Kantian theory, however, *The Foundations* does not fail, rather it offers us a *syntactical* transcendental mechanism which replaces Kant's faculties, and makes the transcendental subject's lack of self-identity explicit: the subject still identifies itself with the manifold of sensations counted as one, but rather than having 'Self=Self' we now have $0=1$, $1=2$, $2=3$, and so on. Both of these modifications give us a transcendental logic more amenable to a Lacanian structure and subject.

IV. THE LOGIC OF THE SIGNIFIER

> From the Kantian *Einheit*, we consider that we pass to [the
> Freudian] *Einzigkeit*.
> (Lacan, Seminar IX)

According to Lacan's classic formulation from the early nineteen-sixties 'a signifier is that which represents the subject for another signifier'.[37] This formulation is taken up again in the late sixties in Lacan's so-called 'discourse of the master',[38] where it is presented in an extremely clear and concise way, and in which we also find a reference to the object (a), lacking in the earlier formulation. The discourse of the master is written as follows, and should be read as a horseshoe movement (∩), from bottom left ($), to bottom right (a):

$$S_1 \;\rightarrow\; S_2$$

$$\text{---} \qquad \text{---}$$

$$\$ \;//\; a$$

In the rest of this article I will sketch out this horseshoe movement, and extract from it some elements of the logic of the signifier which directly build on the preceding pages. The aim of this is to contextualise the logic of the signifier in Kant and Frege's logics and their conceptions of the object.

S_1

We begin not with the split subject, but actually with the instance of the letter, its vertical eruption from out of the void, locating the letter or S_1 at the top left of the schema. We will examine the letter's logical function in more detail later; for now the letter is language's pre-signifying materiality, its components or elements prior to the genesis of meaning. Let us focus on the letter's relation to the subject. If we go back to the two cats sitting on a mat, we saw how the first cat was not an object but an object=x. The subject of the proposition, the two cats, are sutured to the state of affairs by this object=x. The object=x acts as a stand-in or place-holder for a subject yet to emerge, yet which is also grounded in this object=x.

For Lacan the proposition is fundamentally spoken by a subject,[39] following the model of psychoanalysis as the 'talking cure'. In the proposition—my speech—I must identify with something that does not yet exist, namely the words

---

37. Lacan 2006, p. 350.

38. See Lacan 2007.

39. Prioritising speech over writing, Lacan considers language to be fundamentally linked to speech, be it inner speech (and what we would typically call 'thought'), or actual cases of enunciation.

I utter or think prior to them bearing any meaning (more specifically the words that take on the logical function of the 'first cat' or object=x). The letter as suture is the materiality of my speech (or thought), something 'I' must identify with even though it is not me, something which is prior to and constitutive of the emergence of myself as subject of a meaningful proposition.

Miller explicitly argues in 'The Suture (elements of the logic of the signifier)' that the Fregean zero-object is the subject of Lacanian psychoanalysis.[40] Through the 'dead letter' or suture, the (lack of a) subject is counted as one.[41] The subject ($ \mathcal{S} $) not yet existing, the letter (S1) names the lack of a subject (o); it embodies this lack as a positivity, as a one (+1), thus retroactively installing a lack in the subject (-1) from the viewpoint of the number series (language or the Symbolic), due to what Lacan had earlier called an 'error of counting'.[42]

In Lacan's 'structuralist' period the letter would have been more readily associated with the phallus, which the subject becomes identified with thus leading to its lack. For example in *Le séminaire livre IV: la relation d'objet (1956-1957)* the phallus is what the mother lacks since she is deprived of it, and so by identifying with the phallus during the dialectic of recognition of the Oedipus Complex, the subject identifies with a lack. Moreover, it objectively lacks what it identifies with. Arguably from around *Le séminaire livre X: L'angoisse (1962-1963)* onwards, the subject no longer identifies with the phallus but with *itself as lack*, giving rise to the *objet petit a*[43] which is the subject objectified. The subject no longer objectively lacks that which it identifies with, since the lack is purely *subject-ive*. While the phallus had been considered as objectively belonging to the structure of language, and as tying the subject to structure on account of its identification with the phallus, the *objet petit a* is now considered as the insertion of the subject into structure. In Lacan the *objet petit a* is the subject in object-form (as we saw with the zero-object, which Miller calls the subject): it counts the subject as one (object). From the point of view of language this element is a lack since it is not a signifier and so cannot refer to an object (for Miller an object, insofar as it is one, is a signifier[44]). This element marks the lack of an object, from the point of view of language. But objectively this element is an excess since it does not belong to language, unlike the phallus.

The subject identifies itself with language, via the suture or dead letter, inserting excess (+1) into language. But once inside language the subject is actually internally barred from it since the dead letter is excluded from the other signifi-

---

40. Miller 1973, p. 32. 'The impossible object, which the logic of discourse summons as the not-identical with itself [...] we name this object, in so far as it functions as the excess which operates in the series of numbers, the subject'. See the second section of the present article for a reminder of the dynamics of lack and excess in the number series. The object is an excess from the viewpoint of the number series (number counts it as one when it is in fact not one).

41. Ibid., p. 26.

42. See Seminar IX. *L'identification* (unpublished), lesson of 7/3/1962.

43. See Chiesa 2007, for a clear account of these two stages in Lacan's thought.

44. As Miller puts it in Lacan's Seminar XII. *Problèmes cruciaux pour la psychanalyse* (unpublished), lesson of 2/6/1965, signifiers are identical with themselves, which is Frege's definition of a number or quantified object. But for Miller they are only identical with themselves on account of something that is not identical with itself: the $ \mathcal{S} $ as zero.

ers. We saw that the first cat retroactively becomes a one, in our earlier example of two cats sitting on a mat. The first cat, the dead letter, is repressed from number, from the realm of objects. Similarly, the subject is rejected from the sentence it speaks. For Lacan structure becomes non-totalisable, it is not a complete set but constitutively incomplete or ex-centric, just like the finite cardinals.

Miller envisages in Frege's move from the 0 to the 1 the counting of the zero or subject as a number or signifier. The lack of the subject is determined *as* the subject. The subject's lack or absence is counted as a one (as a presence), and thus its absence is given presence: the subject is determined as a subject who is present in language, as an absence (-1). The subject's initial self-determination-as-lack (rather than its lack of the phallus) enables it to be present within the system of language. Rather than simply misidentifying with a phallus which would entail a lack of identity for the subject, the subject is *lured* into identifying with itself as lack.[45] Similarly, in Frege the counting of the zero as a one makes the zero exist in number as a number and subsist in number as a lack, both of which are mutually dependent operations.

$S_1 \rightarrow S_2$

Lacan argues in Seminar IX (1961-1962) that the letter's function must be understood in terms of a *proper name*. The proper name is a privileged signifier since it names something (a subject) that does not exist prior to its own nomination and entry into language. This is something we missed out earlier regarding Frege: for Frege, proper names are already ones and do not require the syntactical calculus of the proposition to be quantified;[46] indeed the latter depends to some degree on proper names. In Seminar IX Lacan considers that every letter has a name, as does Miller, for whom every number functions as the 'unifying name of a set'.[47] There is nonetheless a privileged letter, the proper name, which, building on Russell, Lacan defines as a '"word for particular" a word to designate particular things as such [...] [such as] the "this"'.[48] The proper name is crucial for counting the subject as one. This is true both for one's own proper name, and for the subject of a proposition. In language, the proper name and privileged indexicals such as 'this' have the pre-established form of the *Einheit*: they count as one the subject and provide the pivot for the bi-univocal relations pertaining to the rest of the proposition.

Miller tells us that 'the 1, as the proper name of a number, is to be distinguished from that which comes to fix in a [unary] trait the zero [...] [T]he trait of the identical represents the non-identical'.[49] Lacan's 'unary trait', most fully developed in Seminar IX, refers to *pre-numerical multiplicities without identity* (and as pri-

---

45. See Miller 1973 and Miller 1968.

46. David-Ménard 2009, p. 145, points this out, in connection with psychoanalysis. From a different angle, in 'On Sense and Meaning' (1980) Frege asserts that each complete proposition is itself a proper name.

47. Miller 1973, p. 31.

48. Lacan, Seminar IX. *L'identification* (unpublished), lesson of 20/12/1961. Chiesa (2006) argues that Lacan's notion of the letter, as found in Seminar IX, should be read as an attempt to develop a set-theoretical model of the unconscious.

49. Miller 1973, p. 32.

or to binary or bi-univocal relations). Unary traits are distinctive marks which are not yet signifiers since they do not enter into syntactical relations with other signifiers. As such they are pre-numerical, in Frege's sense.[50] What is interesting here for our purposes is that Lacan explicitly compares the unary trait to the Kantian *Einheit* and manifold of sensations: 'Kant['s] transcendental aesthetic,[51] I believe in it: simply I believe that his is not the right one because precisely it is [...] of a space which first of all is *not one*'.[52] Earlier we saw that in Kant (and Frege) the manifold was counted-as-one and formed as a zero. Similarly, for Lacan the manifold—composed of pre-numerical multiplicities or unary traits—must be counted-as-one. But Lacan is more aware of the deforming character of this count-as-one. Counting the manifold as one (one zero) deforms it since it is 'first of all not one': it is irreducible to cardinal number. Lacan uses the topological figure of the torus (or doughnut) to account for this: counting the manifold as one instates a hole or lack within its very surface. Counting the (set of) unary trait(s) as one thus generates an object-ive lack (-1), rather than merely a zero. The unary trait and its count-as-one not only give the manifold of sensations an organising axis or pivot—a privileged set of material markers—they also react on those very markers, causing them to circumscribe an objective lack in the manifold itself. This lack goes on to function in a way paralleling the object=x.

For Miller, number (the 1) distinguishes itself from the zero, which is 'fixed in a [unary] trait'.[53] The unary trait is counted as a zero (when it is in fact a -1), in order to found the 1, the proper name, which counts the zero (the subject) as one. The zero re-presents the (imaginary) unary trait as a (symbolic) zero counted-as-one by the proper name. As such the zero is an illusion because the manifold and number are of two different orders, contra Frege (and Kant). In Lacan's discourse of the master, S_1 comes to be distinguished from S_2 because unlike S_2, S_1 is a split signifier: originally a unary trait, it is re-presented as a signifier or 1. The unary trait is repressed from language at the same time that it is represented in language by S_1 (the letter or proper name). The split unary trait / S_1 compound is the basis for all other signifiers: they are identical with themselves because the first signifier is not. In the symbolic, the realm of language, S_1 is distinguished from all other signifiers (S_2) and thus is non-identical with them. This makes signifiers as a whole not identical with themselves insofar as S_1 is also a signifier from the viewpoint of S_2. Following Frege's requirements, signifiers must be identical with themselves in order to function in propositions bi-univocally and express objects in states of affairs. However they are not and so they cannot.

$S_1 \rightarrow S_2/a$ and $a \rightarrow \$$

The (imaginary) unary trait's repression from S_2 (and more generally the sym-

---

50. Chiesa (2006) agrees that this notion of number should be understood in terms of axiomatic set theory, which is opposed to Frege's understanding of number on several counts. Unary traits are precisely pre-numerical or illogical for Frege, but numerical for axiomatic set-theory.

51. Kant deals with the sensibility and the manifold in this part of the *Critique of Pure Reason*.

52. Lacan, Seminar IX. *L'identification* (unpublished), lesson of 7/3/1962.

53. See Miller 1973.

bolic) causes it to return (in the real) as the *objet petit a*.[54] In Seminar XIV (1966-1967), Lacan tells us that Russell's paradox (that Frege's zero cannot belong to a set as one of its elements and act as the boundary of a set at the same time) is 'not at all a paradox'.[55] Against Russell's early attempts in logic to develop a metalanguage, Lacan holds that 'there is no Universe of discourse'. The whole is holed and the uni-verse of discourse (the Other or set of all signifiers) lacks at least one signifier (S1).[56] In *The Foundations* Frege had—problematically, for Russell—argued that the zero figures both inside and outside the number series. In Lacan's view, this is actually *required* for any symbolic system to function.[57] Since the zero is dual—being linked both to the unary trait and S1—it straddles the inside and outside of the symbolic or logico-numerical domain, and being dual, it also does not fully belong to any number or set, always having one foot outside, thus saving it from Russell's paradox, which is only a paradox if we consider the zero to be a unitary entity. However, Frege's logic, for Lacan, can only be saved from Russell's paradox if we consider that numbers are signifiers (or letters), and therefore not identical with themselves (since S1 is excluded from S2). Not being identical with themselves (when considered as a w-hole), signifiers cannot logically denote objects in states of affairs, as numbers (which are identical with themselves) had done in *The Foundations*. Therefore, signifiers must denote the *objet petit a*, the logical referent of every (necessarily spoken) proposition. Though, this is after all also the case in Frege, since we saw earlier that in actual fact the zero or object=x is the only thing that is ever counted in a state of affairs.

The *objet petit a* is what distances Lacan's logic of phantasy[58] from *The Foundations*' explicit intentions, as well as from Frege's *Sinn/Bedeutung* distinction, if not from what we have shown can be unearthed in Frege's argument. Lacan tells us that 'the o-object [*objet petit a*] is the first *Bedeutung*, the first referent, the first reality'.[59] *Bedeutung* is Frege's term for the referent of a proposition rather than its signification or meaning (its *Sinn*). All propositions produce signifieds, which are a function of the metonymic displacement of meaning through a chain of signifiers, culminating in a single meaning which signifies the entire proposition.[60] However, below the level of meaning lies a further signified (or referent) which is always the same *objet petit a*, regardless of the sentence at hand.[61] Not only are sig-

---

54. It is tempting to consider Lacan's logic as a *logic of expression*, one that ontologically produces its objects during the very process of describing them. See Jean Hyppolite's *Logic and Existence* (1997).

55. Lacan, Seminar XIV. *La logique du fantasme* (unpublished), lesson of 16/11/1966.

56. This takes us back to the subject as *objet petit a*, inserted into language as an objective excess and a subject-ive lack. See the point I made earlier in this section.

57. Again, the subject as *objet petit a* inserted into structure is objectively a lack (zero-object) and subjectively an excess (zero-concept).

58. It is difficult to tell if this also holds for Miller's logic of the signifier. The zero is considered to be the subject, not the object (a), in Miller, but since the object (a) is the subject in object-form, it is not clear-cut whether or not the object (a) could also be the object of propositions in the logic of the signifier. André Green, for one, identifies the *objet petit a* with the suture, and with the function of the zero, in 'The logic of Lacan's objet (a) and Freudian Theory: Convergences and Questions' (1966), delivered and written around the same time as 'The Suture (elements of the logic of the signifier)'.

59. Lacan, Seminar XIV. *La logique du fantasme* (unpublished), lesson of 16/11/1966.

60. See ibid.

61. Lacan calls this level 'the structure insofar as it is real' (ibid., lesson of 1/2/1967).

nifieds a function of signifiers, but so is the referent, and all propositions generate the same one (the *objet petit a*). The *objet petit a* or *Bedeutung* is connected to phantasy because it has a '"stoppered" [*bouché*] aspect'.[62]. It is tempting to think that if the unary trait generates an objective lack in the manifold (or torus), the *objet petit a* is what attempts to 'stop' up that hole or lack by depositing an objective referent in its place.

Initially the *objet petit a* is the return of the repressed S1, though ultimately it is repressed from the state of affairs it founds, thereby giving rise to the $. Similarly, we saw earlier how the object=x or zero is re-counted in every set or number, all the while being un-presentable in the state of affairs as such. The object of the state of affairs, the *objet petit a*, is the subject in objectified form,[63] but the final stage of the discourse of the master involves this object now being repressed from the state of affairs and separated from the subject ($), who is now split between himself as (conscious) object, and himself as (unconscious) subject.[64] Referring back to our matrix of the discourse of the master, the passage from subject to object terminates in a repression or separation (//) of the object from the subject, and from the state of affairs. In the example of two cats sitting on a mat, the first cat disjunctively sutures the proposition to a state of affairs at the same time that it disappears from this site. While we saw that Frege's subject was out of step with itself, the logical realm nonetheless retained the appearance of clear and distinct perceptions. Arguably, the zero (or *objet petit a*) 'balances' Frege's unbalanced equation (Self=Self+1), by subtracting the +1 of identification. Once we have had one 'revolution' of the discourse of the master (the circular movement from S1 to $), we will have cancelled one numerical degree of imbalance, and created the illusion of an identity between S1 and $ (Self=Self).

Both Lacan and Miller bypass the basic logical paradoxes that one finds in Frege's arithmetical logic because they logically thematise the role played by the subject rather than suturing it, as Frege does. The subject is not identical with itself and thus cannot be completely included in any set. This leads to Russell's paradox only if the subject (zero) is considered to be a single entity, following Kant, rather than two (zero-object and zero-concept, object and subject respectively), following Lacan. Lacan's split subject is itself composed of a subject and an object, rather than two subjects (as in Kant's Self=Self). In a sense, this provides Frege, in Lacan's and Miller's reading, with an axiom of separation,[65] since the elements of a set can belong to but cannot be included in it: the object maintains a disjunctive connection with the subject.[66] It is thanks to Lacan's and Mill-

---

62. Ibid., lesson of 25/1/1967. Briefly, in Seminar XIV the unconscious is structured according to the phantasy $-a. The subject is both connected to and shielded from the *objet petit a*, the 'object-cause' of desire, which both protects the subject against the trauma of lack, *and* frames and enables that very lack (the *lure*).

63. Recall how in the second Lacan the subject is inserted into language or structure (S2) through identification (S1), giving rise to the *objet petit a*.

64. This gives rise to the formula of phantasy: $-a.

65. See note 22 of the present article.

66. This goes some way to accounting for the enduring proximity between Badiou's theory of subjectivity, which is based on axiomatic set theory (which we saw arose partly from Zermelo's axiom of separation, which attempted to save Frege from Russell's paradox), and Miller's, which, in 'The Suture (el-

er's identification of the (already dual) zero with Lacan's split subject that Frege's logic can be saved from the paradoxes it inherited, in part, from Kant's self-identical subject.

BIBLIOGRAPHY

Ayer, A. J., *Russell*, London: Fontana, 1972

Badiou, A., 'Kant's Subtractive Ontology', in *Theoretical Writings*, London: Continuum, 2006a

―― *Being and Event*, London: Continuum, 2006b

―― *Number and Numbers*, London: Polity Press, 2008

Carl, W., *Frege's Theory of Sense and Reference. Its Origins and Scope*, Cambridge: Cambridge University Press, 1995

Chiesa, L., 'Count-as-One, Forming-into-One, Unary Trait, S1', *Cosmos and History: The Journal of Natural and Social Philosophy*, Vol. 2, No. 1-2, 2006

―― *Subjectivity and Otherness: A Philosophical Reading of Lacan*, Cambridge MA: MIT Press, 2007

Currie, G., *Frege. An Introduction to his Philosophy*, Brighton: The Harvester Press, 1982

David-Ménard, M., *Les constructions de l'universel. Psychanalyse, philosophie*, Paris: Quadrige PUF, 2009

Deleuze, G., and Guattari, F., *What is Philosophy?* London: Verso Books, 1994

Dummett, M., *Frege—Philosophy of Mathematics*, London: Duckworth, 1991

Duroux, Y., 'Psychologie et logique', *Cahiers pour l'analyse* (1.2), published by le Cercle d'Epistémologie de l'Ecole Normale Supérieure, 1966

Frege, G., 'Über Sinn und Bedeutung (On Sense and Meaning)', in *Translations from the Philosophical Writings of Gottlob Frege*, Oxford: Basil Blackwell, 1980 [1892]

―― *The Foundations of Arithmetic: A Logico-Mathematical Enquiry into the Concept of Number*, 2nd ed., trans. J. L. Austin, New York: Harper & Brothers, 1960 [1884]

Gardner, S., *Kant and the Critique of Pure Reason*, London: Routledge, 1999

Green, A., 'L'objet (a) de Jacques Lacan, sa logique et la théorie freudienne', *Cahiers pour l'analyse* (3.2), published by le Cercle d'Epistémologie de l'Ecole Normale Supérieure, 1966

Hyppolite, J., *Logic and Existence*, New York: State University of New York Press, 1997 [1952]

Kant, I., *Critique of Pure Reason*, trans. and ed. by M. Weigelt, London: Penguin Classics, 2007 [1787]

Lacan, J., *Le séminaire livre IV. La relation d'objet: 1956-7*, Paris: Seuil, 1998

―― 'The Subversion of the Subject and the Dialectic of Desire in the Freudian Unconscious', in *Ecrits: A Selection*, trans. A. Sheridan, London: Tavistock/Routledge, 2006 [1960]

―――――――――――――――――――――――――――――――――

ements of the logic of the signifier)', is based on Frege's arithmetical logic (plus the Lacanian axiom of separation). See Badiou commenting on his relation to Miller's appropriation of Frege (Badiou 2008, p. 29).

—— *Seminar XVII. The Other side of Psychoanalysis: 1969-70*, London: W. W. Norton & Co., 2007

Miller, J.-A., 'Suture (elements of the logic of the signifier)', in *Screen* 18:4 (Winter 1977-78), trans. J. Rose, 1973 [1966]

—— 'L'action de la structure', *Cahiers pour l'analyse* (9.6), published by le Cercle d'Epistémologie de l'Ecole Normale Supérieure, 1968

Sluga, H., *Gottlob Frege*, London: Routledge, 2008

Metapsychology of Freedom: Symptom and Subjectivity in Lacan

Raoul Moati

INTRODUCTION: REVISITING INTERPELLATION

We now know the central role played by Lacanian psychoanalysis in Althusser's reworking of the concept of ideology inherited from Marx.[1] In many ways, the Freudian theory of the unconscious, and Lacan's return to it, had a decisive influence on Althusser's renewal of the Marxist description of ideological mechanisms' efficiency in subjecting individuals to the established social order. We will be focusing on one of these mechanisms in particular, the Althusserian motif of 'ideological interpellation', since it is directly inspired by Lacan's theory. In fact, the Lacanian theory of subjectivation, as a tight dependence of the subject on the Symbolic order which institutes him, is one of the fundamental sources of inspiration for the Althusserian theory of the subject's constitution through ideological interpellation. For Althusser, ideology is the basis for turning individuals into *subjects*; the French philosopher in fact affirms that '*all ideology hails or interpellates concrete individuals as concrete subjects*, by the functioning of the category of the subject'.[2] By recognising itself in the interpellation that comes to it from an ideological authority (police, state, religion), the individual is constituted as *subject*, and this happens through its subjection to the instituted 'Law', which motivates its interpellation and assigns it a defined subjective position to identify with: 'Ideology "acts" or "functions" in such a way that it "recruits" individuals as subjects among individuals (it recruits them all), or "transforms" individuals into subject (it transforms them all), by this very precise operation which we call *interpellation*, which we can think of in terms of the most basic, everyday police (or not) hailing: "Hey, you there!"'.[3]

As Pascale Gillot[4] pertinently remarks in her book, this mechanism is based on the model of the subject of the unconscious's subjection to the Symbolic Law

---

1. We are referring to the important book by Pascale Gillot, *Althusser et la psychanalyse* (Gillot 2009). We will also draw on the text by Franck Fischbach '"Les sujets marchent tout seuls": Althusser-Butler-Žižek', in Fischbach 2009, pp. 212-232.

2. Althusser 1971, p. 173.

3. Ibid, p. 174.

4. Gillot 2009, p. 122.

proposed by Lacan. In his text on 'Freud and Lacan',[5] Althusser wrote that 'every step man's child climbs up falls under the reign of the Law, under the code of summons, under the code of human and non-human communication', so that 'his "satisfactions" carry in themselves the indelible and constitutive mark of the Law, of human Law's pretences, which like any law are "ignored" by no one'.[6] Moreover, in 'Ideology and Ideological State Apparatuses',[7] in order to describe ideological mechanisms of subjection, Althusser draws on the notion of the 'Other Subject' (with capitals), which is without any doubt directly inspired by Lacan's 'big Other'. Let us remind ourselves that the expression 'Other Subject' is not only the retranslation, in Althusser's lexicon, of the Lacanian 'big Other', but also one which belongs from the very outset to Lacan's teaching, especially the early Lacan (of the 1950s), which Althusser was specifically influenced by.

In his early teachings, Lacan in fact insists on the idea that the big Other effectively defines itself as an Other Subject. In Seminar II, Lacan can thus affirm that 'analysis must aim at the passage of true speech, which joins the subject to another subject, on the other side of the wall of language'.[8]

In Althusser, it is via the interpellation coming from this Other Subject, which Althusser calls, not without continuity with Lacan, 'the big Subject of subjects' (God *par excellence* in religious ideology), that the process of subjective identification in ideological interpellation is accomplished. Besides, in Althusser, the subject, in identifying itself with the interpellation that comes to it from the Other Subject, and in accordance with a mechanism of reciprocity, recognises itself through the Other's recognition, to which it owes its own recognition of self. We can clearly not avoid thinking about Lacan's early communication schemas (notably the L-schema), and about the reciprocal link *constitutive* of the Subject and of the big Other, as 'Other Subject', which they represent.

In the early Lacan, the big Other is in fact defined as an 'Other Subject', whose function is to constitute the subject of the unconscious by its being assigned to a determined symbolic imperative. Yet, such an imperative is only really constitutive of a subject—that is to say it binds itself fully to the symbolic imperative prescribed by the big Other as 'Other Subject'—only insofar as the subject is capable of *taking upon itself* the symbolic imperative, which comes from the Other, in what Lacan calls 'full speech'.[9] 'Full speech' duplicates the institution of the symbolic pact which links the Subject to the big Other as instituting 'Other Subject', and by this very act of language, perfects its subjective assignation to the symbolic imperative which is prescribed to him by the big Other. If we use the famous example given by Lacan of 'full speech', where the subject affirms 'you are my master', this speech has nothing assertive about it;[10] it takes up again, in inverted form, the instituting act of the Other, through which the ac-

---

5. Althusser 1976.

6. Ibid., p. 27 quoted by Gillot 2009, p. 128.

7. This is the final section of *Lenin and Philosophy and Other Essays* (Althusser 1971).

8. Lacan 1991, p. 246.

9. Cf. Lacan, 'The Function and Field of Speech and Language in Psychoanalysis', in Lacan 2006.

10. On this point, we refer the reader to our article, 'The Performative from Ordinary Conventions to the Real' (Moati 2008).

knowledgement of the Other, as my master, guarantees my position of disciple. This taking up again of the instituting act is not in any way an auto-institution; rather, Lacan insists on the *constitutive* dependence of the position of the subject on the 'Other Subject' (or big Other)'s position, from whom the subject receives its own message 'in inverted form'. If the instituting message comes from the Other, it has *instituting effects* starting only from the moment when the subject repeats this instituting speech in its inverted form, which is to say by the accomplishment of a *reciprocal* recognition which ends the instituting process inaugurated by the Other. By recognising the Other as his master, the subject converts the Other's message into *instituting speech*, through which, inevitably, at the same time, the subject reaches its symbolic position of disciple:

> The *You are my woman* or the *You are my master*, which means—*You are what is still within my speech, and this I can only affirm by speaking in your place. This comes from you to find the certainty of what I pledge. This speech is speech that commits you.* The unity of speech insofar as it founds the position of the two subjects is made apparent here. (Lacan 1993, pp. 36-37)

In the early Lacan, it is also important to distinguish between two completely opposed forms of identification: the first is imaginary identification with the Ego, which Lacan reduces to a function of 'misrecognition' ('The subject "mis-recognises" itself in its relation to the mirror'[11]). The second is the identification of the subject with its symbolic imperative, which is to say with its place within the network of signifiers (in the Symbolic Order), and with its position as subject in relation to the symbolic Other. In the early Lacan, the second mode of identification is privileged over the first. Moreover, from a certain moment onwards in Lacan's teaching, more specifically from 1964 and Seminar XI, we can say that Lacan rejects these two options. Starting from this date, the end of the analytic cure, far from still representing the adjustment of the subject to the instituting symbolic order, as was the case in the Lacan of the 1950s, consists in what Lacan calls 'subjective destitution'. How has it been possible to pass from one theoretical position to another, and in such a scenario, how can, in light of this second position, Lacanian theory represent a theoretical apparatus capable of disconnecting subjectivity from its symbolic subjection? We will see that understanding Lacan's dialectics, which he calls 'alienation' and 'separation' in Seminar XI (Ch. XVI), will prove decisive for thinking subjectivity beyond its reduction to the symbolic imperative which interpellates it from the position of the Other. If, for the early Lacan, the finality of the analytic cure amounted to the subject's acceptance of the symbolic imperative which instituted it from the position of the Other, on the contrary, for the later Lacan, it is absolutely clear that this is not the case. It is quite interesting to note that from the moment that Althusser used Lacan's communication schemas, adapting them to the Marxist issues of describing mechanisms of ideological interpellation, Lacan was distancing himself from the absolutism of this model. Taking up again the Marxist concept of 'alienation' within psychoanalysis, Lacan reduced its importance such that it no longer had hegemonic status; in fact, Seminar XI of 1964 is consecrated to a theory about the end of 'alienation',

---

11. Lacan, Seminar IX. *L'identification* (unpublished), lesson of 13/6/1962.

through what Lacan calls 'separation' and 'subjective destitution'. Although Althusser was inspired by Lacan when forging his concept of 'ideological interpellation', we can also understand why, in his theoretical debate with Judith Butler about the possibility of going beyond subjection to an ideological imperative,
Slavoj Žižek could call himself a Lacanian in order to overcome the Althusserian
reduction of the subject to its 'being-interpellated' by the big Other. As for Judith
Butler, although she often refers to Lacan, she draws on Austin's theory of 'performativity', as reworked by Derrida,[12] in what she proposes for the overcoming
of the conditions of ideological interpellation. In the field of contemporary continental philosophy, between Lacan and Derrida (on the topic of 'performativity'),
we can see two competing models being developed to deal with the overcoming
of Althusserian apparatuses of interpellation.

One of the objectives of the present paper is to attempt to answer each of
these philosophers. Thus, although the theoretical thesis which we are trying to
formulate draws on Lacan, and therefore will be closer to Žižek's position than to
Butler's, we will attempt to develop a perspective, using Lacan's theory, which di-
verges from Žižek's position on a number of points. We will attempt to highlight
how Žižek's theoretical apparatus loses sight of what is at stake in the Lacanian
'separation' of the subject from the Symbolic Order. By synthesizing the thought
of Lacan and Hegel, encompassing the clinic of the psychoses and the motif of
'madness' in German Idealism, the Slovenian philosopher defines subjectivity by
its irreducibility to ideological interpellation; we will seek to explain why Žižek's
synthesis is unsatisfactory. However, in order to do this, we will firstly have to
come back to the subversive tension which Butler claims to install in the mechanism of ideological interpellation, notably by using the notion of 'performativity'
inherited from Austin, and reworked under the guidance of Derrida. We will attempt to criticize, on the one hand, Butler's evacuation of the notion of the *subject*, which seems incompatible with the very notion of performativity (and more
generally of symbolic efficiency), and on the other, Žižek's assimilation of subjectivity with the psychotic suspension of the 'night of the world' (Hegel), which
appears to be far from what Lacan means by 'separation', something which, for
us, rather rests on the notion of 'symptom'. On first glance, we can say that from
a Lacanian point of view, Butler's insistence on the subject's irreducibility to apparatuses of interpellation in fact amounts to the exact opposite of the alienation
that such an irreducibility claims to subvert.

I. ALIENATION, INTERPELLATION, IDENTITY

According to Butler, Althusser's theory does not succeed in taking into account
interpellation's failure to exhaustively realize the subjection it aims to achieve.
Thus, Althusserian interpellation will never succeed in fully realizing the subject's identification with its interpellated identity. According to Butler, interpellation, in the Althusserian sense, cannot 'fully constitute the subject it names'.[13]

---

12. For a clarification of Derrida's interpretation of Austin's concept of 'speech acts', we refer the reader to our enquiry into the question in Moati 2009.

13. Butler 1997, p. 129.

The reason Butler puts forward to explain why the subject's identification with its interpellated identity cannot be *exhaustive*, comes down to the irreducibility of the subject's *being* with its *identity*. For Butler, the subject's *being*, in opposition to its *identity*, is defined by its ability to resist any identification. Butler insists on the fact that, far from being assignable to a substantial and positive identification, the subject's being must be understood as 'a potentiality which no interpellation can exhaust'.[14] *Being*, in Butler's sense, would thus amount to not being identical with the identity assigned to me by the Other Subject, such that this crack within the process of interpellation—if it 'saps the subject's capacity for "being' identical with itself"'[15]—engenders the possibility of reforming and resignifying the identity interpellation assigns. For Butler, the subject, on account of the fact that it *is*, manages not to emancipate itself from its interpellated identity—for example so that it can choose another one—but rather to create the distanciation needed to reinvent its identity's significations, giving rise to new forms of subjectivation, allowing there to be as much subversion of the interpellated identity that the subject was primordially subjected to. Also, for Butler, this act of counter-subjection relies on the subjected identity's reiterable gesture of 'performative reconfiguration'. In Butler's work, such a gesture presupposes the recognition of the unsurpassable nature of ideological assignation, or, in Lacanian terms, of the 'alienation' of the symbolic order. Besides, this is what she asserts repeatedly in her work, and notably in *The Psychic Life of Power*, where she can contend that 'all mobilizations against subjection find their resources in subjection'.[16] Yet Lacan, in his reading of Sartre which guides his analyses of the imaginary stage, had shown that the reiteration of the hiatus lying between the subject and its imaginary identity, far from being paradoxical, did not in any way represent the failure of specular alienation, but instead its very *productive* mode, the mode *par excellence* of the identification of the subject with its imaginary identity (or Ego). It is important to remember that, for Lacan, the identification of the subject with its imaginary identity[17] is not only the result of its recognition in a *Gestalt* of its own unified body; properly speaking, this *Gestalt* becomes his (his Ego) only through the intervention of the big symbolic Other, which in this way validates and attaches the subject to its imaginary identity (as we see with the horizontal axis A/a in the L-schema).[18] For Lacan, it is not because the I is irreducible to the Ego that the alienation of the I in the Ego fails; on the contrary, this hiatus opens the *constitutive space* of *imaginary identification*.

The subject is then intercepted, captured by an image which represents its identity, which is never exhaustively *its own*, because it is at the same time always and irreducibly the *other's*. The irreducibility of the subject to its imaginary identity represents *the very mode of the alienation* of one to the other. Also, when Butler claims that the subject's being undermines 'the subject's capacity to "be" identical with itself', she situates her claim in coordinates that are *always already those of iden-*

---

14. Ibid., p. 131.

15. Ibid.

16. Ibid., p. 104.

17. What Althusser, Butler, and Žižek call 'symbolic identity' as social identity comes from Lacan's 'imaginary identity'.

18. Cf. Lacan 1991, p. 246.

tification. We could say that the distanciation of the self from the self is the very mode of identification with oneself. The imaginary effectiveness of identification is not altered by the reopened wound of the self's relation with itself; on the contrary, we can say that it presupposes it to the extent that Lacan presents imaginary identity (from which—intersubjective—social identity is derived, which Althusser and Butler refer to) as the *other's*, even *another's*. Situating oneself at an insurmountable distance, never free from this ego which one is not, *defines* the drama of identification and its specular illusions (which Lacan calls 'misrecognition').

Identification with the Ego can never be exhaustive due to the fact that, for Lacan, the Ego represents the specular other. Yet, this constitutive impossibility of exhaustivity is not an index of the failure of identification, but, on the contrary, the *mode of subjection* of the subject's relation to its imaginary identity. In Lacan, imaginary identification or alienation does not resolve the tension between the subject and its specular other, *it is this very tension*. The conflict which is intrinsic to specular identification is therefore the sign of the *success* of the subject's interpellation by the big Other.

Therefore, from a Lacanian point of view, the Butlerian distinction between being and identity has meaning *only within the coordinates of an accomplished identification*. For this reason, such an apparatus never provides the means for a real neutralization of mechanisms of interpellation. As Žižek remarks, taking Butler's performative reconfigurations of interpellated identity as a starting point, 'the very field of such "transgressions" is already taken into account, even engendered, by the hegemonic form of the big Other', and Žižek insists: 'What Lacan calls "the big Other" are symbolic norms *and* their codified transgressions'.[19]

In other words, the fact of maintaining a certain defiance within one's interpellated identity, far from transgressing it, *perpetuates the subject's subjection to it.*

Thus, the Butlerian apparatus consists of a dramatization *internal to imaginary identification*. As such, it presupposes the *complete accomplishment of the operation of interpellation*,[20] whose symbolic effectiveness is deferred by performative reconfigurations, rather than being neutralized by them.

We can only understand this apparent paradox if we return to the critique of Sartre found in the Lacanian description of the mirror stage. Indeed, at first glance, this critique seems unexpected as Sartre and Lacan fully agree on the idea that the Ego does not represent in any way the *instance of the subject,* but must be understood as one *object* among others, in the general field of objective transcendence. When, in Seminar II, Lacan argues this point, it even appears as if he directly takes it from Sartre; and yet, the most surprising thing is that he defends this thesis only to turn it against its inventor, returning the for-itself of Sartrean consciousness to the ultimate level of identification, from which Sartre, however, thought he could subtract it. In *The Transcendence of the Ego*, Sartre says that the Ego 'is given as an object'.[21] In the same vein, Sartre was able to maintain in *Be-*

19. Žižek 1999, p. 264 (emphasis in original).

20. The identity in which the subject alienates itself is always that of the *other*; the subject alienates itself in it insofar as it does not exhaustively recognise itself there.

21. Sartre 2003, p. 121.

ing and Nothingness, against Bergson, that the Ego always originates from a 'projection of freedom [...] into a psychic object':[22]

> Thus, by a projection of freedom—which we apprehend within ourselves—into a psychic object which is the self, Bergson has contributed to disguise our anguish, but it is at the expense of consciousness itself. (Sartre 2000, pp. 42-43)

In Seminar II, Lacan asserts, like Sartre, that 'the ego is indeed an object. The ego, which one perceives within the field of consciousness as its very unity, is precisely that opposed to which the immediacy of sensation is put into tension'.[23] Yet, despite their apparent theoretical proximity over the status of the ego, if already from 1949 with the 'Mirror Stage' Lacan could assimilate Sartrean consciousness to the ego,[24] it was because the presence of the for-itself to itself described by Sartre under the mode of a being 'being what it is not and not being what it is',[25] sends us back to the self's inadequacy with itself, constitutive of imaginary identification. What Lacan allows us to think, beyond Sartre, is that the subject's alienating reification in the self takes the form of this *presence to itself of the self's non-identity with itself.* According to Lacan, the whole dramatization of imaginary identification rests on such a *discordance.* To surpass the horizon of the ego, it is not sufficient to assert, like Sartre, that

> the *self* therefore represents an ideal distance within the immanence of the subject in relation to himself, a way of *not being his own coincidence* [...] what we shall call *presence to itself* [...] The presence of being to itself implies a detachment on the part of being in relation to itself. (Lacan 2006, p. 77 [our emphasis])

This helps us all the more understand why Lacan redirects identification with the ego to identification with the ideal ego (*Ideal Ich*) which, as such,

> situates [it] in a fictional direction that will forever remain irreducible for any single individual or, rather, that will only asymptotically approach the subject's becoming, no matter how successful the dialectical syntheses by which he must resolve, as *I*, his discordance with his own reality. (Lacan 2006, p. 76)

This enables us to understand the meaning of Lacan's theoretical evolution, who undoubtedly ended up finding the model for 'full speech' outlined in 1954 still too marked by the stigmata of identification, displaced from the imaginary to the symbolic plane (as identification with an imperative). Ten years later, in 1964, the rupture with the plane of identification will demand a reworking of the theoretical and clinical apparatus of 'alienation'. Far from playing one identification against another, Lacan will re-centre the aim of the analytic cure on what he calls in Seminar XI the act of 'subjective destitution'.

As opposed to the postmodern reconfiguration of identity, which feeds alienation rather than freeing itself from it, such an act presupposes the subject's abil-

---

22. Sartre 2000, p. 42.
23. Lacan 1991, p. 50 (our emphasis).
24. Cf. Lacan, 'The Mirror Stage', in Lacan 2006, p. 80.
25. Sartre 2000, p. xli.

ity to separate itself from its interpellated identity, the possibility of which Butler coherently denies insofar as the apparatus of subversion which she proposes remains *internal* to identification: it presupposes its performative outgrowth rather than its overcoming. On the contrary, the Lacanian analytical apparatus does not aim to displace identity (which reinforces identification), but rather aims at 'subjective destitution', which in the very process of its realization entails a destitution of the big Other, considered as an instance of imaginary and symbolic interpellation, producing identifications in which the subject coagulates. This gives us the possibility of conceptualizing a *subject of negativity* beyond the motif of interpellation, a subject of freedom rid of the obstacles which prevented its emergence in Sartre due to his problematic assimilation to the ego of consciousness, considered as *presence to oneself* of a self which does not coincide with itself.

What is the status of this subjectivity? By resorting to the apparatus of language acts, Butler no doubt underestimates the conditions required for performative speech to have symbolic effectiveness. In Austin, among the constitutive conditions needed for the accomplishment of a performative statement (condition A1), the agent must *agree* to play along with convention. Additionally, if Butler were consistent in her manipulation of the notion of the 'performative', she would not be able to reduce the conventions on which the performative act depends to a series of normative procedures producing the subject as effect of their sedimented repetition. One of Butler's arguments consists of showing that by her 'citationality' (a concept she was working on under the patronage of Derrida's interpretation of Austin), the normative discourse which the subject results from can be repeated in other contexts and according to renewed finalities, which are capable of displacing the effects of subjection from the subject to the power which constitutes it. Butler defines what she calls 'the power to act' as the ability of the subject, as effect of normative power, to manipulate the discourse which constituted it, by citing it in order to reconfigure its initial performative/productive force.[26] Yet, the displacement of performativity proposed by Butler causes this notion to no longer play the central role that Austin's notion of the *acceptance* of the subject does. In short, in order to operate, in other words to give speech its performative force, a conventional procedure must, prior to any act of language, *be recognized and accepted* by the agents[27] (without its prior recognition, it is not possible for the procedure to have symbolic/performative force). Once this problematic has been shifted onto the terrain of the unconscious, it seems that Butler misses what is essential to 'alienation' in Lacan's sense, which, however paradoxical it may seem, *comes fundamentally from a form of acceptance which is irreducible to the subject, being the proof of what Lacan calls a 'forced choice'*. For Lacan,

---

26. Cf. Butler 1993.

27. We are dealing with the condition A1 in Austin's *How To Do Things With Words* according to which 'there must exist an accepted conventional procedure having a certain conventional effect, the procedure to include the uttering of certain words by certain persons in certain circumstances' (Austin 1962, p. 26). For Stanley Cavell, the notion of *claim* concentrates on this capacity for accordance or discordance in regards to conventions. What is more, for Cavell, in continuity with Austin and in a claimed proximity with psychoanalysis, it is not possible to subtract the question of ordinary language from the *subject's acceptance* of speaking in the name of the community it belongs to. Cf. Cavell 1979.

the symbolic effectiveness of the subject's alienation *depends* on a prior acceptance by the subject of the symbolic order, without which the order of signifiers *remains symbolically ineffective*, as in psychosis, which results from a denegating choice within the big symbolic Other's instituting power. As we will see later, we cannot understand the meaning of Lacan's assertion that 'the big Other does not exist' if we lose sight of the considerable theoretical modifications Lacan made to the dialectic linking of the subject to the big Other, from 1964 onwards. As we saw, in the Lacan of the 1950s, the big Other was defined as the instituting matrix of the symbolic order, of which the subject of the unconscious was the *effect*. From this perspective, in Lacan's early thought the 'ego' acted as a rampart ('the wall of language'), overseeing the symbolic Other's instituting message. To counter the imaginary luring of symbolic speech, analysis's objective here is to allow the subject to take upon itself, in 'full speech', the symbolic imperative, of which, as subject of the unconscious, it is the effect, by demanding that the analyst occupy the Other's position (and no longer the position of the same, the other). In this context, the failure of the paternal metaphor implies the impossibility of the emergence of the subject of the unconscious considered as a subject *assigned* by the symbolic order.[28] From 1964 and the establishment of the concept of 'forced choice', we must see things in a new light: the Other only exists if the subject *institutes* it as a consistent symbolic order, that is to say grounds it *in a subjective act of acceptance* (the *choice* of a forced choice), on which the *symbolic effectiveness* of the interpellation coming from the Other constitutively depends. Moreover, if the subject depends on the Other as its effect, Butler, in her critique of Lacan,[29] radically fails to see the reciprocal implication entailed by the fact that the symbolic consistency of the big Other (considered as an instance or force of interpellation) depends on a prior acceptance by the *subject* of the forced choice. If Lacan ends by asserting that 'the big Other does not exist', it is because its symbolic force, with which we decode the psychic symptom, only has effectiveness providing there is a *subjective acceptance*, without which its signifying hold on the subject of the unconscious is *null and void*. Ultimately, what Butler fails to take from Austin, and equally from Lacan, is this precondition which is constitutive of *subjectivity*, as much before symbolic-imaginary subjectivation as after it. The subject only takes on its symbolic and imaginary identity through the intervention of the Other if the subject accepts beforehand to institute the Other as a consistent symbolic order. *Subjectivation thus presupposes the subject, it requires this strange state in which the subject precedes its own emergence.* The big Other, through the intervention by which the operation of subjectivation completes itself, presupposes the paradoxical precedence of its *recognition/ acceptance* by the subject in a 'forced choice', without which the symbolic effectiveness of interpellation is *null and void*. The symbolic power of the big Other, its capacity for assigning the subject to a series of symbolic displacements (metaphors and metonymies), engendering decipherable symptoms in the order of the signifier, presupposes a *choice*, without which the subject remains out of reach for the symbolic (psychosis), which is to say outside of the process of subjectivation. This

---

28. Cf. Lacan 1993.
29. Cf. the new introduction to *Bodies That Matter* (Butler 1993).

paradoxical dimension of forced choice, of a choice before any choice, made by a subject before any subjectivity—since as soon as the subject of choice appears, it becomes *the one who has always already chosen*[30]—is for us the *invisible trigger* without which the movement from a logic of fantasy to a logic of the drive in Lacan (which is equivalent to the movement from 'alienation' to 'separation') becomes completely unintelligible.

II. THE MOVEMENT FROM THE 'FANTASY' TO THE 'DRIVE', OR THE SUBJECTIVATION OF FREEDOM

When the subject 'alienates itself' in the symbolic big Other, it confronts what Lacan calls a 'forced choice'. This means that it faces the alternative of 'your money or your life'[31] presented by Lacan: either the subject resigns itself to leading a 'chipped' life, which is to say placed under the aegis of 'symbolic castration', or he rejects this restriction and loses everything, life *and* money. In Seminar XV, Lacan links this alternative with the terms of the Cartesian cogito, whose constitutive maxim he had reformulated as 'I am not where I think, I do not think where I am', which from now on implies a 'forced choice' between being and thinking: 'either I do not think, or I am not'.[32]

In the case of alienation, the subject chooses *to be*, and in such a case, it renounces *thinking*, which implies that in the choice of alienation the subject gains a symbolic identity (the signifier S1[33]), which the repression of its thoughts in the unconscious is correlated with: 'We are never so solid in our being as when we are not thinking'.[34]

On the other hand, if the subject directly chooses thoughts, it cannot be and loses both being and thinking at the same time. The paradox of 'forced choice' paradoxically implies that if in all coherence we want to *choose to think*, we must begin by making the *wrong choice* of being, to the detriment of thought. In other words, the choice of alienation leads the subject to opt for the choice of 'false being',[35] to the detriment of the truth of its unconscious thoughts. Yet, such a *detour* is nonetheless necessary for the subject, if it wants to be able to access them. We can even say that the journey of the dialectical cure coincides with the return of the subject on its 'forced choice', since the analytic operation consists precisely of replaying the scene of 'alienation', this time for the benefit of *thoughts*, and to the detriment of the subject's *being*. The analytic cure in fact aims at what Lacan calls 'separation', which passes through the destitution of the subject alienated in the big Other. This destitution marks the end of the subject's dereliction, having chosen in the repetition of its alienation thought (which is productive of the split subject $, which no longer knows who it is) at the expense of its being.

For Lacan, by means of the cure the subject returns to its initial 'forced choice', opting from now on for *thought* rather than *being*. This is why, contrary to

30. Cf. S. Žižek, 'Why Is Every Act a Repetition?', in Žižek 1992, pp. 74-75.

31. Cf. Lacan 1998, p. 210.

32. Lacan, Seminar XV. *L'acte psychanalytique* (unpublished), lesson of 10/1/1968.

33. This corresponds to the ancient status of the 'Imaginary Ego'.

34. Lacan, Seminar XV, ibid.

35. Ibid.

Althusser's schema of imaginary alienation, in Lacan's schema of symbolic alienation, the meeting of S1 with the couple S1/S2 coming from the Other, does not incite the subject to assume its subjection to the symbolic order (as was still the case for Lacan in the 1950s, in the meeting of the subject with the Other), but to produce the subject's fading. Following Jones, Lacan calls the latter the subject's '*aphanisis*',[36] which remains a first stage on the road towards the destitution of *being* originating in the subject's first forced alienation in the symbolic order. However, the detour by *alienation* remains the first moment of bad choice (the least bad), thanks to which the subject finishes by assuming its first choice *as its own*, and this occurs insofar as in the clinic of alienation it disavows such a choice (by the denial of its being, to the profit of the empty subject ($) of the thinking cogito). The first moment of the choice presupposes a subject which, as soon as it emerges, mistakes itself for the subject *that has always already chosen*. The thesis of a transcendental subject of choice, far from demonstrating that the subject never has a choice, on the contrary allows us to understand why the subject's re-enactment of the drama of its alienation, through the analytic apparatus, does not aim at leading the subject down the road of a symbolic identification to which it is still maladapted (due to the 'wall' of the imaginary), as was the case in the early Lacan, *but to recover itself as the subject of its primordial choice through its disavowal*. In other words, what the clinic of alienation in Lacan allows us to think, is precisely *the subjectivation of this hypothetical X*, preceding all choice, and which, because it is presupposed as the fading substrate of 'forced choice', can still never represent the *subject* of such a choice prior to its alienation.

As Lacan reminds us, what precedes alienation on the side of the subject is nothing else than what he calls 'subject to come':

> The subject is born in so far as the signifier emerges in the field of the Other. But, by this very fact, this—which beforehand was nothing if not a subject to come—fixes itself as a signifier. (Lacan 1998, p. 199)

The passage through alienation is thus required, because such a journey, if it distances the subject from its 'forced choice' in favor of *being*, accomplishes the subjectivation of the *X* prior to its alienation in it. The paradox requires that the subject, by disavowing its first choice (by choosing thought to the detriment of being), *retroactively emerge* as *the still inexistent subject* of its own choice. By disavowing its choice, the subject reappropriates its freedom to choose: it is by assuming its choice as *its* choice, that the subject separates itself from the alienation implied by a choice that has *become its own*.

Said otherwise, the subject emerges as the subject of a primordial forced choice only retroactively *through the act of disavowing* this choice: the disavowal of its choice coincides (following a topological paradox) with its occurrence as subject of such a choice (the one it disavows). This signifies that the subjectivation of the primordial choice is only possible if it coincides with its disavowal. It is exactly in this sense that Lacan speaks alongside Freud about the 'new subject'[37] in the passage from the fantasy to the drive. If we examine closely the moments when

---

36. Lacan 1998, p. 258.
37. Lacan 1998, p. 178.

Lacan insists on the *becoming subject* of the drive, it is evident that in the passage from alienation to separation, the emphasis otherwise put on the Other as principle of causation of the subject's desire, from now on, through the *reflexive* form of the drive and according to a reflexive grammatical circuit, becomes *integrally assumed by the 'I' (which is this 'new subject'), this 'I' henceforth takes upon itself what it previously attributed to the Other. In the passage from the fantasy to the drive, the 'I' must accept from now on that everything it previously attributed to the Other as originary instance of its desire and its symptoms, ultimately and fundamentally resulted from a founding choice through which, henceforth, by the 'traversal of the fantasy', it emerges as its own subject.* The formula 'the big Other does not exist' therefore means that it is possible *for causes to become reasons*, which the clinic of alienation must implement.

In other words, this consists of a subjective conversion: what, by choosing alienation in the Other, the subject considered to be causes (to which the subject was subjected), in the end *becomes reasons*, a conversion which leads to the serialization of belief in the existence of the symbolic big Other (since its causal efficiency was not absolute: its causes could become reasons, or could be causes only on the basis of subjective denial—implying that the existence of the big Other is an illusion). The subject which has chosen alienation *has chosen to disappear as subject of choice*, to the benefit of an external causal order (the big Other). What makes the Other a universe that is not integrally causal is that it results from a denial, that is to say a choice, which implies the possibility for causes to become reasons, which is to say what Lacan calls 'the traversal of the fantasy'.

Thus, this 'new subject' that Lacan talks about following Freud is the subject of the choice that occurs alongside subjectivation, against its 'false being' which emerges from enforced alienation in the symbolic Other. 'Subjective destitution' in Lacan never leads to the nothingness of subjectivity, on the contrary it leads to *the subjectivation of this fading X of choice*, which the clinic of alienation allows *the realization of, which is to say its bringing about in the passage from the fantasy to the drive (the 'traversal of the fantasy')*. It is absolutely clear that this is what explains the reflexive form of the drive in Lacan: through it, the subject integrally accepts that what it attributes to the desire of the Other *ultimately originates from it alone*. The passage from the fantasy to the drive in fact implies that rather than defer its desire to the inner workings of an Other desire in which it would be alienated, the subject ends up accepting that it is the only one to 'have something being done to itself' ['*se faire faire' quelque chose*]. This is why the passage from the fantasy to the drive, or from alienation to separation, completely relies on the grammatical modification by which the subject ends up *taking upon itself what, prior to this passage, it attributed to the Other's desire*. It is a case of retranslating in reflexive terms the answer to the *Che vuoi?* attributed by the fantasy to the Other's desire: in the fantasy, the answer to 'what does he want from me?' is 'he wants to look at me', 'he wants to listen to me'. In the drive, it is a matter of assigning this answer to the *I* through the looping back of the circuit of the Other to its point of departure in the subject: 'I have myself looked at', 'I have myself listened to'. The subjective 'having done to itself' substitutes itself for the absolutes instance of the desire of the Other. This circuit starting from the subject, passing through the Other (in which the fantasy remains), and coming back to the subject (drive), necessarily implies the destitution of the big Other, since its consistency relied on the fact that the subject could still not assume itself as *free subject*, which is to say one capable of attributing *to its own choice* the consistency of the big Other (and through this its 'symbolic effectiveness'). By becoming the subject of this choice, *which is now its own*, it comes to be as a 'new subject', and must take on the crushing responsibility for everything that it used to attribute to the Other. In the drive, the big Other now only represents *the means* (which was previously hidden in the fantasy) by which the subject *has something done to itself* [*se fait quelque chose*]. This is what Lacan means when he affirms in 'Subversion of the Subject': '[S]ince [the Other] doesn't exist, all that's left for me is to place the blame on Γ.'[38]

This allows us to understand why Lacan could define the 'analytical act' as an act conditioned not by alienation but by separation (which supposes the precondition of alienation). It is only from the moment of separation onwards, from the moment when the subject accepts that the consistency of the big Other was only the effect produced by its initial forced choice, that this choice comes about as *forced choice of a freedom*, in the retroactive constitution allowed by the clinic of alienation. After the traversal of the fantasy, the analytical act is defined as *that which only 'authorizes itself by itself', it no longer carries itself out in the name of the Other, or because of the Other*. It is in fact because the big Other, after the traversal of the fantasy, no longer represents the illusory position of the instance of the subject's constitution, that the properly subjective act realizes itself under the auspices of an *authorization of the self by the self of the subject alone*. This means that such an act exposes the subject to its overwhelming responsibility *for which no big Other can be substituted*. In this sense, 'the analytical act' never finds its guarantee and its meaning *a priori* in the big Other, and for this reason such an act can never be attributed to it: the subject's freedom henceforth being irreplaceable and unique. It is because of this radical change of perspective, passing from the primacy of the Other to that of the subject, that for Lacan, as Žižek[39] has clearly shown, *the true act precedes its own conditions of possibility*.[40]

However, the model proposed by Žižek of the 'traversal of the fantasy' implies, with a Hegelian emphasis, the psychotic regression in the 'night of the world':

> One of the lessons of Lacanian psychoanalysis—and at the same time the point at which Lacan rejoins Hegel—is the radical discontinuity between the organic immediacy of 'life' and the symbolic universe: the 'symbolization of reality' implies the passage through the zero point of the 'night of the world'. What we forget, when we pursue our daily life, is that our human universe is nothing but an embodiment of the radically inhuman 'abstract negativity', of the abyss we experience when we face the 'night of the world'.

---

38. Lacan, 'The Subversion of the Subject and the Dialectic of Desire in the Freudian Unconscious', in Lacan 2006, p. 695.

39. Žižek 2002, pp. 152-153.

40. As Adrian Johnston has demonstrated well, Žižek develops this notion of 'act' out of the distinction in Lacan between 'act' and 'action', proposed in the lessons of 15/11/1967 and of 22/11/1967 of Seminar XV. *L'acte psychanalytique.* Cf. Johnston 2009, p. 148 and ff.

And what is the *act* if not the moment when the subject who is its bearer *suspends* the network of symbolic fictions which serve as a support to his daily life and confronts again the radical negativity upon which they are founded? (Žižek 1992, p. 53)

Such a regression appears to us to miss out the decisive stage of the *subject of the symptom*, as we understand it. Žižek makes the repetition of choice equivalent to the psychotic suspense of the symbolic universe, whereas we consider, on the contrary, that by repeating its choice as a disavowal, the subject emerges as *its subject* (which it was not *before this repetition*). Disavowal therefore implies a *radical subjectivation* of the first choice, not its psychotic denegation; here lies all the difference, in Lacan, between psychosis and the fundamental symptom. In fact, the 'new subject' of the drive presented by Lacan represents, from 1964, the forerunner of this identification with the real kernel of the symptom (as unanalysable remainder), which Lacan will seek to develop in a more and more sophisticated way in his Seminar. The acephalous subjectivation which must be born of the drive, beyond the field of the Other, coincides with the irreducibility of the symptom, as principle of satisfaction (*goal*) which fails to satisfy itself with its object/aim (*aim*), which Lacan calls 'jouissance'.

This 'new subject' is the one that assumes the choice of alienation as *its* choice, *the act of taking upon oneself* whose consequence is the separation from the *symbolic order* (and the passage into the self-reflexive field of the drive).

As opposed to the drive-based symptom, the psychotic 'night of the world' thought by Žižek *never produces a new subjectivity, at best it is the annihilation of all prior subjectivity lacking the possibility of renewal*. In fact, the possibility of such a renewal seems to rest on *the subjectivation of the fundamental symptom*, which is to say on a model which opts for the *realization* of the subject *via* alienation and its overcoming, rather than the subject's identification as *suspension* of the symbolic order, in a regression of pure psychotic chaos. According to us, this is the reason why the traversal of alienation *is not equivalent to its suspension*, but to the realization of a *subjective subscription* to the choice of alienation, which necessarily coincides with its extinction, which Lacan calls 'separation'. The subject is no longer subjected to the symbolic Other, insofar as it fully assumes this subjection as coming from *itself*, naming the process of the cure as that by which causes are progressively considered as reasons, a conversion which is only possible *if we presuppose freedom*,[41] i.e. the possibility of the passage from alienation to separation, from the fantasy to the drive. The identification of the subject with the fundamental symptom makes 'separation' possible precisely insofar as it permits us to avoid the false alternative of the 'forced choice' between alienation and psychotic withdrawal.

The psychotic, as opposed to the neurotic, has chosen to *choose*, so that, for

---

41. This presupposition is correlated with the fact that Lacan presents the symbolic order as inconsistent, i.e. as not being an exhaustive principle of determination (under the threat of prohibiting the subject's emergence). For this reason, the subject is reduced to a pure effect of the signifying material. This margin, which is constitutive of subjectivity, requires that analysis orientate itself towards elucidating symptoms produced by signifying causality, at the same time as correlating this with the presupposition of a choice (which is originary and inexistent), which happens to the subject in the 'future anterior', as Lacan formulates it.

the madman, causes *function as reasons from the outset*. That is why Lacan said that 'a madman is the only free man'.[42] The 'madman' is the one who has straight away realized, without passing through the Other, the inefficiency of all causal exteriority pressing itself upon him. In this respect, subjectivation via the drive supposes a circular journey that *converts* causes into reasons, thus implying the reiteration of the gesture by which the subject vacates its fantasy and disinvests the field of the Other. The mistake, however, would be to establish a loss of the component of freedom which would result from the choice of alienation: as we have seen it is indeed by using the latter that the subject renews the subjectivation of its fundamental fantasy, without it coinciding with the 'mad' gesture of the *denegation/foreclosure of the Other* (at the risk of losing the subject, as the effect of a conversion of causes into reasons).

Since the psychotic has chosen, in renouncing the blackmail of forced choice, to lose everything by refusing alienation, it cannot be mistaken for *the separated subject of the drive*, who is fully responsible for everything it attributed to the big Other before its destitution, as organizational (pseudo)-authority over its psychic life. This supposition of a big Other, as external authority determining the subject by pitting it against the formations of the unconscious, masks the *subjective act* at the root of which the choice of the structure played its constituting role. Yet, the paradox is that the aim of the analytic cure is to bring forth this subject of the choice by *the repetition of alienation*. It is by repeating its choice that the subject detaches itself from it in order to emerge precisely as the subject lacking its first choice, which is to say the subject which has chosen alienation, and who for this reason is *solely and fully responsible for its symptomology*. It is the one who is responsible for all consistency granted to the symbolic order, to its effects of identification as well as to its signifiers that symptoms and other formations of such an order organize.

It is thus true and false at the same time to say that a subject pre-exists its alienation, according to the topological paradox of the torus; alienation presupposes the subject's precedence, but such a subject emerges *as subject* only insofar as the structure precedes it, or more exactly insofar as this precession reveals itself and constitutes itself during the process of the cure, *as coming from it*. These could be the first principal elements for the revision of a theory of the subject which allows us to no longer caricaturize Lacan as a thinker of a signifying determinism, in opposition to Sartre, as a thinker of freedom; up to a certain point, the 'traversal of the fantasy' requires an overcoming of 'bad faith', which consists of attributing to the Other what returns to the subject.

Translated from the French by Guillaume Collett

BIBLIOGRAPHY

Althusser, L., *Lenin and Philosophy and other essays*, New York/London: Monthly Review Press, 1971

---

42. Lacan, 'Petit discours aux psychiatres. Conférence au cercle d'etudes dirigé par H. Ey' (1969), unpublished. It is on the basis of this assertion that Žižek elaborates his model of separation, which for us remains problematic, as we have sought to demonstrate. Cf. Žižek 1992, p. 76.

—— *Positions*, Paris: Ed. Sociales, 1976

Austin, J., *How To Do Things With Words*, Cambridge (MA): Harvard University Press, 1962

Butler, J., *Bodies that Matter: On the Discursive Limits of Sex*, London: Routledge, 1993

—— *The Psychic Life of Power*, Stanford: Stanford University Press, 1997

Cavell, S., *The Claim of Reason*, Oxford: Oxford University Press, 1979

Fischbach, F., '"Les sujets marchent tout seuls": Althusser-Butler-Žižek', in F. Fischbach, *Sans objet, capitalisme, subjectivité, aliénation*, Paris: Vrin, 2009

Gillot, P., *Althusser et la psychanalyse*, Paris: PUF, 'Philosophies', 2009

Johnston, A., *Badiou, Žižek and Political Transformations. The Cadence of Change*, Evanston: Northwestern University Press, 2009.

Lacan, J., *The Seminar of Jacques Lacan. Book II: The ego in Freud's Theory and in the Technique of Psychoanalysis*, trans. S. Tomaselli, New York: W.W. Norton and Company, 1991

—— *The Seminar of Jacques Lacan. Book III: The Psychoses*, trans. R. Grigg, London: Routledge, 1993

—— *The Seminar of Jacques Lacan. Book XI: The Four Fundamental Concepts of Psychoanalysis*, trans. A. Sheridan, New York: W.W. Norton and Company, 1998

—— *Ecrits*, trans. B. Fink, New York: W. W. Norton and Company, 2006

Moati, R., 'The Performative from Ordinary Conventions to the Real', in *Lacanian Ink*, 'The Symptom', no. 9, 2008

—— *Derrida/Searle, Deconstruction et langage ordinaire*, Paris: PUF, 'Philosophies', 2009

Sartre, J.-P., *La Transcendance de l'Ego*, Paris: Vrin, 2003

—— *Being and Nothingness. An Essay on Phenomenological Ontology*, trans. H. Barnes, London: Routledge, 2000

Žižek, S., *Enjoy Your Symptom! Jacques Lacan in Hollywood and out*, New York: Routledge, 1992

—— *The Ticklish Subject: The Absent Centre of Political Ontology*, London: Verso, 1999

—— *Welcome to the Desert of the Real! Five Essays on September 11 and Related Dates*, London: Verso, 2002

Wounds of Testimony and Martyrs of the Unconscious: Lacan and Pasolini contra the Discourse of Freedom

Lorenzo Chiesa

> Do you think that things are any better [...] where the desire
> of the Other is based upon what they call freedom, or in oth-
> er words injustice? In a country where you can say anything,
> even the truth, the outcome is that, no matter what you say, it
> has no kind of effect whatsoever.
> (Lacan, *My Teaching*)

I. FREEDOM AS ANTI-CONSERVATIVE EXHIBITIONISM

In a 1970 article entitled 'Unpopular Cinema', now contained in *Heretical Empiricism*, Pier Paolo Pasolini articulates in detail the relationship between the cinematic author and the cinematic spectator in terms of freedom and liberation. To begin with, Pasolini abruptly suggests that freedom is ultimately nothing else than 'the freedom to choose to die'.[1] This is a 'scandalous' yet far from aberrant matter of fact in the case of the human animal. If, on the one hand, nature helps us to live by providing us with an instinct of self-preservation, on the other, it also instils in us a contrary instinct, which Pasolini names 'the desire to die'. The 'oppositional conflict' that consequently arises, which is unconscious and as such unknowable, does not in itself amount to a contradiction, Pasolini contends.[2] If it appears to be one it is because this condition disrupts and even refutes the 'optimistic syntheses' of progressive rationality as epitomised by both mainstream Catholic and Communist notions of life, which similarly consider the latter as a 'duty'—while for Catholicism, 'life is sacred because it was given to us by God', for Communism, 'we need to live in order to fulfil our obligations towards society'.[3]

Against the background of such an oppositional conflict, Pasolini proposes his general definition of the author, which he initially understands in very broad terms by detaching it from any explicit reference to cinema:

---

1. Pasolini 1999a, p. 1600.
2. Ibid., pp. 1600-1601.
3. Ibid., p. 1600.

Authors are those who are entrusted with making this conflict explicit and manifest. Indeed they possess the lack of discretion and the inopportuneness that are necessary to somehow reveal that they 'desire to die' and thus that they do not keep to the rules of the instinct of self-preservation [*istinto di conservazione*]: or, more simply, that they do not keep to CONSERVATIVISM [*conservazione*]. *Freedom is therefore a self-destructive attack on conservativism.* (Pasolini 1999a, p. 1601)

Pasolini then goes on to argue that such an attack on the rules of biological self-preservation and political conservativism—the Italian 'conservazione' has both meanings—is effective only inasmuch as it becomes an *exhibition*. The author's self-destructive act whereby something unknown—suffering and eventually death—is chosen in place of something known—life—is 'meaningless', Pasolini says, if it is not openly disclosed. In other words, the author is an exhibitionist through whom 'freedom presents itself as the exhibition of the masochistic loss of something that was certain. [...] In the inventive act, the author literally exposes himself to others', to their suspicious admiration.[4] In doing so, the author obtains a 'pleasure', which Pasolini himself writes in inverted commas, that is consubstantial with the scopic realisation of the desire to suffer and die before those who watch or read his work.[5]

I believe that at this early stage the originality of the biopolitical dimension of Pasolini's argument—which, as we shall see, he fully unfolds only towards the end of the article in question—is already clearly outlined. In brief, he aims at establishing a political aesthetics whereby anticonservative freedom relies on the 'unpopularity', as Pasolini calls it, of a regressive and potentially lethal exhibitionism. Against the optimistic pseudo-emancipative strategies of liberation adopted by mainstream Catholicism and Communism, the author's scopic confrontation with conservativism should make manifest the importance of an opposition—his own deliberate embracing of the 'oppositional conflict' of the life and death instincts—that is *not* 'progressive', in the sense that it does not progress towards a synthesis. However, quite tellingly, this does not prevent Pasolini from conceiving of the author's masochistic freedom in terms of martyrdom. As he states without reservation, 'freedom can only be manifested by means of a large or small martyrdom. Each and every martyr martyrises himself by means of a conservative executioner'.[6] Such an unexpected specification, the naïvely *Christian* sacrificial logic that it seems to evoke, obliges us to ask ourselves an important question: How does the oppositional conflict promoted and embodied by the author's exhibitionist masochism, now associated with the 'wounds of testimony' of the martyr, concretely avoid the lures of a negative imaginary synthesis?[7]

---

4. Ibid.

5. Ibid.

6. Ibid.

7. Ibid., p. 1602. Pasolini himself reinforces the pertinence of this question when he claims that by 'believ[ing] in what is contrary to life' the author ultimately witnesses to a 'disinterested love *for life*' (ibid., my emphasis). In other words, the contradiction that arises from masochism appears to be aimed at being subsumed under self-preservation; negation is problematically seen as subservient to life.

II. PSYCHOANALYSIS CONTRA THE DISCOURSE OF FREEDOM

Against what is often suggested by simplistic readings, there are few places in Lacan's oeuvre in which he deals extensively with the issue of freedom. It is then all the more remarkable to discover that Pasolini's own specific arguments on this topic are complemented by and further developed in two important lessons from Lacan's Seminars XI and III.

In Seminar XI, in the context of his well-known discussion of the subject's alienation in language and critical assessment of the Hegelo-Kojèvian dialectic of master and slave, Lacan poses freedom as an alternative to life: '*Your freedom or your life!* If [you] choose freedom, [you] lose both immediately—if [you] choose life, you have life deprived of freedom'.[8] In other words, the forced choice that introduces man to slavery also encapsulates the fact that the linguistic subject can only be defined and define himself by means of an alienation into a field that is external to him and thus determines him, that of the symbolic Other—although, as Jacques-Alain Miller spells out in one of his interventions at the seminar, after Freud's discovery of the unconscious, alienation should no longer simply be understood at the level of self-consciousness.[9]

Leaving aside for the moment the important fact that freedom is taken here as synonymous with being while life is regarded as the equivalent of meaning, it is crucial to stress that, elaborating on the notion of forced choice, Lacan comes even closer to Pasolini's own definition of freedom as 'the freedom to choose to die'. The essence of the 'lethal factor' underlying the injunction 'Your freedom or your life!' is for Lacan revealed in the end by the injunction 'Freedom or *death!*', for instance, as it historically emerged during the French Revolution.[10] Facing this injunction, independently of what my decision is, 'I will have both', Lacan argues: not only does the choice of freedom entail that of death—as shown by the fact that throughout the nineteenth century revolutionary insurrections ended up with bloody suppressions and 'the freedom to die of hunger'—but, more surprisingly, the choice of death entails that of freedom. In spite of the identical final result of my decision, if choosing freedom simply means having 'freedom to die', choosing death rather implies in these extreme conditions 'the only proof of freedom that you can have [...] show[ing] you have freedom of choice', that is to say, the freedom to prefer (immediate) death over freedom (*qua* the 'freedom to die') in spite of the thoroughly forced character of the choice.[11] This is why Lacan then provocatively insinuates that the epitome of conservativism, the Ancien Régime master's choice to die (be decapitated) rather than award freedom to his subordinates, should be regarded as *less unfree* than the revolutionary mob's allegedly free choice to die of hunger. In a few words, my impression is that he uses this paradox to put forward the idea that *any* kind of direct and unmediated search for freedom—even the one motivated by the most progressive and egalitarian ideals—leads straight to its opposite.[12]

---

8. Lacan 1998a, p. 212.

9. Ibid., p. 215.

10. Ibid., p. 213.

11. Ibid.

12. In the following lesson of Seminar XI, Lacan significantly adds that the master's freedom to choose to die nevertheless *confirms* his 'radical alienation' (ibid., p. 220). In other words, the uncompromising

I would argue that the discourse based on 'Freedom or death!'—which, as specified in Seminar XI, is nothing less than the discourse of Terror,[13] the unveiling of the lethal factor present in the 'Freedom or life!' that is inextricable from each and every subject's entrance (or failed entrance) into the Symbolic— exactly corresponds to the so-called 'discourse of freedom' heavily criticised by Lacan in Seminar III. The discourse of freedom—that of the slave who, by yelling 'Freedom or death!', chooses freedom over life only to become free to die[14]— does not, according to Lacan, achieve 'the capacity of social action to transform'.[15] In other words, it is limited to 'the pure and simple fact of revolt' and was for this reason abandoned by 'the entire modern revolution'[16] (we can infer that Lacan is here distinguishing the Russian revolution from the 'freedom to die of hunger' which, according to Seminar XI, the choice of freedom amounted to throughout the nineteenth century). Most importantly, Lacan argues that in addition to being ineffectual with regard to its emancipative aims, the discourse of freedom is also profoundly inimical to them: 'Everything [...] that is linked to [the discourse of freedom] is properly speaking the enemy of all progress towards freedom'.[17] Like Pasolini, Lacan also does not fail to specify that the conditions of possibility of such a progress are themselves to be ascertained, that is, we should question freedom's ability 'to animate any *continual* movement in society':[18] progress towards freedom must be detached from progress towards any form of final synthesis that would be approached step by step through an incremental positive continuum.

Moving from these premises, it should come as no surprise that, in the same lesson from Seminar III, psychoanalysis is considered to be just as incompatible with the discourse of freedom as it is with what Lacan names 'common discourse'—Pasolini would call it the 'popular' discourse of the ruling power, the 'conservativism' that is supposedly fought by the advocates of freedom. Furthermore, Lacan believes that psychoanalysis allows us to qualify the discourse of freedom—which is 'always present' in a latent way 'within each of us',[19] essential to modern man as he is structured by a certain conception of his own 'autonomy'[20]—as delusional, basically psychotic. More precisely, Lacan proposes a sort of general parallel between the opposition between psychosis and neurosis and

---

master's alienation—his lack of freedom—in a revolutionary context is not inferior to that of the compliant slave who, in an anti-revolutionary context, is confronted with the master's injunction 'Your freedom or your life!', and opts for a life deprived of freedom. But, most importantly, in both cases, their alienation *coincides* with their freedom of *choice*. Conversely, Lacan's critique targets as much the revolutionary mob's discourse of direct freedom as that of the master's fight for pure prestige in a non-revolutionary context; as Hegel shows, the latter is ultimately as incompatible with freedom as the 'freedom to die of hunger' condemned by Lacan.

13. Ibid., p. 213, p. 220.
14. The same logic could be applied, *mutatis mutandis*, to the master's fight for pure prestige.
15. Lacan 1993, p. 132.
16. Ibid., pp. 132-133.
17. Ibid., p. 133.
18. Ibid. (my emphasis).
19. Ibid., p. 135.
20. Ibid., p. 145.

that between the discourse of freedom and common discourse.[21] Let us first dwell on the second part of the homology. Our modern common discourse is a discourse that, Lacan contends, far from abolishing slavery, generalised it since 'the relationship of those known as exploiters, in relation to the economy as a whole, is no less a relationship of bondage than that of the average man'[22] (using the terminology Lacan will later develop in Seminar XVII, we could say that the new—capitalistic—master, now in the position of truth, has himself been enslaved by the economic knowledge that has knocked him down from the position of agency). This 'generalised bondage' is both the consequence and the precondition of a 'message of liberation' and 'brotherhood', which having historically imposed itself with Christianity, now subsists in 'a state of repression' enforced by common discourse, and is only occasionally brought out in the open by the fleeting rebellions promoted by the discourse of freedom.

Lacan deems that such an asymmetrical relation between the open discourse of freedom and the repressed message of liberation that is inherent to the closed nature of common discourse reflects the way in which psychosis connects with neurosis. While the psychotic is an 'open witness' to the existence of the unconscious, the neurotic only 'gives a closed testimony that has to be deciphered'.[23] Yet, the open testimony offered by the psychotic 'immobilize[s] [him] in a position that leaves him *incapable of restoring the meaning* [sens] *of what he witnesses* and sharing it [with] others'.[24] In this tragic sense, Lacan concludes, 'the psychotic is a martyr of the unconscious', giving the term 'martyr' its original acceptation, that of 'open testimony'.[25] Psychotics as martyrs of the unconscious individualise the rebellious discourse of freedom as idealised freedom from repression/alienation and, with the same move, preclude themselves from undergoing any form of liberation. More technically, what is foreclosed in psychosis together with the possibility of liberation is the Name-of-the-Father, that is, the hegemony of the master. Referring to the equations between life and meaning and between freedom and being proposed by Seminar XI, we could suggest that the martyrs of the unconscious sacrifice the emancipative possibility of acquiring meaning against the background of a more general meaninglessness of human life (that is, in short, a life that language deprives of freedom) in the name of being absolutely free. In doing so, they miscalculate that the mirage of such a freedom is a lure of the Imaginary. As specified in a later lesson of Seminar III, in psychotic martyrdom the ego's 'twin', the ideal ego—that is, the unattainable ideal image which is normally projected by the alienated subject onto the external world—becomes a real 'phantasm [*fantaisie*] that speaks' back to the subject (echoing his thoughts, intervening, naming his actions in the sequence in which they occur) with disastrous consequences.[26] Lacan concludes that the hallucinatory materialisations of this speaking phantasm [*fantaisie*]—

21. See ibid.
22. Ibid., p. 132.
23. Ibid.
24. Ibid. (my emphasis).
25. Ibid.
26. Ibid., p. 145.

the embodiment of the foreclosed master's revenge—clearly differ from the fantasy [*fantasme*] of neurotics.[27]

III. LIBERATION, OR ENJOYING THE OTHER'S FREEDOM

In Seminar III, Lacan appears to confine the 'message of liberation' to what is repressed by neurotics. It amounts to the discourse of freedom reduced to latency by common discourse. If, on the one hand, 'the existence of a permanent discourse of freedom in the modern individual seems to [be] indisputable'[28]—it is itself, on the different level of the unconscious, a 'common' discourse, an ideology, Lacan clarifies[29]—on the other hand, all non-psychotic subjects replace the openness of such a discourse with a 'resigned abandonment to [a] reality' to which they nevertheless 'fail to adjust' fully.[30] In this sense, the *vel* of alienation—the 'or' of the forced choice which should eventually be rendered as a 'neither one, nor the other';[31] neither freedom nor adapted life—seems to be imposing on us a clear-cut alternative between a tenuous attachment to the reality principle—which in our state of generalised bondage is, as we have just said, far from incompatible with the pursuit of so-called 'individual autonomy' and the 'right to happiness'—and psychotic freedom, which in the end amounts to the self-destructive freedom to choose to die. But can the neurotic subject ever temporarily *express* the message of liberation without this necessarily leading to delusional martyrdom? I believe this is precisely the question that Pasolini tackles when he analyses the way in which the unpopular *spectator* reacts to the masochistic exhibition of the author-martyr.

First of all, Pasolini affirms that the spectator is not subservient to the author. In a sense, he is another kind of scandalous author. Like the author, the spectator 'break[s] the order of conservativism which demands either silence or relationship[s] by means of a *common* language';[32] in other words, the spectator masochistically avails himself of 'the same freedom to die' that characterises the author, and in this sense he immolates himself 'in the mixture of pleasure and pain of which the transgression of conservative normality consists'.[33] But most importantly, according to Pasolini, the spectator also differs from the author: the spectator *qua* spectator is able to 'pragmatically *dissociate* his figure from that of the author', or more precisely, from that of the spectator *qua* author.[34] Insofar as the spectator carries out this dissociation, or separation—as a result of which the spectator *qua* spectator is, at the same time, able to *relate* to the author and to himself as an author—he additionally 'enjoys another kind of freedom', or better a liberation, which belongs exclusively to the spectator. Pasolini defines it as,

27. See ibid., p. 144.
28. Ibid., p. 133.
29. Ibid., p. 135 (my emphasis).
30. Ibid., pp. 133-134.
31. Lacan 1998a, p. 211.
32. Pasolini 1999a, p. 1603 (my emphasis).
33. Ibid.
34. Ibid. (my emphasis).

in capital letters, 'ENJOYING THE OTHER'S FREEDOM'.[35] This enjoyment is then further qualified as both:

1. A *codification* of the 'non-codifiable act' carried out by the author, that is, of his 'freedom to choose the contrary of regulatory life';[36]
2. An *objectification* of such a freedom that, while 're-inscribing it in what is sayable', is nevertheless itself not 'integrated' by society.[37]

In other words, Pasolini is describing a signifying relationship between two subjects—one that involves a different form of enjoyment and overcomes the psychotic inability to share freedom with others—which is not recognised as such by the common language, or discourse, of society but remains somehow inherent to it by means of a codification/objectification. He also believes that this anti-social, yet sayable and intersubjective, scopic relationship can better be understood 'under the ambiguous sign of instincts' and, unexpectedly, 'the (non-confessional) religious sign of charity'.[38] Here the spectator's visual charity as an objectification of 'what is non-objectifiable and unrecognisable'[39] is thus both related to the wounds of testimony of the free author-martyr and distinguished from them: 'The negative and creative freedom of the author is brought back to *meaning*— which it would like to lose—by the freedom of the spectator insofar as, I repeat it, the latter consists of enjoying the other's freedom [*godere dell'altrui libertà*]; really, this act is indefinable since it is holy'.[40]

Leaving aside the fact that Pasolini does not really explain why the optimistic synthesis of confessional Catholicism and the naïve sacrificial logic of martyrdom should be replaced by another *religious* notion (the scopic holiness of intersubjective charity), that is, leaving aside the fact that his anticonservative dialectic between the author and the spectator remains gratuitously Christian, I think I am not forcing his argument by suggesting that the liberated spectator ultimately re-inscribes nothing less than what Lacan calls 'the desire of the Other' (which we should bear in mind Pasolini himself understands as a 'desire of pain and death'). The spectator re-inscribes the author's lethal desire, the desire of the Other, but this desire is originally also the spectator's desire; it is precisely insofar as the spectator's desire is the desire of the author-Other that it is possible for Pasolini to initially regard the spectator as being located at the level of the author's freedom to die. By re-inscribing such a self-dissolving and finally de-subjectivised freedom, the spectator establishes a signifying scopic structure that conveys a different, sedated form of enjoyment. As Pasolini observes, this structure of containment is itself ironically a 'pragmatic dissociation', which, in the very same scene, continually splits the spectator between the authoritative codifier of a non-codifiable act and the passive, non-integrable objectification of that act's enjoyment, the enjoyment of the act of the Other. In other words, the spectator as a charitable witness *creates a fantasy*. Interestingly, in a key lesson from Seminar IV that paves

35. Ibid.
36. Ibid.
37. Ibid., pp. 1603-1604.
38. Ibid., p. 1604.
39. Ibid.
40. Ibid.

the way for a close analysis of the function of the veil in subjectivation, not only does Lacan speak of fantasy in terms of witnessing but also elucidates this link by means of a cinematographic simile:

> With fantasy we are in the presence of something that fixes and reduces to the status of a snapshot [...] Think of a cinematographic movement that takes place rapidly and then suddenly stops at one point, freezing all the characters. This snapshot is distinctive of a reduction of the full scene [...] to what is immobilised in fantasy [...] and of which [fantasy] is the support and the *testimony*. (Lacan 1994, pp. 119-120 [my emphasis])

IV. FANTASY: THE SPECTATOR AND THE SCREEN

Although it could easily be argued that Lacan developed the notion of fantasy to a degree of logical and topological complexity that makes it largely depart from Freud's original formulations on the topic, the fact remains that both psychoanalysts agree in considering fantasy as a fundamentally scopic phenomenon. In a seminal article written in 1919, Freud especially emphasises the visual dimension of the final and most accessible stage of beating fantasies, the one a great number of patients who seek analytic treatment admit having indulged in since their childhood and define by means of the phrase 'A child is being beaten'.[41] Freud says that in these confessions 'the child who produces the phantasy appears almost as a *spectator*';[42] in other words, the child no longer appears in his fantasy and is simply, as patients declare, 'looking on'.[43]

We should stress that throughout his article Freud conceives the final stage of fantasy as a *conscious* day-dreaming, which is almost invariably accompanied by masturbation. In this respect, it is instructive to compare his examination of the psycho-sexual motivations that lead to the emergence of the final stage of fantasy with Lacan's understanding of the *social*—or better, socially integrated—role of cinema. Both seem to point at a similar substitutive function of the libido. Lacan once straightforwardly remarked that the structural absence of the sexual relationship, the fact that sexual pleasure is consubstantial with an unbearable enjoyment that is always-already a lack of enjoyment, a pleasure in pain, can be compensated, for example, 'in a darkened cinema [by the] image [of a beautiful woman] on the screen'.[44] To put it bluntly, this is the way in which *non*-creative spectators—the 'popular' spectators who would not partake of what Pasolini calls the author's 'desire to die'—normally relate to the cinematic screen. Likewise, in his 1919 article, Freud affirms that 'sexual excitement' is obtained in fantasy by replacing—and thus repressing—its highly pleasurable yet unsustainable—even scopically—masochistic stage ('I am being beaten by my father') with an only apparently sadistic conscious stage ('A child is being beaten' and, as a spectator, I look on).[45] More specifically, the 'I am being beaten by my father'

---

41. Freud 1919e, pp. 185-186.
42. Ibid., p. 190 (my emphasis).
43. Ibid., p. 186.
44. Lacan 1993, p. 254.
45. Freud 1919e, p. 185.

that makes incestuous sexual love and guilt converge[46] is retroactively substituted in the final conscious, and overtly scopic, stage of the fantasy by a 'My father is beating the child, he loves only me'. Freud promptly acknowledges that while the form of this conscious fantasy is sadistic, the satisfaction it produces continues to be sustained by unconscious masochism.[47]

On this last point, Lacan's more systematic approach to fantasy follows Freud very closely. If his investigation of the possible parallels between the daydreaming function of the cinematic screen and the conscious dimension of fantasy remains after all rather limited, this is because Lacan is primarily interested in directly equating fantasy with a screen and identifying their common structure with that of the repressed *unconscious* as such. With regard to Freud's different phantasmatic stages, Lacan's own notion of fantasy should be related without hesitation to the plainly masochistic stage: as we have seen, such a stage is for Freud himself unconscious—he concedes that 'it has never succeeded in becoming conscious' during the treatment—and 'the most important and the most momentous' of all; although it was never experienced as such by patients and should thus be regarded as a construction of analysis, it is nevertheless a 'necessity'.[48] (In the 1919 article, the masochistic stage follows an initial stage that seems to precede any clear-cut distinction between consciousness and the unconscious, 'perhaps' arises from a 'recollection of events which have been witnessed'[49]—which usually revolve around the birth of a younger sibling—and can be summarised by the phrase 'My father is beating the child *whom I hate*'.[50])

Having said this, in spite of his insistence on the unconscious dimension of the fantasy-screen, Lacan is far from disposing of the role of the spectator: first and foremost, it certainly remains important at an analogical and explanatory level. Insofar as the repressed fantasy-screen is invisible, a detailed analysis of the multifaceted relations between the conscious spectator and paintings or, more sporadically—as we have seen in the quotation from Seminar IV cited above— films, offers a tentative, but useful, approximation to the structure of the unconscious.[51] As we can infer from the arguments Lacan formulates in the sixteenth

---

46. See ibid., pp. 187-189. 'The phantasy of the period of incestuous love had said: "He (my father) loves only me, and not the other child, for he is beating it". The sense of punishment can discover no punishment more severe than the reversal of this triumph: "No, he does not love you, for he is beating you". [...] This being beaten is now a convergence of the sense of guilt and sexual love. *It is not only the punishment for the forbidden genital relation, but also the regressive substitute for that relation*' (ibid., p. 189).

47. See ibid., pp. 190-191. The phrase 'My father is beating the child, he loves only me'—or, 'My father is beating the child (he loves only me)'—which is used by Freud himself, provides us with a better rendition of the substitutive function of fantasy than the phrase 'A child is being beaten', since it preserves the 'he loves only me', that is, the part that has undergone repression, and thus shows how the sadistic-conscious stage continues to be libidinally dependent on the masochistic-unconscious one.

48. Ibid., p. 185.

49. Ibid.

50. Ibid. This first stage—to which Freud hesitates to attribute the characteristics of fantasy (ibid.)— can also be rendered by the phrase 'My father does not love this other child, *he loves only me*' (ibid., p. 187). Freud observes in passing that the third and final—conscious—stage of fantasy resembles the first. But, in the meantime, incestuous love has been repressed. Expanding on Freud, we could suggest that the circuit of fantasy unfolds between 'My father is beating the child *whom I hate*' (first stage) and '*My father is beating the child* (he loves only me)', or, more simply, 'A child is being beaten' (third stage).

51. On this point, see Safouan 2005, pp. 126-127.

lesson of Seminar XIII, given that 'the visual structure [of fantasy], the one on which there is founded any establishment of the subject [...] is logically prior to the physiology of the eye', we (conscious spectators) can only think of it as an invisible screen 'interposed between the subject [the unconscious spectator] and the world' on which 'something is painted'.[52]

In Seminars X and XI, Lacan already extensively refers to the relation between an invisible support and painting to illustrate the scopic functioning of fantasy. Fantasy is described in Seminar X as a 'picture which is located over the frame of a window': the purpose of this 'absurd technique' is precisely 'not seeing what one sees out of the window',[53] that is, the exhibited lack of the desiring Other. The scene depicted by the picture has thus the function of covering an abyss. Seminar XI advances a similar point by contrasting the 'opaque' nature of the screen on which the phantasmatic scene is painted with the geometrical vision we normally adopt in conscious life: the subject is not simply 'a punctiform being that gets his bearings at the geometral point from which the perspective is grasped. No doubt, in the depths of my eye, a picture is being painted. The picture, certainly, is in my eye. But me, I am in the picture [*mais moi, je suis dans le tableau*]'.[54] In other words, our conscious perception of the world as a picture that complies with the rules of perspective must be complemented with what Lacan calls another unconscious 'landscape' that originates from the 'point of the gaze', that is, the desire of the Other.[55] The opaque screen of fantasy is that which 'mediates', in the unconscious, between the point of the gaze and the subject's being in the picture. Or, better, the unconscious is nothing else than this mediation. In both Seminar X and throughout Seminar XI's well-known lessons dedicated to the difference between the (perspectival) eye and the (non-specularisable) gaze, Lacan seems to be primarily interested in stressing the fact that the picture depicted on the opaque—or invisible—screen of fantasy should ultimately be regarded as a defensive scene; more technically, the 'gaze as such', the unmediated desire of the Other, is to be distinguished from the mitigating 'phallic symbol', that is, the 'imaged embodiment [*incarnation imagée*] of the minus-phi $(-\varphi)$ of castration'.[56]

But in what precise sense does the subject manage to keep the exhibited desire (or gaze) of the Other at bay by including himself *in* the phantasmatic picture?[57] I would claim that, for Lacan, the defensive scene made possible by the

52. Lacan, Seminar XIII, *L'objet de la psychanalyse* (unpublished), lesson of 4/5/1966.

53. Lacan 2004, p. 89.

54. Lacan 1998a, p. 96 (my translation; the English translation of this passage is badly mistaken and renders '*mais moi, je suis dans le tableau*' as 'but I am not in the picture'). See also ibid., pp. 86-87: 'What is at issue in geometral perspective is simply the mapping of space, not sight. [...] The geometral dimension of vision does not exhaust, far from it, what the field of vision as such offers us as the original subjectifying relation'.

55. Ibid., p. 96.

56. Ibid., p. 89. Lacan's extensive discussion of anamorphosis in Seminar XI stems from this issue. Anamorphotic paintings such as Holbein's *Ambassadors* make visible the mitigating 'phallic symbol' (which Lacan also calls 'anamorphotic fantasy'). At this stage, it is difficult to say whether painting is still only a technique that, in some circumstances, can provide an analogy for the scopic dimension of the unconscious, or if it somehow makes it partly visible.

57. See also Lacan 1998b, p. 409.

fantasy-screen, independently of its particular traits in different subjects, always portrays the unspecularisable image of the other as a *double*. In other words, the non-perspectival, yet still imaginary other is 'seen' in fantasy as the non-lacking image which owns the part-object lost by the subject, castrated from him (i.e. the minus-phi); the double is thus the imaginary other plus the part-object, or object *a* (as phallic symbol, to use the terminology of Seminar XI).[58] In order to clarify this, both Seminar X and Seminar XI refer to Freud's famous case study of the Wolf-Man, whose repetitive dream, Lacan says, provides us with an excellent example of the 'pure fantasy unveiled in its structure':[59] a window is opened, wolves are perched on a tree and stare at the patient with *his own* gaze (as non-specular remainder of his own body).

This example shows how the lost part-object *a*, first and foremost the phal-licised gaze, is precisely that which veils the void in the Other—his pure desire—who therefore appears as a double in the unconscious fantasy. In the latter, I see myself as the phallicised object—the phallic symbol—of the Other's desire; I see myself *in* the Other in order not to collapse into the pure exhibition of his desire. At its purest, the object of my phantasmatic desire (as a defence) is thus the Other's desire in which I am myself an object. This amounts to the basic (scopic) masochism of the (alienated) subject. In other words, in order to frame—or 'codify', to put it with Pasolini—the desire of the Other, the subject must undergo castration, appear as an object in the Other, and 'this is what is intolerable', the scandal that cannot be integrated by common—con-scious—discourse.[60] From this standpoint, what is fundamentally repressed in the fantasy is the revelation of the 'non-autonomy of the subject', Lacan says.[61] The subject is thus structurally unfree: he can subjectivise himself only at the price of giving up his freedom, that is, of objectifying himself at the place of the exhibition of the Other's freedom. This explains why, despite being that which allows conscious identification (the 'I see myself seeing myself' [*je me vois me voir*][62]), if taken in isolation, the fantasy is *per se* a structure based on a 'rad-ical desubjectivation' due to which 'the subject is reduced to the condition of a *spectator*, or simply an eye'.[63] In interpreting this quotation we should avoid the risk of considering such a (non-geometrical/non-perspectival) vision as a (spec-ular) individuated action: as we have just shown with the example of the Wolf-Man, the fantasy is rather a scene that overcomes the dichotomy between ac-tivity and passivity in which the subject 'makes himself seen'[64] by 'his' gaze as the lost part-object located in the double.[65] Conversely, as Lacan contends in a question-and-answer session of Seminar XI, the object *a* is not simply a passive

---

58. Depending on the context, Lacan uses the term 'object *a*' to designate either the phallic symbol or that which is irreducible to it (i.e., in the field of vision, the 'gaze as such').

59. Lacan 2004, p. 89. Lacan repeatedly returns to the Wolf-Man in Seminar XI (see Lacan 1998a, p. 41, p. 54, p. 70, p. 192, p. 251).

60. Ibid., pp. 122-123.

61. Ibid., p. 60.

62. Lacan 1998a, pp. 80-82.

63. Lacan 1995, p. 125 (my emphasis).

64. See Lacan 1998a, p. 195.

65. '[The wolves'] fascinated gaze is the subject himself' (ibid., p. 251).

'cork', but a photographic 'shutter' [*obturateur*] that actively regulates vision.[66]

It is only in this context that one can make sense of the following enigmatic definition of fantasy provided in Seminar X: 'I would say that the formula of fantasy $ desire of *a* can be translated as "may the Other fade away, faint, before the object that I am as a deduction from the way in which I see myself"'.[67] What fades away in the visual interpassivity of the fantasy is undoubtedly the Other's desire as real lack, the real object *a* of the pure gaze: Lacan can thus propose that the imaginarisation of the object *a* in the fantasy, the 'making oneself seen', defends the subject against anxiety. Yet at the same time in 'framing' anxiety, in being 'the first remedy beyond *Hilflosigkeit*' (i.e. beyond the subject's complete subjection to the desire of the Other), the fantasy is also that which retroactively renders anxiety *effective* on the unconscious level; 'It is the [subject's] constitution of the hostile as such',[68] the birth of what Freud named 'erotogenic masochism' and Lacan rebaptises phallic enjoyment.

Here Lacan both confirms Freud and develops his ideas beyond recognition: in fantasy, the subject is by all means a spectator who enjoys witnessing the fact that he is the author of *his own objectification*; but in spite of the intolerable non-autonomy entailed by this repressed condition, that which would be truly unbearable beyond phantasmatic masochism is the uncorking—or de-shuttering—of the desire of the Other.

V. THE VIRTUAL POINT OF FREEDOM

In Seminar XIII, Lacan further develops his arguments on what one 'sees'—by making oneself seen—in fantasy. Fantasy corresponds to the visual structure of the subject, a screen that both 'hides something' (the desire of the Other) and, for the very same reason, supports for us everything that presents itself;[69] in other words, 'fantasy gives reality its framework'.[70] This point can be clarified as follows: the emergence of fantasy as a supporting screen is the result of the loss of the real object *a*, which here Lacan explicitly identifies again with the gaze (the 'gaze as such' of Seminar XI). Such a loss amounts to nothing less than the division of the alienated subject as a speaking being, his inevitable *Spaltung*.[71] Confronted with the abyssal desire of the Other, the only way in which the subject can then structure himself (i.e. 'frame' reality) is by locating himself precisely at the level of the lack of the Other—his desire—as a failing/lacking subject. More accurately, the object *a* as imaginarised gaze in the fantasy (i.e. as phallic symbol) serves this purpose insofar as it is the paradoxical object that represents the subject as lacking at the place of the Other's lack and, in so doing, simultaneously institutes the subject as a 'tension', a desiring *manque-à-être*. This process can also be considered as a 'superimposition of two lacks [*recouvrement de deux manques*]' which is logically subsequent to alienation (the state of complete helplessness in front of

---

66. Ibid., p. 147 (my translation).
67. Lacan 2004, p. 62.
68. Ibid., p. 91.
69. See Lacan, Seminar XIII (unpublished), lesson of 4/5/1966.
70. Lacan 2001, p. 366.
71. See Lacan, Seminar XIII (unpublished), lesson of 4/5/1966.

the Other) and which, in Seminar XI, Lacan famously names 'separation'.[72] By separating himself, the subject thus manages to defend (*se parer* in French) and engender himself (*se parere* in Latin); he is now able to reply to the question he poses in vain to the Other—the one epitomised by the child's 'You are saying this to me, but what do you want? Why are you telling me this?'—since he 'situates at the point of lack perceived in the Other [...] the answer provided by the previous lack, that concerning his own disappearing [his alienation]'.[73]

In Seminar XIII, Lacan then makes two other important specifications concerning the scopic nature of fantasy:

1. Although the gaze can be understood by means of an analogy (that is, imaginarily) as an anti-imaginary stain from which 'the visual world originates',[74] this very stain is in fantasy far from mutually exclusive with the pictorial, imaginary function at play when we consciously look at a painting or paint it. At this stage, the investigation into the roles of the author and the spectator in art should therefore no longer be considered only as an indirect approach to the functioning of the unconscious. In fantasy, we do in fact have a 'synchronic' montage of imaginary picture and real stain (i.e. the imaginarisation of the object *a*; the formation of the phallic symbol), Lacan says, as a consequence of which the imaginary of fantasy could itself be regarded as real.[75] The unconscious image, which in Seminar IX Lacan already qualified as '*le vrai imaginaire*',[76] possesses a hidden materiality of its own: the latter corresponds to nothing else than the texture of the screen, the frame of the window—to go back to the Wolf-Man example—or the canvas on which the picture and the stain of fantasy are edited together, thus originating a picture *qua* stain and, at the same time, a stain *qua* picture that are as factual as perspectival reality.[77] Following Freud, in Seminar VII, Lacan already spoke of

72. Lacan 1998a, pp. 213-214.

73. Ibid., p. 214 (translation modified). To give a concrete example of what is involved in the passage from alienation to separation, Lacan identifies 'the first object that [the child] proposes for [the] parental desire, [which is] unknown', with the fantasy of his own death or loss. He then proceeds to clinically connect the latter with anorexia, whose basic libidinal scenario would thus be rooted in the question 'Does he want to lose me?' (ibid., p. 214). Following on from this, Massimo Recalcati, a Lacanian expert on eating disorders, has suggested that anorexia should be regarded as a 'separation-against-alienation': 'The anorexic invokes and practices, in an apparently radical way, separation. First of all, this is the separation from the demand of the Other and, more generally, from any possible form of demand. In fact, she does not demand anything and refuses everything. On the other hand, this separation seems to be produced without a loss—which is the structural effect of the signifier's basic grip over the subject; the object *a* seems to remain on the side of the subject rather than being transferred to the field of the Other' (Recalcati 2011).

74. Lacan, Seminar XIII (unpublished), lesson of 4/5/1966.

75. See ibid.

76. Lacan, Seminar IX, *L'identification* (unpublished), lesson of 13/6/1962 ('the true imaginary function [...] is a privileged relation with *a*, object of desire, a term of the fantasy'). In this respect, in Seminar X, Lacan also speaks of 'another kind of imaginarisation' (Lacan 2004, p. 51).

77. We can detect here a crucial elaboration on the equation between the *Gestaltic* Imaginary and the biological Real that governs animal sexuality (i.e. reproduction), which Lacan treated especially in his early Seminars. According to him, this also holds for the human animal as long as we specify that, in the case of *homo sapiens*, the linguistic animal, the equation in question is mediated and made possible only by means of the Symbolic (the phantasmatic phallic symbol). To put it differently, where the speaking being is concerned, the split between conscious *reality* and the unconscious *Real*—with the latter standing for the point of *impossibility* of the Symbolic, the marker of its non-totalizability (i.e., in this context, 'the gaze as such')—amounts to the other side of the *possibilities* (ultimately aimed at reproduction) allowed by

the unconscious in terms of a different kind of (non-specular / non-perspectival) reality based on an 'endopsychic perception';[78] I believe in Seminar XIII he returns to the same issue and now considers the fantasy as an endopsychic picture.

2. The subject ought to put himself at a certain distance from the picture of fantasy. This is a precondition for representation and the physiology of the eye to work (in a non-hallucinatory manner). The subject divided between self-consciousness and the unconscious both pictures his division between S and *a*, his alienation, in fantasy *and* separates himself from it: as Lacan nicely has it, 'the picture is itself a taking of distance, for we do not make a picture of you in the opening of the window in which you are framed'.[79] Most importantly, the subject has 'complete freedom'[80] as regards the standpoint from which he is to relate to the picture or whether he wishes to distance himself from it at all. In other words, 'this distance is arbitrary, it is up to the choice of the one who makes the picture', yet the choice concerning distance is as such 'structural', Lacan says, that is, as we have seen, it is a forced choice.[81] The difference between psychosis and neurosis follows from it.

Bearing these two specifications in mind (i.e. that the—imaginary but non-specular—picture of the unconscious is itself real, and that the subject's distancing himself from this picture is, at the same time, a remaining caught in it—or that separation does not fully overcome alienation, it rather consolidates it), we should emphasise that one of the explicit reasons why, in Seminar XIII, Lacan engages in an extensive analysis of Velasquez's *Las Meninas* is the fact that this painting holds up very well as a 'material object'.[82]

the very same Symbolic—that is, the fact that, via the Symbolic, the *Gestaltic* Imaginary and the 'natural' Real finally coincide also in *homo sapiens*. Lacan's speculation on the Real as the impossible is therefore a continuation and not a refutation—as most Lacanians claim—of his earlier arguments on the animal's biological Real.

78. Lacan 1992, p. 49.
79. Lacan, Seminar XIII (unpublished), lesson of 4/5/1966.
80. Ibid.
81. Ibid., lesson of 11/5/1966.
82. Ibid.

In other words, in both including himself in his painting and detaching himself from it *within the very same painting* (according to the well-established interpretation according to which the painter represented as a spectator in the picture is its author), Velasquez succeeds in representing for us an image as reality. Lacan's fascinating reading proposes that the represented canvas (*Las Meninas* as we see it) 'represents the [hidden] picture' as seen by Velasquez, the canvas represented as unrepresented on the represented canvas of which we can only see the support, the wooden easel.[83] In this precise sense, 'we have in this picture [i.e. the represented canvas] the representation of [the hidden] picture as reality'.[84] Or, to put it bluntly, we now *really* see the image that Velasquez was both painting and contemplating.[85]

According to Lacan, pictorial objects may be considered as representatives of representation. This statement should not be interpreted in a straightforward fashion: they are not simply, following a superficial reading of Plato, copies of copies, copies of representational / perspectival conscious reality: 'The point is not that painting gives an illusory equivalence to the [representational] object'; on the contrary, 'a picture is that kind of appearance that says it is that which gives appearance' and, as such, it competes with the Platonic domain of Ideas.[86] This allows us to understand pictorial objects by means of the Freudian technical notion of *Vorstellungsrepräsentanz*, the representative of representation [*représentant de la représentation*], or placeholder [*tenant-lieu*] of representation, according to Lacan's French translation.[87] Lacan raises the issue of the proximity between pictorial objects and *Vorstellungsrepräsentanz* in both Seminars XI and XIII; certainly, first and foremost, artistic creation has a social value, it is—as Freud pointed out—a form of sublimation in that it appeases and inhibits the spectator's desire through the 'exploitation of the [author's] desire'.[88] However, beyond this 'popular' level—integrated by society, as Pasolini would put it—not only does painting, even the most naturalistic and mimetic, always retain to a certain degree the disquieting presence of the gaze (the desire of the Other)[89] given that when confronted with a picture the subject comes again very close to the scopical dimension in which he establishes himself as such, but, most importantly, there are some rare works that literally '*extract* [...] that something that holds the place of representation'.[90] While in Seminar XI Lacan limits himself to provocatively defining them as 'psychopathological art' and only vaguely refers to expression-

---

83. Ibid.
84. Ibid.
85. It could be argued that we are, on this level, just *passive* spectators of the painting, which the author seems to have already turned into a phantasmatic scenario as a spectator of it. But, as we shall soon see, things could be complicated further: let me anticipate this complication by noticing that Velasquez, and some of the other figures, are actually staring at us, and thus overcome the pacifying enclosure of fantasy, that is, paradoxically make it somehow conscious for us: the gaze as such still erupts from this painting...
86. Lacan 1998a, p. 112 (translation modified).
87. Lacan, Seminar XIII (unpublished), lesson of 11/5/1966; Lacan 1998a, p. 218.
88. Lacan 1998a, p. 111.
89. 'Certainly, in the picture, something of the gaze is always manifested' (ibid., p. 101).
90. Ibid., p. 110 (my emphasis).

ism as an example,[91] it is my contention that his analysis of *Las Meninas* in Seminar XIII is meant to explain in detail how this specific painting functions like a representative [*Repräsentanz*], or placeholder, of conscious representation [*Vorstellung*]—that is, by his own admission, like the phantasmatic unconscious *tout-court*—and even extracts it. Just as *Las Meninas*, a paradigmatic example of what is involved in non-appeasing painting, pictures a hidden canvas as reality on the very same canvas that hides it, so the Vorstellungs*repräsentanz qua* the representative or proxy of representation imaginarises the real of the unrepresentable drive and symbolically inscribes it on the unconscious screen by becoming itself that which is primarily repressed / hidden. Again, what usually passes unnoticed in psychoanalytic critical commentaries on this topic, and can better be grasped by taking into consideration paintings such as *Las Meninas*, is that this imaginarisation of the real, which *is* the unconscious (Lacan has no hesitation in defining the *Vorstellungsrepräsentanz* as what 'essentially determines' the unconscious[92]), should itself be regarded as something that holds up as a material object; *Vorstellungsrepräsentanzen* are *real*, non-specular images that, as signifiers, register the drive on the unconscious screen. As suggested by Lacan, in both *Las Meninas* and *Vorstellungrepräsentanzen* the real and the image in this way 'mutually saturate one another' beyond any possible distinction.[93] In other words, where humans as speaking animals are concerned, the unrepresented drive is only a retroactive postulation just as there is no direct access to 'representation as such'.[94] All that *could* eventually really be shown is 'seen' (as hidden) on the libidinal screen of fantasy. But here Velasquez takes a step further and actually *shows* this thanks to his 'extraction' of the placeholder of representation: Velasquez makes his fantasy be seen; with the very same move, he causes a collapse of representation and the triumph of the gaze of the author (which, in *Las Meninas*, implacably stares at us, and not at the canvas).

It should be added that, in Seminar XIII, Lacan explicitly speaks of the structural screen on which the picture of fantasy is painted in terms of *Vorstellungsrepräsentanz*: 'Before defining what is involved in representation, the screen already announces to us […] the dimension of the representative of representation. Before the world becomes representation, its representative—I mean the representative of representation—emerges'.[95] As we have seen, in the same Seminar, Lacan also spells out the importance of the relation between the scopical subject's personal positioning with regard to the picture of fantasy and the existence of a structural choice on his part: this point can fully be appreciated only if it is read together with the argument about the alternative between freedom and life—which should rather be conceived as a 'neither one, nor the other'—advanced in Seminar XI. As a matter of fact, in a couple of usually underestimated passages from Seminar XI, Lacan goes as far as explicitly linking the issue

---

91. Ibid., p. III, p. 109.

92. Lacan 1998a, p. 60.

93. Lacan, Seminar XIII (unpublished), lesson of 11/5/1966. This argument should also be related to what I explained in note 77 above.

94. Lacan, Seminar XIII (unpublished), lesson of 4/5/1966.

95. Ibid.

of freedom and of the subject's structural choice with the *Vorstellungrepräsentanz*. One particular answer he gives to André Green is especially revealing and worth quoting in full:

> The point at which we capture the resumption of the *Vorstellungsrepräsentanz* [*le point où se branche la reprise du Vorstellungsrepräsentanz*]—and this is of great importance [...]—is the [...] *virtual point of the function of freedom*, in as much as the choice, the *vel*, is manifested there between the signifier and the subject. [...] I illustrated this by means of an opening on what we could call the misadventures [*avatars*] of this freedom, which in the final resort, is never, of course, rediscovered by any serious individual. (Lacan 1998a, p. 227 [my translation and emphasis]).

'Serious individuals', that is, non-psychotic subjects, never 'rediscover' freedom and its disastrous vicissitudes—which Lacan discusses once again in the same lesson through a revisitation of the Hegelian master's self-refuting struggle for pure prestige[96]—since, by choosing meaning over being, opting for the alienated life dictated by the signifier which makes the subject fade away, in short, by *creating* a fantasy—after having overlapped this subjective fading with the Other's lack in separation—they, as it were, tune into the *Vorstellungsrepräsentanz* and always stay on its wavelength. Freedom survives only as a 'virtual point' around which the very existence of the alienated-separated subject as divided between the unconscious fantasy and self-consciousness revolves. Although this position can temporarily be occupied by switching off, or 'extracting' the *Vorstellungsrepräsentanz*, such a 'traversal of the fantasy'—to use a more well-known phrase that expresses the same process, that is, nothing less than the aim of psychoanalytical treatment—does not ever accomplish a rediscovery of freedom. From a slightly different perspective, this means that the virtual point of the function of freedom should definitely not be confused with what would satisfy the neurotic demands of the 'message of liberation' evoked in Seminar III. While the latter is a concrete component of the modern subject's unconscious, and subsists in a state of repression that is the counterpart of modernity's condition of generalised bondage, the virtual status of the former logically pre-dates the subject's very entrance into language, not to mention his differentiation between consciousness and the unconscious. Considering the fact that, in Seminar XI, as is frequently the case, Lacan is above all addressing practicing analysts—his discussion of alienation and separation emerges during an exploration of the notion of the transference—it would be sensible to suggest that, like in Seminar III, the very general idea that he intends to put forward is that psychoanalysis has nothing to do with the *discourse* of freedom, while nonetheless—and this is the novelty with respect to Seminar III—it aims at the extraction of the *virtual* point of freedom. As he candidly puts it at one point in the very same lesson that we are scrutinising, freedom is a fantasy *par excellence*.[97] But fantasies, including that of freedom, can be traversed, and this retains a certain liberating effect. It is now a matter of establishing what such liberation precisely amounts to.

---

96. Ibid., pp. 219-220.
97. Lacan 1998a, p. 219.

VI. LIBERATION AS SUBJECTIVISED SUBJECTION

According to Lacan, fantasy dissolves when the Other's desire (including that of the analyst during psychoanalytic treatment) becomes too proximate; as a consequence of this, the subject acquires a *positive* image of lack, Lacan says in Seminar X.[98] In other words, the hidden phantasmatic window, or screen, is made visible and opens itself onto the void, the non-totalizability of the Symbolic, normally concealed by the subject's specular projections (which are themselves supported by the unconscious picture). Concomitantly, 'the absence where we are' beyond specularity is revealed, scopically exhibited in its true nature, as a 'presence elsewhere', a 'pound of flesh', the part-object *a* (the image of lack) that we are for the Other's desire.[99] This moment thus corresponds to the fleeting surfacing of the part-object, the scopical appearance of the double which looks at the subject with the subject's own gaze. Said otherwise, this is the appearance of the disappearance of the subject's own fantasy in self-consciousness, the intolerable appearance of his being nothing other than the non-autonomous phantasmatic object of the Other's desire: the 'conscious' appearance of the fantasy therefore necessarily coincides with its demise and with the concomitant (at least temporary) loss of self-consciousness. Here, the non-psychotic subject has the possibility of reaching the *virtual* point of freedom, the manifestation of the *pre*-subjective forced choice between being—the mythical non-alienated subject—and meaning—the subject alienated in the Other (or better, reading Seminar XI's schema of alienation closely,[100] between being as non-meaning—the disappearance of subjectivity in psychosis—and the non-meaning of meaning—the neurotic emergence of subjectivity which is gained only at the price of the *Spaltung* between self-consciousness and the unconscious).

What matters the most in this regard is that, as Lacan maintains in another lesson of Seminar XI, the virtual point of freedom can ultimately be attained in the specific—transference based—setting of psychoanalysis (and not as the result of a mere existential crisis)[101] only *retroactively* when the signifying logic of fantasy—that of the non-meaning of meaning—is itself *reinstated* as such after the traversal. As a matter of fact, in his answer to Green, Lacan speaks of the *re*sumption, or rerun, of the *Vorstellungsrepräsentanz*. In other words, the virtual point of

98. Lacan 2004, p. 75.

99. Ibid., p. 60.

100. See Lacan 1998a, p. 211.

101. A paradigmatic example of the dissolution of the fantasy in a non-psychoanalytical context is, for Lacan, Hamlet's rejection of Ophelia in the so-called 'Nunnery scene' of the play, his 'I did love you once [...] get thee to a nunnery'. As he points out in Seminar VI, 'Ophelia is completely dissolved *qua* love-object'; she is 'no longer treated as she should be, as a woman. She becomes for him the bearer of children and of every sin', an embodiment of fecundity as such, the equivalent of the phallus. That is to say, Hamlet assumes Ophelia in consciousness as a phallicised double; as we have seen, the emergence of the components of fantasy brings about the fact that 'the object is reintegrated into its narcissistic framework', into the ego. Lacan thus concludes that 'a nunnery could just as well at the time designate a brothel [...] The whole dialogue with Ophelia is indeed about woman conceived here uniquely as the bearer of this vital tumescence which is a question of cursing and putting an end to' (see Lacan 2013, pp. 363-382). Although this issue would require a much longer discussion, we can tentatively suggest that the dissolution of the fantasy outside of psychoanalysis is not a traversal insofar as the appearance of the components of fantasy and of the master-signifier that kept them together is not interpreted.

freedom is always only actualised as *virtual* since 'what, in effect, grounds, in the meaning [...] of the subject, the function of freedom is strictly speaking [a] signifier'.[102] However, and this is decisive, such a 'primary signifier' must be understood as a signifier that 'kills all [previous] meanings'.[103] It will then be more correct to suggest, as Lacan indeed does, that this signifier grounds the function of freedom 'in the meaning *and* radical non-meaning of the subject'.[104] The only alternative to being psychotically free is the alienated freedom of the subject who, facing again the pre-subjective forced choice between being and meaning, does not limit himself to prefer meaning over being, but actively chooses the non-meaning of meaning over being as non-meaning—in this way, 'meaning survives only deprived of that part of non-meaning that is, strictly speaking, that which constitutes, in the realisation of the subject, the unconscious'.[105] Non-psychotic freedom is therefore the retrospective instant of a transitory liberation that annuls meaning while paving the way for the imposition of a new 'primary signifier': this pure virtuality is the freedom of the fantasy as opposed to what Seminar III called the delusional egological phantasms of freedom.[106]

Let us dwell on this crucial conclusion by unravelling the notion of the traversal of the fantasy—which, in Seminar XI, Lacan mentions only in passing—and especially of the contiguous concepts of non-meaning and separation. In psychoanalysis the decomposition of the fantasy—the appearance of its components that brings about a subjective disorganisation (that is, the joining up of the unconscious part-object *a* with the conscious ego as image of the other)—is artificially induced by the analyst and accompanied by an interpretation. The latter always consists of isolating the kernel of the subject, 'an irreducible signifier' that corresponds to that which is 'originally repressed', as nonsensical.[107] Lacan returns here to the example of the Wolf-Man and states that the wolves staring at the subject from the window do not only *represent* his loss (i.e. function as a phallic symbol) but, beyond this, 'their fascinated gaze is nothing less than the subject himself'.[108] The subject emerges as subjected to the traumatic non-meaning of this primary signifier, which psychoanalysis can isolate yet is unable to articulate any further.[109]

But in order to fully grasp what psychoanalysis accomplishes when it circumscribes the nonsensical primary signifier by means of the traversal of the fantasy it is important to carefully reconstruct the dialectical relation between meaning and non-meaning as it unfolds during the subject's ontogenesis in alienation and separation. In alienation as an ontogenetical stage that logically precedes separation, the forced choice of meaning over being originally 'con-

---

102. Lacan 1998a, p. 252.

103. Ibid.

104. Ibid., (my emphasis).

105. Ibid., 211.

106. In brief, psychoanalysis should therefore at all cost avoid to transform the double, which invariably appears for a moment when the fantasy is dissolved, into what Seminar III designated as the 'ego's twin'.

107. Lacan 1998a, pp. 250-251.

108. Ibid., p. 251.

109. Ibid. See also Lacan 1998b, p. 394.

demns the subject to appearing exclusively in [a] division', that is to say, on the one hand, he appears as a disappearance, a fading (*aphanisis*), while, on the other, concomitantly, he 'appears as *meaning*, produced by the [primary] signifier'.[110] This happens insofar as, in alienation, the primary signifier represents the subject for another signifier, the S2, which is itself responsible for the fading of the subject.[111] We should not lose sight of the fact that two signifiers are already operative at this level, that of alienation (at one point, Lacan even—misleadingly—identifies the alienated subject—prior to separation—with the S2, that is, the 'cause of his disappearance').[112] The novelty brought about by separation involves precisely a problematisation of this primary representation $S_1 \rightarrow \$ \rightarrow S_2$,[113] and of the division between meaning and fading that it sustains, in that such a second logical stage of subjectivation identifies this very representation with the *non-meaning* of the Other. Through separation the subject (divided in alienation between meaning and fading as a consequence of his choice of meaning over being) 'finds the weak point of the signifying articulation's primitive couple', that is, the presence of the unknowable desire of the Other/Mother 'beyond or within what she says, orders, what she brings out as meaning'.[114] In other words, in exposing the non-meaning of meaning, in encountering the lack of the signifying Other, the subject retroactively returns *as a subject* to 'the initial [pre-subjective] point', that of the forced choice, a point that in this context Lacan calls 'his lack as such'.[115] He is careful to distinguish its irreducibility, which he also names the 'lack of his *aphanisis*' [*le manque de son aphanisis*],[116] from the more circumscribed *aphanisis* that emerged in alienation as a *dialectical counterpart to meaning*. The latter, 'the aphanisic effect of the binary signifier' produced by $S_1 \rightarrow \$ \rightarrow S_2$—which in Seminar XI is repeatedly equated with the *Vorstellungsrepräsentanz*—is, through separation, that which is repressed as primary; it amounts to 'the central point of the *Urverdrängung*—of what, from having passed into the unconscious, will be, as Freud indicates in his theory, the point of *Anziehung*, the point of attraction, through which all other repressions will be possible'.[117] It is therefore not enough to identify what is primarily repressed with the S1, as Lacan himself does at times. His hesita-

110. Lacan 1998a, p. 210.

111. See ibid., p. 218.

112. Ibid.

113. It would be more accurate to designate this primary representation as a *presentation* of the subject's drives, since no *Vorstellung* is as yet involved at this stage, only the *Repräsentanz* (in the Lacanian sense of the representative that logically precedes representation). For the same reason, $S_1 \rightarrow \$ \rightarrow S_2$ should rather be rendered as $S_1 \rightarrow S \rightarrow S_2 \rightarrow \$$ (where S stands for the mythical subject of drive, which Lacan at times refers to as the *asujet*).

114. Ibid., p. 218 (translation modified).

115. Ibid., p. 219.

116. Ibid. This crucial phrase could be understood in two complementary senses, namely, both as 'the *lack* of his *aphanisis*', a condition of lack that precedes, or lacks, *aphanisis* / fading, and, at the same time, as 'his *aphanisis*' lack', the presence of a lack within *aphanisis* that cannot be contained by the alternation between meaning and fading that determines alienation. The first sense is more appropriate for describing the condition in which the pre-subjective choice between being and meaning emerges, while the second better conveys the passage from alienation to separation, that is, the subject's (re-)discovery of the desire of the Other.

117. Ibid., pp. 218-219.

tions, if not contradictions, regarding which signifier ultimately constitutes the *Urverdrängung*—in some lessons of Seminar XI he explicitly makes this Freudian notion depend on the S1, in others on the S2[118]—could perhaps be solved by suggesting that the S1 as primarily repressed is in the end the *binary* signifier S1→$ →S2. Maybe we should here clarify Lacan's ambiguities and distinguish the S2 *stricto sensu* (i.e., as we have just seen, the cause of the subject's *meaningful* disappearance in alienation) from what he himself calls on different occasions the 'binary signifier' (i.e. the overall *meaninglessness* of meaning—of alienation as a dialectic between meaning and fading—which is repressed thanks to separation). Returning to the Wolf-Man and going beyond Lacan, we could put forward the hypothesis that the primary repression of the S1, the nonsensical equation of the subject with the pure gaze of the Other (which psychoanalysis then isolates, extracts), is really put into place only retroactively by the repression—as a separation that grants a subjective foundation—of the binary signifier S1→$ →S2, that is, by the emergence of the phantasmatic $-a, an unconscious 'I make myself seen by the wolves' gaze as *my* gaze'.

I wish to stress this point once more: against common readings, separation as a *liberation* from the aphanisic effect—Lacan is adamant on this: 'What the subject has to free himself of is the aphanisic effect of the binary signifier'[119]—goes together with *repression*. Thanks to the elimination (or at least suspension) of meaning, separation as an 'intersection'[120] of non-meaning—i.e. of the element that belongs to both the set of being and to that of meaning in Lacan's schema[121]—prepares the establishment of the fantasy. The overlapping of the two lacks (of the subject and of the Other) which we have discussed earlier as Lacan's most succinct definition of separation and as the basis of fantasy should more precisely be understood as the overlapping, covering, or suturing of the *non-meaning* of meaning (the senselessness of the signifying Other) with *being* as non-meaning (the disappearing of the failed, psychotic subject who chooses being over meaning as *subjectively* experienced in retrospect *qua* the 'lack as such' by the non-psychotic subject at the moment of the encounter with the Other's desire; the subject can thus properly be regarded as a *manque à être*).

It is only on this basis that we can make sense of Lacan's claim according to which the becoming unconscious of the binary signifier 'constitutes the subject in his freedom with regard to all meanings, yet this does not mean that he is not *determined* [by] dialecticised significations in relation to the desire of the Other'.[122] As he puts it even more clearly in a much earlier lesson of Seminar XI, which is usually not associated with his discussion of separation although it explicitly introduces this theme for the first time, the subject as an insubstantial, nonsensical indetermination is, at the same time, 'strictly speaking *determined* by the very separation that determines the cut of *a*, that is to say, the fascinatory el-

---

118. Ibid., pp. 218-219 and pp. 251-252.
119. Ibid., p. 219.
120. Ibid., pp. 213-214.
121. See ibid., p. 211.
122. Ibid., p. 252 (translation modified) (my emphasis).

ement introduced by the gaze'.[123] Separation thus works as a bridge—or a vanishing mediator—between free indetermination (the *virtual* point of freedom) *qua* the suspension of the meaning of the Other and its subjective re-determination as alienated existence in the new *meaning* of the Other's meaninglessness. Alienation follows the forced and mythical (pre-subjective) choice between being and meaning; separation follows alienation by suspending meaning; but meaning, that is, alienation, follows—or better, sublates, i.e. preserves by overcoming—separation. Lacan is unequivocal on this point: 'In the relation of desire to desire', that of the subject's desire to the Other's desire as it is established thanks to separation, 'something of alienation is preserved, but not with the same elements—not with the S1 and the S2 of the first couple of signifiers, from which I deduced the formula of alienation', that is, the aphanisic effect issued from S1→$, →S2.[124] Alienation is rather preserved after separation with the following elements:

> On the one hand, what has been constituted on the basis of primal repression, of the fall, the *Unterdrückung*, of the binary signifier, and, on the other hand, what appears initially as lack in what is signified by the couple of signifiers, in the interval that links them, namely the desire of the Other.
> (Lacan 1998a, p. 236 [translation modified])

In other words, alienation as directly caused by the binary signifier should be differentiated from but also related to alienation as caused by the repression of the very same binary signifier, an alienation that takes into account that the Other—which is by now constituted as a *set* of signifiers that can logically work only if it does not signify itself[125]—or better his desire, is itself alienated, inconsistently split between meaning and non-meaning. To sum up, alienation after separation is equal to the disjunctive synthesis of the fantasy, its logical 'torsion' of the 'non-reciprocity' between being and meaning that characterised alienation before separation.[126]

Finally, how should we understand the place of psychoanalysis within the sequence alienation → separation → alienation? The last lesson of Seminar XI leaves little doubt about this: the traversal of the fantasy as the aim of the treatment amounts precisely to a new separation, a separation from separation in alienation, a retroactive *un*-determination of the re-determination of indetermination, of the *meaning* of meaninglessness brought about by separation *qua* the fantasy. But Lacan also importantly specifies that isolating a non-interpretable non-meaning in interpretation as the end of analysis should not itself be regarded as non-meaning.[127] Otherwise any interpretation would do and psychoanalysis would be at best a manipulative form of psychological suggestion. The isolation of non-meaning accomplished by the traversal of the fantasy is rather itself a vanish-

---

123. Ibid., p. 118 (translation modified) (my emphasis). In one of the last lessons of Seminar XI, Lacan restates this point even more concisely: 'Through the function of the *objet a*, the subject separates himself off' (ibid., p. 258).

124. Ibid., p. 236 (translation modified).

125. See ibid., p. 249.

126. See ibid., p. 215.

127. See ibid., p. 250.

ing mediator, like the separation (the *se parer*) that it deposes, and cannot be thought independently of a new alienation, a new subjection of the subject to the signifier.

Much has been written about the subject of the drive that would be brought to light following the traversal of fantasy, and its supposed liberating effects *beyond alienation*. However, Lacan is not even interested in testing the plausibility of this possibility, certainly not in Seminar XI. He liquidates the topic in just one paragraph by saying that the hypothetical subject of the drive as such does not fall within the field of psychoanalysis.[128] On the contrary, he argues that the 'loop' of fantasy must be 'run through' several times: this is for him what Freud meant by 'working-through' (*durcharbeiten*).[129] True, at one point, Lacan is also tempted to juxtapose, in passing and in the conditional mood, the subject of the drive with the analyst, his desire.[130] And yet two pages after this, in the very last paragraph of Seminar XI, he comes to the firm conclusion that 'the desire of analysis is not a pure desire'. Rather, 'it is a desire to obtain absolute difference, the difference that intervenes when, confronted with the primordial signifier, the subject comes for the first time in a position to subject himself to it [primordial signifier]'.[131] Again, for Lacan, psychoanalysis is consecrated to the *subjective* attainment of an absolute difference, the virtual point of freedom, which manifests itself retroactively by means of a new *subjection* to the signifier.[132]

---

128. 'How can a subject who has traversed the radical phantasy experience the drive? This is the beyond of analysis, and has never been approached' (ibid., p. 273).

129. Ibid., p. 274.

130. 'This is the beyond of analysis, and has never been approached. Up to now, it has been approachable only at the level of the analyst, in as much as it *would* be required of him to have specifically traversed the cycle of the analytic experience in its totality' (ibid., pp. 273-274, my emphasis). It is not a random terminological coincidence if, throughout his works, Lacan mostly, if not exclusively, speaks of the *desire* of the analyst, not of his drive…

131. Ibid., p. 276 (my translation). This fundamental passage is one of the most often quoted by critics in discussions regarding the status of desire, drive, and fantasy in Lacanian theory. For Anglophone readers, the problem is that the translation is completely unreliable. This serious limitation has not as yet been spelled out sufficiently. First of all, Lacan speaks of a '*désir de l'analyse*', the desire of *analysis*, and not of the 'analyst's desire', as the translator wrongly renders it. Although I cannot treat this issue in detail here, it is clear that we are not dealing with an insignificant change, especially considering the fact that, as we have just seen, a few pages earlier, Lacan explicitly treated the *analyst*'s desire in terms of its hypothetical attainment of the 'beyond of analysis'. Any attempt at understanding the way in which Lacan articulates the relation between desire and drive, as well as thinks the end of analysis, must take this shift into account. Secondly and most importantly, what intervenes—or also, 'takes place', 'occurs' (the French *intervenir* has all these meanings)—at the moment when the subject is confronted with a primordial signifier, is *absolute difference*. The French is unequivocal on this: '*Le désir de l'analyse n'est pas un désir pur. C'est un désir d'obtenir la différence absolue, celle qui intervient quand, confronté au signifiant primordial, le sujet vient pour la première fois en position de s'y assujettir*' (Lacan 1973, p. 307). '*Celle qui*' cannot grammatically be related to desire, which is what the English translator does: 'The analyst's desire is not a pure desire. It is a desire to obtain absolute difference, a desire which intervenes when, confronted with the primary signifier, the subject is, for the first time, in a position to subject himself to it'. Analysis desires to obtain absolute difference, and, at the moment of the traversal of the fantasy, absolute difference does indeed take place, yet the *desire* to obtain absolute difference does *not* ever as such take place during the treatment. The mistaken translation ultimately encourages the reader to understand the desire of absolute difference as the taking place of pure desire, of a desire *qua* absolute difference, ultimately of a vitalist differential drive (a 'free' One of difference) which would be unleashed at the end of analysis. This is the opposite of what Lacan is saying: the absolute difference he is focusing on as the (repeatable) aim of analysis is nothing else than the primordial +/− of the signifier's hold on the subject, the cipher of which is a materialist dialectical two.

132. In his contribution to the present volume, Raoul Moati thus rightly argues that 'the paradox is that

In order to avoid any misunderstanding, I wish to make it clear that I deem this position to be far from expressing a pessimistic, if not altogether conservative, stance on the possibilities of subjective change. As I have claimed elsewhere, Marx's own notion of freedom can be considered to be ultimately dependent on a retroactive and asymptotic dialectic of *dis*-alienation, of *liberation*, a never-ending reduction of passivity that nonetheless cannot help reiterating alienation. In addition to being the insubstantial presupposition of the human animal's substantiality, of his inevitable self-estrangement in language, alienation is also, first and foremost, a subjective positing, the *consequence* of the possibility of the perpetual renewal of a historical-emancipative project, which in spite of stemming from the animality of the human animal as a speaking animal, cannot be limited to it.[133]

VII. CODA: AVOIDING THE *LAGER*, OR, TOWARDS A *LOTTA CONTINUA*

We have seen how both Lacan and Pasolini understand the freedom of the subject/author as the 'exhibition of [a] masochistic loss',[134] which for Lacan corresponds to the appearance of the object *a*. Conversely, we have also highlighted the way in which both of them refuse to detach this act as a free act from its retroactive reinscription in what is sayable albeit not integrated by common discourse: for freedom to take its virtual place, 'the negative and creative freedom of the author [needs to be] brought back to *meaning*'.[135] In other words, the author survives only through the re-codifying creation of the spectator.

Since Pasolini never explicitly mentions the idea of fantasy in his discussion of the aesthetical-political dialectic between the author and the spectator, it is all the more interesting that, in the very last sentence of 'Unpopular Cinema', he conceives of the emergence of freedom in terms of the 'reapparitions of Reality', a real which he clearly distinguishes from everyday reality and the control Power normally exercises over it.[136] If, on the one hand, Pasolini says, 'each and every Power is evil', on the other, a '"less-bad" Power' [*un Potere 'meno peggio'*] would be one that 'would take into account' the reapparitions of Reality as liberating im-

---

the aim of the analytic cure is to bring forth [the] subject of choice by the *repetition of alienation*' and that 'it is by repeating its choice that the subject detaches itself from it in order to emerge precisely as the subject lacking its first choice'. However, he then draws three conclusions that clash with the reading of alienation, separation, and freedom that I am advancing: 1) the singular, unrepeatable repetition of alienation would result in the final 'extinction' of alienation, that is, in separation; 2) the 'new subject' emerging from this process of victorious dis-alienation would correspond to an *actual* 'subject of freedom'; 3) such a subjectivation of freedom as a separation from the symbolic order would replace once and for all the logic of fantasy with that of the acephalous drive. I fail to see how these propositions can be understood within Lacanian psychoanalysis. Especially with regard to the last, would the permanent replacement of the fantasy with the acephalous drive not lead to *psychosis*, or at best to *pure perversion* (as Moati himself seems to hint at when he insists on the notion of disavowal, the disavowal of the subject's primordial choice through which he would recover himself)?

133. See especially Chiesa 2010, pp. 44-67, and Chiesa 2012, pp. 135-151.

134. Pasolini 1999a, p. 1601. Pasolini even speaks of the 'almost *sexual* effect of transgressing the code as the exhibitionism of something that has been violated' (ibid., p. 1608) (my emphasis).

135. Ibid., p. 1604.

136. Ibid., p. 1610.

ages, and then '*re*-constitute rules'.[137] In this way, such a power would oppose to-day's ruling discourse of conservativism, which is no longer that of the traditional Master's repression, but rather that of the falsely transgressive discourse of Capital's hedonistic consumerism, its '*unconscious and real* ideology'[138] (that is to say, the 'message of liberation' which, according to Seminar III, is inherent to our current condition of universalised—liberal-democratic—bondage).

At this stage, it should be apparent that what is more generally at stake in the openly political conclusion of 'Unpopular Cinema' is a denunciation of the role of transgression as brandished by the hegemonic discourse of (capitalistic) freedom. By now transgression tends to be completely reactionary and, at the same time, uselessly self-destructive: the more it is incorporated by Power, the less the author's martyrdom manages to pose a social threat to its abnormal norms. Pasolini therefore believes that in order to fight this state of affairs we should first and foremost 'keep ourselves alive, and maintain the code in force'; more to the point, if we fail to tame our authorial desire to die, 'suicide creates a void which is immediately filled in by the worst quality of life', as shown by the fact that 'restorations always found themselves on [...] a general nostalgia for a code that was violated too badly'.[139] Here Pasolini is not only agreeing with Lacan's critique of pure desire—from which psychoanalysis should be distanced—and of acephalous rebellion—the freedom to die of hunger—but also attempting to delineate a practical political agenda for countering a ruling Power that, by enjoining wannabe authors to radically transgress its code, has finally unveiled its true anarchic foundations.[140] Complicating Lacan's identification of the suicidal-psychotic discourse of freedom with the discourse of Terror, Pasolini thus puts forward his basic strategy by means of a programmatic question: 'After all, isn't it possible to be an extremist without for this reason being a fanatic or a terrorist?'[141]

To put it differently, for Pasolini, it is a matter of inventing a form of extremist transgression that somehow transgresses precisely the imperative to transgress. While transgression is undoubtedly an essential component of liberation—which in fact can only be achieved by breaking with the norms of biological preservation and political conservativism—it becomes antitransgressive as soon as we 'advance beyond the front of transgression', 'the firing line', Pasolini claims, and find ourselves on the 'other side', in enemy territory.[142] At this point, we immediately get confined into a compartment or, more precisely, 'gathered in a *Lager*, a concentration camp [...] where *everything is transgression* and the enemy has disappeared'.[143] In other words, radical transgression finally resolves itself into a new kind of totalitarian and extremely homogenising Power, which can be epitomised by the anomie of the *Lager*. According to Pasolini, those who decide to transgress

---

137. Ibid. (my emphasis).

138. Pasolini 1999b, p. 322.

139. Pasolini 1999a, p. 1608.

140. Giorgio Agamben's notion of the state of exception and his ethics of testimony are much indebted to Pasolini's political thought, which he knows well (see especially Agamben 2005 and Agamben 2002).

141. Pasolini 1999a, p. 1609.

142. Ibid.

143. Ibid., pp. 1609-1610.

in the name of liberation are consequently faced, in the last resort, with a choice between, on the one hand, the fanatical and terroristic identification of Power with its dissolution, which, in the name of freedom, inevitably leads to the construction of a *Lager*, and, on the other hand, an extremist *lotta continua*, a 'continuous struggle', which, beyond any optimistic synthesis, renounces the idea of redemptive reconciliation and stresses the retroactive character of dis-alienation while moving the firing line further and further:

> Victory over a transgressed norm is soon re-included in the code's infinite possibility of modification and broadening. What is important is not the moment of the realisation of invention but that of invention. Permanent invention, continuous struggle. (Pasolini 1999a, p. 1610)[144]

BIBLIOGRAPHY

Agamben, G., *Remnants of Auschwitz: The Witness and the Archive*, New York: Zone Books, 2002

—— *State of Exception,* Chicago: Chicago University Press, 2005

Chiesa, L., 'Christianisme ou communisme? L'hégélianisme marxien et le marxisme hégélien de Žižek', in R. Moati (ed.), *Autour de Slavoj Žižek. Psychanalyse, Marxisme, Idéalisme Allemand*, Paris: Presses Universitaires de France, 2010

—— 'Umano, inumano e umanesimo nella *Critica della ragion dialettica*', in *aut aut*, 353, 2012

Freud, S., (1919e), 'A Child Is Being Beaten', in *SE 17*

Lacan, J., *Les quatre concepts fondamentaux de la psychanalyse*, Paris: Seuil, 1973

—— *The Ethics of Psychoanalysis,* London: Routledge, 1992

—— *The Psychoses. Book III*, London: Routledge, 1993

—— *Le séminaire. Livre IV. La relation d'objet*, Paris: Seuil, 1994

—— *The Four Fundamental Concepts of Psycho-analysis*, London: Vintage, 1998a

—— *Le séminaire. Livre V. Les formations de l'inconscient*, Paris: Seuil, 1998b

—— 'Allocution sur les psychoses de l'enfant', in *Autres écrits*, Paris: Seuil, 2001

—— *Le séminaire. Livre X. L'angoisse*, Paris: Seuil, 2004

—— *My Teaching*, London: Verso, 2008

—— *Le séminaire. Livre VI. Le désir et son interprétation 1958-1959.* Paris: Éditions de La Martinière, 2013

Pasolini, P. P., 'Il cinema impopolare', in *Saggi sulla letteratura e sull'arte. Tomo primo*, Milan: Mondadori, 1999a

---

144. Pasolini is here outlining a Communist project that departs from the optimistic synthesis of doxastic Marxism, which he criticised at the beginning of 'Unpopular Cinema'. The notion of *lotta continua* was crucial to the homonymous extra-parliamentary Italian organization of the 1970s and early 1980s. In spite of his repeated denunciations against the 'linguistic vulgarity' of the far-left extremism that followed 1968 in Italy, that is to say, of its adoption of the technical language of neo-capitalism (see, for instance, Pasolini 1999b, pp. 248-249 and pp. 437-439), Pasolini showed on several occasions that he openly supported *Lotta continua*. Famously, he lent for some time his name as editor-in-chief of the movement's journal in order to circumvent an Italian law that required every newspaper to prove its 'reliability'. Starting from autumn 1970, a few months after he wrote 'Unpopular cinema', Pasolini also participated in the shooting of *Lotta continua*'s *12 dicembre*, a long documentary about the so-called 'strategy of tension' of those years (available at http://www.youtube.com/watch?v=p6lEU2sVLuY).

—— *Saggi sulla politica e sulla società*, Milan: Mondadori, 1999b

Recalcati, M., 'Hunger, Repletion, and Anxiety', in *Angelaki: Journal of the Theoretical Humanities*, Volume 16, number 3, 2011

Safouan, M., *Lacaniana. Les séminaires de Jacques Lacan. 1964-1979*, Paris: Fayard, 2005

The Field and Function of the Slave in the Écrits

Justin Clemens

> It is claimed that self-interest will prevent excessive cruelty; as
> if self-interest protected our domestic animals, which are far
> less likely than degraded slaves, to stir up the rage of their sav-
> age masters.
> (Darwin, *The Voyage of the Beagle*)

My thesis in this essay is that the figure of the slave is integral to Lacanian psychoanalysis from first to last. This thesis is both simple and unoriginal. Its pertinence derives from the concerted incapacity of commentators, both pro- and
hostile to Lacan, to sustain this integral status. One symptomatic index of this
incapacity can be located in the indices to nominally Lacanian texts, in which
any entry for 'the slave' regularly fails to appear. If it does appear, it is always insofar as it is a correlate or subheading for 'the master' or 'master-signifier' and,
almost as often, insofar as it is referred to Lacan's uptake of 'The Master-Slave
dialectic' of Hegel. Not only does this constitute a severe misunderstanding of
the stakes of Lacanian psychoanalysis, but it necessarily involves falsifying the
stakes of Lacan's relationship to philosophy (not to mention much else). If there
is only the space here to give the most minimal indications of the status of the
slave — indeed, as my title promises, I will almost entirely restrict my comments
to evidence found in the *Ecrits* — it is nonetheless worth beginning with a grim-
ly quantitative rhetorical question. Is there a single seminar of Lacan's in which
the problem of the slave does not occupy a key place?

Certainly, it is undeniable that Jacques Lacan was strongly influenced by Alexandre Kojève's interpretation of G.W.F. Hegel's 'master-slave dialectic'. Lacan
and Kojève were friends, and at one stage even planned to write an article together in 1936 on the differences between Freud and Hegel's theories of desire.
Through painstaking archival research, Elisabeth Roudinesco has even shown
that 'Lacan's specific reading of Freud arose out of his attendance at Kojève's
seminar on *The Phenomenology of Spirit* and follows directly from questions asked in
the review *Recherches philosophiques*'.[1] Lacan was, moreover, very attentive to phi-

---

1. Roudinesco 2003, p. 27. Moreover, 'Documents from this period show that in July 1936 Lacan
intended to collaborate with Kojève in writing a study dealing with the same philosophical principles

losophy, even if he sometimes professed to despise it, and references to the philosophical tradition run throughout his work. Finally, Lacan develops concepts that are, at the very least, compatible with philosophical thinking, and which can be taken up, contested, extended and applied by philosophy in its own way.

I think that almost everything about this picture is insufficient—if not downright misleading and pernicious. If Lacan was indeed 'influenced' by Kojève's interpretation, the word 'influence' remains an *asylum ignorantiae* if not further specified. I would prefer to say: Lacan treats philosophy as an enemy to be combated, right from the start; precisely because of this, he attacks it, just as Lenin recommended, 'at its strongest point'. Hegel is that 'strongest point'. Because he is also a psychoanalyst, however, Lacan's attack cannot be a head-on attack. As he reminds his interlocutors in Seminar XX, there's never any point in 'convincing' anybody.[2]

Lacan's 'attack' is therefore rather of the following kind. Philosophy orients us towards the proper objects and terms of study, but does so in a way that falsifies their import, and, in doing so, functions to exacerbate misunderstandings. Psychoanalysis needs to 'subvert'—a crucial term in the Lacanian armature—philosophy's operations, since psychoanalysis, in line with its own affirmation of the powers of discourse, has no standing nor authorization in the public world. Nor can it gain such a standing, except at the cost of its own self-betrayal. What psychoanalysis might do, though, is, from a position of weakness, exacerbate the routines of philosophy to the point at which the latter literally *shows itself* in its operations and aims; that is, shows itself as something other than the alibis of truth, knowledge and friendship would allow. Moreover, psychoanalysis can and must lose its public struggle against philosophy, if it is not to lose itself. *In* its failure, however, psychoanalysis works to sustain modes of 'speaking' (or 'writing' or 'gesture', there's nothing in these distinctions here) that engage further inventions of freedom within discourse. As such, psychoanalysis is above all a praxis, a praxis whose ethics are those of 'free association'. From Seminar I, Lacan could not be more emphatic regarding the singularity of psychoanalysis as a science of singularity, one, moreover, that is perpetually open to revision in its constitutional refusal of philosophical system.

Lacan was always very clear about this, and also very clear that this clarity would inevitably be occluded as a matter of course. For psychoanalysis, the subject is 'split', that is, constitutively inconsistent, and therefore constitutionally foreign to any form of philosophical mastery. People think they think. They even think they think they think. They think they think what they think. And they think they know why they think what they think. Psychoanalysis thinks this too, but thinks it subversively. People do think like this, precisely because they—we,

---

as those found in the Marienbad lecture and later in the article in the *Encyclopédie*. The study was to be entitled 'Hegel and Freud. An attempt at a comparative interpretation'. The first part was called 'The genesis of self-consciousness,' the second, 'The origin of madness,' the third, 'The essence of the family'. In the end, the study was never written. But in the fifteen pages that survive in Kojève's handwriting we find three of the major concepts used by Lacan in 1936: the I as subject of desire; desire as a revelation of the truth of being; and the ego as site of illusion and source of error' (Roudinesco 2003, p. 28).

2. Lacan 1998.

I—can't think any differently. We can't think differently, because what it means to think is thought for us by the signifiers that deploy us. Philosophy, to the extent that it has managed to inscribe its ontological obsessions within language, will always essay to effect a recapture of what evades, subverts or evacuates philosophical conceptuality. Yet Lacan ceaselessly develops and refines his position on just what this recapture might mean throughout his career. If it is impossible to provide a full account of the mutations to which Lacan submits his rethinking of the problem of the master, in this article I will point to a few of his critical steps.

Lacan evidently chose his words, or, rather, his *signifiers*, very carefully. So it's worth asking why Lacan comes to designate the signifier-signifier the *master*-signifier. What does it mean to be a 'master' of this kind? After all, a 'master' can be opposed to a slave, a serf, a student, an apprentice, or even an actor. On the other hand, a master can be allied with or differentiated from a father, a leader, a lord or a sovereign—quite a ragtag collection of putative rulers. A master also implies a certain relation to self. My thesis is that Lacan's use of the word *master* not only has a number of implications, but that its significance shifts quite radically over the course of his work. First, its crucial correlate is the slave, not a student. To be a master for Lacan isn't just to be a schoolmaster; it means, first and foremost, being a slave-master, a master of slaves. Law, politics and economics are all enshrined in this structure, whose logic is ultimately established and delivered by the structure of signification. Second, the emergence of the thought of this opposition between master and slave lies in philosophy, specifically Hegelian philosophy, and, vis-à-vis Lacan himself, in his own initial encounter with Hegel by means of Kojève's notorious seminars on the *Phenomenology of Spirit* in 1930s Paris. Third, Lacan himself will use the term master as a way to finally differentiate himself, not only from Freud's account, but from his own. The master-signifier ultimately comes to supplant those of the father, phallus or leader, for reasons that are complex and overdetermined, but which hinge on the issue of the consistency of psychoanalysis in a new media age. These three points need to be taken together. None of them would be particularly novel to Lacanians, but I would like to emphasize something about the master that remains under-examined, though it is crucial throughout Lacan's career: his analysis of *slavery*, on which he insists from first to last, even though it undergoes certain highly significant shifts.

As far as I have been able to ascertain, the word 'slave' (*esclave*) appears twenty times in the *Écrits*, and the word 'slavery' (*esclavage*) once.[3] Unsurprisingly, the word 'master' (*maître*), by contrast, appears far more frequently in the *Écrits*; 'mastery' (*maîtrise*) eighteen times, *maîtresse* eight times, most often as an adjective (e.g., *les lignes maîtresses*), and 'to master' (*maîtriser*) once.[4] If it's worth at least pointing to this rather disproportionate distribution, this shouldn't prevent us from examining Lacan's uses of the slave further.

---

3. Lacan 1966. All further reference will be to Lacan 2005, including page references to both the English and French editions.

4. The term *maître* appears on the following pages of the French Ecrits: 21, 32-33, 38, 65, 121-23, 27, 152, 162, 168, 179, 181, 241, 244, 249, 292-94, 304, 313-16, 320, 330, 345, 348-349, 351, 356, 371, 379, 396, 419, 424, 432, 452, 475, 477, 486, 536, 588, 634, 699, 754, 757, 807, 810-11, 824, 826, most often in connection with the themes of teaching, ancient politics, and the Hegelian dialectic.

Let's examine a few of the uses of these terms. In 'Aggressiveness in Psycho-analysis' (1948), Lacan writes:

> A child who beats another child says that he himself was beaten; a child who sees another child fall, cries. Similarly, it is by identifying with the other that he experiences the whole range of bearing and display reactions—whose structural ambivalence is clearly revealed in his behaviours, the slave identifying with the despot, the actor with the spectator, the seduced with the seducer. (Lacan 2005, p. 92 / Lacan 1966, p. 113)

> Before Darwin, however, Hegel had provided the definitive theory of the specific function of aggressiveness in human ontology, seeming to prophesy the iron law of our own time. From the conflict between Master and Slave, he deduced the entire subjective and objective progress of our history, revealing in its crises the syntheses represented by the highest forms of the status of the person in the West, from the Stoic to the Christian, and even to the future citizen of the Universal State. Here the natural individual is regarded as nil, since the human subject is nothing, in effect, before the absolute Master that death is for him. The satisfaction of human desire is possible only when mediated by the other's desire and labour. While it is the recognition of man by man that is at stake in the conflict between Master and Slave, this recognition is based on a radical negation of natural values, whether expressed in the master's sterile tyranny or in work's productive tyranny. The support this profound doctrine lent to the slave's constructive Spartacism, recreated by the barbarity of the Darwinian century, is well known. (Lacan 2005, pp. 98-99 / Lacan 1966, p. 121)

> The question is whether the conflict between Master and Slave will find its solution in the service of the machine, for which a psychotechnics, that is already yielding a rich harvest of ever more precise applications, will strive to provide race-car drivers and guards for regulating power stations. (Lacan 2005, p. 99 / Lacan 1966, p. 122)

There are therefore two major senses in which Lacan is mobilising the resources of the signifier 'slave' in these presentations: 1) as exemplifying a law of projective reversal, of projection as dissimulated reversal: I experience what I do to you as if you had done it to me or vice-versa; 2) as a Hegelian *philosopheme*, as marking the origin of human ontology in a struggle, but, notably in a struggle for 'recognition' or 'prestige', founded on a 'radical negation of natural values'. A particular phenomenon of *mis*recognition, in other words, regulates both senses of the slave. The truth of intersubjective relations inverts itself as part of its integral operations; this inversion is the medium of an irreducible antagonism; technology is a symptom of this antagonism. The problem of technology is raised integrally in the question of the slave, the invention of which category was of course an ancient category of technology; by comparison, our 'objectifying' world demands a 'psychotechnics' (perhaps what is now dominant as Cognitive Behavioural Therapy and psychopharmacology?) as a correlate. Finally, one cannot miss that, at least in this account of Lacan's, Hegel's philosophy mis-speaks of the *imaginary* functions of the self. If Hegel is right to identify the master-slave dialectic as crucial, some of its routines (the irreducible narcissistic-aggressiveness it marks), and its essentially anti-natural character, his analysis takes place at the cost of mistaking the relationship between philosophy and the world. Philosophy at once pinpoints something essential, but miscomprehends it, not least because it ultimately seeks to suture truth to knowledge.

This early position of Lacan partially derives from his encounter with Kojève. Kojève, who was Alexandre Koyré's brother-in-law and Wassily Kandinsky's nephew, had studied under Karl Jaspers, before ending up in Paris. His central work in this context is not really a book at all; it is basically an assemblage of texts and lecture-notes taken by the great French writer Raymond Queneau, at Kojève's seminar at the École des Hautes Études. The seminar was attended by Raymond Aron, Georges Bataille, Maurice Merleau-Ponty, Eric Weil, Aron Gurwitsch, André Breton, and Lacan, among others. In a superb twist of contingency, the lectures were only given in the first place because Koyré was off to Egypt for a couple of years, and had invited Kojève to take his seminar for him. Kojève, then, proceeded on his reading of Hegel with extreme violence.

As Michael Roth comments, 'it would be a complete mistake to try to understand or evaluate Kojève's work on the basis of its faithfulness to Hegel'.[5] What, then, was crucial about this seminar? It:

1. identified Hegel as the crucial philosopher of modernity;
2. identified the anthropological elements as crucial to Hegel's philosophy;
3. identified temporality as crucial to this anthropology;
4. identified the master/slave dialectic as crucial to this temporality;
5. identified the struggle for recognition as crucial to the master/slave dialectic;
6. identified the epitome of this struggle in the self-seizure of self-consciousness as such;
7. identified self-consciousness as such as finalised at the 'end of history'.

These identifications—despite their obvious failings as a reading of Hegel—are nonetheless compelling in the detail given them by Kojève. Human being only properly begins when humans are willing to risk their animal, biological existence in a fight to the death for pure prestige, that is, recognition by the other; the winner, who becomes master, is the one willing and able to stare death, the absolute master, full in the face, and, in this total risk of life, dominates the other who, fearful, has decided it would be better to live at any price than die; the master, however, is then condemned to enjoyment. For not only does he not get the recognition that he craved, except as recognition by an inferior (which is no real recognition at all), but his reward is enjoyment, the enjoyment of the fruits of the slave's labour, without truth; the slave, on the other hand, forced to toil at matter, comes, in the course of his enforced labours, to transform the world really, and, in this transformation, comes to know the truth of matter. Note that 'recognition' here is not recognition of/by something real, but of a nothingness, of the desire of the other, a desire directed towards another desire.

---

5. See Roth 1985, p. 295.

The End of History is a controversial thesis to say the least. In the second edition to the commentary on Hegel, Kojève notes that:

> If Man becomes an animal again, his arts, his loves, and his play must also become purely 'natural' again [...] But one cannot then say that all this 'makes Man happy'. One would have to say that post-historical animals of the species Homo sapiens (which will live amidst abundance and complete security) will be content as a result of their artistic, erotic and playful behaviour, inasmuch as, by definition, they will be contented with it. But there is 'more'. 'The definitive annihilation of Man properly so-called' also means the definitive disappearance of human discourse (*Logos*) in the strict sense. (Kojève 1969)

For Kojève, then, the 'end of history' does not mean that things don't continue to happen. What it means, however, is that, in accordance with a reading of Hegel that sees the dialectic of knowledge concluding with an immanentization of all relations in the absolution of Spirit, which is absolute as no longer articulated with any contradictions whose dynamic leads to irreversible developments, we see a paradoxical reconciliation of humanity with its natural animality. As such, language (*logos*, reason) will no longer project ideals that drive man forward through false starts and illusions, but will be resolved back into the pleasures of the body itself as forms of purposiveness-without-purpose.

It is *against* this philosophical sense of an End to Man's becoming that Lacan develops his own position. As such, the properly 'structuralist' Lacan remains locked in a struggle with Hegel regarding ends. As Charles Shepherdson writes:

> Lacan's early seminars (1953-55) are marked by a prolonged encounter with Hegel, who had a substantial and abiding effect not only on his account of the imaginary and the relation to the other (jealousy and love, intersubjective rivalry and narcissism), but also on his understanding of negation and desire while leading to the logic of the signifier. (Shepherdson 2003, p. 116)[6]

Indeed, the important *écrit* 'The Subversion of the Subject and the Dialectic of Desire' (delivered 1960, but first published 1966) begins with a reference to the *Phenomenology of Spirit*. First presented at a conference entitled '*La Dialectique*', organised by Jean Wahl, the paper proceeds to distinguish psychoanalysis from philosophy, and both from science. Psychoanalysis properly speaking subverts the nature of the subject as it is delivered by philosophy. For Lacan, 'we expect from Hegel's phenomenology' the 'marking out [of] an ideal solution—one that involves a permanent revisionism, so to speak, in which what is disturbing about truth is constantly being reabsorbed, truth being in itself but what is lacking in the realization of knowledge'.[7] But scientific theories 'do not, in any way, fit together according to the thesis/antithesis/synthesis dialectic';[8] rather, science abolishes the subject altogether. Freud emerges in the non-space of this deadlock:

---

6. See also Huson 1996, pp. 56-78.

7. Lacan 2005, p. 675 / Lacan 1966, p. 797.

8. Lacan 2005, p. 675 / Lacan 1966, p. 798.

In Hegel's work it is desire (*Begierde*) that is given responsibility for the minimal link the subject must retain to Antiquity's knowledge if truth is to be immanent in the realization of knowledge. The 'cunning of reason' means that, from the outset and right to the end, the subject knows what he wants.

It is here that Freud reopens the junction between truth and knowledge to the mobility out of which revolutions arise.

In this respect: that desire becomes bound up at that junction with the Other's desire, but that the desire to know lies in this loop. (Lacan 2005, p. 679 / Lacan 1966, p. 802)

For Lacan, what goes wrong in the end with Hegel is not that the latter hasn't touched on a number of fundamental propositions—for example, that language divides man from animal, that 'the word is the murder of the thing,' or the powers of negation cannot be ignored if one is to even begin to take account of singularities—but that 'the reason for Hegel's error lies in his rigour'.[9] What this means is that *Bewusstsein* covers over the split in the *Selbst* produced by the external opacity of the shifter 'I', which no knowledge can contain. Hegel fails to note the 'generic prematurity of birth' in humankind (the 'dynamic mainspring of specular capture'), the fact that death is not the Absolute Master (being split between 'two deaths'), and the *jouissance* of the slave (that loss itself and not merely recognition is what is at stake in the struggle, insofar as it is the index of a surplus-pleasure).

Note, too, that the theme of 'the end of history' is immediately subverted by the possibility of an analysis that is 'interminable'. One can see how Lacan implicitly maintains: 1) there is and can be no 'end' to history; 2) 'history' itself is a *post-facto* reconstitution of events that necessarily effaces the operations of self-effacement essential to the subject; 3) 'history' therefore cannot function as any 'determination in the last instance' or as the ultimate place of the taking-place of events. The 'unconscious', as Freud insisted, is characterised by its 'untimeliness', and in a number of senses. First, its activity always comes as a shock, whose effects are in excess of their causes, or rather retroactively create a cause which they dissimulate; second, the materials from which the unconscious is composed are not chronologically-organised, and nor are they even in principle able to be so-organised; third, the unconscious withdraws itself from any possible positive knowledge. Excess, disorganisation, unknowability: rather than history, then, Lacan emphasizes the radical 'loopiness' of revolutions (something he will of course continue to do in different ways throughout his career), directed by the Freudian revelation that 'truth' and 'knowledge' have to be held apart on the condition of the unconscious. Psychoanalysis affirms the loopiness-without-end of subjectivity, its incessant de-totalisation and its a-conceptuality. Indeed, Lacan will at one point formalise the operations of fantasy as $S \lozenge a$ (that the subject is correlated with an object-cause of desire): the unconscious is structurally Other, a diacritically-defined treasury which is an eccentric locus, and in which the fundamental signifier (the 'phallus') is always lacking from its place. Yet what Lacan's assault on dialectical teleology also means is this: slavery will always be with us, and it is us.

---

9. Lacan 2005, p. 685 / Lacan 1966, p. 810.

But what is most determining in the present context is that at this stage of his work the slave—the subject of the signifier—*is not really correlated with the master at all*. This may seem like a preposterous remark. Yet what's important here is that the 'mastery' of which Lacan most often speaks is correlated with the ego, that is, with the imaginary. As Lacan says: 'we analysts deal with slaves who think they are masters'.[10] Mastery is thus an imaginary function; slavery is a symbolic one. The subject is a subject insofar as it subsists in a state of servitude, servitude to the signifier. As Lacan puts it, suggesting that, with respect to the Freudian doctrine of the death-drive, a *savoir* is involved without any possible *connaissance*,

> in that it is inscribed in a discourse of which the subject—who, like the messenger-slave of Antiquity, carries under his hair the codicil that condemns him to death—knows neither the meaning nor the text, nor in what language it is written, nor even that it was tattooed on his shaven scalp while he was sleeping. (Lacan 2005, p. 803 / Lacan 1966, p. 680)

When he arrives at his destination, the tattoo that the slave bears will be read, and enacted; this slave-messenger will be put to death. The critique of the Hegelian master-slave dialectic is pursued: 'it is not enough to decide the question on the basis of its effect: Death. We need to know which death, the one that life brings or the one that brings life'.[11] And this requires a recourse to Freudian doctrine again: Freud's Father is a dead Father, and this is, in Lacan's terms, of course the 'Name-of-the-Father'. For Lacan, 'the Father the neurotic wishes for is clearly the dead Father [...] But he is also a Father who would be the perfect master of his desire'.[12] A fantasy, evidently, a fantasy of mastery whose very form of demand actively works against its satisfaction. The Master-Slave dialectic is rather a Phallus-Slave a-dialectic.

So what, finally, has to be emphasized is that it is *sex* that returns to subvert the master-slave relationship that it founds. If there is something that Lacan doesn't substantially seem to change his mind about, it's this. Moreover, this has a bearing upon analytic attentiveness itself. If psychoanalysis thinks the problem of the master-slave and the consequences of sexual difference by being *sui generis*, its singularity is not monotony: psychoanalysis is only itself because it was called into being by a certain kind of speech, a hysterical demand for love. The insistence of psychoanalysis, as well as its emergence, is conditioned by hysteria. Hysteria itself is a response to this primary aspect of discourse, that of the servitude of humanity to signification. To some extent, this also reproduces a dictum of Hegel's, to the effect that 'woman is the eternal irony of community', as the latter remarks in *The Phenomenology of Spirit* regarding, of all things, the character of Antigone. In any case, we now have a fundamental topic (the phallus-slave relation), a theme of subversion (the hysterical subversion of a sexual dis-organisation that it thereby reveals), and a *différend* (psychoanalysis against philosophy).

This approach is at once consecrated and transformed with Seminar XVII. Why? Because there the master returns, as correlated with but differentiated

---

10. Lacan 2005, p. 242 / Lacan 1966, p. 293.
11. Lacan 2005, p. 686 / Lacan 1966, p. 810.
12. Lacan 2005, p. 698 / Lacan 1966, p. 824.

from the slave, and the relation between master, slave and knowledge is at the heart of that seminar. What is the Master? He is not a person, not simply, anyway, but more fundamentally a signifier. He is, in what we could call Lacan's post-1968 '*mathemations*', an S1. How to speak of him, then? After all, the conceptual tools we have to speak about him derive primarily from philosophy, and philosophy itself is a master's discourse—if, as Lacan says, a 'subtle' one. We must avoid philosophy, then, but how? And, furthermore, even if we do, how then do we evade another form of discourse, one that is just as fundamental as the master's, that of the 'university'? For S1 can only be an S1 because of S2, the signifiers of knowledge. The Master doesn't know, but addresses himself to those who do. Who are these little S2s, then? They are slaves, if knowing slaves. A slave is always a slave of knowledge, in subjective and objective senses of the genitive. If, as we know from the notorious Seminar XX, 'there is no sexual relationship', analysis doesn't for that deny the existence of all relationships. Indeed, if there are relationships between human beings, if there is indeed any basis for a social bond, they all share a fundamental basis: S1–S2, the Master and the Slave. At the origin of language, there is the pure command without content, to which is correlated a knowledge of dependence. The cost, of course, is that of the splitting of the speaking being, marked by castration and by death. Like 'primitive accumulation' for Marx, the master-slave relationship is at the origins of the subject for Lacan.[13]

If I have had no time here except to designate the brute way-stations of Lacan's development, I want to end by reiterating that the problematic of slavery is there in Lacan from first to last. Ultimately, man is a slave to the signifier. And, as Lacan knows, the ancient slave's speech could only have a legal bearing if it had been extracted through torture. To be a speaking being for Lacan is thus not to be free, but enslaved; and the very act of speaking is itself not freedom but evidence of coercion. 'Free association' is therefore literally an impossible affair. This is partially why, in the end, the entire elaborate edifice of Lacanian approaches to philosophy ends up by coming down on the side of the slave against philosophy, or, rather, on psychoanalysis as a non-revolutionary but essentially rebellious discourse that takes the side of the slave revolt against the master. This slave revolt is not Spartacist, but Antigonian, if I can put it like that. The hysteric is the ethical hero in this regard: one can never abolish the structures of mastery for Lacan, but one can at least assault in words the law of language, that is, by finding a master to rule over.

BIBLIOGRAPHY

Huson, T., 'Truth and Contradiction: Reading Hegel with Lacan', in S. Žižek (ed.), *Lacan: The Silent Partners*, London: Verso, 2006

Kojève, A., *Introduction to the Reading of Hegel*, ed. A. Bloom, trans. J.H. Nichols, NY and London: Basic Books, 1969

---

13. As Marx points out, vis-à-vis Adam Smith, 'this primitive accumulation plays approximately the same role in political economy as original sin does in theology' (Marx 1986, p. 873). It is with respect, however, to primitive accumulation, that Marx notes that violence and force are integral to its operation, that is, 'extirpation, enslavement and entombment': 'Force is the midwife of every old society which is pregnant with a new one. It is itself an economic power' (ibid., p. 916).

Lacan, J., *Écrits*, Paris: Seuil, 1966

—— *Encore: The Seminar of Jacques Lacan, Book XX. On Feminine Sexuality, The Limits of Love and Knowledge, 1972-1973*, ed. J-A. Miller, trans. with notes B. Fink, New York: W.W. Norton, 1998

—— *Écrits*, trans. B. Fink with H. Fink and R. Grigg, New York: Norton, 2005

Marx, K., *Capital*, Vol. 1, trans. B. Fowkes, Harmondsworth: Penguin, 1986

Roth, M. S., 'A Problem of Recognition: Alexandre Kojève and the End of History', *History and Theory*, Vol. 24, No. 3, 1985

Roudinesco, E., 'The mirror stage: an obliterated archive', in J.-M. Rabaté (ed.), *The Cambridge Companion to Lacan*, Cambridge: CUP, 2003

Shepherdson, C., 'Lacan and philosophy', in J.-M. Rabaté (ed.), *The Cambridge Companion to Lacan*, Cambridge: CUP, 2003

The School and the Act

Oliver Feltham

On the lawns sloping away from the University of Sydney I watched a friend-ship disintegrate in front of my eyes. One friend had announced he was leaving for Melbourne to study psychoanalysis as a non-institutional praxis. The other friend would not be left behind and would continue to militate for a deconstructive praxis on the margins of the university. At a certain point the argument was no longer about convincing. That point was an accusation: Lacan is a pig, how could you follow him? The pig had swallowed the friend. I chose to follow a few years later. Our school was dissolved in acts.

To act for a school—is this the desire of philosophy?

> It is on the basis of the subversion of the subject that we have
> to rethink the notion of act.[1]
> (Lacan, Seminar XV)

Thus Lacan formulates the stakes of his seminar on the psychoanalytic act. Two months later the Movement of the 22nd of March begins at the Nanterre campus. Replace 'the subject' with 'society' in the formula, and one has a universal prescription for the events of May: It is on the basis of the subversion of *society* that we have to rethink the notion of act.

Lacan was in no way innoculated from the events of May 1968.[2] The student leader Daniel Cohn-Bendit was invited to speak to the Ecole de la Cause Freudienne, Lacan signed a letter of support for the students and he suspended his seminar on the 15th of March in line with a strike pronounced by the Teacher's Union. In his eyes, the stakes of the protests went well beyond what Raymond Aron diagnosed as a juvenile bourgeois psychodrama. Nothing less than a transformation in the registers of desire and knowledge was involved: for Lacan structures did walk in the street.[3]

---

1. All translations by O. Feltham. References to Seminar XV. *L'acte psychanalytique* (unpublished) are to the unofficial pdf transcript to be found on the website; http://gaogoa.free.fr/SeminaireS.htm

2. I am indebted to Jean-Michel Rabaté's excellent article '1968 + 1: Lacan's *Année Erotique*' (Rabaté 2006).

3. Lacan, Seminar XV. *L'acte psychanalytique* (unpublished), lesson of 15/5/1968.

During that year Lacan's own seminar was subject to change. He insists that his target audience consists of qualified analysts but he often notes, to his dismay, that the senior analysts of his school are absent. They have been replaced by an influx of young students from his host institution, the *Ecole Normale Supérieure*. Lacan's reactions waver between bemusement and belligerence; he wagers that the students come because they feel—unlike in the Faculty of Letters—that something is at stake in his teaching, it could have consequences.[4] And it did: in the Spring of 1969 the new director of the Ecole Normale expelled Lacan's seminar. This caused one more in a series of displacements that added up to institutional homelessness. During one session Lacan sarcastically dismisses a desire on the part of his colleagues to be housed in the Faculty of Medicine. Neither at home in the Faculty of Letters nor in the Faculty of Medicine, the place of his teaching also caused problems inside his own school.[5]

What was thus at stake in Lacan's own seminar, in his presence and in the constitution of his audience, was also the articulation of truth and knowledge—with regard to the reproduction of his school, *l'Ecole française de psychanalyse*. Who would join the school, to strengthen its numbers? What did it take to become a member? What exactly did the school transmit?

At the end of the *Nicomachean Ethics*, Aristotle grapples with the same question: who could understand his teaching, to whom was it properly transmitted? Throughout the work he has claimed that its end is not further study, not an increase in knowledge, but correct action. It is a treatise that is designed to have a practical effect, to lead its readers to live virtuous lives. Moral philosophy thus positions itself as a *propadeutic* to correct action. However there are limits to this propadeutic. In the final chapter Aristotle tardily issues a drastic caveat: if the reader does not already have a noble soul, and if they are not already posing the question of how to act in the right way, then they are a lost cause for ethics. This is quite different to the primitive Christian church with its universal proselytism. In Aristotle there is no drive to convert anyone regardless of the state of their soul. The field of prospective candidates is limited from the outset. Only the already chosen can choose themselves and be schooled in virtuous action. And Aristotle was a founder of one of the first schools, the Lyceum.

The question of preparing someone to act correctly is inseparable from the question of the school, and of its continued existence. A school positions itself as a propadeutic to life as a virtuous citizen. Psychoanalysis can also be positioned as a propadeutic to a life as a virtuous citizen. Indeed Freud advises that the analyst request the patient to refrain from any life-changing action during the time of treatment; no decisions to marry for example, no choices of a profession. Action is prohibited during the time of analysis and deferred until afterwards: once the patient has been analyzed. This appears less draconian if one remembers that the duration of an analysis was a little shorter back then. Indeed action is placed quite differently during the analysis itself; Lacan notes that psychoanalysis may be understood as the recuperation of the hidden meaning of human ac-

---

4. Ibid., lesson of 22/11/1967. See also Lacan 2001, p. 346.
5. Lacan 2001, p. 298.

tions.[6] Not only is the meaning hidden, but often the subjects involved are not aware that their behaviour constituted an action. The first analytic concepts of action are thus those of unconscious action—acting out, and the *acte manqué* (the misfired act), as Freud details in the *Psychopathology of Everyday Life*. In the case of the restitution of the existence and meaning of unconscious acts, action is thus placed as what has already happened and it is a question of discovering the orientation of such action. However, as Lacan points out, it is the interpretation of the analyst that properly constitutes a behaviour as an *acte manqué*, and for this reason the real subject of the action is the analyst. Thus even when it is a case of diagnosing the analysand's actions, the analysand does not properly act. And so action can only really occur—and here psychoanalysis repeats the Aristotelian position of the school—after the completion of the analysis.

However, it is precisely during the very seminar on the psychoanalytic act—the one interrupted by the events of May 1968—that Lacan claims that psychoanalysis is not only a propadeutic but an *exemplar* of action: 'the psychoanalytic act [...] can shed some light on the act without qualification'.[7] Addressing the newcomers in his audience he states: 'The psychoanalytic act directly concerns those who do not make psychoanalysis their profession'.[8] In his summary of the seminar, reproduced in *Autres Ecrits*, he offers a definition: 'The act—any act, not just psychoanalytic—takes the place of a saying, and it changes the subject of that saying'.[9] He gives examples of such acts from the field of politics: Caesar crossing the Rubicon, the Jeu de Paume and then the night of the 4th of August during the French Revolution, the days of October 1917—in each case new signifiers were unleashed upon the world. The efficacy of the act, he explains, has nothing to do with the efficacy of war, or of making in any sense: it lies rather in its signifying something new, and thus inaugurating something.[10] But these historical acts are mere examples: the exemplar, theorized at length, is the psychoanalytic act. Indeed there is an entire history of the subject's position in relation to the act—a history marked by Aristotle, Descartes, Kant, Hegel and Marx—a history in which psychoanalysis has not yet taken its proper place, a place to be carved out by Lacan.[11]

What immediately strikes the casual reader of Seminar XV is the similarity between this history and that mapped out in his seminar on the ethics of psychoanalysis eight years previously. Lacan himself remarks that the projects of the two seminars are paired in some fashion.[12] They are paired—this is my hypothesis—in that their project is the same: to give, in the phrasing of Seminar VII, 'the young person setting himself up as an analyst [...] a backbone for his action'.[13]

---

6. Lacan 1992, p. 312.

7. Lacan, Seminar XV (unpublished), lesson of 20/3/1968. See also Lacan 2001, p. 375.

8. Ibid., lesson of 22/11/1967.

9. Lacan 2001, p. 375.

10. Lacan, Seminar XV (unpublished), lesson of 10/1/1968.

11. Ibid., lesson of 24/1/1968.

12. Ibid., lesson of 29/11/1967.

13. Lacan 1986, p. 226 (my translation). See also Lacan 1992, p. 192. All references in the body of the text to this seminar will be to the English edition.

Seminar VII is centered upon action: Lacan situates psychoanalysis as a descendent of the tradition of moral philosophy. The task of psychoanalysis, he says, 'given our situation as men' is to determine 'what [we] must [...] do to act in the right way'.[14] The whole first half of the seminar is spent on the question 'what orientates human action?' But why do the two seminars share the same project? This suggests that Seminar VII is in some manner incomplete. And yet it is one of the most satisfying of Lacan's seminars to read, since it does appear to come to a conclusion. It announces an ethics of psychoanalysis—the principle 'do not give up on your desire'—and it identifies the space of that ethics as tragic through a reading of Sophocles' *Antigone*. Seminar XV, on the other hand, is definitely incomplete: Lacan explains that he didn't manage to teach half of what he wanted to.[15]

Repetition of the project, implicit and explicit incompletion: what exactly is at stake in giving a backbone to the action of young analysts? Our hypothesis will be that it is the question of the school; and particularly the hesitation between propaedeutic and exemplar for the position of the subject of psychoanalysis with regard to the act.

I. ARISTOTLE AND ACTION WITHIN THE *POLIS*

In this question it is the confrontation with Aristotle that is crucial. Seminar VII begins with a reading of the *Nicomachean Ethics* and its model of ethical action. Lacan reconstructs Aristotle's argument in the following manner. Human action is orientated by the sovereign good, an 'ultimate point of reference'.[16] The good can be identified with pleasure inasmuch as pleasure is 'a sign of the blossoming of an action'.[17] This identification is not immediately obvious in Aristotle. A few steps need to be restituted: he defines man's sovereign or highest good as *eudaimonia*—prospering or flourishing—which is in turn defined as acting according to reason and virtue. Since to act in a virtuous manner is man's highest good, such action cannot be carried out for any other external end; it is thus what he terms *eupraxia*, action whose end is itself. Much later on in the *Nicomachean Ethics* Aristotle remarks of actions whose ends are themselves that 'pleasure completes the activity that unfolds'.[18] Lacan concludes that for Aristotle pleasure is thus a natural orientation, a 'signal', and so in some manner it grounds human beings in reality. This is a point that Lacan insists on: in Aristotle the good, which is identified with pleasure, defines an adequacy to reality for human beings.[19] It serves as a striking contrast with Freud, for whom the pleasure principle, as a principle of homeostasis, operates so as to insulate the subject from reality.

The second major thesis in Lacan's interpretation of the *Ethics* is that like other works of moral philosophy it 'refers to an order that is initially presented

---

14. Lacan 1992, p. 19.

15. There is one saving grace, though: 'My discourse was not interrupted by something unimportant; it was interrupted by something [May '68] that called into question—in an infantile manner, to be sure—a dimension that is not without a relation to the act' (Seminar XV, lesson of 19/6/1968).

16. Lacan 1992, p. 36.

17. Lacan 1992, p. 27.

18. No doubt referring to *Nichomachean Ethics*, Book X, 4, 8. I owe this reference to Jean Ansaldi's *Lire Lacan: L'éthique de la psychanalyse* (Ansaldi 1998).

19. Lacan 1992, p. 13, p. 34, p. 36.

as a science, *episteme*, a science of what is to be done, an uncontested order which defines the norm of a certain character, *ethos*'.[20] This is curious. There is an order for Aristotle—an order of goods—but there is precisely no science of what is to be done; *phronesis* (practical wisdom, prudence), he states, is not a science.[21] Yet the science at stake for Lacan, of course, is that of Aristotle's own discourse, that of moral philosophy, the *orthos logos*, the correct discourse. The order, Lacan continues, is 'gathered together [...] in a sovereign Good, a point of insertion, of attachment and convergence, wherein the particular order is unified with a more universal knowledge, where ethics gives onto politics'.[22] This order is thus the order of goods which Aristotle constitutes as follows: all activities are carried out for the sake of something, a good. The good is what occurs at the end of the activity. Some ends are carried out in order to bring about another end—a saddle is completed in order to then facilitate horse riding. Hence the multiplicity of goods can be organized into hierarchical series. These series can in turn be unified into one encompassing hierarchy inasmuch as there is a good which encompasses all other goods: the sovereign good. Lacan states that this order of goods—defined by philosophy—'defines the norm of a certain character'. Shortly afterwards he claims that Aristotle addressed his ethics to an ideal type: the master, who 'left the control of his slaves to his steward in order to concentrate on a contemplative ideal'.[23] Aristotle's prospective student—one of the happy few possessing a noble soul—is thus a prospective master, an Athenian aristocrat.

In the first book of the *Metaphysics* Aristotle determines the place of philosophical knowledge via an analogy: philosophical knowledge is to technical knowledge as an architect is to manual-laborers; the architect commands and has a vision of the whole whereas the laborer works without knowing what he is doing. The philosopher arrogates for himself the position of the master: the master who will transmit his knowledge, via a teaching, to prospective masters—to youth whose action does not yet have backbone.

But there is a problem. Philosophy is missing something: the knowledge of the master. As mentioned above, there is no science of action. Aristotle defines virtue—it is a mean between two extremes—and he names the virtues: courage, temperance, liberality, magnificence, etc. What he cannot do is explain how the mean can be determined for a particular action. In other words, there is no rule which explains how the rule must be applied. In his magnificent study *La prudence chez Aristote*, Pierre Aubenque shows that in the absence of any philosophical explanation Aristotle is forced to defer to existing practice.[24]

> Virtue, then, is a state that decides, consisting in a mean, the mean relative to us, which is defined by reference to reason, that is to say, to the reason by reference to which the prudent person would define it. (*Metaphysics*, II, 6, 1107a1)[25]

20. Ibid., p. 22.
21. See Aristotle, *Nicomachean Ethics*, Book VI, 8.
22. Lacan 1992, p. 22.
23. Lacan 1992, p. 23.
24. Aubenque 1963.
25. See also 9, 1109b14.

Aristotle thus *supposes* the existence of such ethical knowledge in the possession of the *phronimom*, the prudent person. His example is Pericles, a master if anyone was. The philosophical science of what is to be done is flawed with an in-
dexical deferral to existent supposed mastery. Aristotle's school for masters does
not possess but supposes the knowledge of the master: no slight anticipation of
Lacan's 'supposed subject of knowledge'.

The final piece in Lacan's reading of Aristotle is that he is the author of the
idea of a macrocosm—and thus of a microcosm—insofar as the ethical sphere
is harmoniously articulated with the political sphere, which in turn is an imita-
tion of the cosmos.[26]

Lacan's position with regard to the Aristotelian construction is one of dia-
metrical opposition. Based on an interpretation of Freud's concept of the pleasure
principle and the reality principle he states there is no sovereign Good. He claims
that there are no grounds for a microcosm-macrocosm articulation.[27] In short,
the subject of psychoanalysis is fundamentally conflictual and inadequate to the
real: pleasure does not provide human beings with a grounding in nature, precisely the opposite.[28] On the basis of Freud's arguments in *Civilization and its Discontents*, Lacan claims there is no harmonious articulation of such an individual
with the collective: his or her attempts to satisfy the superego's demands to con-
form to society's requirements only cause those demands to increase in their cru-
elty. He then goes on to construct a psychoanalytic theory of what orientates human action—*das Ding*, and its stand-ins. The problem is that this theory, which
occupies a large part of the seminar, remains in the register of diagnosis: such is
the symptom, such is the sublimation that has orientated the analysand's action
so far. Furthermore, in denying the existence of Aristotle's macrocosm, Lacan entirely elides the name and the nature of that macrocosm: the *polis*, the city-state.

Aristotle's fundamental contribution to political philosophy is the identification of the individual good with the collective good. Plato had already made such
an identification in the *Republic* but it was via an analogy: the separate parts of
the human soul had to be articulated in a balanced manner just like their corresponding parts in the city. Aristotle's identification, in contrast, is not analogical
but metonymic. The sovereign good of the city is the good of the most inclusive
of partnerships.[29] It is the final good: that for the sake of which everything else
in the city is done. As the sovereign good it is complete or self-sufficient: nothing else is required; 'by itself alone [it] renders life desirable and lacking in nothing'.[30] Yet the supreme good of the city not only *has* the property of self-sufficiency but it *is* self-sufficiency. A city is self-sufficient not just when it assures the
conditions of life for all those in its partnership, but when it assures the good life.
The sovereign good of the individual also shares the properties of finality and
self-sufficiency but it is identified as prosperity, as acting well for the sake of acting well; in other words as the good life.

---

26. Lacan 1992, p. 22.
27. Ibid., p. 13, p. 34, p. 92.
28. Ibid., p. 28, p. 35.
29. See Aristotle, *Politics*, I, 1.
30. Aristotle, *Nichomachean Ethics*, I, 7.

How does Aristotle articulate these two identical sovereign goods, the individual and the collective? If an individual acts so as to contribute to the overall self-sufficiency of the city then his action figures solely as an instrumental means to an end. It does not fulfil the citizen's sovereign good, since it is carried out for an external end, not for itself. However there is an alternative to instrumentalism in the articulation of ends: the part-whole relationship. When a virtuous action is a means—carried out for the sake of the city's self-sufficiency—this does not erase its character as an end. Actions are thus not instruments but immediately part of achieving the highest good of self-sufficiency. That is, it is not individuals who form the parts of the city, but actions.[31] Moreover, according to Aristotle's 'organicism' or 'holism' the whole is prior to its parts. Without the city there is no action, without the macrocosm no microcosm. Hence the *polis* for Aristotle is not simply the incidental end of a series of instrumentally linked actions like a supply chain. In the *Nicomachean Ethics* the *polis* is also the agent and the space of action. In his account of factionalism and the rise and fall of various types of regime in the *Politics* Aristotle actually provides, under the name of the *polis*, a theory of the reception of actions.

To provide a psychoanalytic model of action beyond propadeutics, Lacan must thus not only name a principle for action but also theorize the space of its occurrence. That is, if there is no macrocosm, no polis, then what is the space of action? And how may that space be theorized without supposing a master of knowledge?

These are not abstract questions for Lacan. Contemporary psychoanalysis in the form of American ego psychology reproduces the Aristotelian solution. It supposes a knowledge of the master in the possession of the analyst. According to Lacan it manipulates the transference so as to adjust the analysand's ego to the supposedly more objectively aligned ego of the analyst. This is a repetition of Aristotle inasmuch as it enforces adequacy to reality in the form of a certain order; in other words, it enforces social conformity.

The question is once the Other is barred, where does action occur? And to complicate matters further, how does such action articulate with the psychoanalytic school?

II. THE ACT AS LEAP: LUTHER AND THE CHURCH

The complete answer to this knot of questions around action, transmission and the school is not to be found in Seminars VII or XV but rather in Lacan's 'Proposition of October 1967', the proposition of the pass.

The pass is Lacan's controversial answer to the question of the reproduction of the school, the training of analysts and the transmission of clinical knowledge. In my interpretation what is at stake in the proposition of the pass is whether or not a school can accommodate action. Alain Badiou charges that there are two fundamental acts in Lacan, one philosophical—'I found, alone as I have always been…'—and the other antiphilosophical—'I dissolve'.[32] Can there be any other

31. Aristotle, *Politics*, 1253a80.

32. Badiou, 'Lacan et le réel', p. 60. See also Badiou's year-long seminar on Lacan and antiphiloso-

actions with regard to the school than foundation or dissolution? Can one act *for* or *within* a school? Without completely destabilizing it?

The training of analysts presented a problem for Lacan. In other professions, such as medicine or architecture, a candidate must demonstrate mastery of a corpus of knowledge and a set of techniques before being granted the symbolic title of 'doctor' or 'architect'. One's qualifications as a professional are guaranteed by a state institution. In Lacanian terms, one's being—as a doctor, an architect—is guaranteed by the big Other. As we well know, after various scandals in the medical profession concerning drug trials without properly informed consent, this is no protection against charlatanism in practice. However, it does constitute a legal protection and it considerably facilitates taking out professional insurance. But what qualifications will serve for the psychoanalyst? Is there a state exam they might pass or fail?

Lacan's doctrine is very clear on this point: there is no status of being an analyst that is guaranteed by the big Other. 'Psychoanalyst', he says—unfortunately for those who would like a brass plaque outside their door—is not a predicate.[33] His teaching is addressed to psychoanalysts but he cannot simply say 'there are psychoanalysts'; rather it is the case that there is some psychoanalysis.[34] Admittedly, if one were to define the being of a doctor by the activity of actually diagnosing and curing diseases, then it would also be impossible to say 'there are doctors': one could say, 'there is some doctoring…' At the level of the mastering of a corpus of knowledge and technique, Lacan says the analytic act is not grasped at the level of the universal.[35] In other words there is no technical prescription for what to do faced with a particular moment in a particular analysand's discourse. As a result there are no textbooks for the analyst's education, save, as Freud suggests, all of literature. What basis then for qualification? The principle, Lacan states, is that the analyst is only authorized on the basis of himself.[36] This would appear to leave an open door to charlatanism: surely anybody could then announce that he or she is a psychoanalyst. In principle perhaps, but in practice no; there are no psychoanalysts without analysands Lacan says—it takes two to tango (if not four).[37] And in order to have analysands one must have built a reputation. Nevertheless Lacan does modify his principle by adding four crucial words: 'the analyst is only authorized on the basis of himself […] and a few others'.[38] A 'few others' do not make up an institution: a few others are what is at stake in the pass, and in an analysand's family history. But before examining the pass, it's important to understand why Lacan insists on self-authorization.

phy in 1994-95 archived on François Nicolas' website www.entretemps.asso.fr/Badiou/seminaires.htm

33. Lacan, Seminar XV (unpublished), lesson of 7/2/1968.

34. See Lacan 2001, p. 378.

35. Ibid., p. 379. See also; 'If there is something that analysts most instinctively reject it's the idea that "all knowledge of psychoanalysis qualifies the psychoanalyst" […] for a precise reason: the status of knowledge is suspended to the point that it is excluded from any subsistence of the subject, and the psychoanalyst cannot in any way summarize the whole proceedings, being only the pivot and instrument' (Lacan, Seminar XV [unpublished], lesson of 20/3/1968).

36. See Lacan 2001, p. 243.

37. Lacan, Seminar XV (unpublished), lesson of 7/2/1968.

38. Lacan, Seminar XXI. *Les non-dupes errent* (unpublished), lesson of 5/4/1974.

As he formulates it in Seminar XV, the end of analysis is a moment during which the analysand realizes that there is no subject who possesses knowledge of their being. This is the end of the transference: there is a 'fall' of the analyst from the position of the supposed subject of such knowledge to that of rejected waste, a leftover. The same realization can be formulated in terms of castration. The analysand comes to accept that there is no essential kernel of their being, no ultimate experience to possess, no perfect situation to find oneself in, no ideal partner to have. The original enjoyment they search for behind every fantasy or identification is not only lost but impossible. Their being is that of a lack of being; this is the status of the subject of desire, of the continual change of objects of desire. As such there is no being of the subject to be known; there is no final truth of the subject to be found in the Other, amongst the treasure-house of signifiers. These realizations amount to no less than a shift in the registers of truth and knowledge, a shift that Lacan identifies as essential to the analytic act. In becoming an analyst, one knows there is no guarantee via the Other of one's status: and so one may only authorize oneself on the basis of oneself... and a few others.

It is at the moment of the shift in the articulation of truth and knowledge that the *exemplary* nature of the psychoanalytic act manifests itself. During Seminar XV Lacan circles around and around this point like a bee—the act of becoming an analyst involves the realization of the illusion of the supposed subject of knowledge. Yet the prospective analyst persists in wanting to take up, or support, this illusion, with their own being, in clinical practice: 'supposing the very lure which for him is no longer tenable'.[39] Not only that, but prospective analysts accept that they will be struck, at the end of each of the analyses they conduct, with the same unbeing (*désêtre*) as they struck their analysts.[40] Lacan says, 'the subject institutes himself as analyst knowing full well that at the end of an analysis he will come to the place of *objet a* as reject'. The end of the action of becoming an analyst is thus subjective destitution. And then he asks, quite simply, 'how can such a leap be made?'[41]

It is this leap that illuminates the act in general. Lacan claims that the subject of an action always ends in the position of detritus: there is no hero of action, or if there is a hero, he or she is precisely a tragic hero. Continuing the analogy between psychoanalysis and tragedy he explores in Seminars VII and VIII, Lacan claims that at the end of a tragedy one always finds the *objet a* alone on stage, exposed.[42] Early on in the seminar Lacan reworks this idea in the following manner:

> It is a common dimension of the act, to not bear in its instant the presence
> of the subject. The passage of the act is that beyond which the subject will
> refind its presence as renewed, but nothing else. (Lacan, Seminar XV [unpublished], lesson of 29/11/1967)

This is almost an optimistic version: beyond the act the subject is renewed. The accent is not placed on subjective destitution but rather on the 'passage of

39. Lacan 2001, p. 376.
40. Lacan, Seminar XV (unpublished), lesson of 10/1/1968.
41. Ibid., lesson of 21/2/1968.
42. Ibid.

the act' as destitute of the subject. The act itself is blind. This is what Lacan calls the leap. Alain Badiou calls it the 'irreducibility of the act' in Lacan's antiphilosophy.

Shortly after he asks 'how can this leap be made?', Lacan says 'I explored the nature and status of this leap in my text "The Proposition" on the pass'.[43] Without explaining this reference he continues by saying one cannot speak directly of this leap, but that one can say, for instance, that it involves 'an act of faith in the supposed subject of knowledge after knowing that psychoanalysis can never base itself in a science that is teachable in a professorial manner'.[44] In the previous session he refers this act of faith to Luther's quarrel with the Catholic Church over the question of faith versus works as justifying man before God. The reference to Luther is not incidental. It also occurs in the Ethics seminar in regard to the fundamentally corrupt nature of man's works and his relation to this world.[45] Lacan's problem—how to guide action without rigidifying it in norms—is actually quite close to Luther's. Luther intends to subtract Christian action from the institutional guarantees and rites of the church, guarantees that he sees as a sure sign of corruption, of hypocrisy, of self-sufficiency before God. In turn Lacan says 'authorizing oneself is not the same as auto-ritualizing oneself'.[46] For Luther it is faith alone in Christ as the Savior, the faith of the inner man, that justifies man before God, and will naturally and spontaneously lead to good works. However, this subtraction leaves Luther—and the entire reformation—with a problem: how can one organize a church if any institutional rites are corrupt and if all men are priests?

In *The Freedom of a Christian* Luther's solution is utopic: the church will arise if we serve our neighbors:

> The good things we have from God should flow from one to the other and be common to all, so that everyone should 'put on' his neighbor and so conduct himself towards him as if he were in the other's place [...] That is what Christ did for us [...] A Christian lives not in himself but in Christ and his neighbor. (Luther 1962, pp. 79-80)

The church—which will provide a space and a collective name for a Christian's actions—will thus emerge as a happy fraternity from a particular kind of action: action *for* the neighbor.

Here we find an answer to my opening question: to act for a school is not necessarily the desire of philosophy. Rather it is to think like a Christian. Indeed in the latter half of the Ethics seminar, which is devoted to identifying the space of psychoanalytic action, Lacan engages in a critical exercise, pinpointing and rejecting all rival spaces of moral action: society (the American way in psychoanalysis); nature (the pastoral illusion); and the neighbor (Christianity and philanthropy). Basing his critique on Freud's protestations against the Christian imperative in *Civilization and its Discontents*, Lacan argues

---

43. Ibid., lesson of 21/2/1968.
44. Ibid.
45. Lacan 1992, p. 92, p. 97, p. 122.
46. Lacan 2001, p. 308.

What I want is the good of others in the image of my own—then the whole thing deteriorates to the point of it becoming 'What I want is the good of others in the image of my own provided that it depends on me'. (Lacan 1992, p. 187)

This is an acute and disturbing observation in an epoch when charities behave like multinational corporations. For Lacan, the obstacle to these projections of the imaginary is quite simply the neighbor's jouissance—the Somalian warlord and his hijacking of aid convoys.[47]

If one abstracts from the neighbor's jouissance for a moment, one can link Luther's church to another solution to the problem of the space of action, and that is the republican school. The fundamental tenet of the republican school—and this is precisely why it is in perpetual crisis—is that the school is the *polis*. The school prepares the student to become a citizen by already constituting the school as a city-state, a microcosm. But for Lacan the *polis* is dead, and any school modeling itself after the polis will be subject to the vicissitudes of what Freud termed the band of brothers, the happy few. It is tempting, given Alain Badiou's harsh critique of Lacan's thought of action, to charge, in return, that Badiou's own philosophy, despite all of his precautions, projects beyond its borders the existence of a band of brothers, of a school that is seamless action, in his recent concept of a body of truth emerging subsequent to an event.[48]

The other reference Lacan makes to Luther in Seminar XV is to a conception of the act that will dissolve all churches, all supposed bodies of truth. It is found in the debates over religious toleration in the sixteenth and seventeenth centuries:

The act says something. This dimension has always been known: it is enough to look at pregnant formulas, formulas that have acted such as 'act according to your conscience'. This is a turning point in the history of the act: to act according to one's conscience: why and before whom? Nor can one eliminate, inasmuch as the act ends up testifying to something (conscience?), the dimension of the Other. (Lacan, Seminar XV [unpublished], lesson of 17/1/1968)

'Freedom of conscience' was a rallying call for the radical parties in the English Civil War. Philosophers—Spinoza, Locke—took up this cause under the banner of 'religious toleration'. They argued that a governmental policy of religious toleration would not pave the way to anarchy if a crucial distinction was made: the distinction between the internal actions of faith and the external actions of civil obedience. An Anabaptist, say, who objected to the papal ceremony of Archbishop Laud's Anglican Church, could perform the rites required by the state church whilst internally disagreeing with them: this split is termed 'passive obedience' and it desubjectifies action. John Locke in the *Letter on Toleration* took one step further. He redefines a church as a voluntary association: one can-

---

47. Ibid., p. 194.

48. Such a charge would be inaccurate. Nevertheless, at an immediate rhetorical level, the earlier concept of a generic truth procedure would be less susceptible to such an accusation. See my *Alain Badiou: Live Theory* (Feltham 2008) for an exegesis of the latter concept.

not be born into a church, one must choose it as an adult. If, as an adult, one decides that the church one has joined in order to gain one's eternal salvation is not capable of assuring that end, if one's conscience is in conflict with church practices, then one can withdraw one's allegiance and join another more promising church. In this he anticipates the position of the subject of capitalism: investing and withdrawing investment in joint-stock companies according to the promise of the market.[49] Locke thus shows that 'acting in accordance with one's conscience'—the historical result of Luther's teaching—is not only a formula for the dissolution of a church, but also for the foundation of a new church.

And so after the Reformation the Christian idea of acting for another does not secure a place for action inside the collective—the church, the school—but gives rise, again, to actions of foundation and dissolution. Hence the proliferation of congregation; Baptists, Anabaptists, Familialists, Quakers, Ranters—so many schools continually giving rise to further schools.

If one can no longer act for a school—after the death of the *polis*, and the death of the neighbor (of the Catholic Church)—is it possible to act within a school?

III. THE PASS AS SPACE FOR THE BEING OF AN ACT

The analytic act is that of becoming an analyst. Lacan's apparatus for this passage is the pass. With regard to acting according to one's conscience he says: 'Nor can one eliminate, inasmuch as the act ends up testifying to something (conscience?), the dimension of the Other'. He will build the pass around testimony. As such its action will take place in the Other. The 'passage of the act'—the leap, that from which the subject is absent—cannot be anything other than its unfolding, its consequences. Lacan says of his actual proposition of the pass that its consequences will decide whether it is an act.[50] So the being of the act consists in its consequences. He also says that it is within the pass that 'the act could be grasped in the time it produces'.[51]

The thesis is thus that the pass constitutes a space for action within the school, a space for the unfolding of its consequences, for the renewal of the subject, which is also a time for the act. Before describing the details of the apparatus, let me address a few doubts. It is well known that the institution of the pass within the psychoanalytic school very much turned out to be an act. It had many consequences, and indeed it does not seem to stop having consequences, from the resistance Lacan encountered when trying to have it adopted by his school to his own disappointment in its operation ten years later, to its repeated arraignment as suspect in the provocation of irremediable splits in Lacanian schools. Not an auspicious past: it seems as though the pass was one more 1960s failure in institutional experiments, to be ranked alongside the kibbutz and the commune.

However for some failures it is possible to write an apology; in other words,

---

49. See my *An Anatomy of Failure: Philosophy and Political Action* (Feltham 2013) for an expansion of this argument.

50. See Lacan 2001, p. 261.

51. Ibid., p. 266.

to show that it was no such thing. Indeed of the pass Lacan writes that it 'never succeeds so well as when it fails' which seems to indicate that it has a rather peculiar functioning.[52] In the pass, in order for an analysand to become an analyst of the school he or she must transmit his or her experience of analysis to two 'passers' who will then transmit this testimony in turn to a jury.[53] The jury will then decide whether the analysand has passed. This decision is based on the quality of the testimony: has the analysand developed sufficient psychoanalytic knowledge of their own case—and thus recuperated the hidden meaning of their actions? But the requirements for a successful pass are even more demanding. The knowledge the analysand has developed must be sufficiently articulated to survive its passage through the two passers. If the analysand does not clearly articulate and organize their understanding of their own analysis, the risk is that his or her testimony will be distorted when it is transmitted by the two passers: much like the game called Chinese whispers. There have been many accounts written by 'passers' of their experience of the pass and they often write of having to confront their own desire when transmitting the analysand's testimony. Distortion, in other words, is another name for the work of the desire of the Other in the transmission of action.

What remedy against the desire of the Other in the transmission of the action of analysis? From the candidate or prospective analyst's point of view, the only safeguard is clear conceptual articulation of their testimony to the point of formalization. This is where the doctrine of the pass meets the doctrine of the matheme.[54] Famously, in *Encore*, Lacan says 'the matheme is our goal, our ideal'. Why? Because it alone guarantees complete transmission.[55] The success of the action of the pass thus depends on the analysand's capacity to formalize their knowledge of their symptoms, their traversal of the fantasy, their experience of castration—in short, on their capacity to formalize the hidden meaning of their actions, to generate a matheme of the success and failure of previous actions. But what is transmitted is not the matheme alone but also the process of generating the matheme and the difficulties the analysand encountered in doing so given the diverse material produced during the analysis.

Lacan says the being of the act is constituted through consequences. The action at stake in the pass is that of testifying to one's understanding of one's own psychoanalysis. If one does so successfully, that action becomes that of actually becoming an analyst, passing, being recognized as an analyst of the school. These consequences all belong to the symbolic order. To testify to one's experience as an analysand is to inscribe those signifiers that emerged during the analysis within the symbolic order. The pass is thus an apparatus that stages the inscription of an action within the symbolic order. In so far as this inscription and its modality is not automatic, but passes through the subjectivity of 'a few others', the consequences of the action are exhibited in all of their contingency. Thus

---

52. Ibid., p. 265.
53. See ibid., p. 255.
54. I owe this idea to a discussion with Samo Tomšič, a most contemporary Lacanian.
55. Lacan 1998, p. 119.

if the being of an act is constituted through its consequences, the apparatus of the pass stages the contingent being of the act. Not only does it stage but it fore-grounds, it exacerbates, it intensifies such contingent being through triple layers of inscription: first the analysand speaks, then the passers speak, and finally the jury speaks. The multiplication of stages of inscription lends the action temporal-ity and opens up the possibility of difference between the inscriptions; thus com-plicating and prolonging its being. It is quite possible for the jury to decide that on the evidence of the passers the analysand has not come to a sufficiently clear understanding of the stakes of their own analysis to become an analyst of the school. In this case the action of attempting the pass, of trying to become an ana-lyst, is not a failure; it is simply unfinished, and it furnishes much material for the analysand's further tasks of understanding and subsequent attempts at the pass.

The structure of the pass with its layers of consequences encourages the emergence of a specific ethics, of an orientation for the candidate's action. This is an ethics of speaking well in order to ensure the maximum coherence between the three levels of inscription. In its combination with the action of passing such speech, such testimony is in perfect accordance with Lacan's definition of prax-is in Seminar XI: the treatment of the real by means of the symbolic. The pass is thus clearly an avatar of the polis: it explicitly stages the reception of actions, its parts are constituted from actions and it maintains its own existence through the judgment of actions.

In Seminar VII Lacan critiques and dismisses Aristotle's conception of the polis; yet in doing so leaves open a gap in his own conception of psychoanalyt-ic action. He has named an ethical imperative—do not cede upon your desire—but he has no theory of the reception of action. This will become a concern as Lacan confronts the question of the psychoanalytic school and the transmission of psychoanalytic knowledge. In Seminar XV he oscillates between two concep-tions of the school: as propadeutic or exemplar for action, either the school pre-pares the citizen to act or the school is already a microcosm of the polis. If, as I have argued, Lacan finally provides an account of the space of the reception of action in his invention of the pass, on what side does he fall? Propadeutic or ex-emplar? Indeed, if analytic action is already an exemplar, then let us ask how does any apparatus of transmission and testimony like the pass articulate action with the school? According to analytic action as exemplar, let us recall, all true action is inaugural. That is, all true action takes the place of a saying by intro-ducing new signifiers to the world. All action ends by renewing the subject.

The initial evidence surrounding the pass in the psychoanalytic school dis-courages any attempt to think its exemplary value. Indeed if one were to ask, given the nature of action, whether it can be accommodated within a school; if one were to ask if the apparatus of the pass permits one to act within a school, the response would appear to be negative. Lacan himself states in a 1978 text, 'Assises de Deauville', that he is disappointed in the pass; he has concluded that psychoanalysis is untransmissible and that each psychoanalyst must invent it anew. It is well-known in the subsequent history of Lacanian schools that the pass itself played a large part in generating splits in those schools and thus fragmenting and weakening Lacan's contribution to the field of Freudian psychoanalysis. In itself this is not particularly surprising. In *The Essay Concerning Human Understanding* Locke points out that everyone disagrees over the judgment of the nature of an action, and that in such judgment the only criteria or standard that can be employed is common usage. That is, one should refer to how the linguistic community usually names such actions. A further difficulty is then encountered in that it is very difficult in particular cases to determine just what the correct usage is—in Lacanian terms, there is no metalanguage of use. Here Locke suggests that correct usage is always assumed to be that of a recognized authority, in short a master. Here we find ourselves back in Aristotle's problem of determining the nature of practical wisdom: it is what practically wise men, masters like Pericles possess. If, in practice, the judgment of difficult cases is referred to the usage of masters, then it constitutes an evident trigger for the emergence of the discourse of hysteria. It is just such a discourse that drives the formation of splits in a school. Lacan condemned Aristotle's articulation of action with the *polis* according to a microcosm-macrocosm linkage. If dysfunction at the level of the pass leads to dysfunction and factionalism within the school then ironically Lacan has introduced just such a microcosm-macrocosm logic with his invention of the pass.

But is it not the protest of a beautiful soul to dismiss the apparatus of the pass just because it has been associated with splits in psychoanalytic schools? What kinds of collectives do not split? Surely it is only state institutions with no subjective investment or multinational corporations that avoid splits. Institutions have their budgets cut and corporations are sold off or taken over by foreign capital, but neither are subject to splits. Rather, the only collectives that are subject to splits are those in which there has been a true teaching, and thus a subjective investment and a transmission of genuine action. In short, the only collectives subject to splits are schools. To condemn splits in the name of peace and tranquility is to condemn oneself to a life in an eternal tearoom with thick lace curtains and stale biscuits. Let us accept that there is no way of accommodating true acts within a school, and thus there is no school *for* the act. Rather, each act is its own school. Inversely, a school must be incessantly founded again and again: as Leibniz says of God's creation, it fulgurates, punctually and infinitely. Furthermore, according to this line of thinking, the pass is the same as the school which in turn is the same as the *polis*. There is no distinction between the school and an external sphere or context. The exemplarity of the act becomes identification: there is no outside with which the act, or indeed the school, could be articulated.

Nietzsche and Philippe Lacoue-Labarthe ask: what is modern tragedy? If we are correct in our conclusion, modern tragedy is the psychoanalytic school. Just as Aristotle says of action in tragedy, the psychoanalytic act is indivisible—unlike technical production, analytic action has no finite parts, it is one. And just as action in tragedy psychoanalytic action is irreversible.[56] In the absence of any encompassing *polis* the pass thus leads to separation, division and the multiplication of schools—and this, literally, is a tragedy.

---

56. See Lacan 2001, p. 265.

But this conclusion is not yet fully dialectical. And so another step must be taken.

In Lacan's thought of the act not only is there the moment of exemplary pulverization wherein every action becomes its own school but there is also the moment of propadeutics, the moment in which actions both prepare further actions and assume the existence of prior actions. In short, every action—and its pass—presumes the existence of a school just as the succession of finite ordinals within an infinite limit ordinal supposes the existence of a limit ordinal which is both beyond the reach of that succession and that in which the succession occurs.[57] Hence an action is not identical with but included in its school. The school is not purely a propadeutic for action, preparing for action in the outside world, but neither is action in the school a pure exemplar, collapsed in upon itself. An action within an apparatus of multiple inscription and judgment, like the pass, is not only an exemplar but a propadeutic; that is, it prepares subsequent actions. To accommodate an action within the school, to pass it, is to actively assume its symbolic consequences, its relative successes and failures, its capacity to engender further actions. The pass is an eminently democratic institution in that, first, one does not need to be a senior member of a school to be on the jury or to be one of the two passers. It is democratic inasmuch as the multiplication of stages of inscription encourages the emergence of different and unforeseen consequences. In Seminar XV Lacan says:

> In every act there is something that escapes the subject and which will end up having some effect at the end of the act. The very least one can say is that what he has to realize in the accomplishment of the act—which is the realization of himself—is veiled. (Lacan, Seminar XV [unpublished], lesson of 13/3/1968)

As a multiple mechanism of transmission the pass registers those consequences of the act that escape the subject. It is in assuming these unpredictable consequences that the subject renews itself and its position. The school, as *hypokeimenon* or support of transmission, can also be renewed through the act by the assumption of the latter's consequences. A minimal difference between the school and its encompassing context—*the polis*—is introduced by the occurrence of these unpredictable consequences, yet to be assumed. Hence the act expands the school within the *polis*.

Against the critique of the whole in the name of the local and the particular—which is but one more variant on possessive individualism—we must learn again to expand and totalize our schools in order to maintain them. This is the ultimate act of friendship.

BIBLIOGRAPHY

Ansaldi, J., *Lire Lacan: L'éthique de la psychanalyse*, Nîmes: Les editions du champ social, 1998

Aubenque, P., *La prudence chez Aristote*, Paris: P.U.F, 1963

Badiou, A., *Being and Event*, trans. O. Feltham, London: Continuum, 2006

---

57. See Chapter 14 of Badiou 2006.

Feltham, O., *Alain Badiou: Live Theory*, London: Continuum, 2008

—— *An Anatomy of Failure: Philosophy and Political Action*, London: Continuum, 2013

Lacan, J., *Le séminaire livre VII: L'Ethique de la psychanalyse*, Paris: Seuil, 1986

—— *The Ethics of Psychoanalysis 1959-60: The Seminar of Jacques Lacan Book VII*, trans. D. Porter, London: Routledge, 1992

—— *Autres écrits*, Paris: Seuil, 2001

—— *The Seminar of Jacques Lacan. Book XX (1972-73). On Feminine Sexuality, the Limits of Love and Knowledge*, J.-A. Miller (ed.), B. Fink (trans.), New York: W.W. Norton, 1998

Luther, M., *The Freedom of a Christian* in *Martin Luther: Selections from his Writings*, J. Dillenburger (ed.), New York: Anchor Books, 1962

Rabaté, J.-M., '1968 + 1: Lacan's *Année Erotique*', in *Parrhesia*, no. 6, 2009.

Lacking Subjects and the Subject of Lack: Basaglia and Lacan

Alvise Sforza Tarabochia

I. INTRODUCTION

The Italian psychiatrist Franco Basaglia (1924-1980) is best remembered for his revolutionary practice in the asylums of Gorizia, Colorno and Trieste, where, by introducing a community approach and open-door policy, he overcame the backward psychiatry (characterised by possibly lifelong internment and questionable treatments such as shock therapies) that was still common in Italy after World War II. His efforts started in 1961 and culminated with the approval of Law 180 in 1978, which abolished all public residential facilities for mental health care in Italy and restricted the possibility of involuntary hospitalisation.

Basaglia's revolutionary practices and Law 180 itself were guided by his philosophical self-education, and by an enduring loyalty to theoretical rather than strictly clinical-psychiatric notions, which he drew not only on his early influences such as Heidegger, Sartre, and Merleau-Ponty but also from Foucault, and, possibly, from his psychoanalyst collaborators, such as Michele Risso. This aspect of Basaglia's path to Law 180 is often overlooked to the point of being neglected.

It is to this extent that in this paper I will analyse Basaglia's theory of the subject and I will do so by contrasting and comparing it to Lacan's. It is necessary, therefore, before I begin my analysis, to clarify two crucial questions.

Why is it important to single out Basaglia's theory of the subject over other aspects of his work, such as his criticism of traditional organicist psychiatry and institutionalism?

Why is it necessary to bring Lacan in the picture in the context of defining Basaglia's theory of the subject? After all, Basaglia was rather critical of psychoanalysis,[1] and his theories could be much more readily relatable to other think-

---

1. Basaglia's criticism of psychoanalysis pivots around three main points: 1) psychoanalysis is too tied to the naturalistic determinism of the drive and the economy of the libido (Basaglia 1953, p. 6); 2) it emphasizes desires, while the central issues with psychiatric patients are primary needs (Basaglia 1978, pp. 349-350); 3) it is a 'class science' in different ways: 'lower' classes cannot afford psychoanalysis; it aims at normalizing and socializing the neurotic; it is strongly loyal to a theoretical and institutionalized frame-

ers who directly influenced him.

Singling out Basaglia's theory of the subject is important for several reasons. From 1953 to 1961 Basaglia works in a University Clinical Practice, where, by his own admission, only the rich mentally ill could be treated. The orientation is purely organicist: there is no psychotherapeutic approach, all illnesses are diagnosed through the already dated Kraepelinian system, treatment is strictly limited to the few medicines available—such as chlorpromazine—and to shock therapies—such as insulin coma and ECT. In this context Basaglia begins to be interested in Jaspers, Binswanger and Minkowski's works, whose approach could be summarised in the very loose definition of 'phenomenological psychiatry': instead of looking for the underlying organic causes of mental illness (which were and still are impossible to ascertain), one has to focus on the *phenomena* (the manifestations) of the illness and, following the Dyltheian distinction, try to *understand* rather than *explain* how these manifestations relate to the patient's subjectivity and the surrounding world.[2]

In the writings of this period Basaglia develops a theory of the subject much indebted to this phenomenological/existentialist tradition: for instance, he regards the subject as *Dasein* in its constitutional relationship with the surrounding world, the Heideggerian being-in-the-world. Suddenly, in 1961, Basaglia abandons the University, for reasons that are still debated, and, in a career-suicidal move, becomes director of a public asylum.

After three years of silence, this experience results in the publication of the 1964 article 'La distruzione dell'ospedale psichiatrico'—literally: 'The Destruction of the Psychiatric Hospital'. In this text, the notion of subjectivity that he had developed earlier seems to have disappeared: having apparently abandoned his interest in the limited setting of the one-to-one psychiatric encounter with the patient, Basaglia seemingly becomes concerned with the damaging effects that the asylum as a *total institution*—in Goffman's terms[3]—has on the inmates, how to overcome it, and eventually envision a psychiatric clinical practice that does not rely *at all* on physical constraint, locked doors, involuntary hospitalisation and so on. Furthermore, such psychiatric clinical practice should be made available to both the rich who could afford a private facility, and the destitute, the poor, who, when suffering from a mental ailment, were doomed to the asylum.

This is, for Basaglia, not only a shift from a private facility to a public one, from private to public psychiatry, from a reforming intent that invests psychia-

---

work that overshadows the needs of the individual, etc. These reservations show a rather limited grasp of psychoanalysis, and a marked disregard for Lacan's psychoanalytic theory. For further comments on Basaglia's take on psychoanalysis see: Kantzà 1999; Stoppa 1999; Polidori 1999; Colucci and Di Vittorio 2001; Benvenuto 2005; Viganò 2009; Recalcati 2010.

2. Dilthey distinguishes between explaining [*Erklären*] natural facts and understanding [*Verstehen*] human subjects. According to him (1976, p. 88), 'explanation, the methodological approach of the physical sciences, aims at subsum[ing] a range of phenomena under a causal nexus by means of a limited number of unambiguously defined elements'. Human studies 'differ from the [physical] sciences because the latter deal with facts which present themselves to consciousness as external and separate phenomena, while the former deal with the living connections of reality experienced in the mind' (ibid., p. 89). Hence human sciences are 'based on mental connections' which, although we might as well be able to explain, we should also and especially *understand*: 'We explain nature but we understand mental life' (ibid., p. 89).

3. Goffman 2007.

try in its one-to-one aspect of contact with the patient to the political intent of re-forming the laws that regulate public psychiatric health care. It is also a shift in theoretical framework. Basaglia begins to study and apply the theories of thinkers such as Goffman and Foucault, thinkers who are interested much more in the wider mechanisms of social control, in the role that institutions play in society, than on the individual and subjective experiences of the patients.

While Basaglia's choice of abandoning the university, and his reforming and revolutionary work in the asylum have been largely analysed, the shift in theoretical framework has always been overlooked, regarded as a simple consequence of Basaglia's change in focus and interests. I think differently, more in line with Leoni's position.[4] Some notions underpin all of Basaglia's reflection, from his early one-to-one clinical psychiatric studies to his struggle against institutional psychiatry and eventually to the phrasing of Law 180. Hence, to answer my first question on the importance of Basaglia's theory of the subject, I would like to point out that this theory is pivotal, precisely because it links almost seamlessly all the phases of Basaglia's reflection. Beginning with his very first works Basaglia theorises what is that indissolubly ties the subject to otherness: I will call it a 'constitutional lack of the subject', the paradoxical impossibility, loosely put, for any human being to be 'oneself', to perceive oneself as a self outside of a relationship with the other. This constitutional lack of the subject is exploited in power relations, in the functioning of the psychiatric institution and in the asylum, and in the mechanisms of social control, but is also central in Basaglia's theory of psychosis. The constitutional lack of the subject is what defines his notion of subjectivity throughout his work, in the one-to-one relationship with the patients and in the reforming work that will lead to Law 180.

Despite such an indissoluble relationship with intersubjectivity, Basaglia's subject is not an epiphenomenon of intersubjectivity, as can instead be concluded if we follow for instance Foucault's reflection on psychiatry, society and individuality to its most extreme ramifications. In brief we could say that Foucault (a central influence for Basaglia's social and political work) very often—and I would say *always* when he refers to psychiatry—puts forward a pessimistic conception of the individual subject.[5] All human beings are always-already 'trapped' in a certain subjectivity and individuality. What we believe to be our own self is, in fact, only a product (or by-product) of power (whether disciplinary or biopower), a power that is exercised in such a diffuse way that it is eventually internalised to the point of producing the very idea of subject/individual/self with which we always-already identify. Hence, as Rovatti puts it, there is no 'way out'[6] of this subject; there is no possible liberation from a condition of subjection to power in Foucault's work.

On the contrary, as Kirchmayr has pertinently noted, Lacan 'maintains the interrogation on the subject alive well beyond its "disappearance", which was

4. Leoni 2011.

5. I refer the reader to my 2013 monograph, *Psychiatry, Subjectivity, Community. Franco Basaglia and Biopolitics*, for a more articulated analysis of Foucault's pessimistic take on subjectivity *vis-à-vis* Basaglia's.

6. Rovatti 2008, p. 219. All translations from Italian sources, including all of Basaglia's quotes, are mine, unless otherwise stated.

sanctioned in several different ways by structuralism'.[7] Lacan's subject is indeed constitutively intertwined with otherness, but it is much more than just a product of power relations in which we are always-already alienated. Indeed, we are all alienated into the Other, constitutively losing, as Lacan puts it, our very *being* as individual subjects—but it is precisely through this loss that we *actively* enter intersubjectivity. While for Foucault the very idea of subject is a means by which we are subjected to *power*, for Lacan to be a subject is to be subjected to *language*, and ultimately, to have the possibility of taking active part in the Other. This is, in brief, the answer to the second question. Why Lacan? Because Lacan offers a notion of subjectivity intrinsically related to intersubjectivity, without reducing the subject to being an epiphenomenon of power relations. Arguably, this could also be the outcome of say Heidegger's *Dasein* and his notion of being-in-the-world. Yet Lacan's theory of the subject seamlessly feeds not only into a *clinical practice*, that is psychoanalysis, but also into a strong stance of *institutional criticism*, which we can see, for instance, in his theory of the four discourses in Seminar XVII.[8] We can also see it informing his variable length sessions, which in 1953 made him resign from the *Société Parisienne de Psychanalyse* (SPP) and join the *Société Française de Psychanalyse* (SFP), as well as in the continuous struggles he had with the *International Psychoanalytical Association* (IPA).

For reasons of space constraint, this paper explores only the first aspect, that is to say, it focuses on a comparative analysis of Basaglia's and Lacan's theory of the subject in connection to their theory of psychosis, limiting for the time being the analysis of the institutional criticism of both authors and especially their possible impact on clinical practice. This first step is pivotal to establish that while Foucault—certainly much more than Lacan—has been a central influence for Basaglia's anti-institutional endeavours, it would be far too restrictive to limit his theory of the subject to Foucault's pessimistic stance. What is more, this would hinder the possibility of recognising how much Basaglia's theory of the subject transcends his seemingly abrupt shift of interest from the doctor/patient relationship to institutional psychiatry, and informs both his clinical approach and his work of de-institutionalisation—without discontinuity.

Re-evaluating Basaglia's theory of the subject is also crucial to understand how much of his legacy survives today, in the declaredly post-Basaglian work of deinstitutionalisation that is still carried out in the Italian *Centri di Salute Mentale* and by authors loyal to Basaglia's teachings. Finally, it is central to understand Basaglia's and his legacy's theoretical proximity to seemingly far psychiatries such those inspired by McGinn's externalist conception of the mind[9]—that tend to view mental patients in terms of relations with the surroundings, integrating behavioural and psychodynamic approaches—or Leader's markedly Lacanian psychoanalytic clinical approach to the treatment of psychoses.[10]

---

7. Kirchmayr 2009, p. 41.
8. Lacan 2007.
9. McGinn 1989.
10. Leader 2011.

To begin with, I will give an overview of the notion of subject according to Lacan, and, having established a logical and ontogenetic primacy of intersubjectivity over subjectivity, I will show how this applies to Basaglia's conception of the subject as early as his very first papers. I will then show how both authors maintain that in the 'normal' ontogenesis of the subject a constitutional and constitutive relationship is established between intersubjectivity and subjectivity and how deviations from the establishment of this relationship can and usually have pathogenetic outcomes. I will then dwell on how Basaglia's definition of psychosis and neurosis relies on his theory of the subject and how these are intimately related to the same distinction as it is drawn in psychoanalysis, especially in Lacan's theory.

II. SUBJECTIVITY AND INTERSUBJECTIVITY

It goes without saying that my outline of the most important characteristics of the subject according to Lacan will be necessarily limited, not only for reasons of space constraint, but also and especially because it is a notion that undergoes a continuous evolution in Lacan's own writings.

Let us start then with the definition of Barred S ($), the split, barred subject: broadly speaking, the subject divided between a conscious ego and the unconscious, between otherness and subjectivity;[11] and, strictly speaking, the subject split by the shaping action of language in what is commonsensically misinterpreted as its most intimate dimension, i.e. the unconscious. As Lacan repeatedly posited, 'the unconscious is the Other's discourse'.[12] There are many reasons for this: because we speak a language that pre-exists us (it belongs to the Other), because we are constantly influenced by what others say, etc. But this holds good especially because every human being was born from the Other and inside the Other: the child's parents have chosen a name for him before his birth, his symbolic space is already invested with the parents' desires, which, in turn, derive from their own parents and have been formulated in a language that long pre-existed them. We come into being inside a symbolic space that pre-exists us. To this extent, the subject, strictly speaking, *is* this space, that is to say, it is the effect of what Lacan calls the *signifier* (S1) that represents the subject to all other signifiers (S2).[13]

Therefore, speaking of a subjectivity that precedes otherness and intersubjectivity is impossible, as there is no such thing. There is no subject *per se*, without the other or outside of the other. To this extent, Lacan states that:

> Man cannot aim at being whole (at the 'total personality', another premise with which modern psychotherapy veers off course), once the play of displacement and condensation to which he is destined in the exercise of his functions marks his relation, as a subject, to the signifier. (Lacan 1958, p. 581)

The Lacanian subject hence lacks the very possibility of being whole in itself, an independent individual subject, outside of the Other and without the Other.

---

11. Lacan 1958.
12. Lacan 1957, p. 10.
13. Lacan 1964, p. 708.

The subject is constitutionally lacking or, even better, as Chiesa contends, the Lacanian subject is a subject of lack.[14]

Subjectivity can be regarded as a relationship with this lack of wholeness. In Chiesa's words, 'Lacan's subject amounts to an irreducible lack [...] which must *actively* be confronted and assumed'.[15] Loosely put, the subject becomes such by subjectifying lack, that is to say, by becoming *in* the Other, *in* the Symbolic, *in* language: in other words, by becoming what S1 represents to S2 and abandoning imaginary wholeness and independence.

It is to this extent that Lacan and Basaglia stances draw near.

Since his 1953 article 'Il mondo dell'incomprensibile schizofrenico', Basaglia maintained that 'the subject exists only insofar as he "is" in the world'[16]—testifying to his early existentialist influences. In this article, Basaglia brings this consideration to the conclusion that human beings are unable to know themselves, to define themselves as individual subjects outside of the relationship with the other. I would call this impossibility to establish a direct reflexive relationship, the 'constitutional lack of the subject'—although Basaglia himself did not use the Italian word for lack, *mancanza*, in this precise context. This lack urges the establishment of a relationship with the other, which will shape and create the subject. As Basaglia remarks in 'Su alcuni aspetti della moderna psicoterapia: Analisi fenomenologica dell'"incontro"':

> Only when man feels the need for a human relationship he becomes such [...] wanting to be oneself, that is to say perceiving oneself as a full and accomplished personality, always presupposes the reciprocal opening up to another self. (Basaglia 1954, p. 35)

The lack of the subject is co-extensive with a constitutional need for the other, the need for recognition—Lacan's Kojèvian notion that the subject's desire is the desire for recognition by the other. If this recognition does not take place, the very process of subjectification, the ontogenesis of the subject, is halted. But Basaglia goes even further. Not only do we become subjects only when we open ourselves to the shaping action of the other: Otherness constitutes our psychic dimension *tout court*. In the same article Basaglia argues that

> when we refer to the 'psychic' we are not necessarily referring to something subjective and individual, because the individual does not only partake of himself, but also of everything that surrounds him. These surroundings are not only the environment but something that surpasses him and invests all other human entities, an *interhuman* dimension of which all beings partake. (Basaglia 1954, p. 43)

Arguably, according to Basaglia, it is impossible to outline a subjective dimension unrelated to the other: outside of a relationship with the other there is no subject. This is also clear in the articles that Basaglia dedicates to depersonalisation and hypochondria, where he posits that both symptoms derive from a

---

14. Chiesa 2007, p. 6.
15. Ibid.
16. Basaglia 1953, p. 5.

lack of relationship with the world and the other.[17] When this external pole is absent, the sick person is unable to define himself as a subject.

Of course, these ideas are not exclusive to Basaglia or Lacan, but come from a phenomenological-existentialist legacy, to which both are somehow related. What draws Basaglia and Lacan nearer is that, according to the former, this *inter-human* dimension, which constitutes the subject, finds its most appropriate manifestation in *language*. As Basaglia puts it, 'we believe that one of the most meaningful expressions of human nature is "language"'.[18] Yet language is not to be understood as an 'instrument that can express our ideas and our concepts',[19] that is, conscious speech. Language is 'the most genuine expression that man has in his inter-human relationships because it can be regarded as the projection of the individual onto the world'.[20] In language and through language human beings are enabled to become subjects *in* the world, *in* the Other.

To sum up, Basaglia shares with Lacan the idea that intersubjectivity logically (and ontogenetically) precedes subjectivity, in that there is an intersubjective dimension that defines and shapes the subject. To a certain extent this is also Foucault's position, as he regarded individuality and subjectivity as effects of power relations. However, Basaglia's and Lacan's stances go beyond Foucault's. Foucault's definition of subject is paradoxically de-subjectifying: the subject is nothing substantive; it is *only* an effect of power relations, an *effect* of a dominant otherness. Neither Basaglia's nor Lacan's subjects are substantive, but according to both the subject *is* this very lack of substance; the constitutional lack of subjectivity is in both authors raised to the most intimate and pivotal characteristic of being subjects (and of being *tout court* I would add). While Foucault's subject is, properly speaking, a lacking subject, Lacan's and Basaglia's subject is, rather, a subject of lack, a subjectivised lack.

III. ALIENATION, *APHANISIS*, SEPARATION, *ALTERITÀ* AND *ALIENITÀ*

The constitutive relationship between the subject and the intersubjective dimension, the Other, is established by means of *alienation*, to which Lacan dedicates an important lesson of Seminar XI. According to Lacan, alienation 'condemns the subject to appearing only in [a] division', which means that the subject can only appear 'on the one side as meaning, produced by the signifier', on the other as '*aphanisis*', namely, a disappearance.[21] Alienation is what the subject undergoes to appear in the field of the Other. The signifier manifests the subject to the Other but in doing so it also reduces

---

17. Basaglia 1956a; 1956b; 1957.
18. Basaglia 1953, p. 9.
19. Ibid.
20. Ibid.

21. Lacan 1998, p. 210. *Aphanisis* ('disappearance' in Ancient Greek) is a notion that Lacan borrows from Ernest Jones (Lacan 1998, p. 207). While in his 1927 article 'The Early Development of Female Sexuality' Jones (1927) defines *aphanisis* as the disappearance of sexual desire, for Lacan, it is a disappearance of the subject *tout court*. Lacan's discussion of Jones' conception of *aphanisis* can be found in Seminar VI (1958-1959) (Lacan 2013).

the subject in question to being *no more* than a signifier, to petrify the subject in the same movement in which it calls the subject to function, to speak, as subject. (Lacan 1998, p. 207)

Fink reads this process as alienation into the Other's desire, inasmuch as, since birth, the subject is *caused* by the desire of his parents.[22] Lacan summarises alienation in the logical disjunction *vel* (which corresponds to the grammatical compound *either...or...*): the subject *vel* the Other, being *vel* meaning.[23]

If the subject 'chooses' to be, he disappears from the field of the Other, he can no longer be recognised, he ceases to exist insofar as he refuses his *signifier.* Clearly, it is not a matter of consciously choosing or accepting one's own *aphanisis* and one's own alienation in the Other. It would be better to refer to this as an implicit imposition, which is part of the ontogenesis of the subject. As Fink correctly notes, the best possible way to refer to alienation would be a 'forced choice [...] (which is something of an oxymoron)'.[24] One does not choose to submit to the other 'if one is to come to be as a subject' but submission to the other still 'maintains its status as a choice' because it is still 'possible to refuse subjectivity',[25] for instance in the case of psychosis. In order to exist the subject must accept to *mean*, to be a *signifier* thrown in the field of the Other. Yet in this case, the subject 'survives only deprived' of something: his own being.[26] That is to say,

> it is of the nature of this meaning, as it emerges in the field of the Other, to be in a large part of its field, eclipsed by the disappearance of being.
> (Lacan 1998, p. 211)

In the very alienation in the Other, the subject *disappears* as such, he undergoes an *aphanisis.* In Lacan's words, 'the subject manifests himself in this movement of disappearance'.[27] The *aphanisis* of the subject *qua* being makes of the subject a 'place-holder within the symbolic order',[28] because the subject 'cannot indicate himself there except *qua* disappearing from his position as subject'.[29]

This aphanisic process does not imply that subjectivity ultimately amounts to nothing. On the contrary, it portrays the process through which subjects accept to be 'subdued by the Other', a process that implies 'the loss of oneself' but also the eventual 'advent as a subject'.[30] Outside of the Other, there can be no such thing as a subject, even if the participation to the Other entails a paradoxical disappearance (*aphanisis*) of subjectivity itself.

In the ontogenesis of the subject, alienation is followed by what Lacan calls 'separation'.[31] The subject enters the symbolic order through alienation, which

---

22. Fink 1997, p. 50.
23. Lacan 1998, p. 211.
24. Fink 1997, pp. 49-50.
25. Ibid.
26. Lacan 1998, p. 211.
27. Ibid., pp. 207-208.
28. Fink 1997, p. 53.
29. Lacan 2013, p. 501.
30. Ibid., p. 50.
31. Lacan 1998, p. 213.

amounts to the imposition of an 'either...or...', i.e. 'either being or being part of the Other': by choosing to be part of the Other, the subject accepts his constitutional lack of being. At a second stage, i.e. separation, the subject recognises that the Other is also lacking. In Lacan's words, 'a lack is encountered by the subject in the Other',[32] first of all in the first Other that the child meets: the mother. Only when the mother shows to be herself lacking, to be herself desiring, can the subject properly become *barred*: in attempting 'to fill the mOther's lack', the subject effectively lodges 'his or her lack of being *(manque-à-être)* in that "place" where the other is lacking'.[33] In other words, in separation, the child discovers that the mother herself *desires*, and his desire thus becomes the desire of being the object of the mother's desire: 'Desire is always desire of the Other' is one of Lacan's best known Kojèvian/Hegelian refrains. In other words, when a lack is encountered in the Other, human beings desire to become what is lacking to the Other. Desire is established as desire *of* the Other in all its possible meanings: the Other is the object of one's desire; one desires to become the object of the Other's desire; one desires the object that the Other desires.

Separation also establishes a fundamental 'trust' in the symbolic order that will henceforth regulate all relationships with the Other and with oneself. As Leader puts it:

> The child must find a way to show that the mother is herself subject to a force beyond her. Otherwise the child is left entirely at the mercy of her power. (Leader 2011, p. 58)

> Anticipating her responses, a basic trust may be established between mother and child, which involves repressing the very idea that her actions depend on her will. This is a faith in the symbolic order as such, a fundamental foothold that makes the mother-child relation subordinate to the symbolic law that we care for our offspring. (Leader 2011, p. 59)

It is to this extent that Lacan plays on the word separation, from the Latin *separare*: on the one hand, *se-parare*, to separate, as in to separate oneself from the Other or being separated from the engulfing relationship with the (m)Other by the severing action of the Name-of-the-Father; and also to parry oneself, as in to defend oneself or be defended from the drive and egoistic whims of the Other, by evoking and trusting a set of rules that—by regimenting both one's and the Other's desire—guarantees the very possibility of a relationship in the first place. On the other hand, *se-parere*, to engender oneself, to put oneself into the world.[34]

In the article 'Corpo, sguardo e silenzio' Basaglia describes two possible ways of being in a relationship with others.[35] He calls them *alterità (otherness / being other)* and *alienità ('alienity' / being alien)*. The subject can choose to accept the presence of the other and with it the fact that were it not for this presence the subject would not be able to be a subject at all (choosing *alterità*). Otherwise, one could attempt to remove oneself completely from being exposed to the determining presence of

---

32. Ibid., p. 214.

33. Fink 1997, p. 54.

34. Lacan 1998, p. 214.

35. Basaglia 1965a, pp. 31-33.

the other. In this case, one would unfailingly fall into a state of *alienità*. In this distinction Basaglia is echoing Sartre:

> I thereby recognize and affirm not only the Other but the existence of my Self-for-others. Indeed this is because I can not not-be the Other unless I assume my being-as-object for the Other. The disappearance of the alienated Me would involve the disappearance of the Other through the collapse of Myself. [...] But as I choose myself as a tearing away from the Other, I assume and recognize as mine this alienated Me. (Sartre 1978, p. 285)

The very noun *subject* elicits this idea: one becomes and is a subject insofar as one is subjected/subjects oneself to the presence of the other. This presence actively objectifies the subject, makes him an object of its gaze, thus setting in motion the process of subjectification. Removing oneself from the objectifying power of the other would entail the collapse of one's self, while accepting to be at the mercy of the Other *corresponds* to the ontogenesis of the subject:

> Man cannot carry out an act of reflection on himself if not through the gaze of the other: the gaze of the other, as intermediary that references me to myself, makes me aware of myself. (Basaglia 1965a, p. 32)

Alterità is thus, strictly speaking *subjectivity* itself, and we can say it is 'chosen' only inasmuch as the only alternative to it is no advent of subjectivity, whereby, and I will return to this shortly, subjectivity collapses into a state of *alienità*: by emphasising to the utmost the distance from the other, that is, by rejecting the constitutional relationship with the Other, there is, strictly speaking, no subject. This is what Basaglia calls *alienità*, a state in which the non-subject is assaulted by the Other, in a condition of 'promiscuity in which the other [...] presses relentlessly on [*urge senza tregua*]'.[36]

In Lacanian terms we could call such 'choice of the other', this step towards the achievement of *alterità*, the moment of *aphanisis* of subjectivity *qua* being, the symbolic alienation into the signifier that represents the subject to the Other. Loosely speaking, in this step the subject becomes the only 'thing' he could ever be (a 'placeholder' in the field of the Other) by letting his illusion of a unitary, unique, independent and substantial subjectivity fade. The advent of subjectivity presupposes the assumption of one's own constitutional lack, which amounts, simply put, to the fact that we cannot be without the other.

Yet while the condition of *alterità* certainly involves choosing to be at the mercy of the other's gaze, it also demands, according to Basaglia, to establish a *gap*, an *intervallo* he calls it, between the subject and the other. In Lacan's terms, this is the achievement of *separation*: on the one hand, a lack is recognised in the Other as much as in oneself and desire is established as desire of the Other, promoting intersubjectivity and thus subjectivity; on the other, the subject defends itself against the engulfing and devouring relationship with the other. In the state of *alienità* there is no such gap: one tries to make this gap limitless, to distance the other completely, to *be* without the other, and as a consequence the gap collapses, and, with it, the very possibility of subjectivity.

---

36. Ibid., p. 31.

The moment man loses the possibility of seeing and accepting oneself [...] through the objectivation granted by the presence of the other, he loses the possibility of overstepping multiplicity to place oneself in opposition; he thus loses the reciprocity of the encounter with the other, who invades his space [...] man loses his own alterity and alienates himself. (Basaglia 1965a, p. 37)

In this condition, man is unable to differentiate himself from the other. As Lacan maintains, 'the relation of the subject to the Other is entirely produced in a process of *gap*. Without this, *anything* could be there'.[37] The gap between the subject and the Other is what allows the process of alienation to constitute the subject, allowing him to take active part in the Other, without entailing a complete *fading into* the Other. The subject does not amount to *nothing*, on the contrary, the subject *is* the signifier that represents him to the Other. This is one of the reasons why Chiesa can affirm that the Lacanian subject is '*not* a *lacking* subject' but a '*subjectivised lack*', a lack that 'must *actively* be confronted and assumed'.[38]

IV. PSYCHOSIS AND NEUROSIS

If lack is not subjectivised, if, in Basaglia's terms, one falls into a state of *alienità*, then there usually are pathological consequences in psychiatric terms. According to Stoppa, it is precisely in their respective interpretations of psychosis that Lacan's and Basaglia's theories converge.[39] As he puts it, the crucial moment in the subject's ontogenesis is the moment when otherness is assumed, inasmuch as otherness is 'woven into' the subject itself. Stoppa suggests that, according to both Basaglia and Lacan, the aetiology of psychosis lies in the fact that the assumption of this constitutional otherness does not take place.[40]

In brief, according to Lacan, psychosis amounts to the *foreclosure*, or radical rejection (*Verwerfung*), of the Name-of-the-Father. In order to understand the connection of such foreclosure with the ontogenesis of the subject and its relationship to the Other, we must briefly turn to the Oedipus complex. While Lacan in Seminar XI does not explicitly link them to the Oedipus complex, alienation and separation, being stages in the ontogenesis of the subject, should be read together with its phases. Separation is the crucial moment that establishes the subject's entrance in the symbolic order, that is to say, the advent of the subject as such. It is also, to a certain extent, Lacan's original interpretation of Freud's formulation. According to Freud, the resolution of the Oedipus complex amounted to the sanctioning of the prohibition of incest, enacted by the father's separation of the child from the mother—the Oedipal *no*. In this separation the father gives the first notion of law to the child, the first limit to his previously uncontrolled libido. According to Lacan, the function Name-of-the-Father does not only put libido under control, it also, and especially, protects the child from the devouring relationship with the mother. It separates the child, not only regulating his libido, but also 'showing' him that the mother's libido too is regulated by, as Leader puts it, a force be-

---

37. Lacan 1998, p. 206.
38. Lacan 2007, p. 6.
39. Stoppa 1999, p. 113.
40. Ibid.

yond her: a force that regulates all desires and thus all relations—the Other. The Name-of-the-Father thus inaugurates the symbolic order for the child, whose existence is henceforth equivalent to the existence of S1.

Foreclosure of the Name-of-the-Father thus means that no *separation* has taken place, the symbolic order has not been established, and there has been no advent of subjectivity. Foreclosure discriminates between neurosis and psychosis. As Freud posits, the aetiology of neurosis is grounded in the process of repression (*Verdrängung*):[41] what takes place in a neurotic patient is a 'return of the repressed' in the form of the neurotic symptom. Hence, neurosis pertains to the symbolic dimension in Lacanian terms, in that the set of neurotic symptoms is a language that speaks (although in a displaced fashion) of the repressed unconscious.

On the contrary, the psychotic has not *repressed* an unconscious desire/memory but foreclosed the very possibility of subjectivity and otherness. In psychosis, it is not the repressed that returns as a symptom but the *foreclosed* that returns, in the Real, as *hallucination*. In psychotic phenomena there is no gap, no space for subjectification that can protect the subject from the traumatic and hallucinatory intrusion of the Real. In Lacan's words, 'something that has been rejected from within, reappears without', or, better still, 'something [that] is not symbolised [...] is going to appear in the *real*'.[42] Due to the foreclosure of the primordial signifier and the consequent impossibility of taking part in the symbolic order—that is to say of *actively symbolising the Real*—the subject is unable to mediate his relationship with the Real and with others through the symbolic dimension. The psychotic,

> for want of being able in any way to re-establish his pact with the other, [...] substitutes for symbolic mediation a profusion, an imaginary proliferation, into which the central signal of a possible mediation is introduced in a deformed and profoundly asymbolic fashion. (Lacan 1997, p. 87)

It is therefore indeed a kind of fracture with otherness that characterises psychoses, yet it is not a simple disavowal of the Other, as it could happen for instance in perversion: the psychotic lacks the very primordial signifier that would have enabled him to actively enter the symbolic order, and thus lacks in the first place the very possibility of recognising an Other to disavow.

This radical fracture between the subject and the Other that, nevertheless, allows the subject to be somehow included in the Other, is precisely where Basaglia's theory of psychoses converges with Lacan's. I believe that, in distinguishing neurosis from psychosis, especially in the 1966 article 'L'ideologia del corpo come espressività nevrotica', Basaglia is heavily relying on psychoanalysis, despite his declared aversion to it. Interestingly, Basaglia claims to be drawing on the psychiatrist Heinz Häfner[43] (1961) in defining the difference between neurosis and psychosis. According to Basaglia, the neurotic tries to maintain a rela-

---

41. Freud 1915.

42. Lacan 1997, p. 81.

43. Heinz Häfner (born 1926) is a German psychiatrist, director of the Central Institute for Mental Health in Mannheim. Häfner is responsible for the reform of psychiatry in Germany, which humanised psychiatric assistance and introduced a community centred mental health care.

tionship with the other (unable to live his own body, the neurotic must 'build an image [...] capable of tying him [...] to the other from which he cannot stand being excluded').[44] This is what he refers to, using Häfner's words, as 'neurotic expressivity':[45] remaining 'within the limits of everyday organisation', the neurotic tries to 'dominate the demands that erupt, elaborating them as a compromise'.[46] While the neurotic's 'expressive actions' try to convey such 'erupting demand', this is bound to remain 'unsatisfied, even at the very moment it is communicated'.[47] It seems to me that Basaglia is avoiding a psychoanalytical vocabulary almost on purpose, as these 'erupting demands' retain all the characteristics of unconscious desires according to Freud's formulation: the neurotic represses an unconscious desire, which then returns expressed in the compromise formation of the symptom, because repression is never completely successful. The symptom is always a mere compromise and is therefore bound to be unsatisfactory, insofar as it deviates from the original unconscious content that was to be expressed.[48]

On the other hand, psychosis is not expressive, i.e. a psychotic symptom does not express an 'underlying erupting demand', or an unconscious desire. Psychotic actions are not 'expressive actions' but 'actions of psychopathic break':[49] the distance from the other 'must be maintained and the breaking action is an expression of the effort required by its maintenance'.[50] By radically breaking with the other, the psychotic does not experience the distance between himself and the other as a space of subjectification (the *intervallo* that allows human beings to be in an intersubjective relationship without losing themselves into the other). On the contrary, the psychotic completely loses his distance and precipitates himself into the other: this is the apparently paradoxical outcome of Basaglia's theory of *alterità/alienità*. It is only in maintaining a *distance* with the other that I can acknowledge myself as, in turn, *other*. This *intervallo*, this gap between me and the other enables me to establish the unavoidable relationship with the other: this is a state of *alterità*. Yet this distance cannot be a complete fracture with otherness, because that would cause a state of *alienità*: by refusing to be in a relationship with the other (that paradoxically I would refuse precisely to safeguard to the utmost my *distance* from the other, make it insurmountable, protect myself from the other) I lose this *intervallo* and fade into the other. This was already clear in the 1953 article 'Il mondo dell'incomprensibile schizofrenico', where Basaglia defined this situation as the 'narrowing' of the psychotic existence.[51] According to Basaglia, the psychotic is 'ravaged by the other's gaze, by the other's world, that reifies, condenses and repels him':[52] the psychotic 'objectifies himself precisely when he believes he is subjectifying himself to the utmost'.[53] That is to say, the psychotic tries to es-

---

44. Basaglia 1966, p. 73.
45. Ibid.
46. Ibid., p. 74.
47. Ibid.
48. Freud 1923, p. 242.
49. Basaglia 1966, p. 73.
50. Ibid., p. 74.
51. Basaglia 1953, p. 15.
52. Basaglia 1965a, p. 36.
53. Basaglia 1963, p. 10.

tablish an insurmountable fracture with the other, in order to safeguard his illusory individual and substantial subjectivity; in doing so, he loses the *intervallo* and becomes the object of the other. Both the psychotic and the neurotic have troubles accepting their *alterità* and therefore they fall into a state of *alienità*. While the neurotic alienates in an image, in the 'actions of neurotic expressivity', which allow him to entertain an (inauthentic) relationship with the other, the psychotic completely breaks with otherness and refuses to be a part of it. As Lacan puts it, 'if the Other is removed from its place, man can no longer even sustain himself in the position of Narcissus'.[54] Without a relationship with the Other, there can be no subject.

V. CONCLUSIONS

In his later texts, Basaglia's theory of psychosis sternly veers towards social and political concerns, for instance highlighting the pathogenetic component of society itself; exclusion and poor economic conditions as the leading causes of mental illness; and the potential that 'political' interventions have of improving the conditions of the mentally ill—a potential which was realised with the psychiatric reform law of 1978. Yet it is also clear and sometimes overlooked in critical literature that Basaglia was never an anti-psychiatrist; he never denied the concrete existence of mental illness as a bio-psycho-social entity; and he never thought psychosis was just the by-product of an unjust/imbalanced/intolerant society—as if changing society alone could cure mental illness. Throughout his years of political commitment, while he did express reservations on his early therapeutic approaches such as Binswanger's *Daseinsanalyse*, he never disavowed his studies on subjectivity and always regarded psychosis as a complex product of biological, psychological and social interactions: one of the possible outcomes of the encounter between intersubjectivity and subjectivity, that is to say, one of the possible outcomes of the ontogenesis of the subject. Thus, spelling out Basaglia's theory of the subject and how it informs his theory of psychosis is not an abstract exercise that invests only his early career, but sheds new light also on his anti-institutional—but never anti-*psychiatric*—practices.

What is clear is that, as Leader very aptly puts it, 'a psychoanalytic theory of psychosis does not imply a psychoanalysis of psychotic subjects'.[55] Such a remark holds all the better for the above considerations: highlighting the proximity of Basaglia's theory of subjectivity and psychosis with Lacan's does not necessarily entail that psychoanalysing psychotic subjects would be a good idea, or that Basaglia had a clinical psychoanalytic approach in mind. This proximity does though open up further promising lines of investigation that might eventually inform a clinical practice within the context of de-institutionalisation. Numerous authors have already pointed this out, stressing how staging the 'missed dialogue'—to borrow Colucci and Di Vittorio's fortunate expression—between Basaglia and Lacan could be productive on many different levels.[56] To date, no

---

54. Lacan 1955, p. 460.
55. Leader 2011, p. 294.
56. Colucci and Di Vittorio 2001, p. 288.

study develops this suggestion further and I might be replicating the same vagueness by leaving my conclusions open to further research. One idea, though, stands out: Basaglia has been extensively studied *with* Foucault, to the point that a bond of reciprocal jealousy between them was theorised.[57] While it is indisputable that Basaglia's work of reform owed much to Foucault's analysis of psychiatry and disciplinary power, I find it very important to highlight that Basaglia's theory of the subject steers clear of the impasses Foucault stumbles into. Granted, the latest Foucault—in *The Courage of Truth*[58] for instance—acknowledges possible counter-hegemonic practices of subjectification. Yet he was never able to relate them to the spectrum of psychiatric practices, having found there *exclusively* a subjected and powerless subject, the by-product of power relations. A 'counter-hegemonic', if you will, psychiatry cannot be envisioned starting with Foucault's notion of subject. Yet it can be and has been envisioned on the grounds of Basaglia's theory of the subject. The crucial difference is, as I have shown, that between a lacking/empty subject and a *subject of lack*: a difference that can have, and this in my opinion emerges clearly in comparison with Lacan, a marked resonance in clinical and anti-institutional practices.

BIBLIOGRAPHY

Basaglia, F., 'Il mondo dell'"incomprensibile" schizofrenico attraverso la "Daseinsanalyse". Presentazione di un caso clinico', in Ongaro Basaglia, F., ed. (1981) *Scritti*, Vol. 1, Turin: Einaudi, 1953

——— 'Su alcuni aspetti della moderna psicoterapia: Analisi fenomenologica dell'"incontro"', in Ongaro Basaglia, F., ed. (1981) *Scritti*, Vol. 1, Turin: Einaudi, 1954

——— 'Il corpo nell'ipocondria e nella depersonalizzazione. La coscienza del corpo e il sentimento di esistenza corporea nella depersonalizzazione somatopsichica', in Ongaro Basaglia, F., ed. (1981) *Scritti*, Vol. 1, Turin: Einaudi, 1956a

——— 'Il corpo nell'ipocondria e nella depersonalizzazione. La struttura psicopatologica dell'ipocondria', in Ongaro Basaglia, F., ed. (1981) *Scritti*, Vol. 1, Turin: Einaudi, 1956b

——— 'L'ipocondria come deformazione dell'"Erlebnis" individuale nel fenomeno di depersonalizzazione', in Ongaro Basaglia, F., ed. (1981) *Scritti*, Vol. 1, Turin: Einaudi, 1957

——— 'Ansia e malafede. La condizione umana del nevrotico', in: Ongaro Basaglia, F., ed. (2005) *L'utopia della realtà*, Turin: Einaudi, 1963

——— 'La distruzione dell'ospedale psichiatrico come luogo di istituzionalizzazione', in: Ongaro Basaglia, F., ed. (2005) *L'utopia della realtà*, Turin: Einaudi, 1964

——— 'Corpo, sguardo e silenzio. L'enigma della soggettività in psichiatria', in: Ongaro Basaglia, F., ed. (2005) *L'utopia della realtà*, Turin: Einaudi, 1965

——— 'L'ideologia del corpo come espressività nevrotica', in: Ongaro Basaglia, F., ed. (2005) *L'utopia della realtà*, Turin: Einaudi, 1966

---

57. Di Vittorio 1999.
58. Foucault 2011.

—— 'Introduzione a "Lo Psicanalismo"', in Ongaro Basaglia, F., ed. (1981) *Scritti*, Vol. 1, Turin: Einaudi, 1978

Benvenuto, S., 'Psichiatria e critica della tecnica. Franco Basaglia e il movimento psichiatrico anti-istituzionale in Italia', in *Psichiatria e psicoterapia*, XIV(3), 2005

Chiesa, L., *Subjectivity and Otherness. A Philosophical Reading of Lacan*. Cambridge (MA): MIT Press, 2007

Colucci, M. & Di Vittorio, P., *Franco Basaglia*. Milan: Bruno Mondadori, 2001

Di Vittorio, P., *Foucault e Basaglia. L'incontro tra genealogie e movimenti di base*. Verona: Ombre Corte, 1999

Dilthey, W., 'Ideas about a Descriptive and Analytical Psychology', in Rickman, H.P. (ed.), *Selected Writings*, Cambridge: Cambridge University Press, 1976

Fink, B., *The Lacanian Subject: Between Language and Jouissance*, Princeton (NJ): Princeton University Press, 1997

Foucault, M., *The Courage of Truth: The Government of Self and Others*. New York (NY): Palgrave MacMillan, 2011

Freud, S. (1915). 'Repression', in *SE 14*

—— (1923). 'Two Encyclopaedia Articles: Psychoanalysis and the Libido Theory', in *SE 18*

Goffman, E., *Asylums: Essays on the Social Situation of Mental Patients and Other Inmates*, New Brunswick: Aldine Transaction, 2007

Häfner, H., *Psychopathen*, Berlin: Springer, 1961

Jones, E., 'The Early Development of Female Sexuality', in *International Journal of Psychoanalysis*, 8, 1927

Kantzà, G., 'Il punto d'impasse', in *La Psicoanalisi*, 25, 1999

Kirchmayr, R., 'A cosa può servirci l'*objet (petit) a*', in *aut aut*, 343, 2009

Lacan, J., 'On a Question Prior to Any Possible Treatment of Psychosis', in Fink, ed. and trans. (2007) *Écrits: the First Complete Edition in English*, London: W.W. Norton, 1955

—— 'Seminar of "the Purloined Letter"', in Fink, ed. and trans. (2007) *Écrits: the First Complete Edition in English*, London: W.W. Norton, 1957

—— 'The Signification of the Phallus', in Fink, ed. and trans. (2007) *Écrits: the First Complete Edition in English*, London: W.W. Norton, 1958

—— 'Position of the Unconscious', in Fink, ed. and trans. (2007) *Écrits: the First Complete Edition in English*, London: W.W. Norton, 1964

—— *The Psychoses. The Seminar of Jacques Lacan, Book III, 1955-1956*, translated by Russell Grigg, London: W.W. Norton & Co., 1997

—— *The Four Fundamental Concepts of Psychoanalysis. The Seminar of Jacques Lacan, Book XI, 1963-1964*, translated by Alan Sheridan, London: W.W. Norton & Co., 1998

—— *The Other Side of Psychoanalysis. The Seminar of Jacques Lacan, Book XVII, 1969-1970*, translated by Russell Grigg, London: W.W. Norton & Co., 2007

—— *Le séminaire. Livre VI. Le désir et son interprétation 1958-1959*. Paris: Éditions de La Martinière, 2013

Leoni, F. (ed.), *Franco Basaglia. Un laboratorio italiano*. Milan: Bruno Mondadori,

2011

Leader, D., *What is Madness?* London: Penguin, 2011

McGinn, C., 'Can We Solve the Body-Mind Problem?', in *Mind, New Series*, 98(391), Jul., 1989

Polidori, F., 'Una prassi che interroga l'etica', in *La Psicoanalisi*, 25, 1999

Recalcati, M., 'Lo snodo Sartre, Basaglia e Lacan', in *Franco Basaglia e la filosofia del 900*, Milan: Bema, 2010

Rovatti, P.A., 'Il soggetto che non c'è' in Galzigna, M., ed. *Foucault, Oggi*, Milan: Feltrinelli, 2008

Sartre, J.P., *Being and Nothingness; an Essay on Phenomenological Ontology*, translated by Hazel E. Barnes, New York: Pocket Books, 1978

Sforza Tarabochia, A., *Psychiatry, Subjectivity, Community. Franco Basaglia and Biopolitics*, Oxford: Peter Lang, 2013

Stoppa, F., 'Basaglia, la comunità terapeutica e l'enigma della soggettività' in *La Psicoanalisi*, 25, 1999

Viganò, C., *Psichiatria non psichiatria. La follia nella società che cambia*, Rome: Borla, 2009

Contributors

Matteo Bonazzi is a research fellow at the University of Milan-Bicocca and teaches Critique of Mass Media Communication at SUPSI (Lugano, Switzerland). He is a member of *Orbis Tertius*, a research group on the contemporary imaginary, and of the Lacanian School of Psychoanalysis in Milan. Bonazzi is the author of several books, including *Il Libro e la scrittura. Tra Hegel e Derrida* (Mimesis, 2004), *Scrivere la contingenza. Esperienza, linguaggio, scrittura in Jacques Lacan* (ETS, 2009), and, with F. Carmagnola, *Il fantasma della libertà. Inconscio e politica al tempo di Berlusconi* (Mimesis 2011).

Lorenzo Chiesa is Professor of Modern European Thought and Co-director of the Centre for Critical Thought at the University of Kent at Canterbury (UK). He is the author of, among other books, *Subjectivity and Otherness: A Philosophical Reading of Lacan* (MIT Press 2007) and *Der Möglichkeitspunkt der Freiheitsfunktion. Essays zu Politik, Ästhetik und Psychoanalyse* (Merve Verlag Berlin 2014). His new monograph on Lacan (*The Not-Two: Logic, Love, and God in Lacan*) is forthcoming with MIT Press.

Justin Clemens is a Senior Lecturer in the School of Culture and Communication at the University of Melbourne, and the secretary of the Lacan Circle, Melbourne. He is the author (with Jon Roffe) of *Lacan Deleuze Badiou* (Edinburgh University Press 2014). His other publications include the co-editorship of *Jacques Lacan and the Other Side of Psychoanalysis* (Duke UP 2006) with Russell Grigg and, most recently, the *The Jacqueline Rose Reader* (Duke UP 2011) with Ben Naparstek and *Alain Badiou: Key Concepts* (Acumen 2010) with A. J. Bartlett.

Guillaume Collett holds a Ph.D. in French Studies from the University of Kent and in Psychoanalysis from the University of Paris VII. His thesis is on Deleuze, Lacan, Spinoza, and anti-humanism. He has recently co-edited a special issue of *Deleuze Studies* on philosophical practice. Currently, he is working on a monograph tentatively entitled *Immanence and Language: Deleuze and the Lacanian School*, and on a co-edited book on Deleuze and transdisciplinarity. He has translated articles, chapters, and booklets on psychoanalysis and philosophy.

Felix Ensslin holds the Chair of Aesthetics and Art-Mediation at the State Academy for Fine Arts in Stuttgart, Germany. He is a curator (exhibitions include *Regarding Terror: The RAF-Exhibition* with Klaus Biesenbach and Ellen Blumenstein at the KW Institute for Contemporary Art, Berlin) and stage-director (he worked at the German National Theatre, Weimar). He is the editor of the book series *Subjektile* published by Diaphanes and a founding member of *pli-Psychoanalyse nach Lacan*. His publications include *Between Two Deaths* (Hatje Cantz, 2007) and *Spieltrieb: Was bringt die Klassik auf die Bühne? Schillers Ästhetik heute* (Theater der Zeit, 2006). A book-length study on Luther and Lacan is forthcoming with Diaphanes.

Oliver Feltham coordinates the Philosophy Program at the American University of Paris. He has published on the work of Alain Badiou and Jacques Lacan, notably translating Badiou's *Being and Event* and writing a monograph *Alain Badiou: Live Theory*, both with Continuum Books. He researches in the fields of early modern philosophy, the history of metaphysics, psychoanalysis and the philosophy of theatre. His most recent book is *Anatomy of Failure: Philosophy and Political Action* which compares the model of political action found in the thinking of the Leveller-agitators of the New Model Army during the English Revolution to the sovereign and contractual models of political action found in the philosophies of Thomas Hobbes and John Locke.

Adrian Johnston is a Professor in the Department of Philosophy at the University of New Mexico at Albuquerque and an Assistant Teaching Analyst at the Emory Psychoanalytic Institute in Atlanta. He is the author of *Time Driven: Metapsychology and the Splitting of the Drive* (2005), *Žižek's Ontology: A Transcendental Materialist Theory of Subjectivity* (2008), and *Badiou, Žižek, and Political Transformations: The Cadence of Change* (2009), all published by Northwestern University Press. With Catherine Malabou, he has co-authored a book on affects entitled *Self and Emotional Life: Philosophy, Psychoanalysis, and Neuroscience* (Columbia University Press 2013). His most recent book is *Prolegomena to Any Future Materialism* (Northwestern, 2013).

Michael Lewis is Senior Lecturer in Philosophy at the University of the West of England, Bristol, United Kingdom. He is the author of *Derrida and Lacan: Another Writing* (Edinburgh University Press 2008), *Heidegger Beyond Deconstruction: On Nature* (Continuum Books 2007), *Heidegger and the Place of Ethics* (Continuum Books 2005), and *Phenomenology: An Introduction* (Continuum Books 2010) (with Tanja Staehler).

Raoul Moati obtained his Ph.D. in philosophy from the University of Paris 1, Panthéon-Sorbonne, and is currently an Assistant Professor in the Department of Philosophy of the University of Chicago. He is the author of *Žižek, Marxisme et psychanalyse* (PUF 2012) (with Ronan de Calan), *Derrida/Searle, déconstruction et langage ordinaire* (PUF 2009), and the editor of *Autour de Slavoj Žižek. Psychanalyse, Marxisme, Idéalisme Allemand* (PUF, 'Actuel Marx', 2010).

Alvise Sforza Tarabochia is a Lecturer in Italian Studies at the University of Kent at Canterbury (UK) and the author of the monograph *Psychiatry, Subjectivity, Community. Franco Basaglia and Biopolitics* (Peter Lang 2013). He is also a member of the Centre for Critical Thought at the University of Kent, and of the editorial board of *European Journal of Psychoanalysis*. He has recently edited an issue of *EJP* entitled *The End* (2014).

Alenka Zupančič is a full-time researcher at the Institute of Philosophy of the Slovenian Academy of Sciences and Arts and a visiting professor at the European Graduate School (EGS) in Saas-Fee, Switzerland. She has written extensively on psychoanalysis and philosophy. She is the author of numerous articles and several books, including *Ethics of the Real: Kant and Lacan* (Verso 2000), *The Shortest Shadow: Nietzsche's Philosophy of the Two* (MIT Press 2003), *The Odd One In: On Comedy* (MIT Press 2008), and *Why Psychoanalysis: Three Interventions* (Aarhus University Press 2008).

www.ingramcontent.com/pod-product-compliance
Lightning Source LLC
Chambersburg PA
CBHW020702270326
41928CB00005B/221